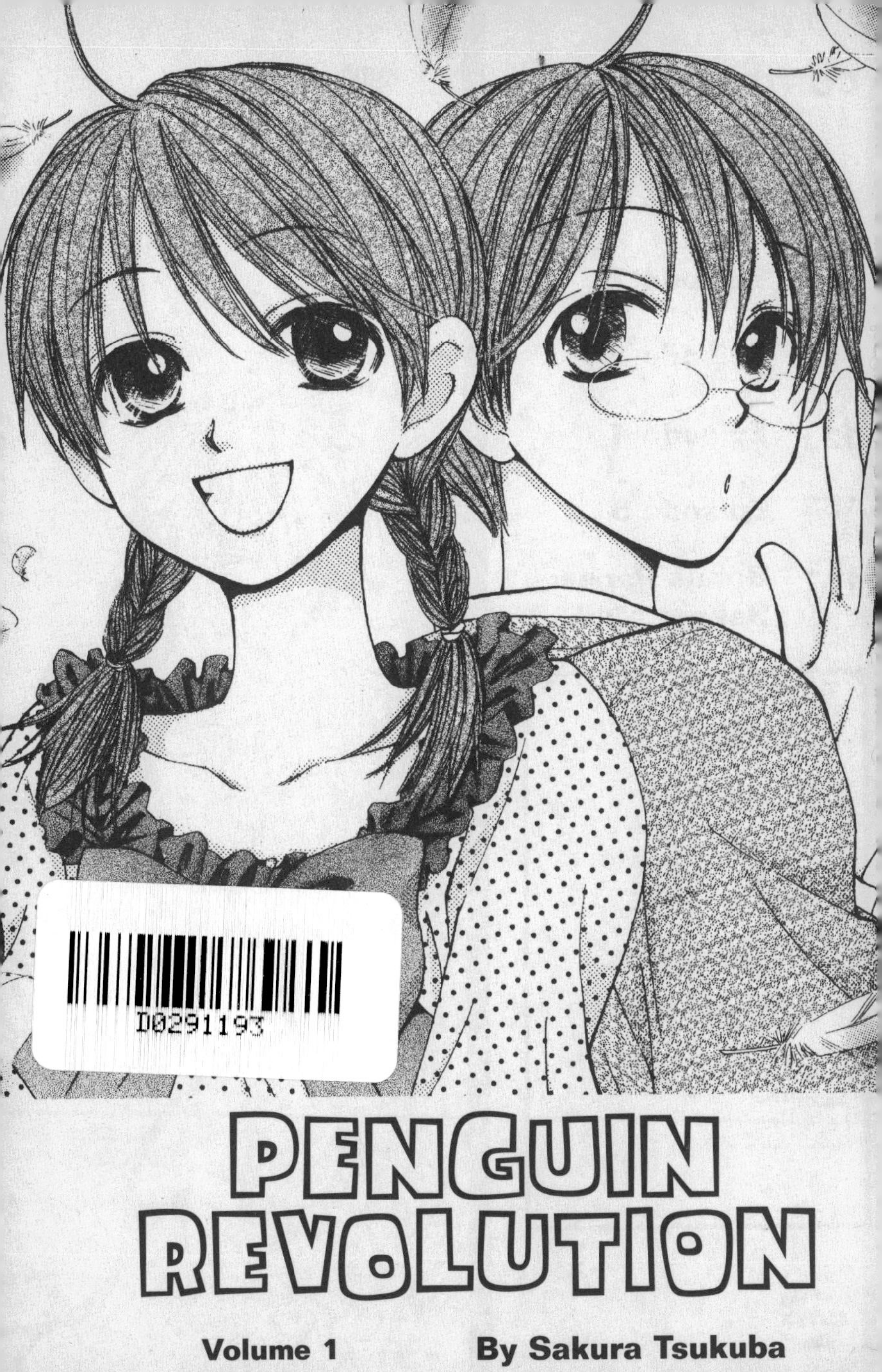

PENGUIN REVOLUTION

Volume 1 **By Sakura Tsukuba**

CONTENTS

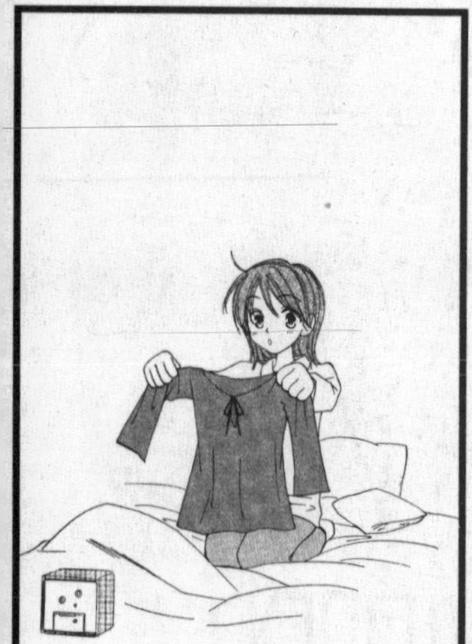

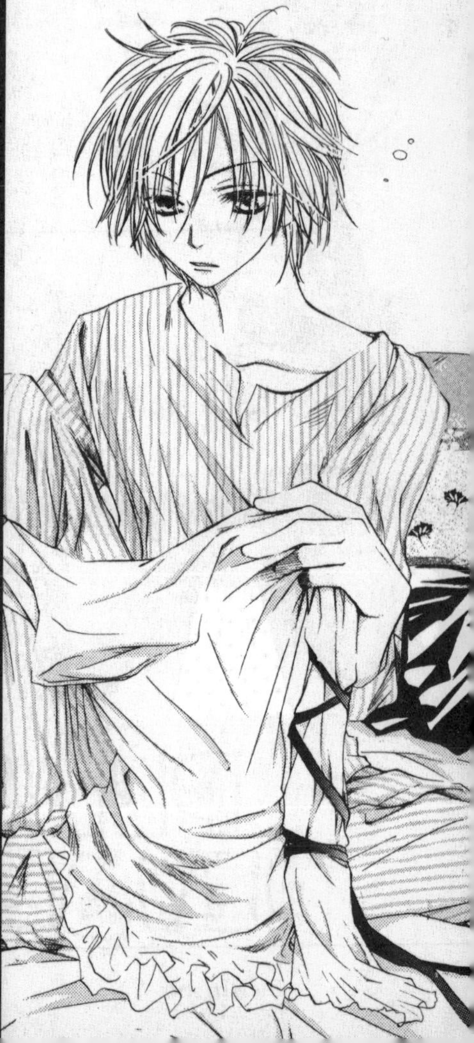

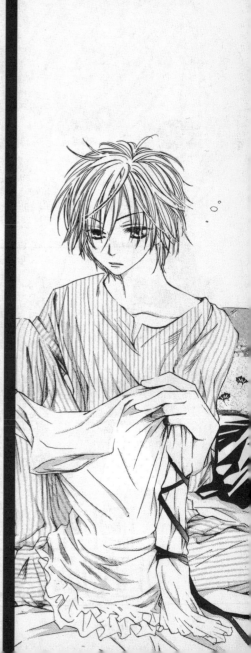

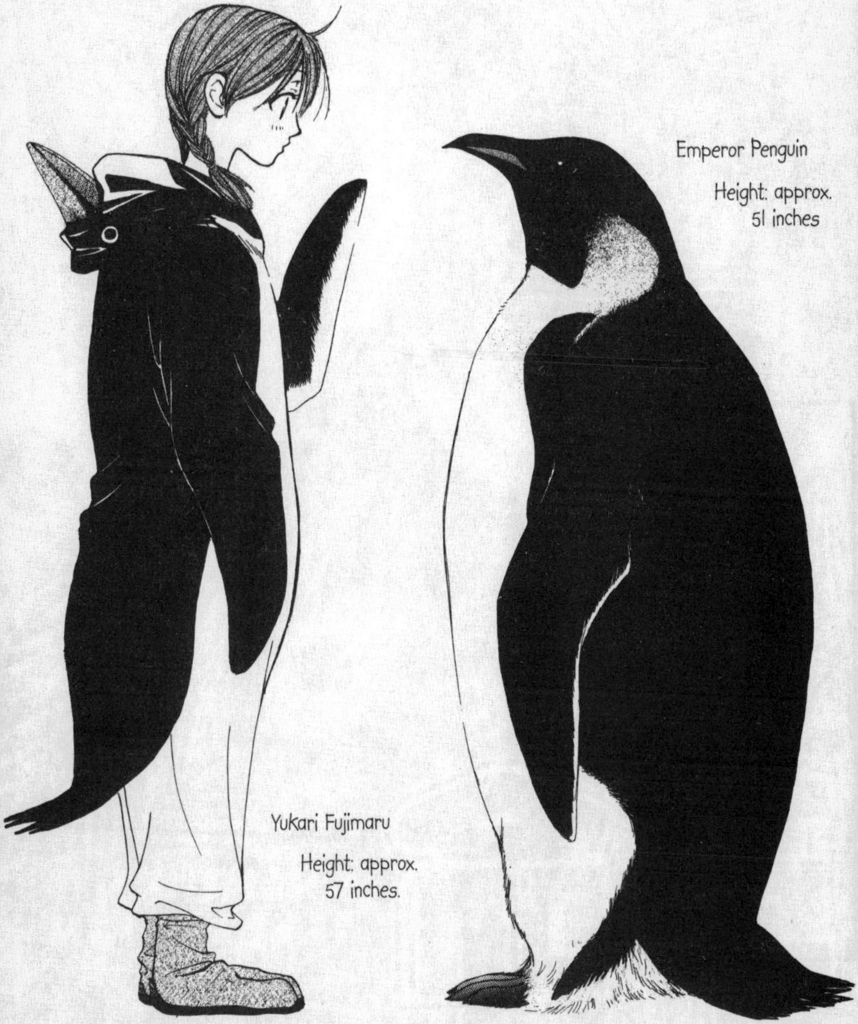
Emperor Penguin
Height: approx. 51 inches
Yukari Fujimaru
Height: approx. 57 inches.

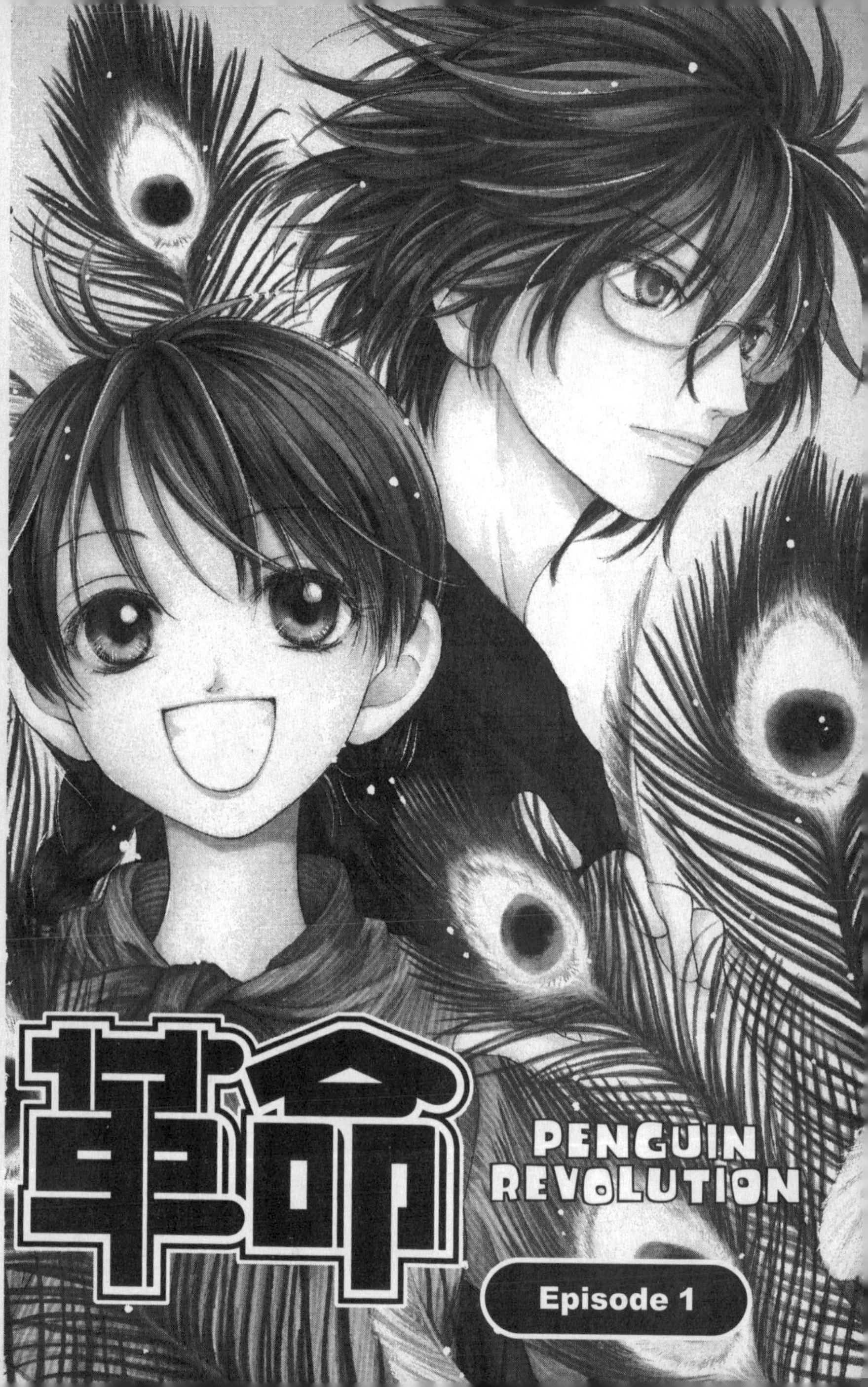
PENGUIN
REVOLUTION
Episode 1

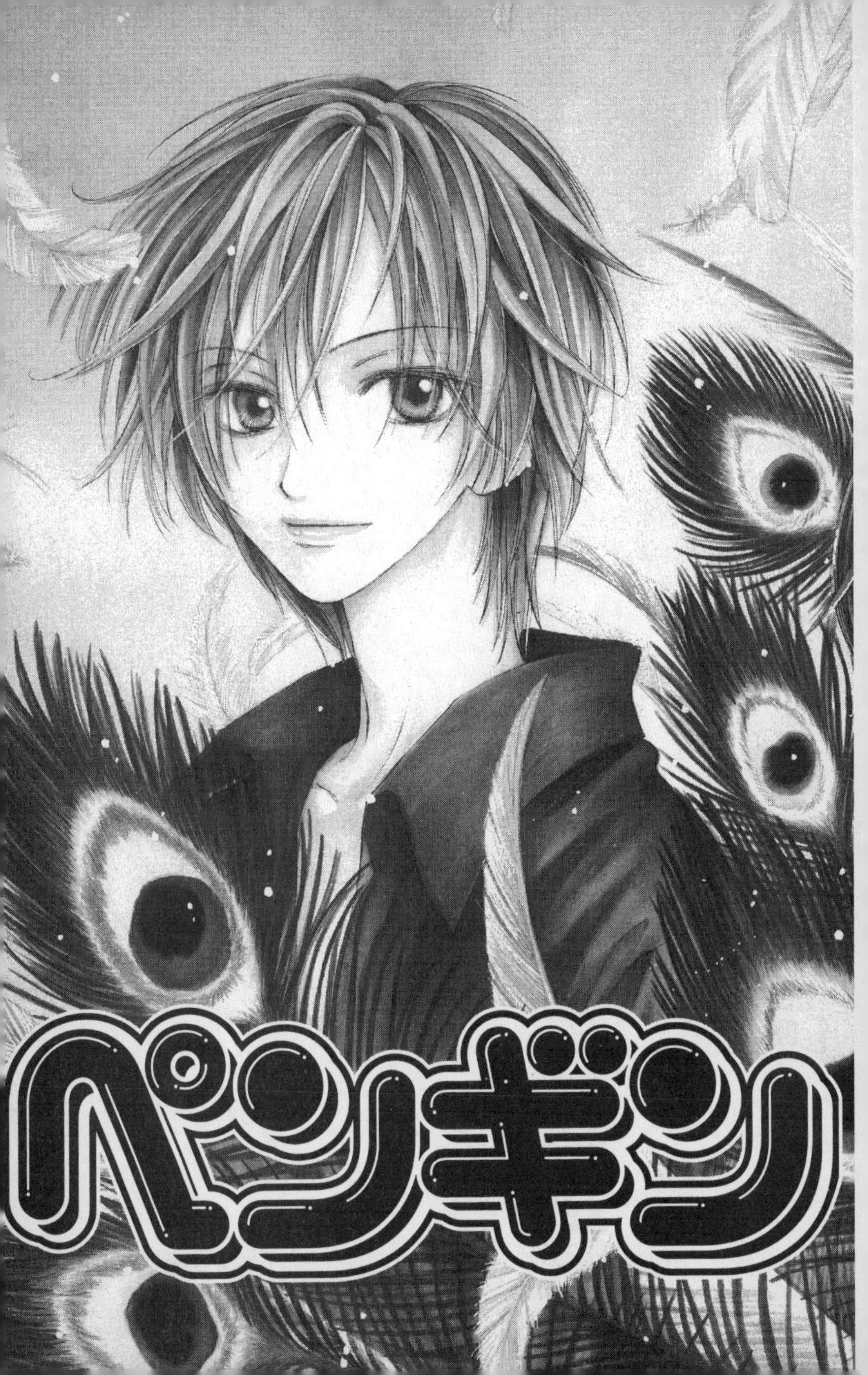
ペンギン

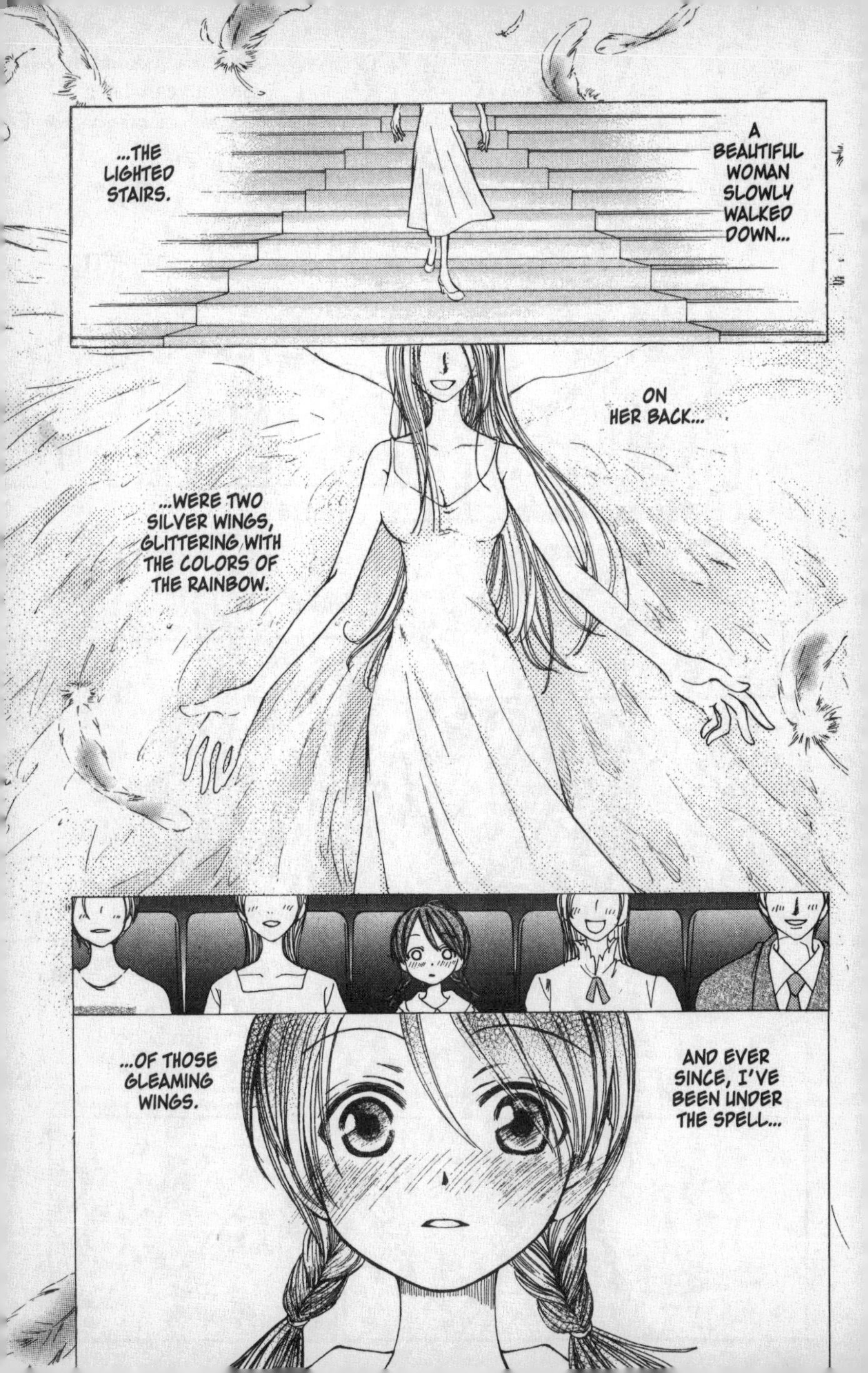
A BEAUTIFUL WOMAN SLOWLY WALKED DOWN...
...THE LIGHTED STAIRS.
ON HER BACK...
...WERE TWO SILVER WINGS, GLITTERING WITH THE COLORS OF THE RAINBOW.
AND EVER SINCE, I'VE BEEN UNDER THE SPELL...
...OF THOSE GLEAMING WINGS.

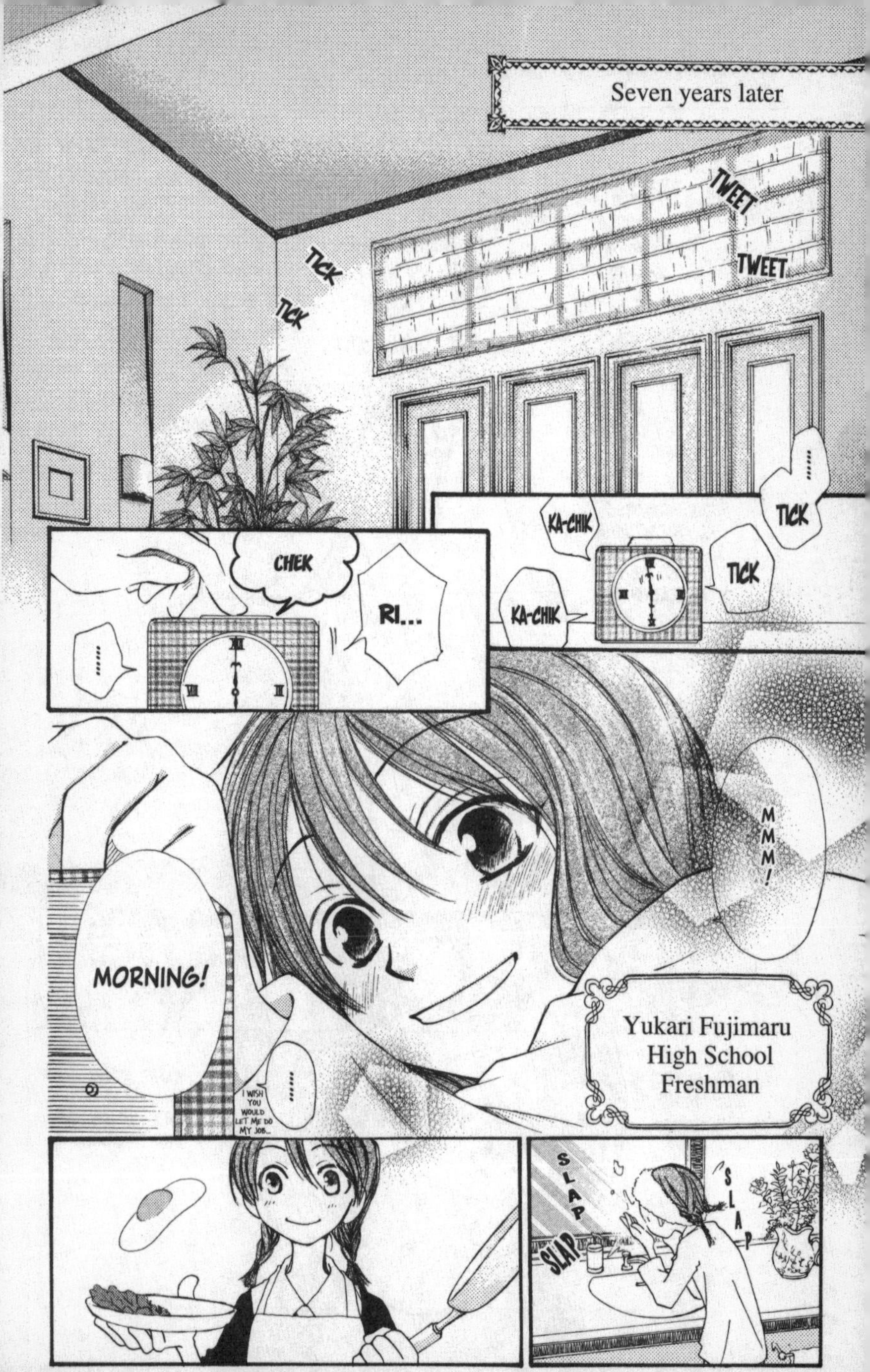
Seven years later
TWEET
TWEET
TICK
TICK
......
TICK
TICK
KA-CHIK
KA-CHIK
RI...
CHEK
......
MMM!
Yukari Fujimaru
High School
Freshman
MORNING!
......
I WISH YOU WOULD LET ME DO MY JOB...
SLAP
SLAP
SLAP
SLAP

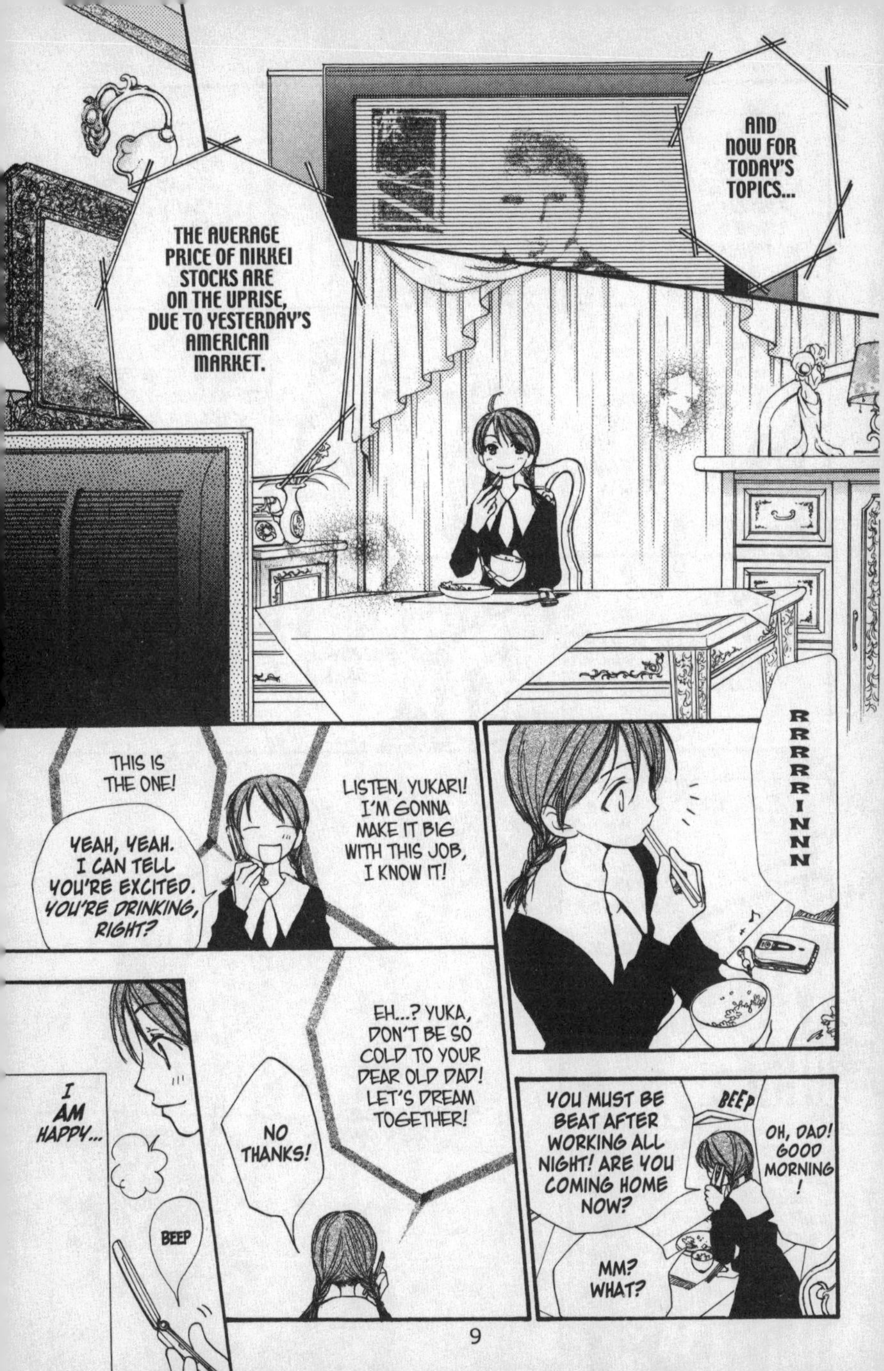
AND NOW FOR TODAY'S TOPICS...
THE AVERAGE PRICE OF NIKKEI STOCKS ARE ON THE UPRISE, DUE TO YESTERDAY'S AMERICAN MARKET.
RRRRRINNN
LISTEN, YUKARI! I'M GONNA MAKE IT BIG WITH THIS JOB, I KNOW IT!
THIS IS THE ONE!
YEAH, YEAH. I CAN TELL YOU'RE EXCITED. YOU'RE DRINKING, RIGHT?
BEEP
OH, DAD! GOOD MORNING!
YOU MUST BE BEAT AFTER WORKING ALL NIGHT! ARE YOU COMING HOME NOW?
MM? WHAT?
EH...? YUKA, DON'T BE SO COLD TO YOUR DEAR OLD DAD! LET'S DREAM TOGETHER!
NO THANKS!
BEEP
I AM HAPPY...

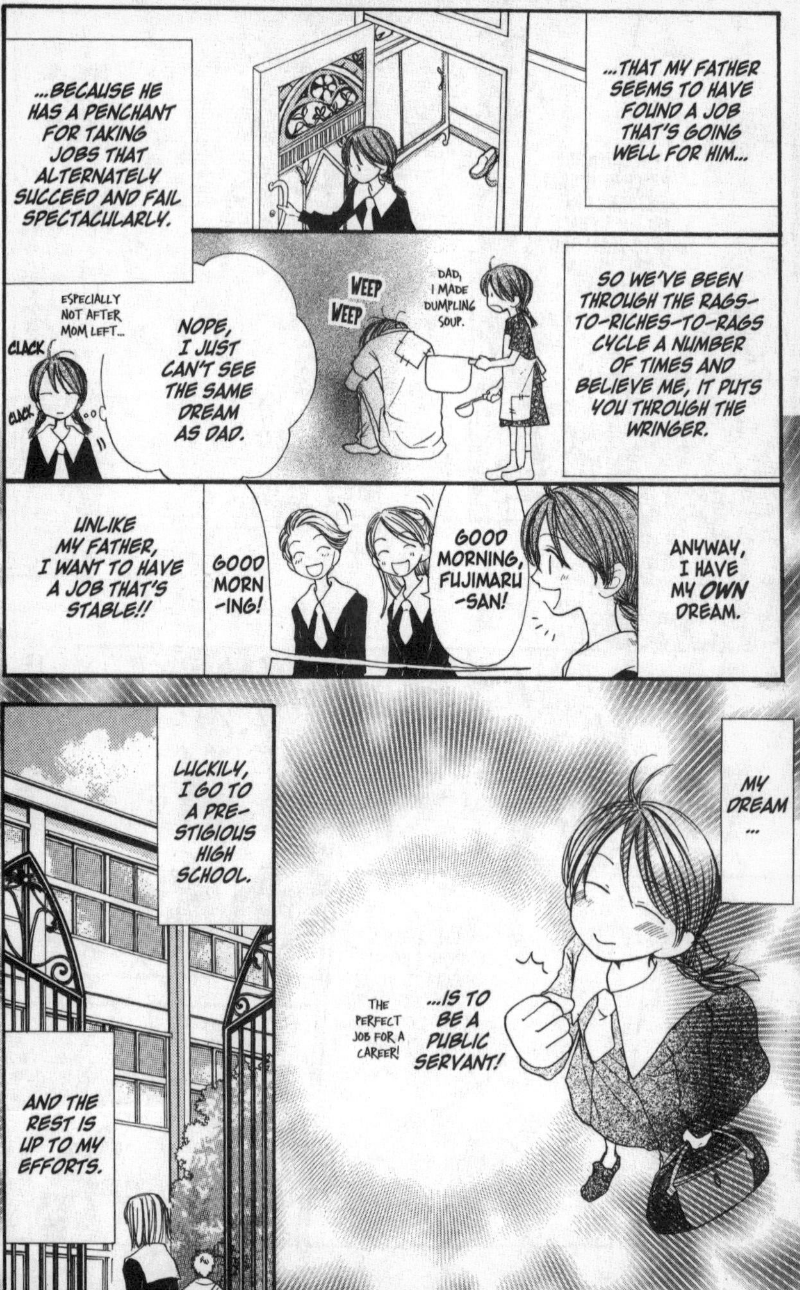
...THAT MY FATHER SEEMS TO HAVE FOUND A JOB THAT'S GOING WELL FOR HIM...
...BECAUSE HE HAS A PENCHANT FOR TAKING JOBS THAT ALTERNATELY SUCCEED AND FAIL SPECTACULARLY.
SO WE'VE BEEN THROUGH THE RAGS-TO-RICHES-TO-RAGS CYCLE A NUMBER OF TIMES AND BELIEVE ME, IT PUTS YOU THROUGH THE WRINGER.
DAD, I MADE DUMPLING SOUP.
WEEP
WEEP
NOPE, I JUST CAN'T SEE THE SAME DREAM AS DAD.
ESPECIALLY NOT AFTER MOM LEFT...
CLACK
CLACK
ANYWAY, I HAVE MY OWN DREAM.
GOOD MORNING, FUJIMARU-SAN!
GOOD MORN-ING!
UNLIKE MY FATHER, I WANT TO HAVE A JOB THAT'S STABLE!!
MY DREAM...
...IS TO BE A PUBLIC SERVANT!
THE PERFECT JOB FOR A CAREER!
LUCKILY, I GO TO A PRE-STIGIOUS HIGH SCHOOL.
AND THE REST IS UP TO MY EFFORTS.

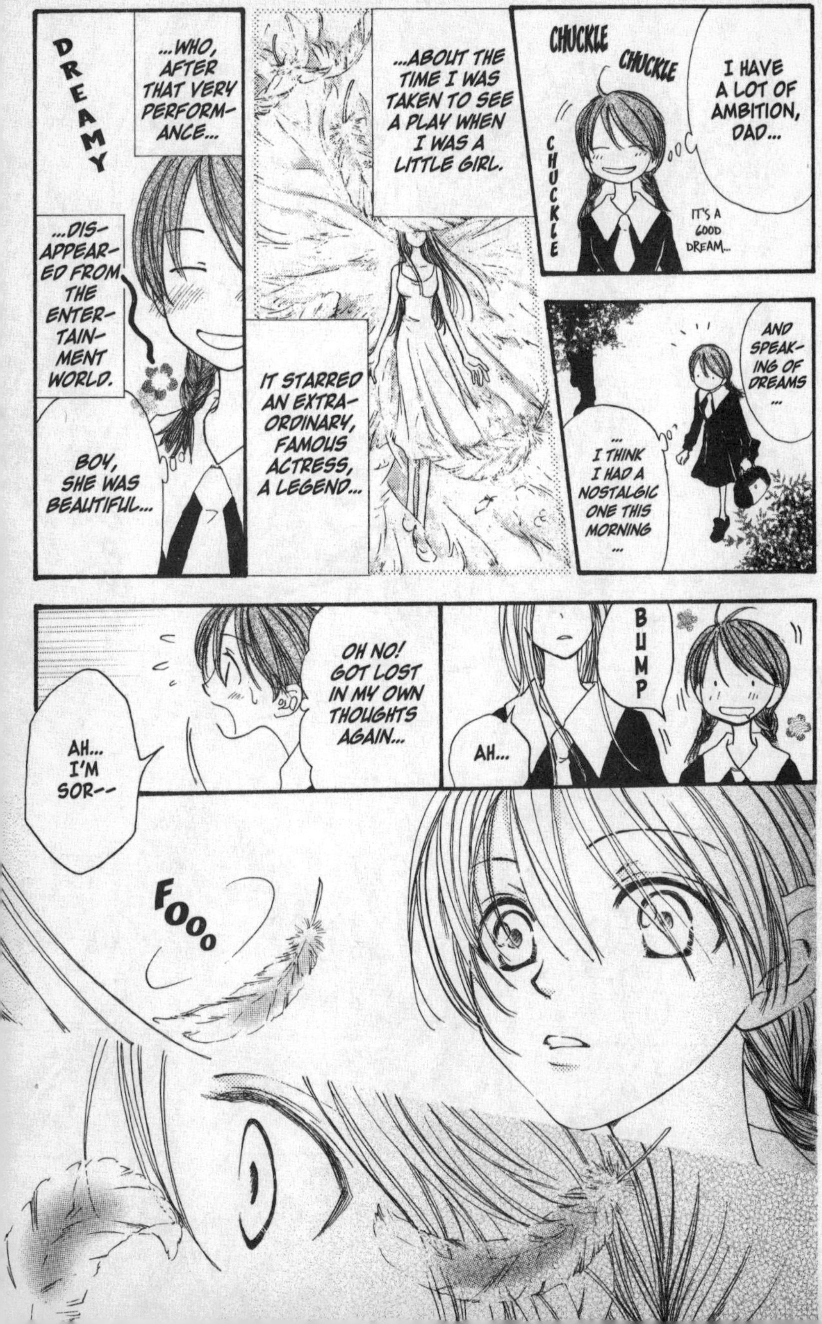
I HAVE A LOT OF AMBITION, DAD...
CHUCKLE CHUCKLE
CHUCKLE
IT'S A GOOD DREAM...
AND SPEAKING OF DREAMS...
...I THINK I HAD A NOSTALGIC ONE THIS MORNING...
...ABOUT THE TIME I WAS TAKEN TO SEE A PLAY WHEN I WAS A LITTLE GIRL.
IT STARRED AN EXTRA-ORDINARY, FAMOUS ACTRESS, A LEGEND...
...WHO, AFTER THAT VERY PERFORM-ANCE...
DREAMY
...DIS-APPEAR-ED FROM THE ENTER-TAIN-MENT WORLD.
BOY, SHE WAS BEAUTIFUL...
BUMP
AH...
OH NO! GOT LOST IN MY OWN THOUGHTS AGAIN...
AH... I'M SOR--
FOOO

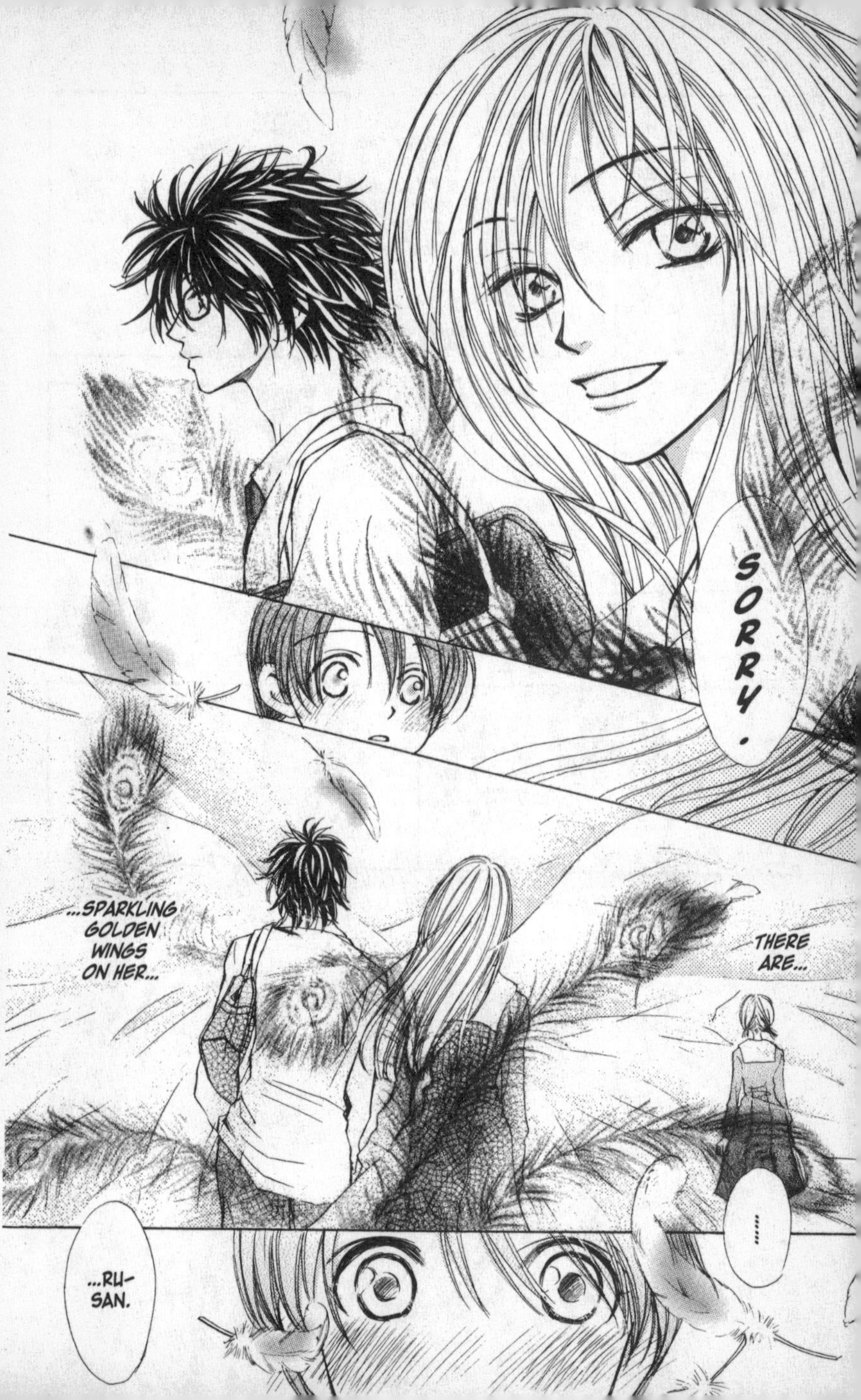
SORRY.
THERE ARE...
...SPARKLING GOLDEN WINGS ON HER...
......
...RU-SAN.

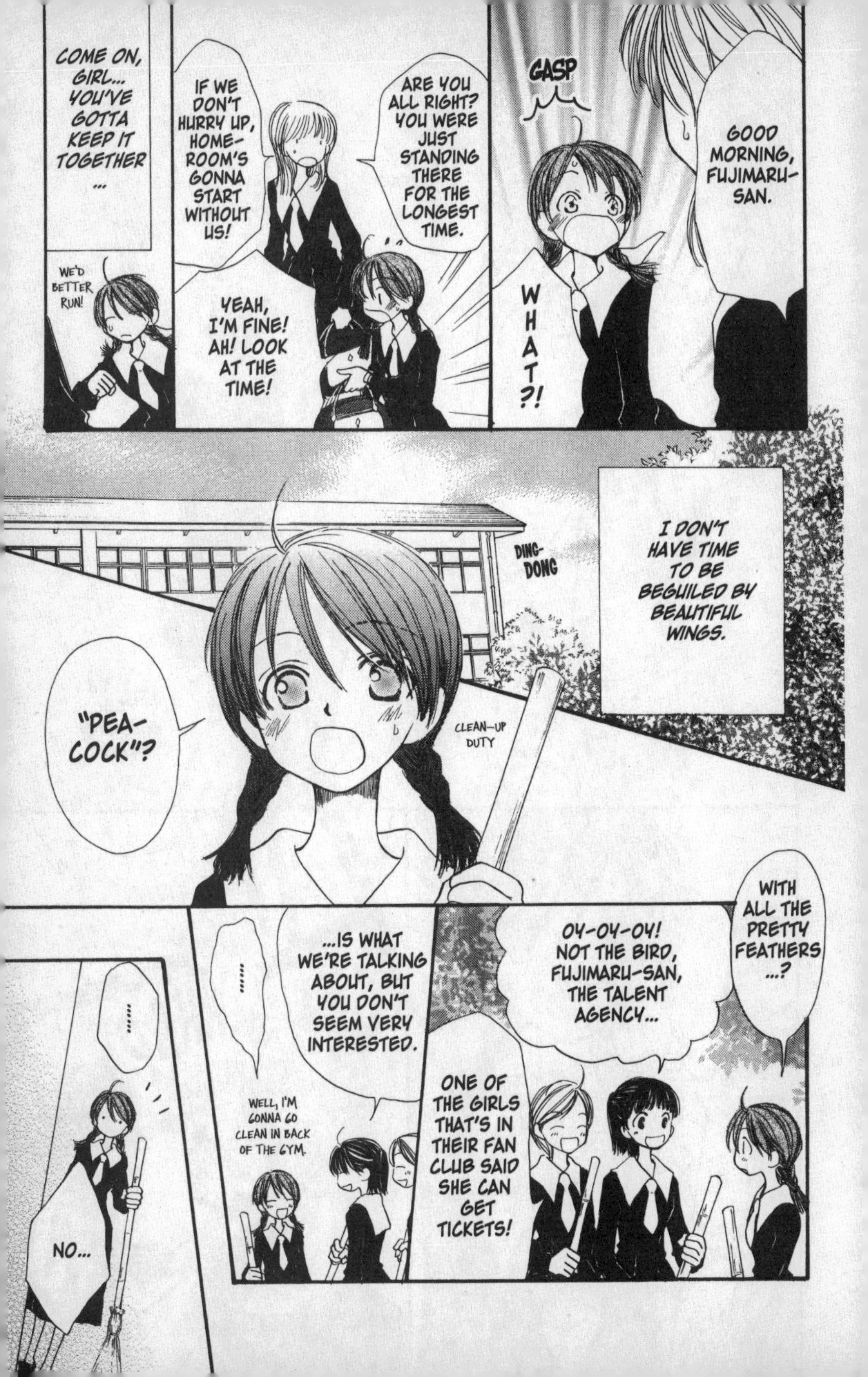
GOOD MORNING, FUJIMARU-SAN.
GASP
WHAT?!
ARE YOU ALL RIGHT? YOU WERE JUST STANDING THERE FOR THE LONGEST TIME.
IF WE DON'T HURRY UP, HOME-ROOM'S GONNA START WITHOUT US!
YEAH, I'M FINE! AH! LOOK AT THE TIME!
COME ON, GIRL... YOU'VE GOTTA KEEP IT TOGETHER...
WE'D BETTER RUN!
I DON'T HAVE TIME TO BE BEGUILED BY BEAUTIFUL WINGS.
DING-DONG
CLEAN-UP DUTY
"PEA-COCK"?
WITH ALL THE PRETTY FEATHERS...?
OY-OY-OY! NOT THE BIRD, FUJIMARU-SAN, THE TALENT AGENCY...
ONE OF THE GIRLS THAT'S IN THEIR FAN CLUB SAID SHE CAN GET TICKETS!
...IS WHAT WE'RE TALKING ABOUT, BUT YOU DON'T SEEM VERY INTERESTED.
......
WELL, I'M GONNA GO CLEAN IN BACK OF THE GYM.
......
NO...

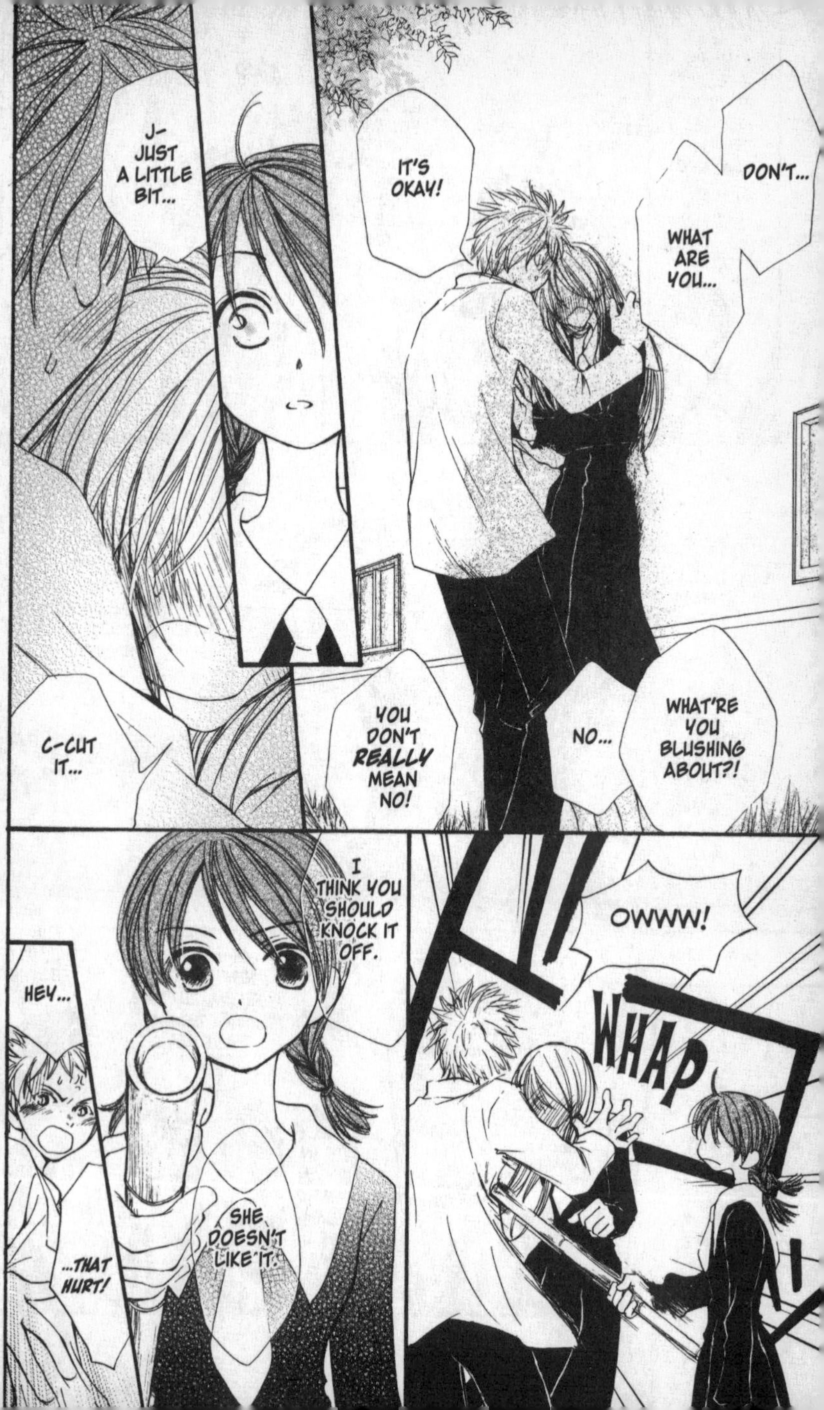
DON'T...
WHAT ARE YOU...
IT'S OKAY!
WHAT'RE YOU BLUSHING ABOUT?!
NO...
YOU DON'T REALLY MEAN NO!
J- JUST A LITTLE BIT...
C-CUT IT...
OWWW!
WHAP
I THINK YOU SHOULD KNOCK IT OFF.
HEY...
SHE DOESN'T LIKE IT.
...THAT HURT!

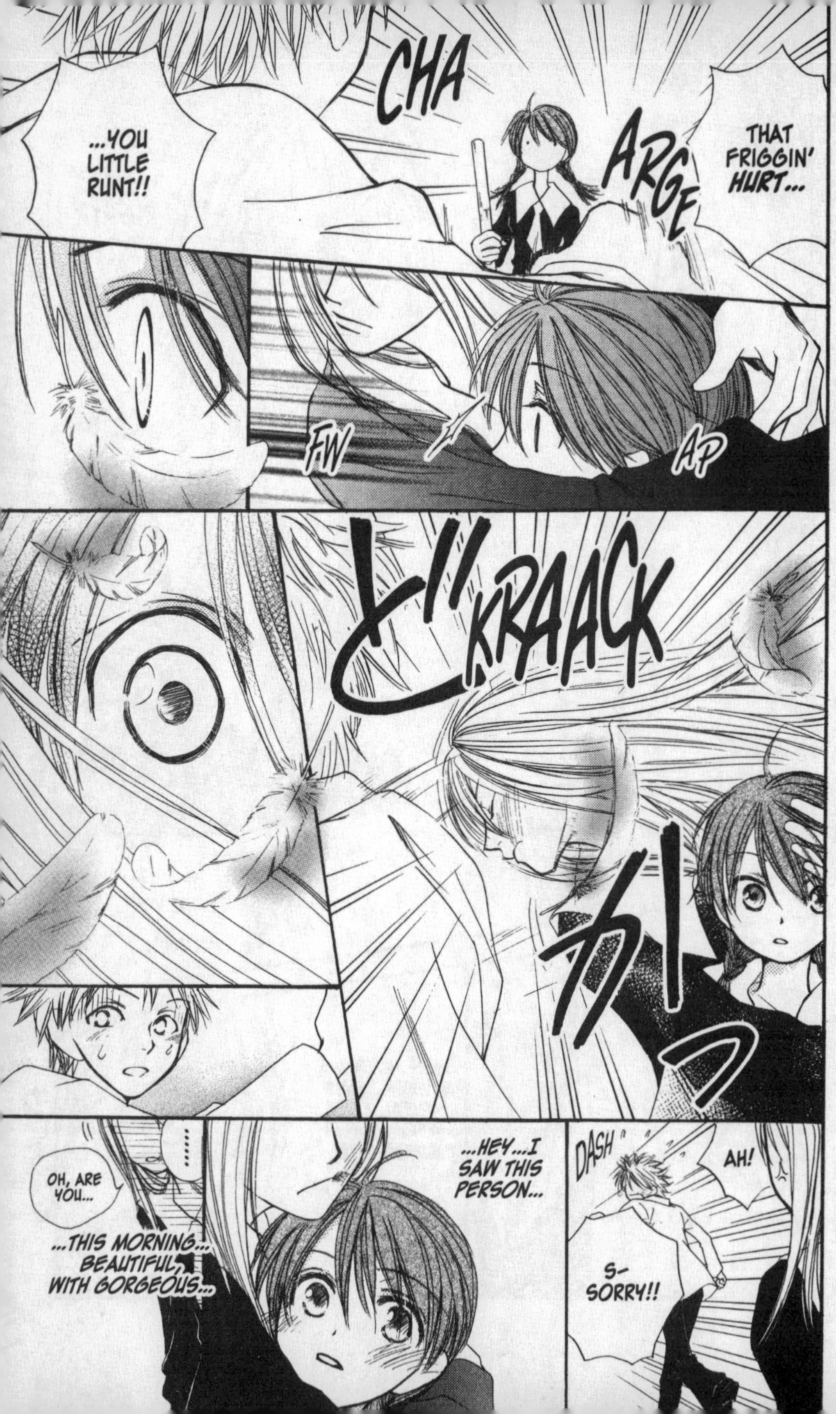
THAT FRIGGIN' HURT...
CHA
ARGE
...YOU LITTLE RUNT!!
FW
AP
KRAACK
AH!
DASH
S-SORRY!!
...HEY...I SAW THIS PERSON...
......
OH, ARE YOU...
...THIS MORNING... BEAUTIFUL, WITH GORGEOUS...

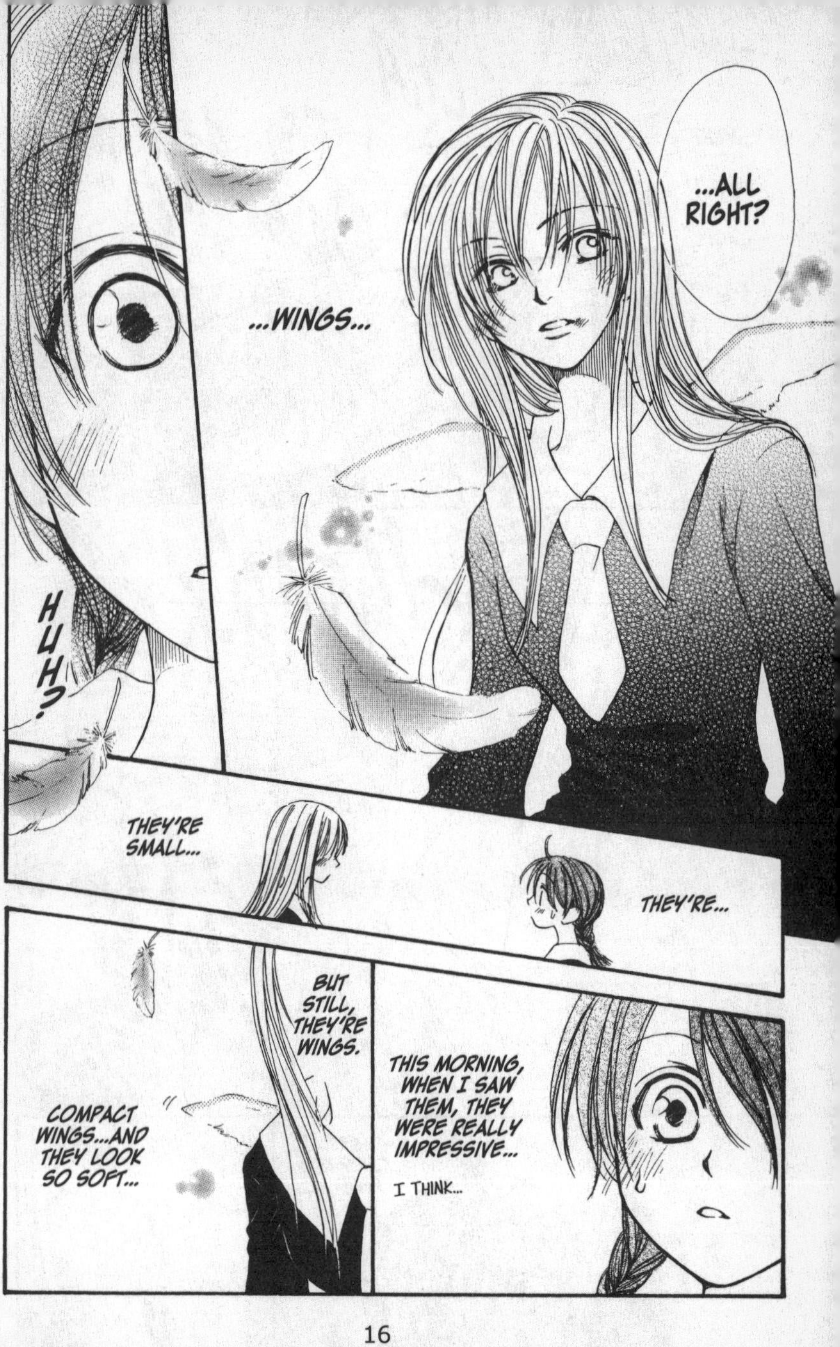
...ALL RIGHT?
...WINGS...
HUH?
THEY'RE...
THEY'RE SMALL...
THIS MORNING, WHEN I SAW THEM, THEY WERE REALLY IMPRESSIVE...
I THINK...
BUT STILL, THEY'RE WINGS.
COMPACT WINGS...AND THEY LOOK SO SOFT...

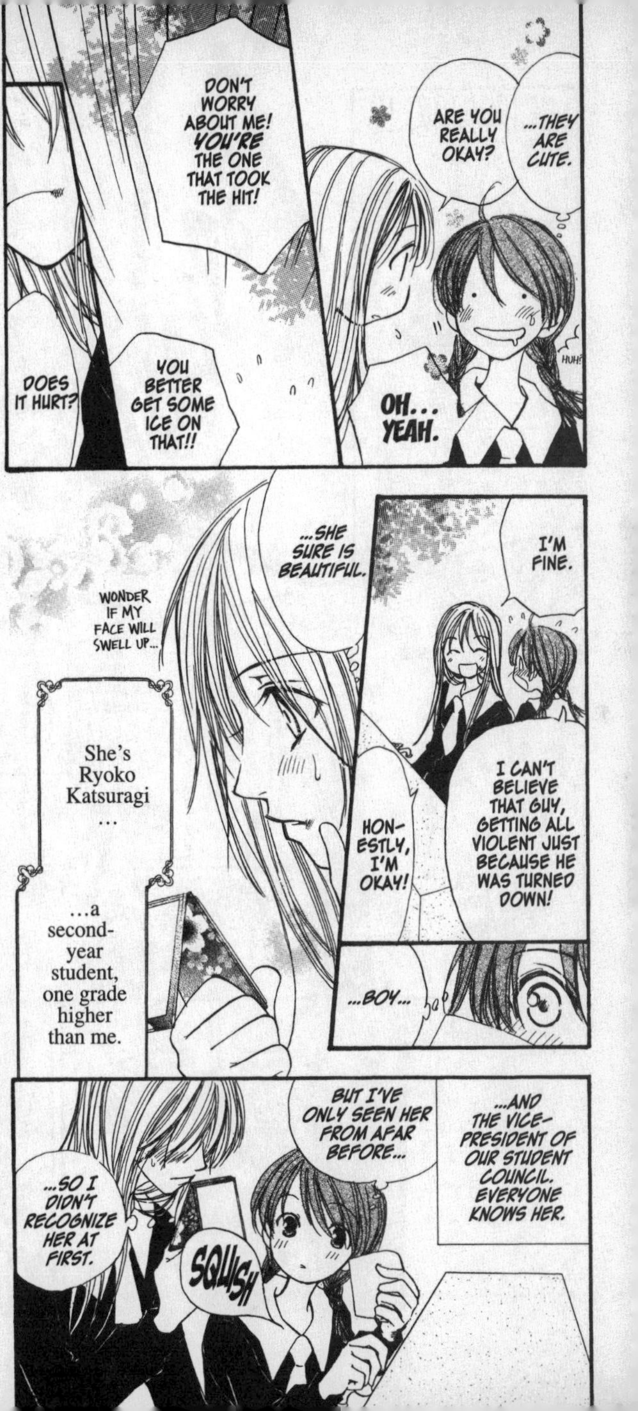
...THEY ARE CUTE.
ARE YOU REALLY OKAY?
HUH?
OH... YEAH.
DON'T WORRY ABOUT ME! YOU'RE THE ONE THAT TOOK THE HIT!
YOU BETTER GET SOME ICE ON THAT!!
DOES IT HURT?
I'M FINE.
I CAN'T BELIEVE THAT GUY, GETTING ALL VIOLENT JUST BECAUSE HE WAS TURNED DOWN!
HON-ESTLY, I'M OKAY!
...BOY...
...SHE SURE IS BEAUTIFUL.
WONDER IF MY FACE WILL SWELL UP...
She's Ryoko Katsuragi ...
...a second-year student, one grade higher than me.
...AND THE VICE-PRESIDENT OF OUR STUDENT COUNCIL. EVERYONE KNOWS HER.
BUT I'VE ONLY SEEN HER FROM AFAR BEFORE...
...SO I DIDN'T RECOGNIZE HER AT FIRST.
SQUISH

1/4 Sakura Mail

Part 1

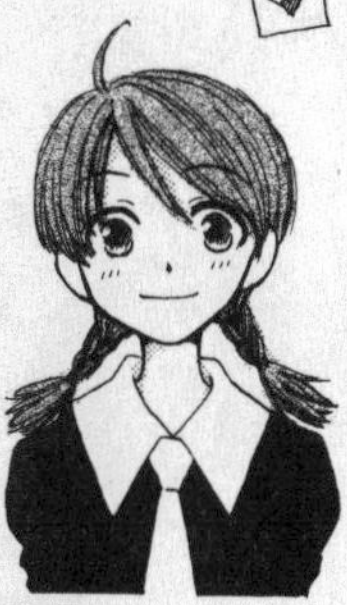

Hi! I'm Sakura Tsukuba. Whether you're a first-time reader of my stories or have read my work before, thank you for picking up this book!! Welcome to "Penguin Revolution!!" I had always wanted to do a series about a character or characters with some kind of talent and had been searching for ideas when I got sidetracked by and fixated on the entertainment world. So now we have a story about an idol!!

To be continued

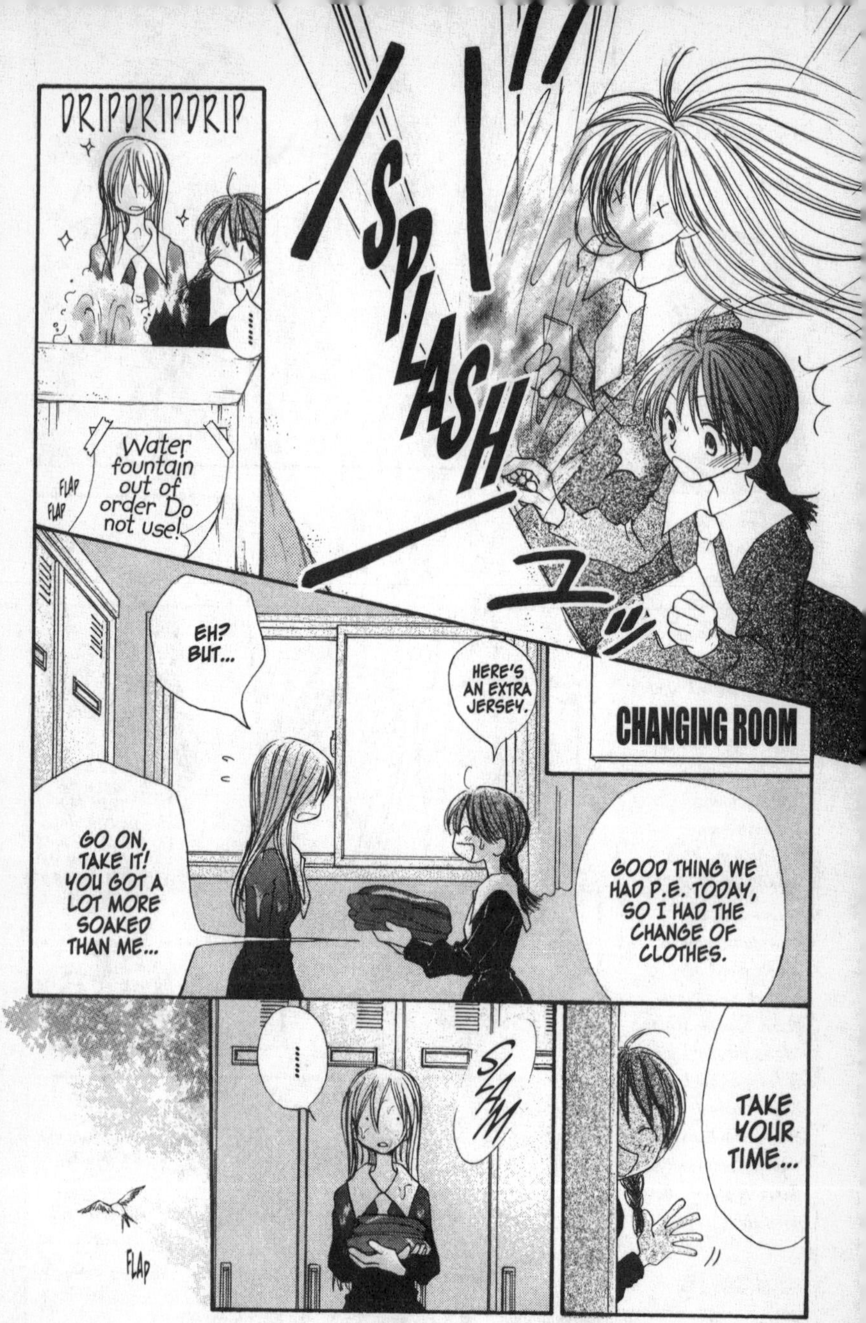
SPLASH
ユッ
DRIPDRIPDRIP
......
Water fountain out of order Do not use!
FLAP FLAP
CHANGING ROOM
HERE'S AN EXTRA JERSEY.
EH? BUT...
GOOD THING WE HAD P.E. TODAY, SO I HAD THE CHANGE OF CLOTHES.
GO ON, TAKE IT! YOU GOT A LOT MORE SOAKED THAN ME...
TAKE YOUR TIME...
SLAM
......
FLAP

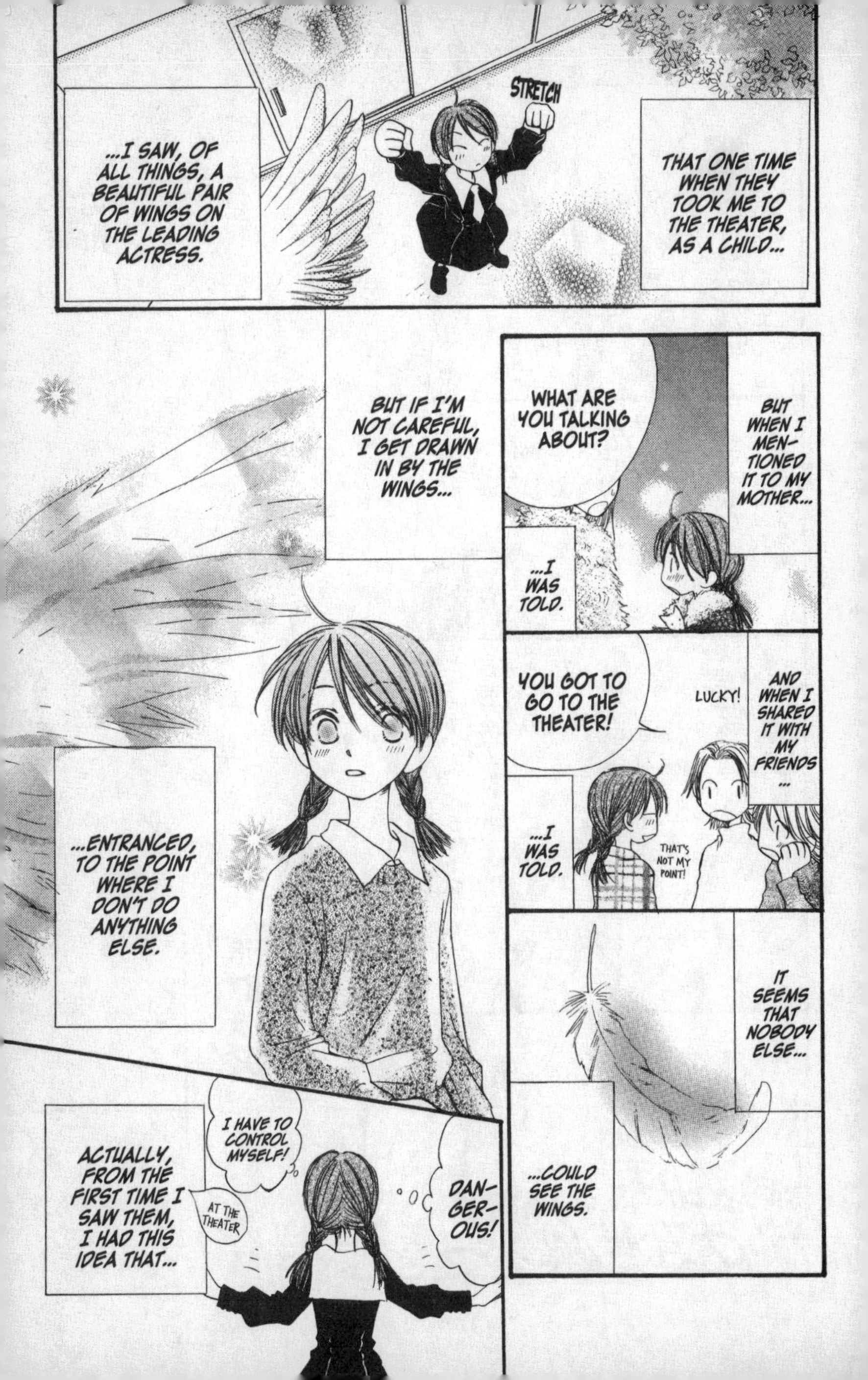
THAT ONE TIME WHEN THEY TOOK ME TO THE THEATER, AS A CHILD...
STRETCH
...I SAW, OF ALL THINGS, A BEAUTIFUL PAIR OF WINGS ON THE LEADING ACTRESS.
BUT WHEN I MENTIONED IT TO MY MOTHER...
WHAT ARE YOU TALKING ABOUT?
...I WAS TOLD.
AND WHEN I SHARED IT WITH MY FRIENDS ...
LUCKY!
YOU GOT TO GO TO THE THEATER!
THAT'S NOT MY POINT!
...I WAS TOLD.
IT SEEMS THAT NOBODY ELSE...
...COULD SEE THE WINGS.
BUT IF I'M NOT CAREFUL, I GET DRAWN IN BY THE WINGS...
...ENTRANCED, TO THE POINT WHERE I DON'T DO ANYTHING ELSE.
DAN-GER-OUS!
I HAVE TO CONTROL MYSELF!
AT THE THEATER
ACTUALLY, FROM THE FIRST TIME I SAW THEM, I HAD THIS IDEA THAT...

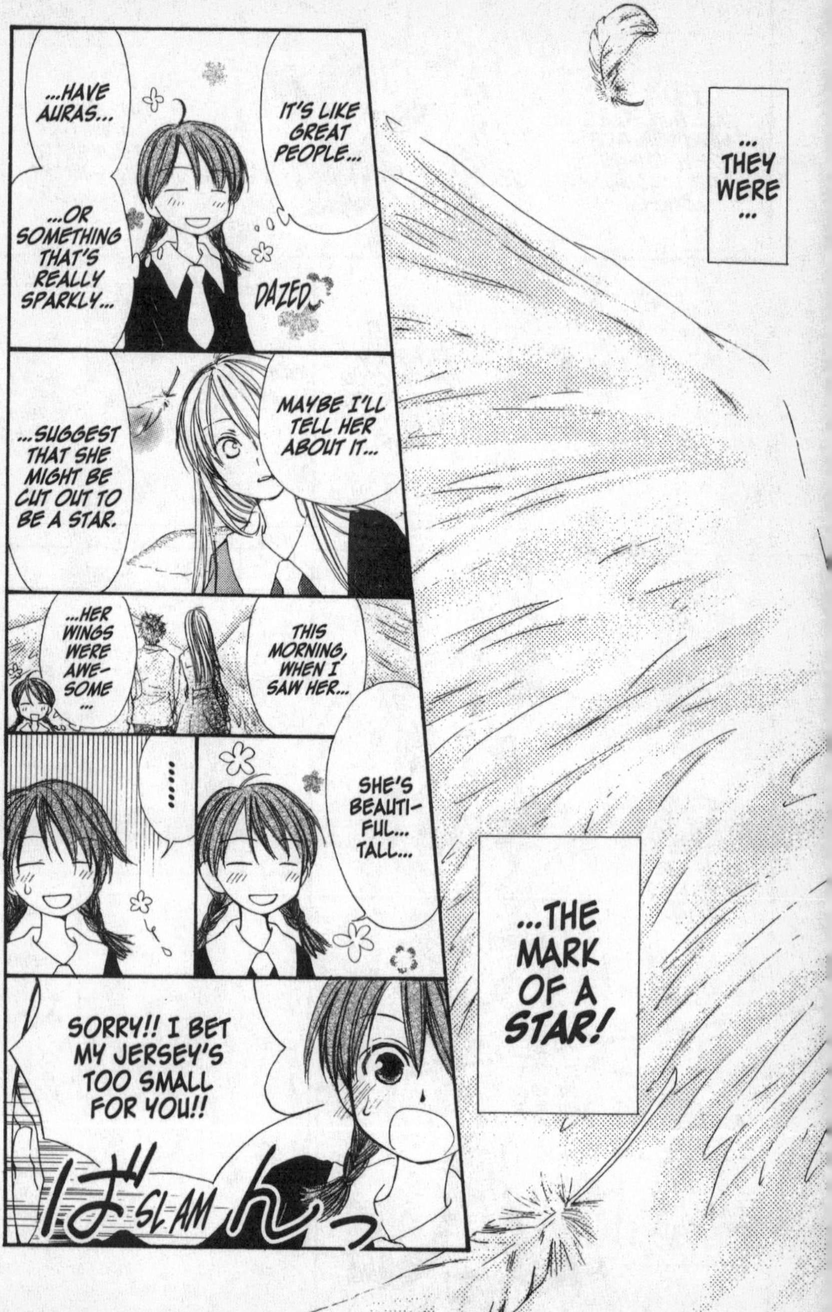
...THEY WERE...
...THE MARK OF A STAR!
IT'S LIKE GREAT PEOPLE...
...HAVE AURAS...
...OR SOMETHING THAT'S REALLY SPARKLY...
DAZED
MAYBE I'LL TELL HER ABOUT IT...
...SUGGEST THAT SHE MIGHT BE CUT OUT TO BE A STAR.
THIS MORNING, WHEN I SAW HER...
...HER WINGS WERE AWE-SOME...
SHE'S BEAUTI-FUL... TALL...
......
SORRY!! I BET MY JERSEY'S TOO SMALL FOR YOU!!
ばSLAMんっ

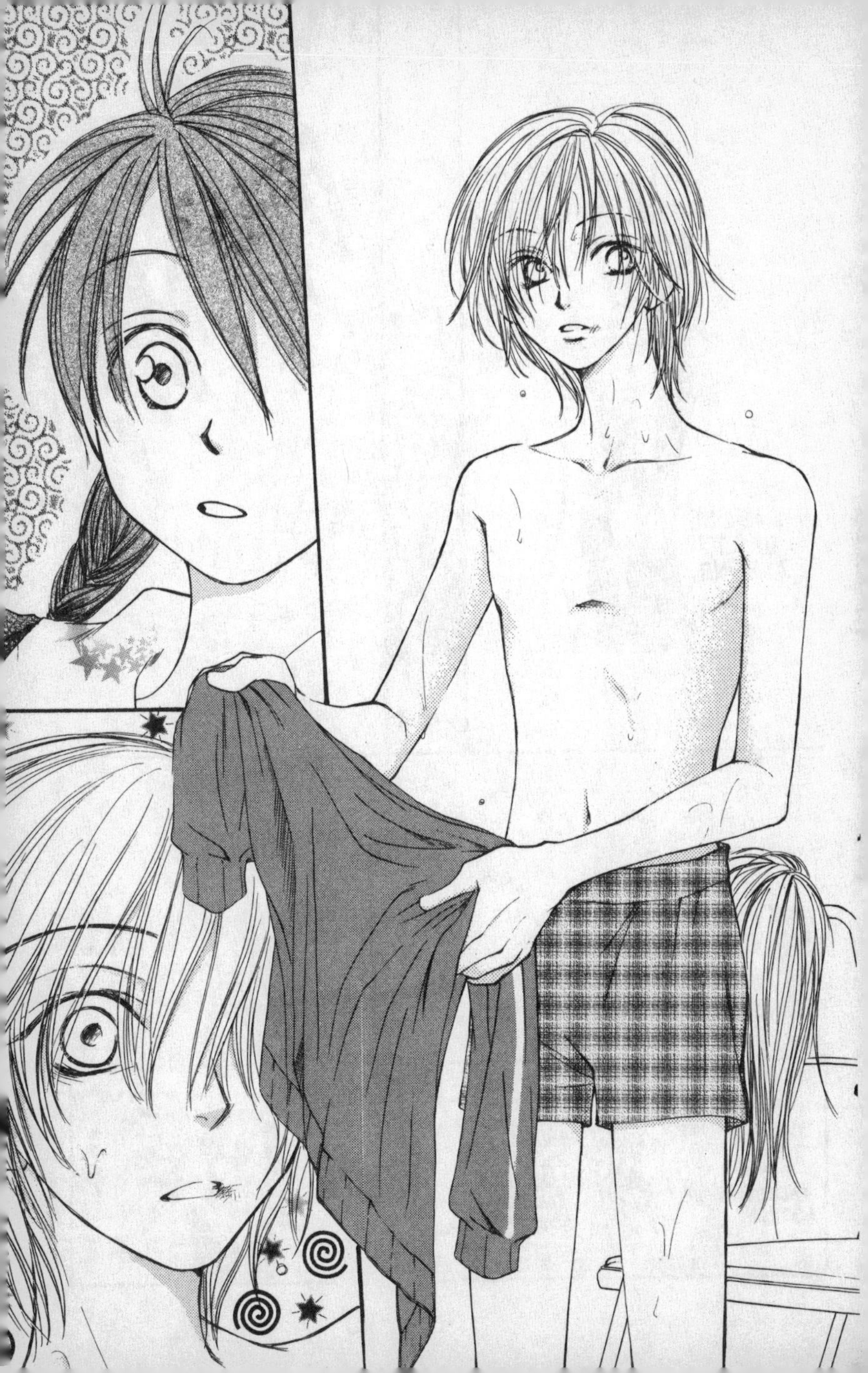

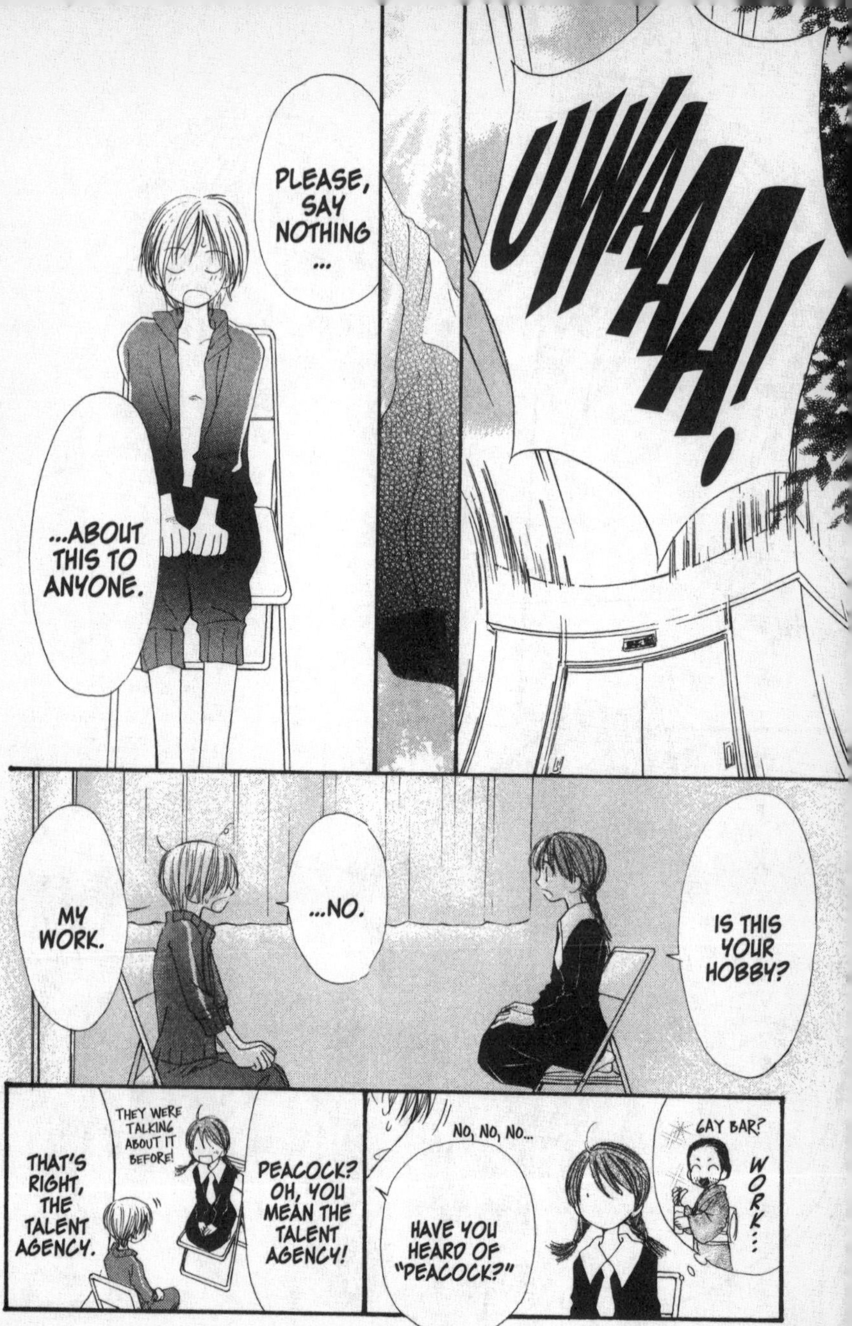
UWAAA!
PLEASE, SAY NOTHING ...
...ABOUT THIS TO ANYONE.
IS THIS YOUR HOBBY?
...NO.
MY WORK.
WORK...
GAY BAR?
NO, NO, NO...
HAVE YOU HEARD OF "PEACOCK?"
PEACOCK? OH, YOU MEAN THE TALENT AGENCY!
THEY WERE TALKING ABOUT IT BEFORE!
THAT'S RIGHT, THE TALENT AGENCY.

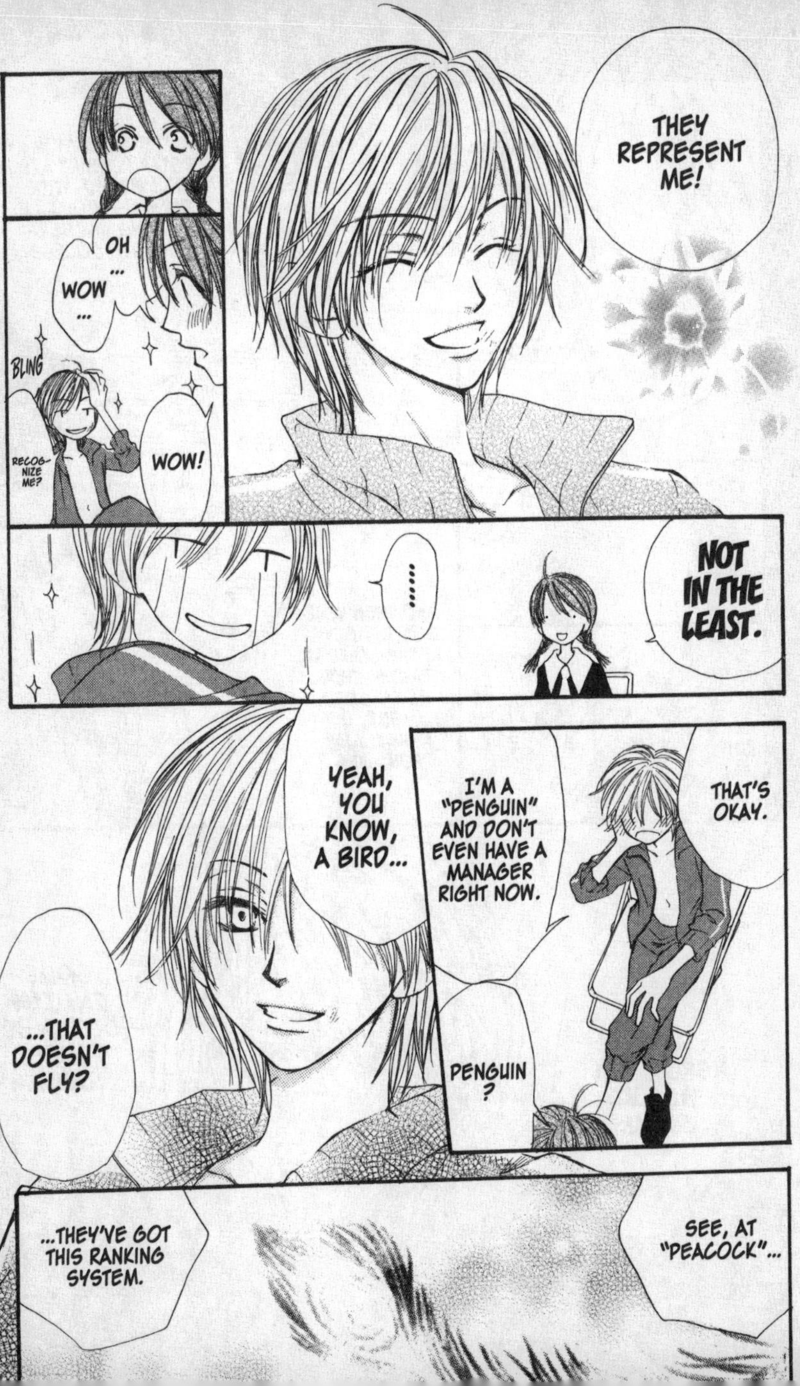
THEY REPRESENT ME!
OH ... WOW ...
WOW!
BLING
RECOG-NIZE ME?
NOT IN THE LEAST.
......
THAT'S OKAY.
I'M A "PENGUIN" AND DON'T EVEN HAVE A MANAGER RIGHT NOW.
PENGUIN?
YEAH, YOU KNOW, A BIRD...
...THAT DOESN'T FLY?
SEE, AT "PEACOCK"...
...THEY'VE GOT THIS RANKING SYSTEM.

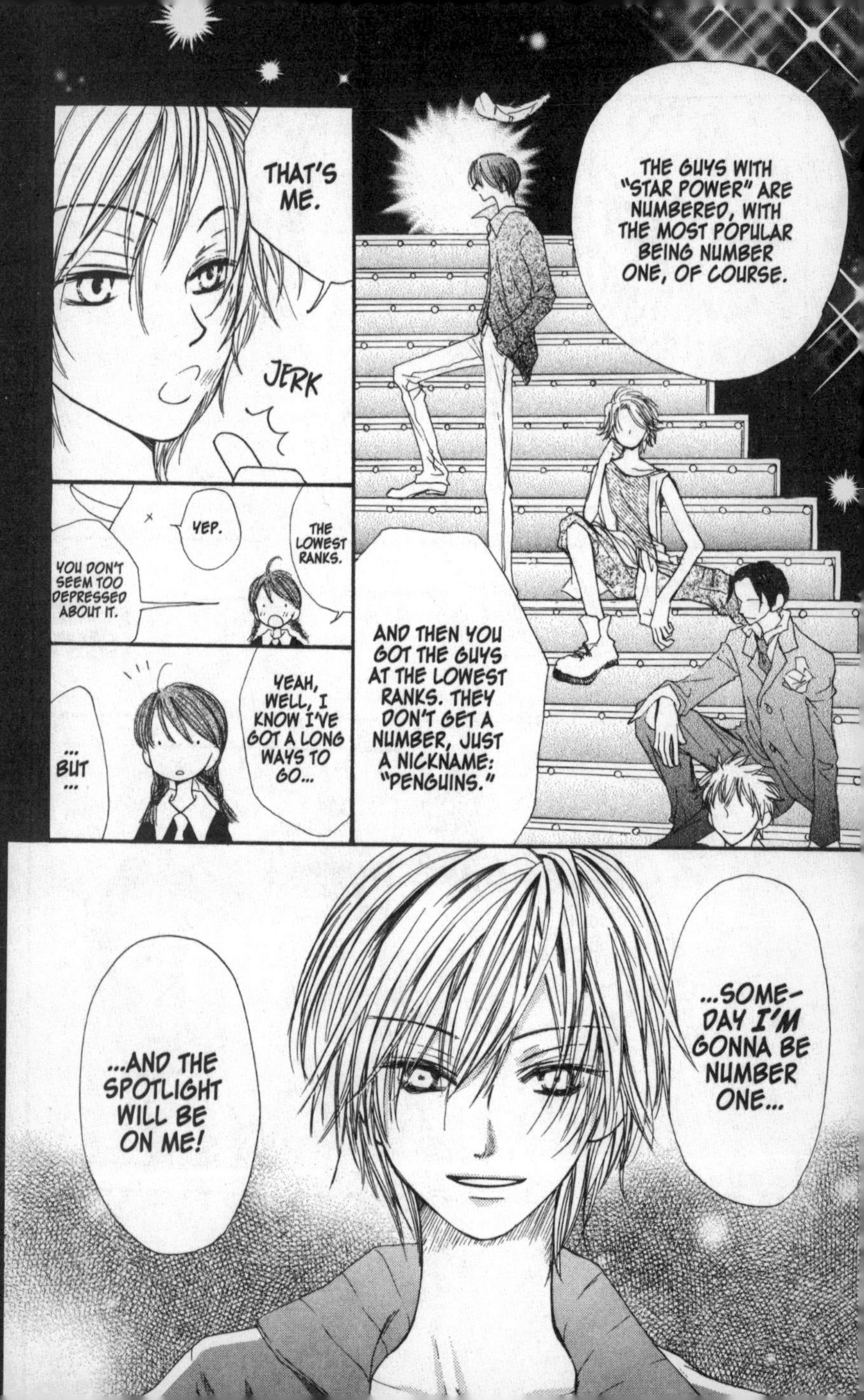
THE GUYS WITH "STAR POWER" ARE NUMBERED, WITH THE MOST POPULAR BEING NUMBER ONE, OF COURSE.
AND THEN YOU GOT THE GUYS AT THE LOWEST RANKS. THEY DON'T GET A NUMBER, JUST A NICKNAME: "PENGUINS."
THAT'S ME.
JERK
THE LOWEST RANKS.
YEP.
YOU DON'T SEEM TOO DEPRESSED ABOUT IT.
YEAH, WELL, I KNOW I'VE GOT A LONG WAYS TO GO...
... BUT ...
...SOME-DAY I'M GONNA BE NUMBER ONE...
...AND THE SPOTLIGHT WILL BE ON ME!

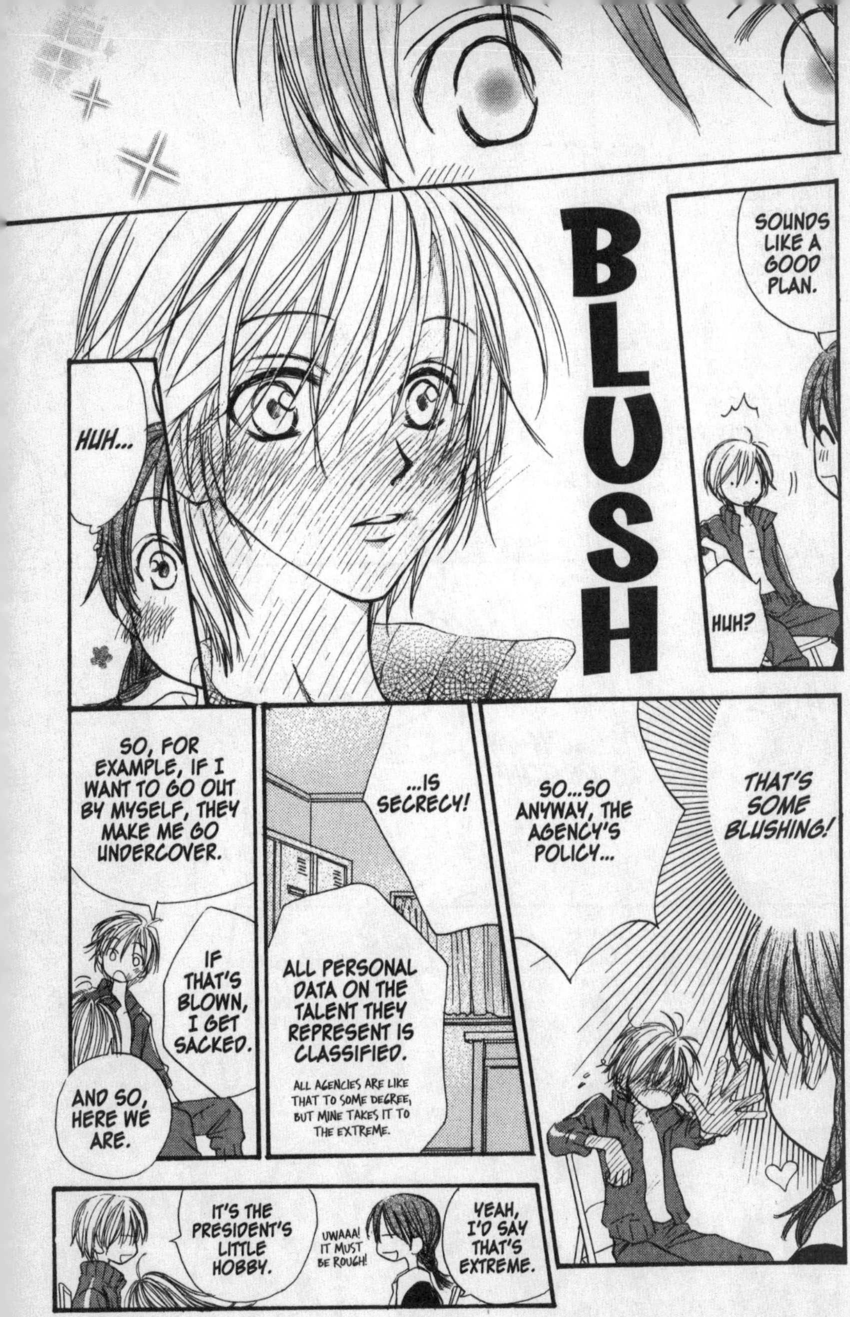

SOUNDS LIKE A GOOD PLAN.
HUH?
BLUSH
HUH...
THAT'S SOME BLUSHING!
SO...SO ANYWAY, THE AGENCY'S POLICY...
...IS SECRECY!
ALL PERSONAL DATA ON THE TALENT THEY REPRESENT IS CLASSIFIED.
ALL AGENCIES ARE LIKE THAT TO SOME DEGREE, BUT MINE TAKES IT TO THE EXTREME.
SO, FOR EXAMPLE, IF I WANT TO GO OUT BY MYSELF, THEY MAKE ME GO UNDERCOVER.
IF THAT'S BLOWN, I GET SACKED.
AND SO, HERE WE ARE.
YEAH, I'D SAY THAT'S EXTREME.
UWAAA! IT MUST BE ROUGH!
IT'S THE PRESIDENT'S LITTLE HOBBY.

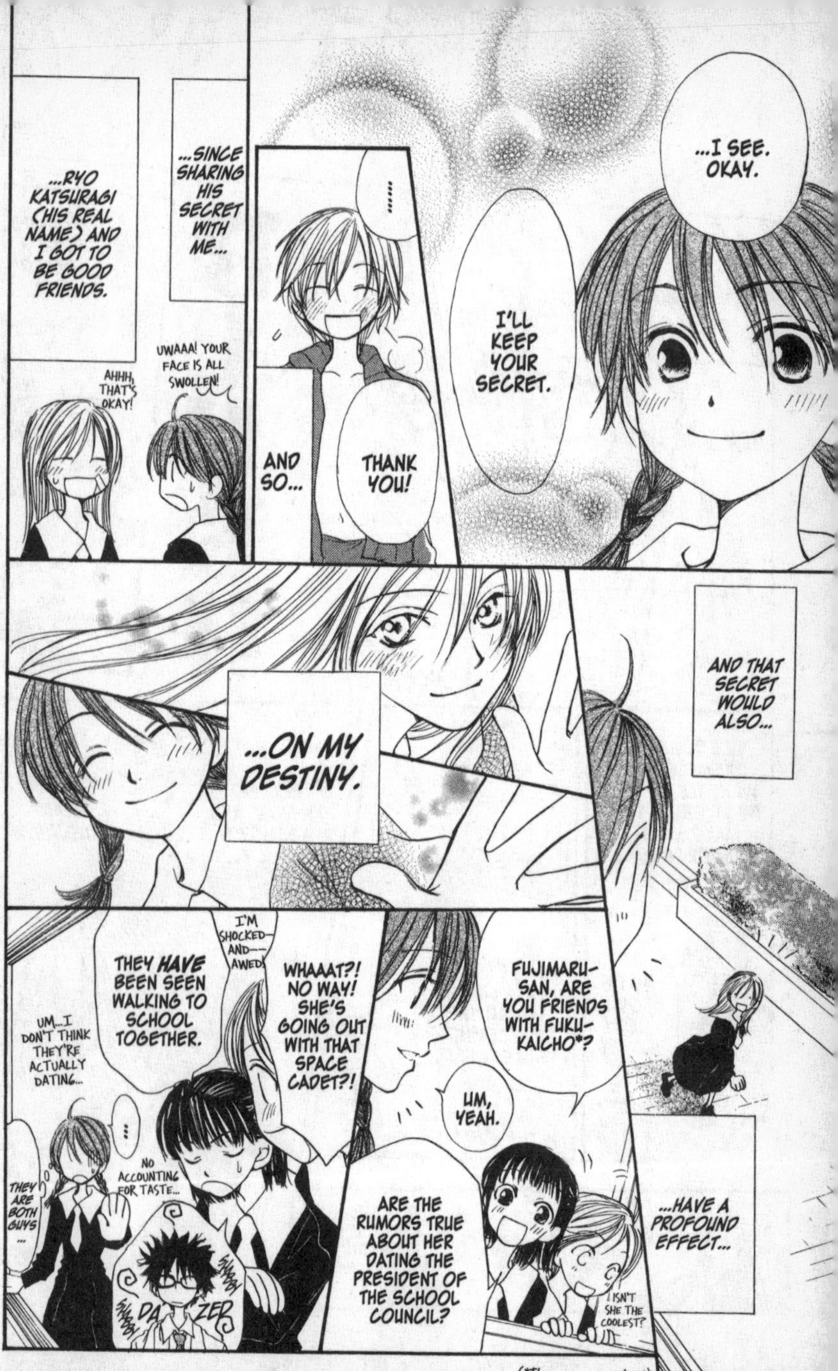
...I SEE. OKAY.
I'LL KEEP YOUR SECRET.
......
THANK YOU!
AND SO...
...SINCE SHARING HIS SECRET WITH ME...
...RYO KATSURAGI (HIS REAL NAME) AND I GOT TO BE GOOD FRIENDS.
UWAAA! YOUR FACE IS ALL SWOLLEN!
AHHH, THAT'S OKAY!
AND THAT SECRET WOULD ALSO...
...HAVE A PROFOUND EFFECT...
...ON MY DESTINY.
FUJIMARU-SAN, ARE YOU FRIENDS WITH FUKU-KAICHO*?
UM, YEAH.
ARE THE RUMORS TRUE ABOUT HER DATING THE PRESIDENT OF THE SCHOOL COUNCIL?
ISN'T SHE THE COOLEST?
WHAAAT?! NO WAY! SHE'S GOING OUT WITH THAT SPACE CADET?!
I'M SHOCKED AND—AWED!
THEY HAVE BEEN SEEN WALKING TO SCHOOL TOGETHER.
UM...I DON'T THINK THEY'RE ACTUALLY DATING...
...
NO ACCOUNTING FOR TASTE...
THEY ARE BOTH GUYS...
SHABBY
SHABBY

(*The vice-president)

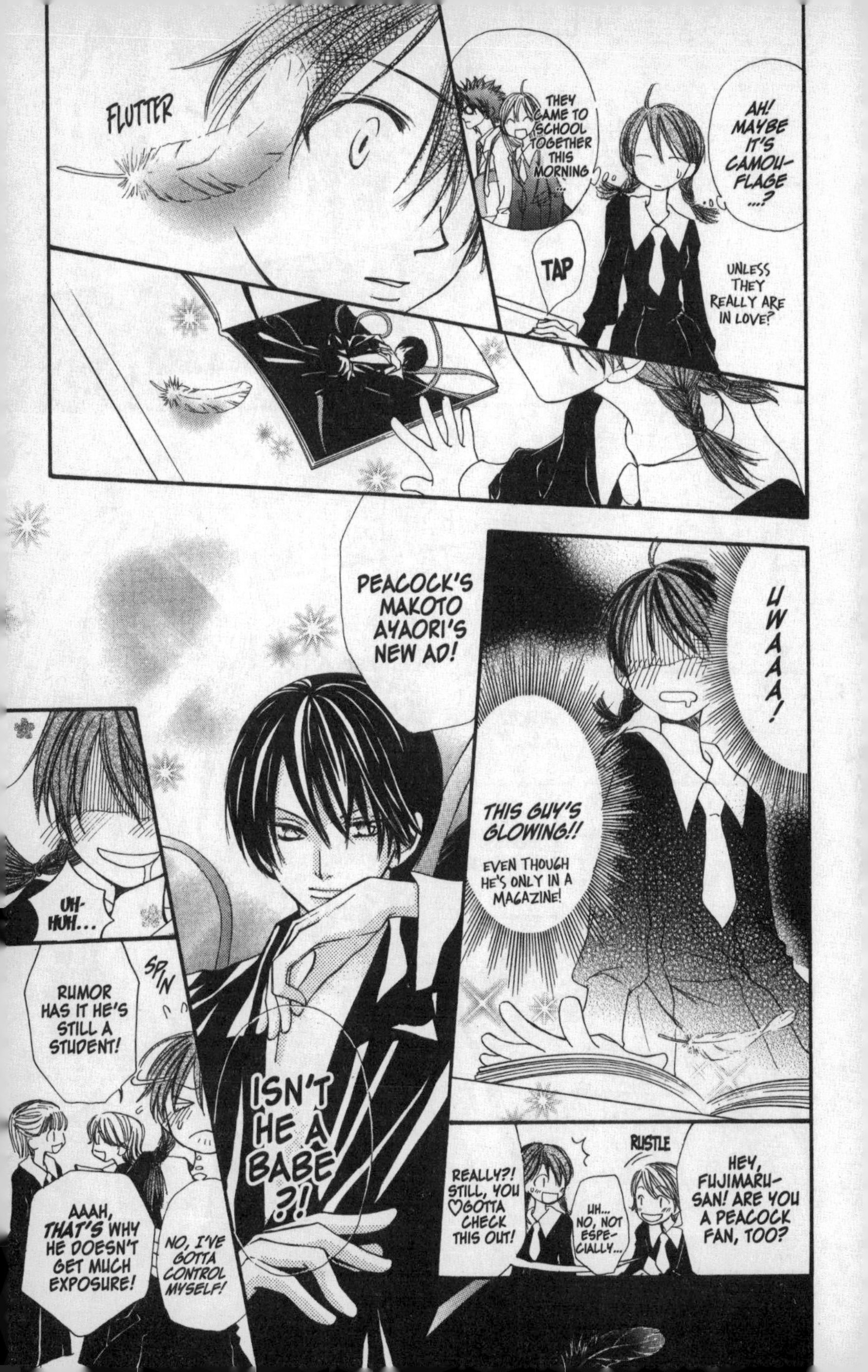
AH! MAYBE IT'S CAMOUFLAGE ...?
THEY CAME TO SCHOOL TOGETHER THIS MORNING ...
UNLESS THEY REALLY ARE IN LOVE?
TAP
FLUTTER
UWAAAA!
THIS GUY'S GLOWING!!
EVEN THOUGH HE'S ONLY IN A MAGAZINE!
PEACOCK'S MAKOTO AYAORI'S NEW AD!
ISN'T HE A BABE?!
HEY, FUJIMARU-SAN! ARE YOU A PEACOCK FAN, TOO?
RUSTLE
UH... NO, NOT ESPECIALLY...
REALLY?! STILL, YOU GOTTA CHECK THIS OUT!
UH-HUH...
SPIN
RUMOR HAS IT HE'S STILL A STUDENT!
NO, I'VE GOTTA CONTROL MYSELF!
AAAH, THAT'S WHY HE DOESN'T GET MUCH EXPOSURE!

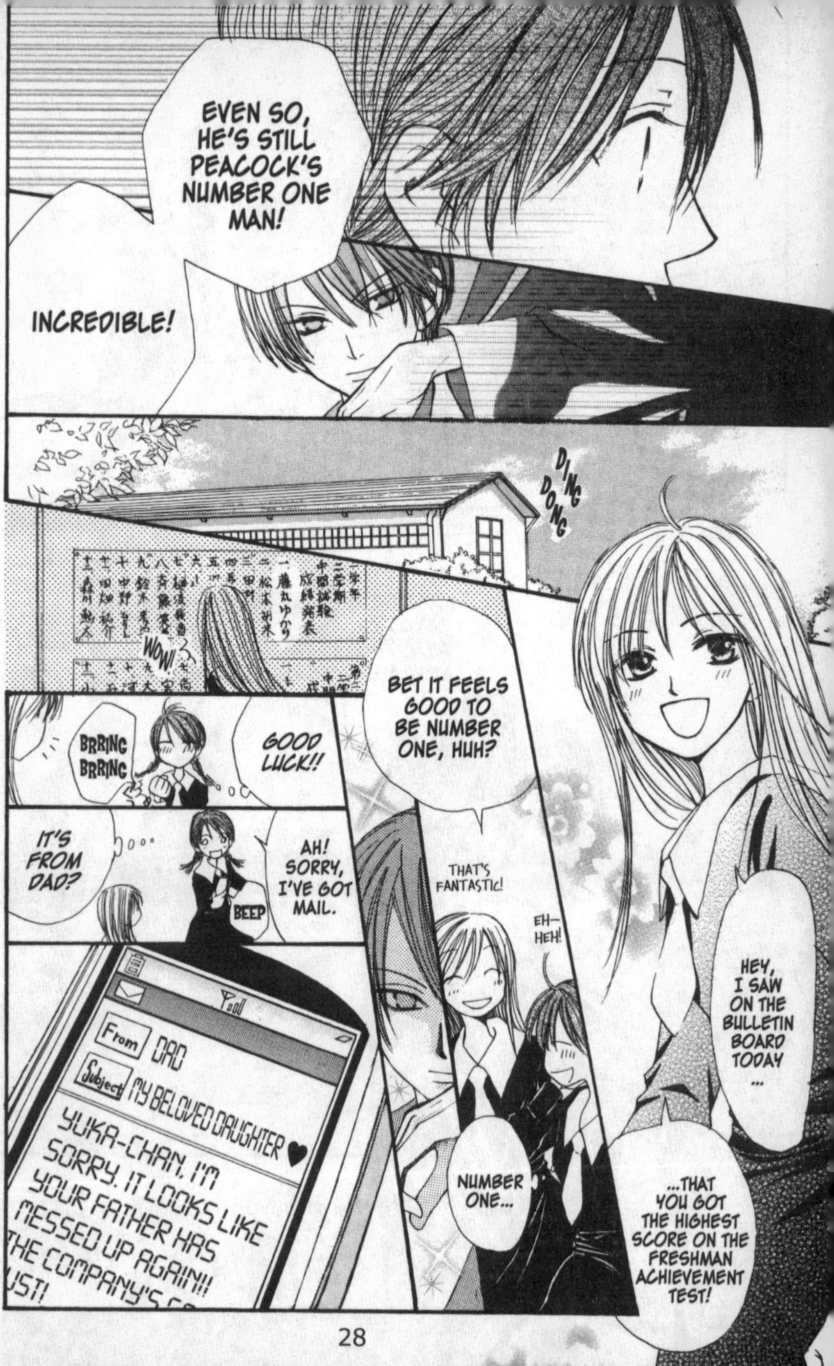
EVEN SO, HE'S STILL PEACOCK'S NUMBER ONE MAN!
INCREDIBLE!
DING DONG
WOW!
HEY, I SAW ON THE BULLETIN BOARD TODAY ...
...THAT YOU GOT THE HIGHEST SCORE ON THE FRESHMAN ACHIEVEMENT TEST!
BET IT FEELS GOOD TO BE NUMBER ONE, HUH?
THAT'S FANTASTIC!
EH-HEH!
NUMBER ONE...
GOOD LUCK!!
BRRING BRRING
AH! SORRY, I'VE GOT MAIL.
BEEP
IT'S FROM DAD?
From DAD
Subject MY BELOVED DAUGHTER ♥
YUKA-CHAN, I'M SORRY. IT LOOKS LIKE YOUR FATHER HAS MESSED UP AGAIN!!! THE COMPANY'S

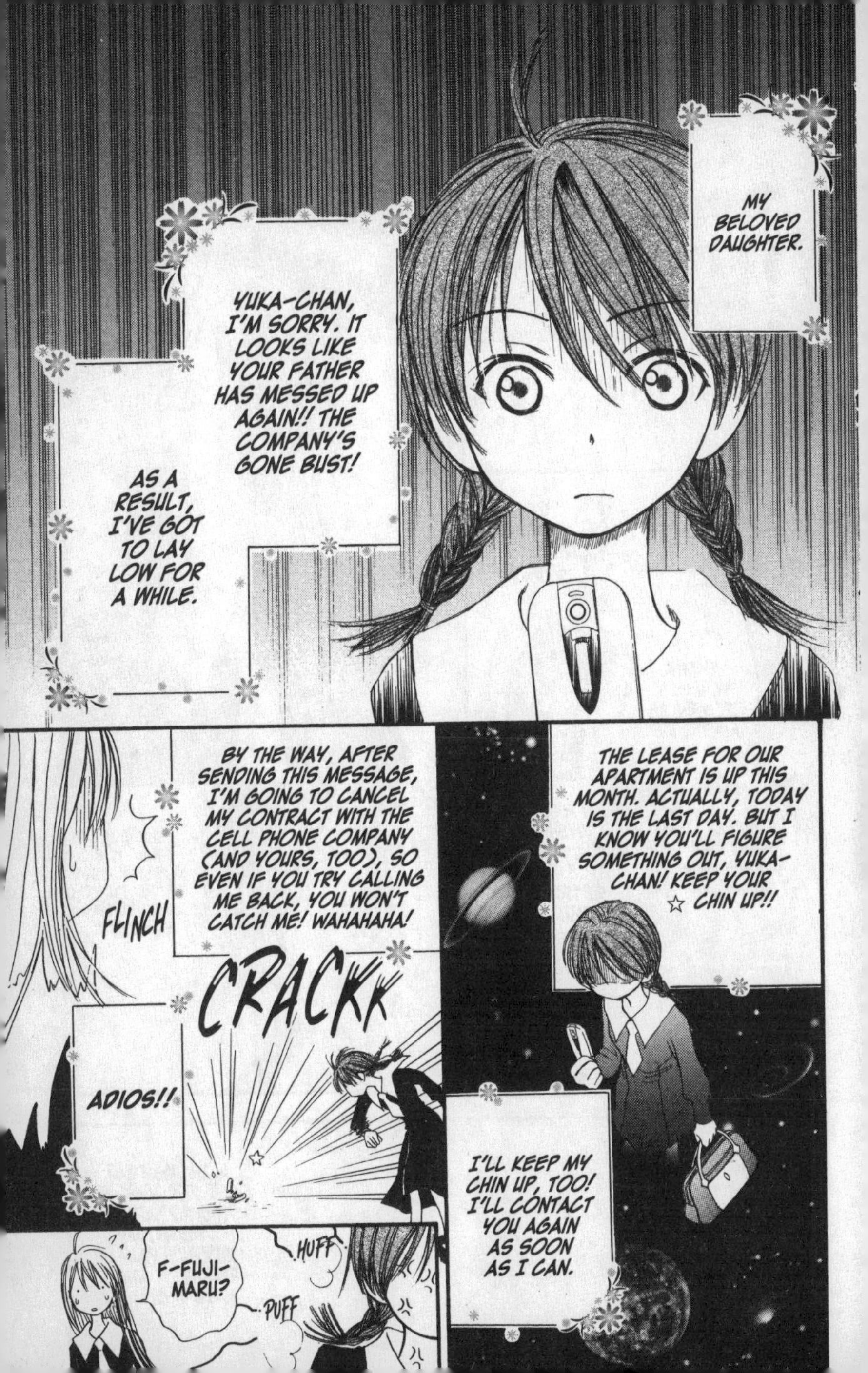
MY BELOVED DAUGHTER.
YUKA-CHAN, I'M SORRY. IT LOOKS LIKE YOUR FATHER HAS MESSED UP AGAIN!! THE COMPANY'S GONE BUST!
AS A RESULT, I'VE GOT TO LAY LOW FOR A WHILE.
THE LEASE FOR OUR APARTMENT IS UP THIS MONTH. ACTUALLY, TODAY IS THE LAST DAY. BUT I KNOW YOU'LL FIGURE SOMETHING OUT, YUKA-CHAN! KEEP YOUR ☆ CHIN UP!!
I'LL KEEP MY CHIN UP, TOO! I'LL CONTACT YOU AGAIN AS SOON AS I CAN.
BY THE WAY, AFTER SENDING THIS MESSAGE, I'M GOING TO CANCEL MY CONTRACT WITH THE CELL PHONE COMPANY (AND YOURS, TOO), SO EVEN IF YOU TRY CALLING ME BACK, YOU WON'T CATCH ME! WAHAHAHA!
FLINCH
CRACKK
ADIOS!!
HUFF
PUFF
F-FUJI-MARU?

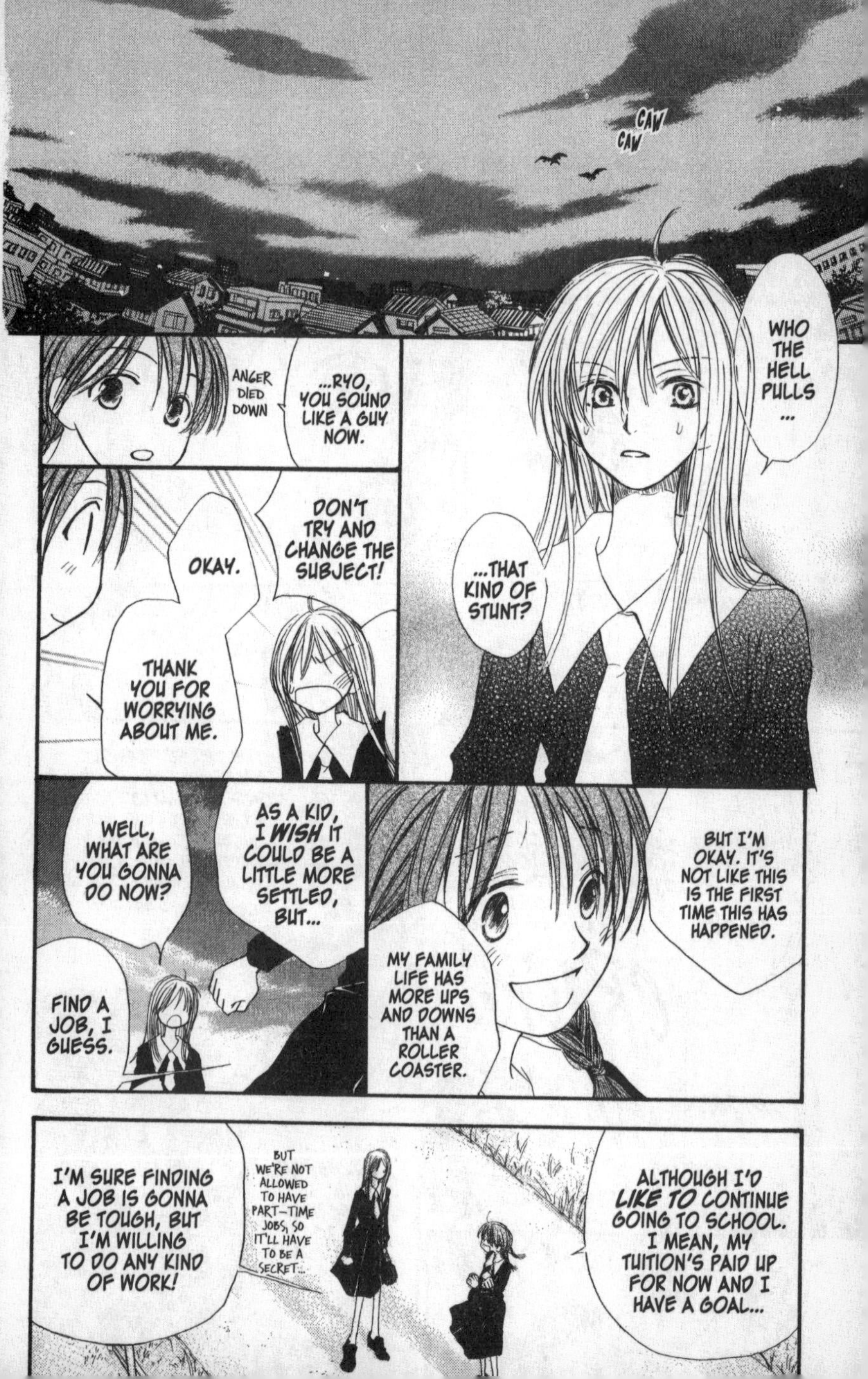
CAW
CAW
WHO THE HELL PULLS...
...THAT KIND OF STUNT?
...RYO, YOU SOUND LIKE A GUY NOW.
ANGER DIED DOWN
DON'T TRY AND CHANGE THE SUBJECT!
OKAY.
THANK YOU FOR WORRYING ABOUT ME.
BUT I'M OKAY. IT'S NOT LIKE THIS IS THE FIRST TIME THIS HAS HAPPENED.
MY FAMILY LIFE HAS MORE UPS AND DOWNS THAN A ROLLER COASTER.
AS A KID, I *WISH* IT COULD BE A LITTLE MORE SETTLED, BUT...
WELL, WHAT ARE YOU GONNA DO NOW?
FIND A JOB, I GUESS.
ALTHOUGH I'D *LIKE TO* CONTINUE GOING TO SCHOOL. I MEAN, MY TUITION'S PAID UP FOR NOW AND I HAVE A GOAL...
BUT WE'RE NOT ALLOWED TO HAVE PART-TIME JOBS, SO IT'LL HAVE TO BE A SECRET...
I'M SURE FINDING A JOB IS GONNA BE TOUGH, BUT I'M WILLING TO DO ANY KIND OF WORK!

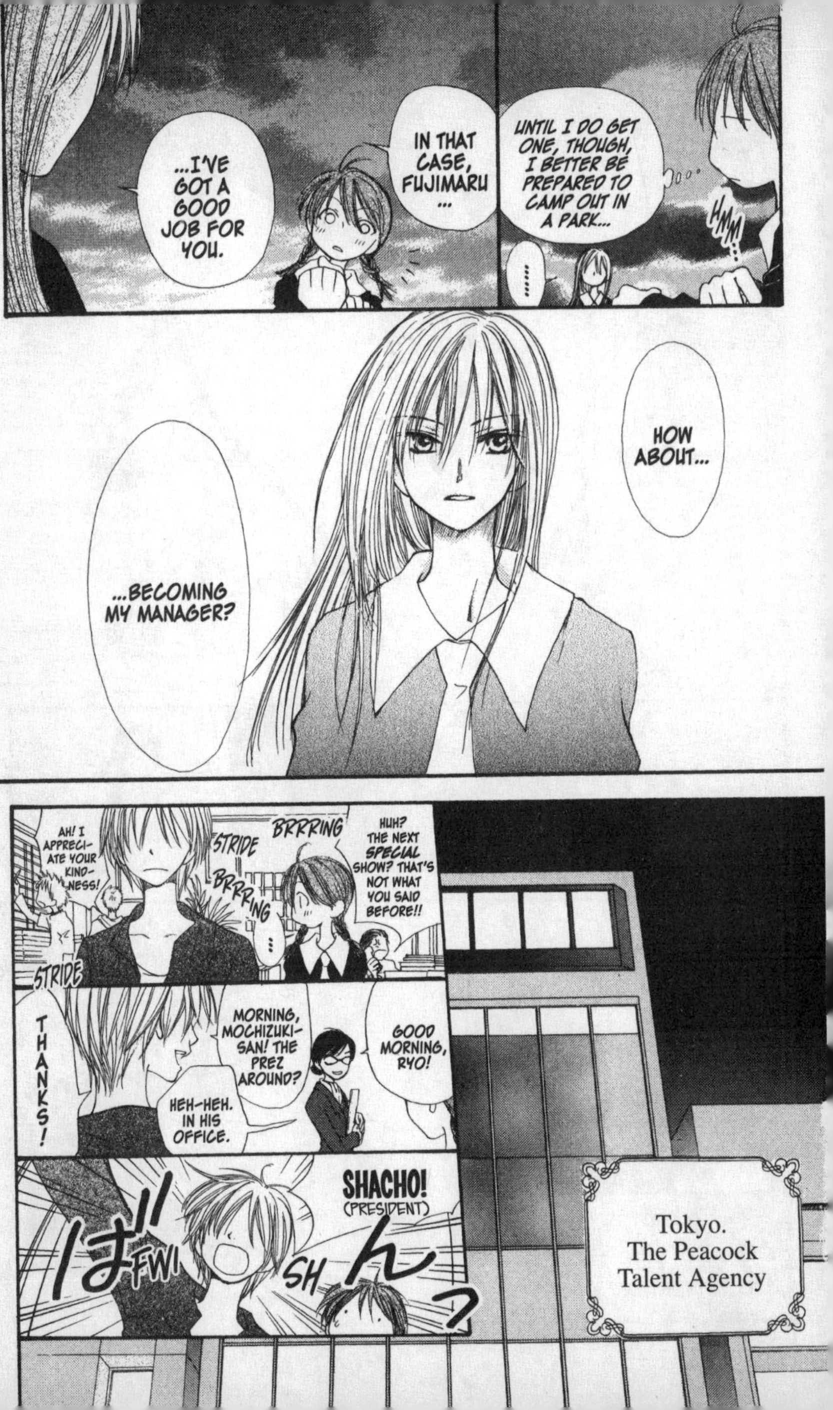
UNTIL I DO GET ONE, THOUGH, I BETTER BE PREPARED TO CAMP OUT IN A PARK...
HMM
......
IN THAT CASE, FUJIMARU ...
...I'VE GOT A GOOD JOB FOR YOU.
HOW ABOUT...
...BECOMING MY MANAGER?
Tokyo. The Peacock Talent Agency
HUH? THE NEXT SPECIAL SHOW? THAT'S NOT WHAT YOU SAID BEFORE!!
BRRRING
STRIDE
BRRRING
...
AH! I APPRECIATE YOUR KINDNESS!
STRIDE
GOOD MORNING, RYO!
MORNING, MOCHIZUKI-SAN! THE PREZ AROUND?
HEH-HEH. IN HIS OFFICE.
THANKS!
SHACHO! (PRESIDENT)
ばFWI SHん

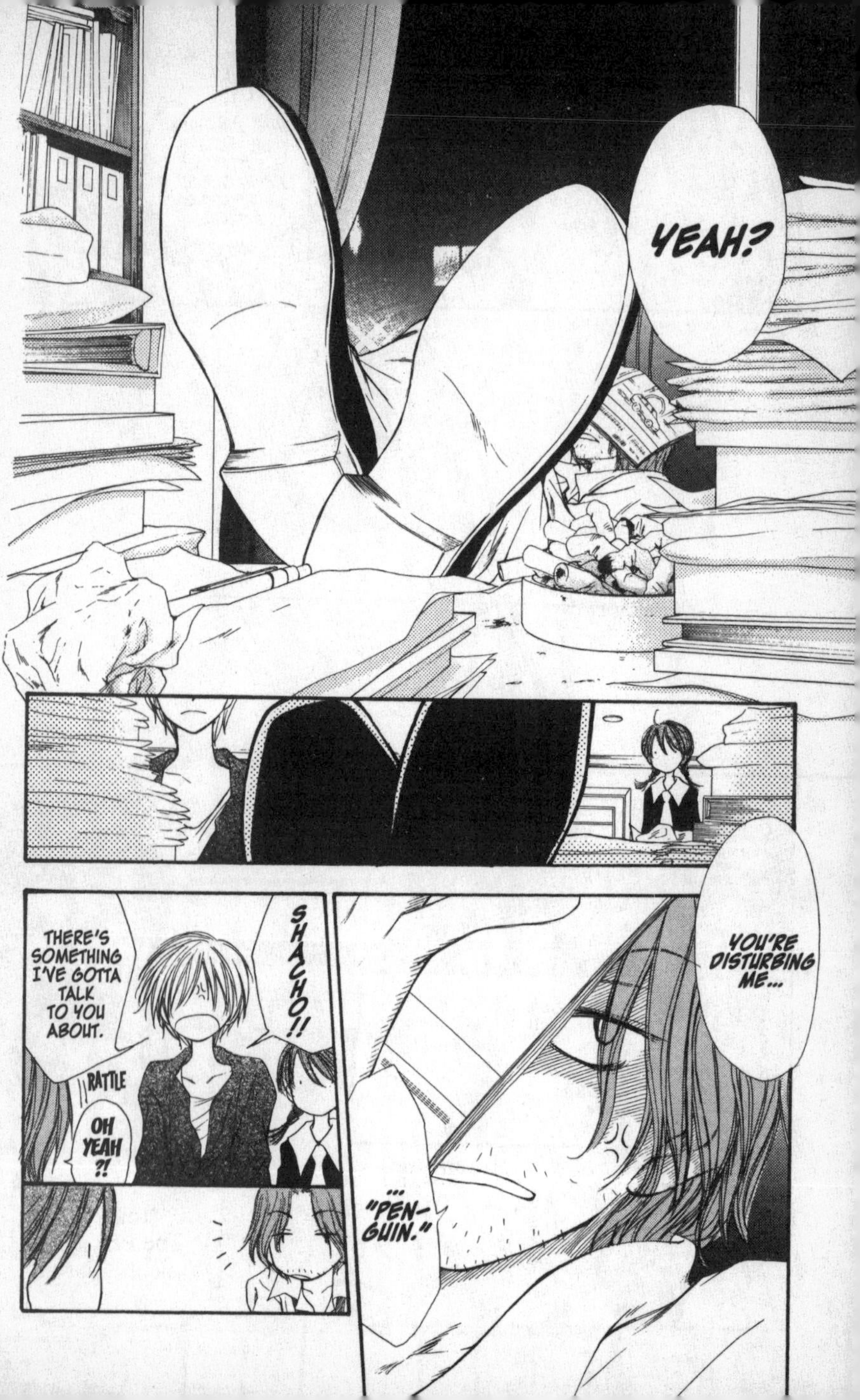
YEAH?
YOU'RE DISTURBING ME...
..."PEN-GUIN."
SHACHO!!
THERE'S SOMETHING I'VE GOTTA TALK TO YOU ABOUT.
RATTLE
OH YEAH?!

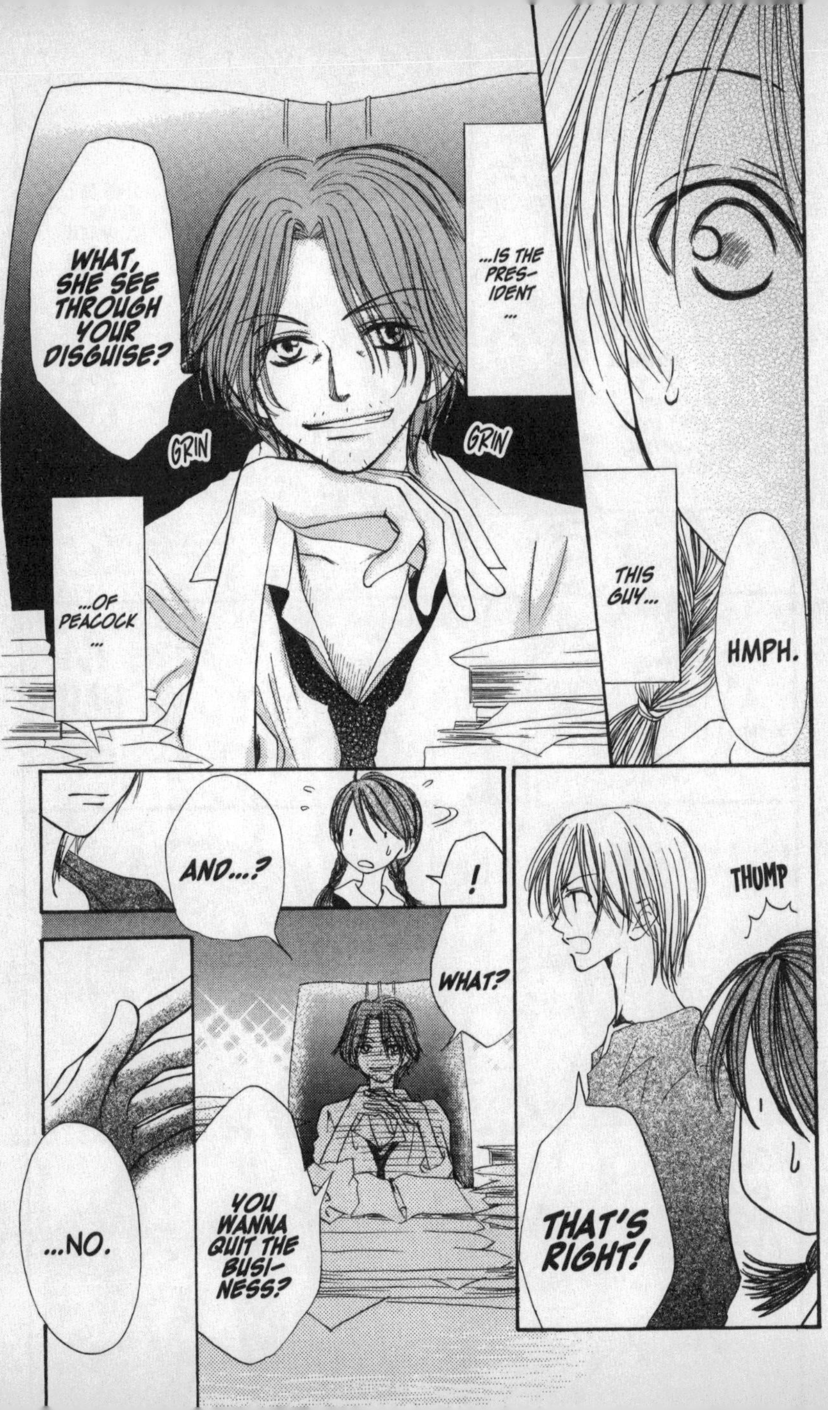
THIS GUY...
HMPH.
...IS THE PRES-IDENT ...
WHAT, SHE SEE THROUGH YOUR DISGUISE?
GRIN
GRIN
...OF PEACOCK ...
THUMP
THAT'S RIGHT!
!
AND...?
WHAT?
YOU WANNA QUIT THE BUSI-NESS?
...NO.

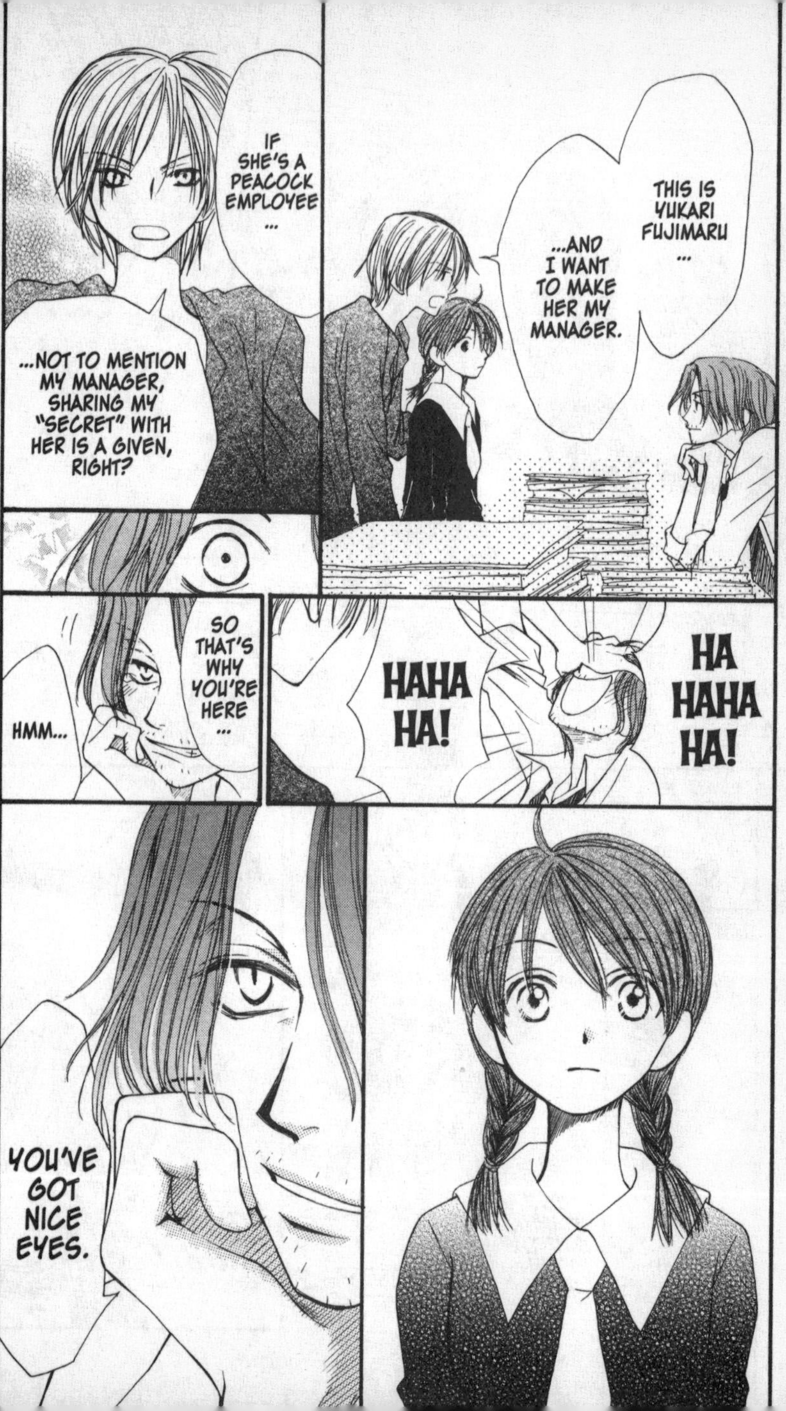
THIS IS YUKARI FUJIMARU...
...AND I WANT TO MAKE HER MY MANAGER.
IF SHE'S A PEACOCK EMPLOYEE...
...NOT TO MENTION MY MANAGER, SHARING MY "SECRET" WITH HER IS A GIVEN, RIGHT?
HA HAHAHA HA!
HAHA HA!
SO THAT'S WHY YOU'RE HERE...
HMM...
YOU'VE GOT NICE EYES.

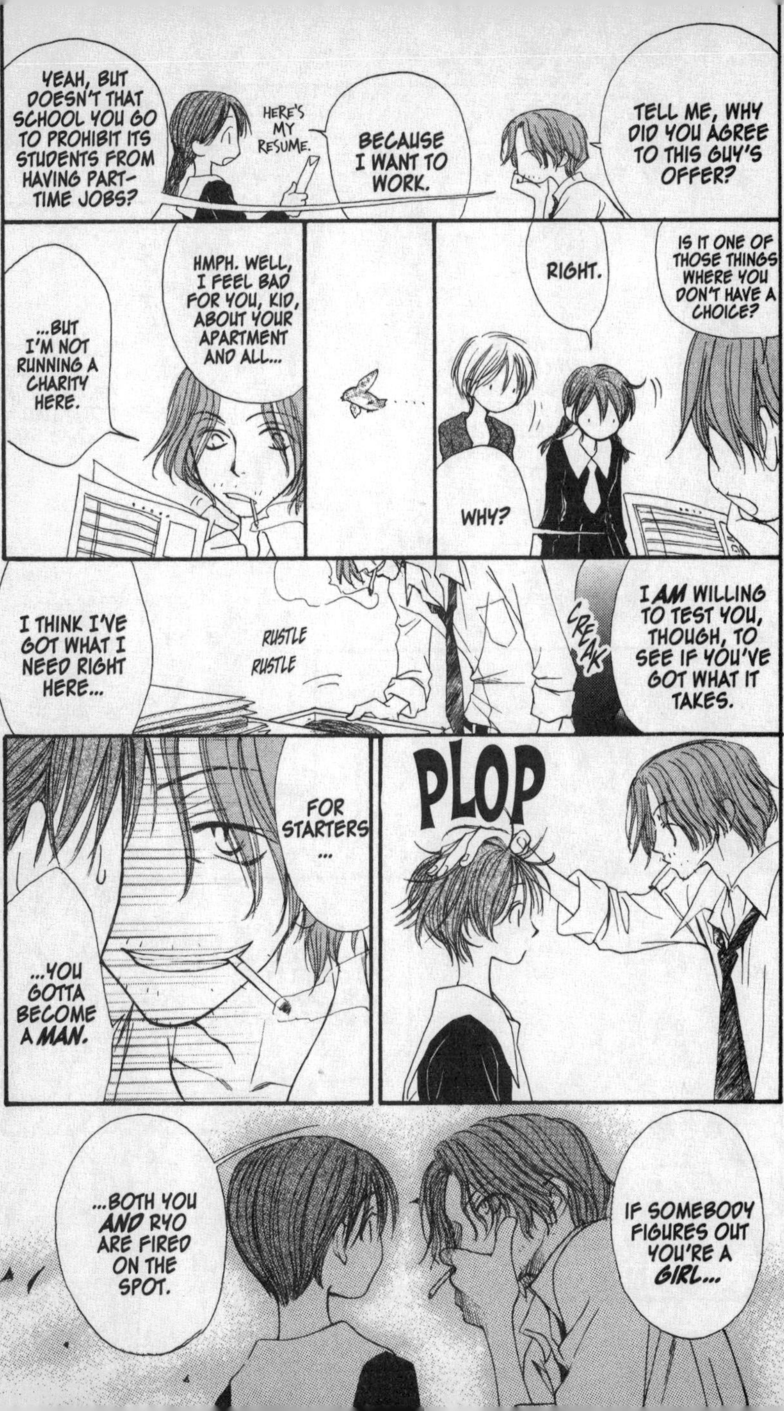
TELL ME, WHY DID YOU AGREE TO THIS GUY'S OFFER?
BECAUSE I WANT TO WORK.
HERE'S MY RESUME.
YEAH, BUT DOESN'T THAT SCHOOL YOU GO TO PROHIBIT ITS STUDENTS FROM HAVING PART-TIME JOBS?
IS IT ONE OF THOSE THINGS WHERE YOU DON'T HAVE A CHOICE?
RIGHT.
WHY?
HMPH. WELL, I FEEL BAD FOR YOU, KID, ABOUT YOUR APARTMENT AND ALL...
...BUT I'M NOT RUNNING A CHARITY HERE.
I AM WILLING TO TEST YOU, THOUGH, TO SEE IF YOU'VE GOT WHAT IT TAKES.
CREAK
RUSTLE
RUSTLE
I THINK I'VE GOT WHAT I NEED RIGHT HERE...
PLOP
FOR STARTERS...
...YOU GOTTA BECOME A MAN.
IF SOMEBODY FIGURES OUT YOU'RE A GIRL...
...BOTH YOU AND RYO ARE FIRED ON THE SPOT.

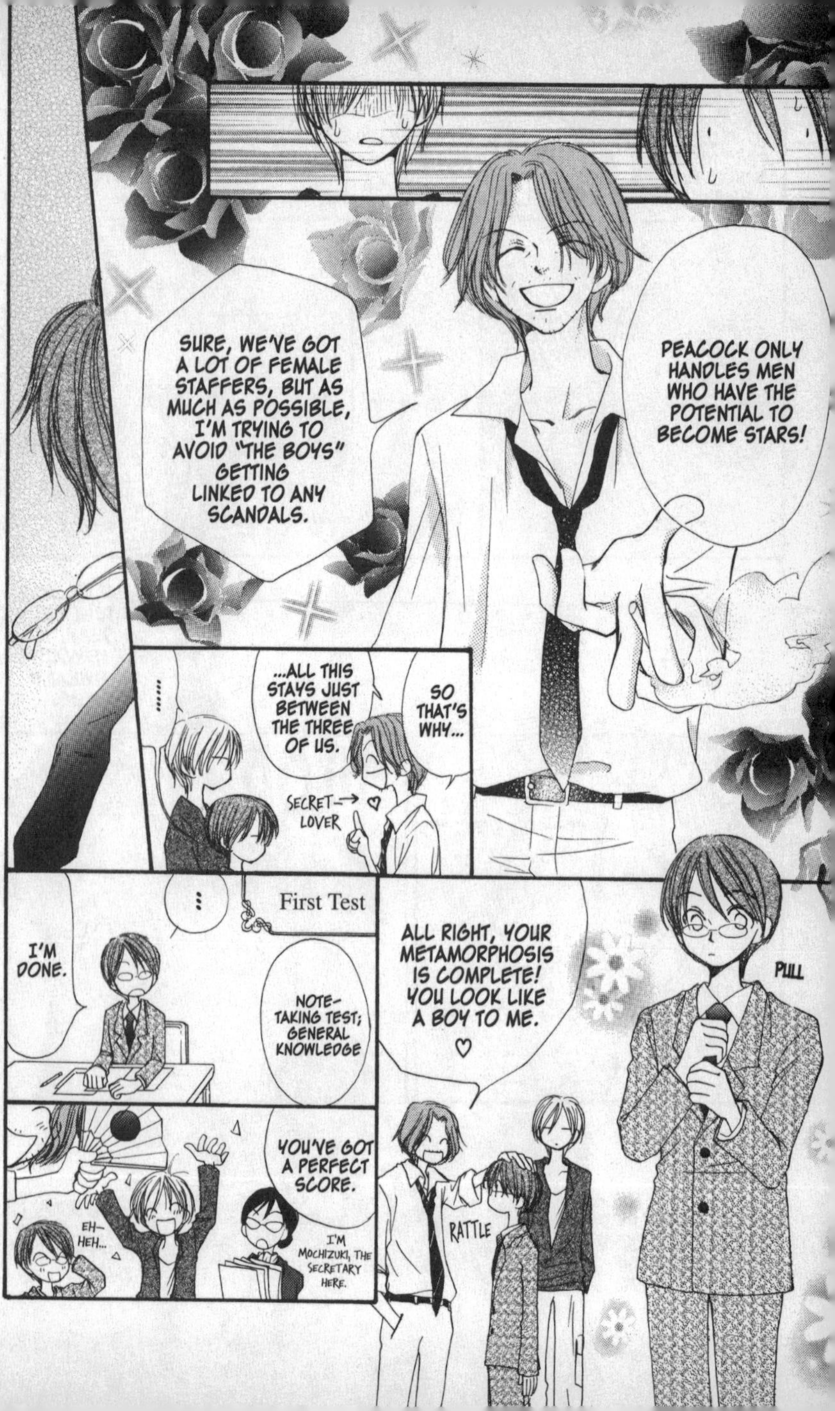
PEACOCK ONLY HANDLES MEN WHO HAVE THE POTENTIAL TO BECOME STARS!
SURE, WE'VE GOT A LOT OF FEMALE STAFFERS, BUT AS MUCH AS POSSIBLE, I'M TRYING TO AVOID "THE BOYS" GETTING LINKED TO ANY SCANDALS.
SO THAT'S WHY...
...ALL THIS STAYS JUST BETWEEN THE THREE OF US.
SECRET-LOVER
......
PULL
ALL RIGHT, YOUR METAMORPHOSIS IS COMPLETE! YOU LOOK LIKE A BOY TO ME. ♡
RATTLE
First Test
...
NOTE-TAKING TEST; GENERAL KNOWLEDGE
I'M DONE.
YOU'VE GOT A PERFECT SCORE.
I'M MOCHIZUKI, THE SECRETARY HERE.
EH-HEH...

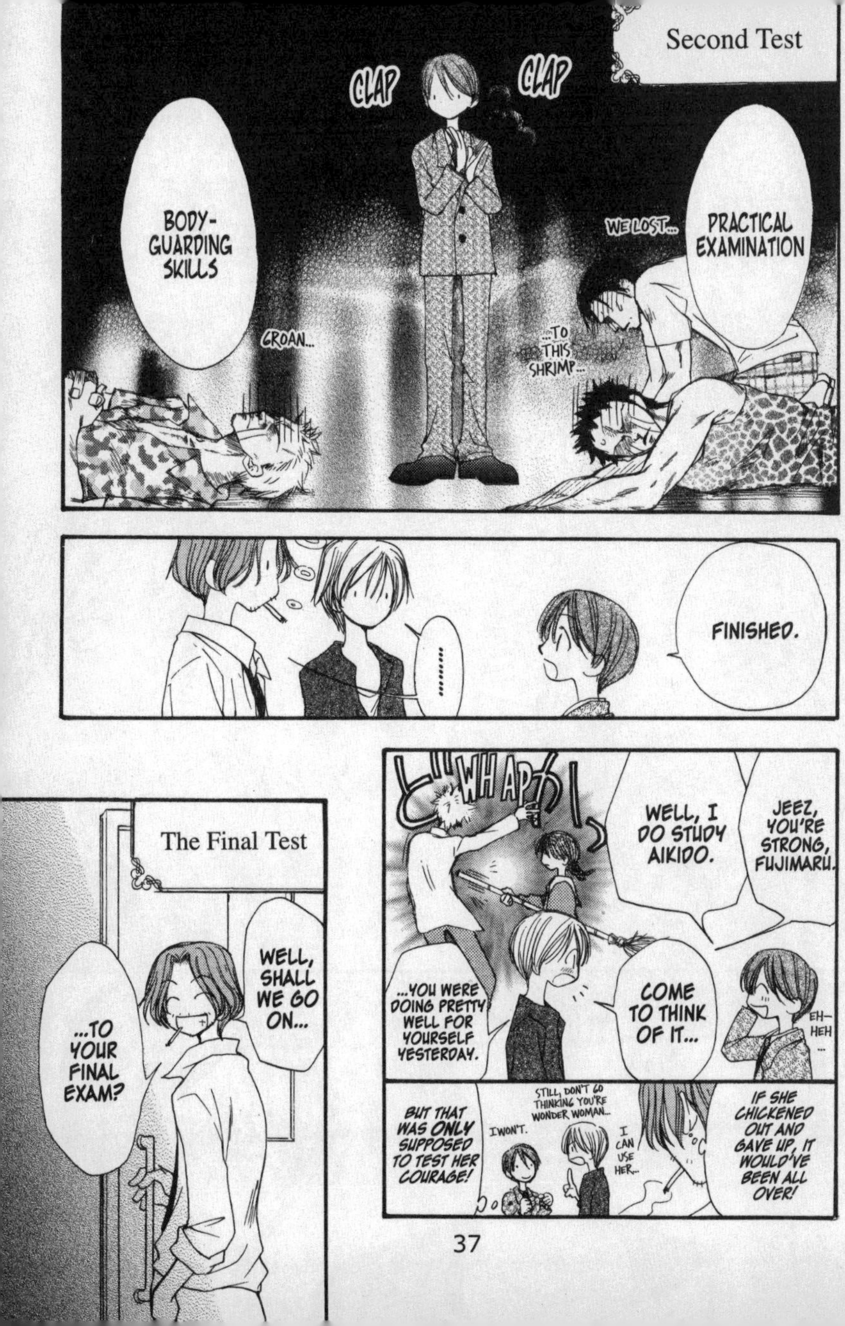
Second Test
CLAP
CLAP
PRACTICAL EXAMINATION
WE LOST...
...TO THIS SHRIMP...
BODY-GUARDING SKILLS
GROAN...
FINISHED.
......
WHAP
JEEZ, YOU'RE STRONG, FUJIMARU.
WELL, I DO STUDY AIKIDO.
EH-HEH...
COME TO THINK OF IT...
...YOU WERE DOING PRETTY WELL FOR YOURSELF YESTERDAY.
IF SHE CHICKENED OUT AND GAVE UP, IT WOULD'VE BEEN ALL OVER!
I CAN USE HER...
STILL, DON'T GO THINKING YOU'RE WONDER WOMAN...
I WON'T.
BUT THAT WAS ONLY SUPPOSED TO TEST HER COURAGE!
The Final Test
WELL, SHALL WE GO ON...
...TO YOUR FINAL EXAM?

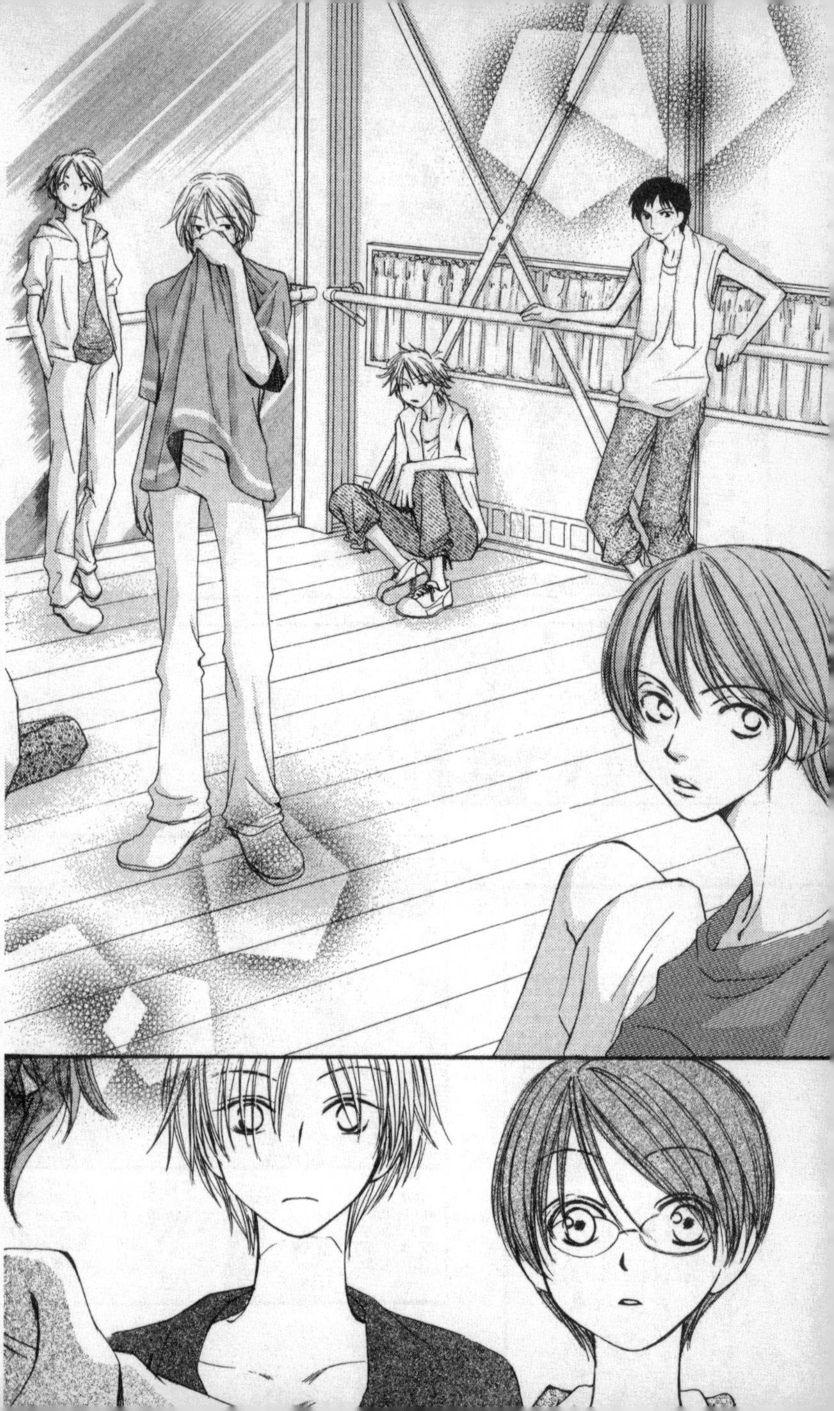

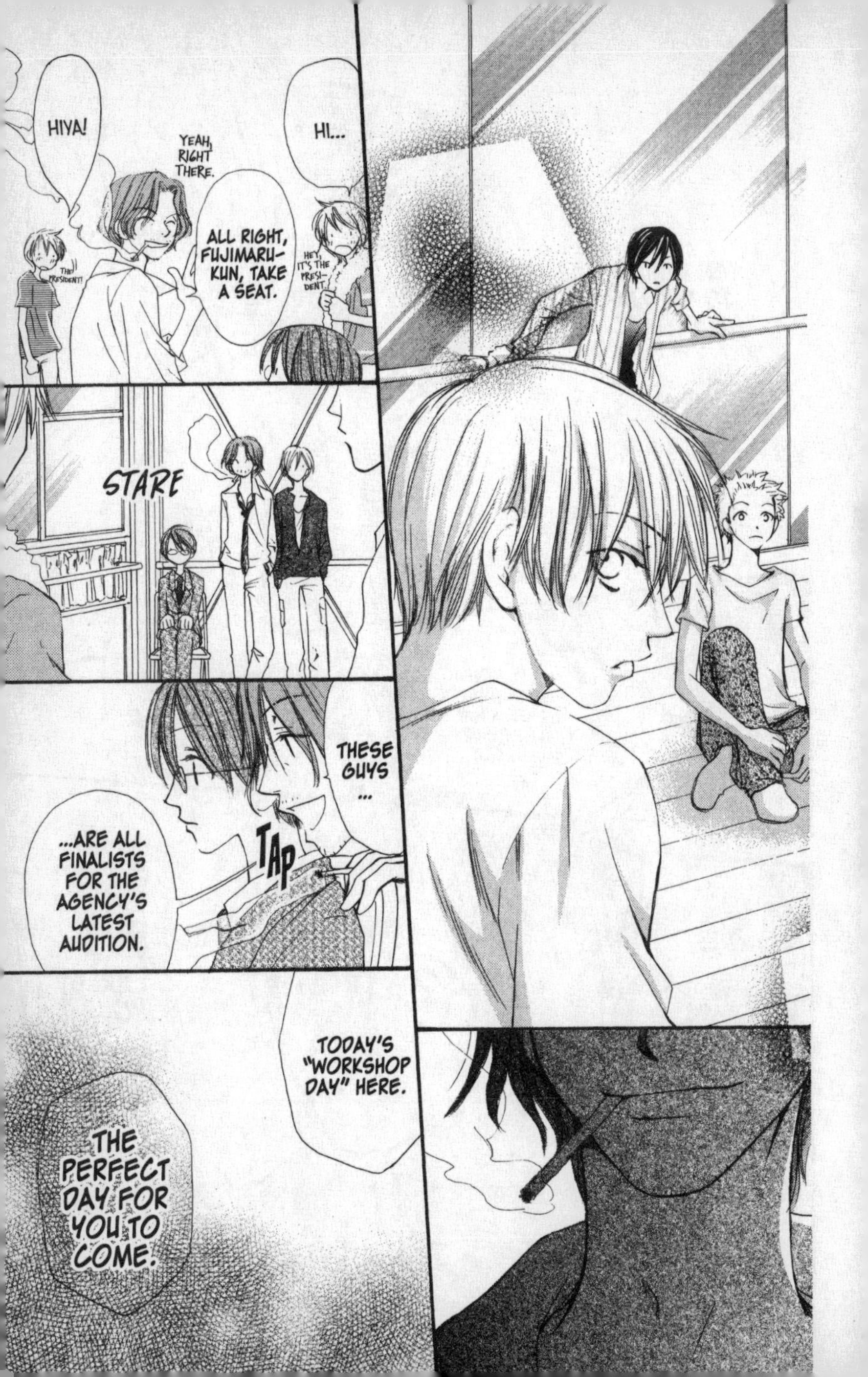
HI...
ALL RIGHT, FUJIMARU-KUN, TAKE A SEAT.
HEY, IT'S THE PRESIDENT.
YEAH, RIGHT THERE.
HIYA!
THE PRESIDENT!
STARE
THESE GUYS...
...ARE ALL FINALISTS FOR THE AGENCY'S LATEST AUDITION.
TAP
TODAY'S "WORKSHOP DAY" HERE.
THE PERFECT DAY FOR YOU TO COME.

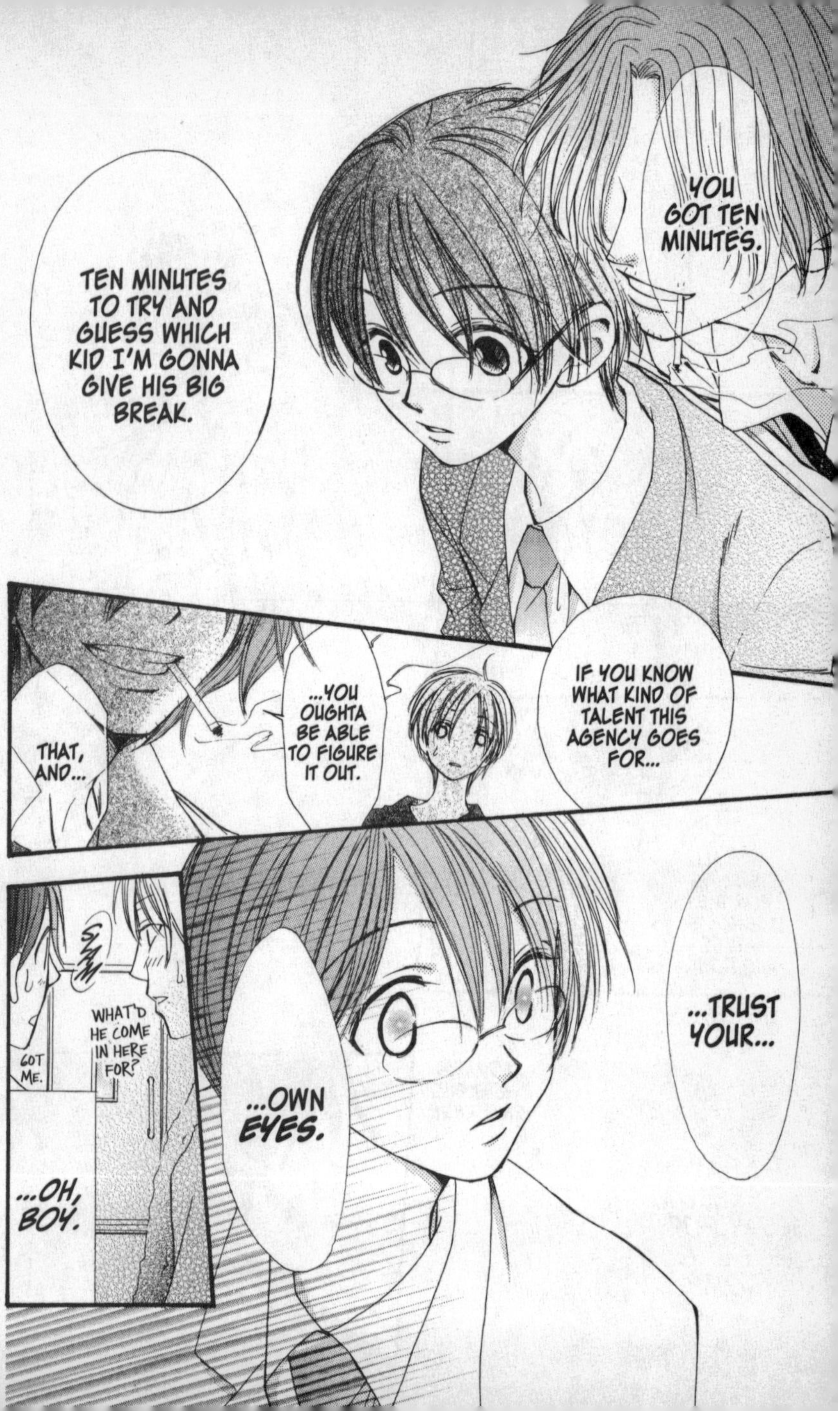
YOU GOT TEN MINUTES.
TEN MINUTES TO TRY AND GUESS WHICH KID I'M GONNA GIVE HIS BIG BREAK.
IF YOU KNOW WHAT KIND OF TALENT THIS AGENCY GOES FOR...
...YOU OUGHTA BE ABLE TO FIGURE IT OUT.
THAT, AND...
...TRUST YOUR...
...OWN EYES.
SLAM
WHAT'D HE COME IN HERE FOR?
GOT ME.
...OH, BOY.

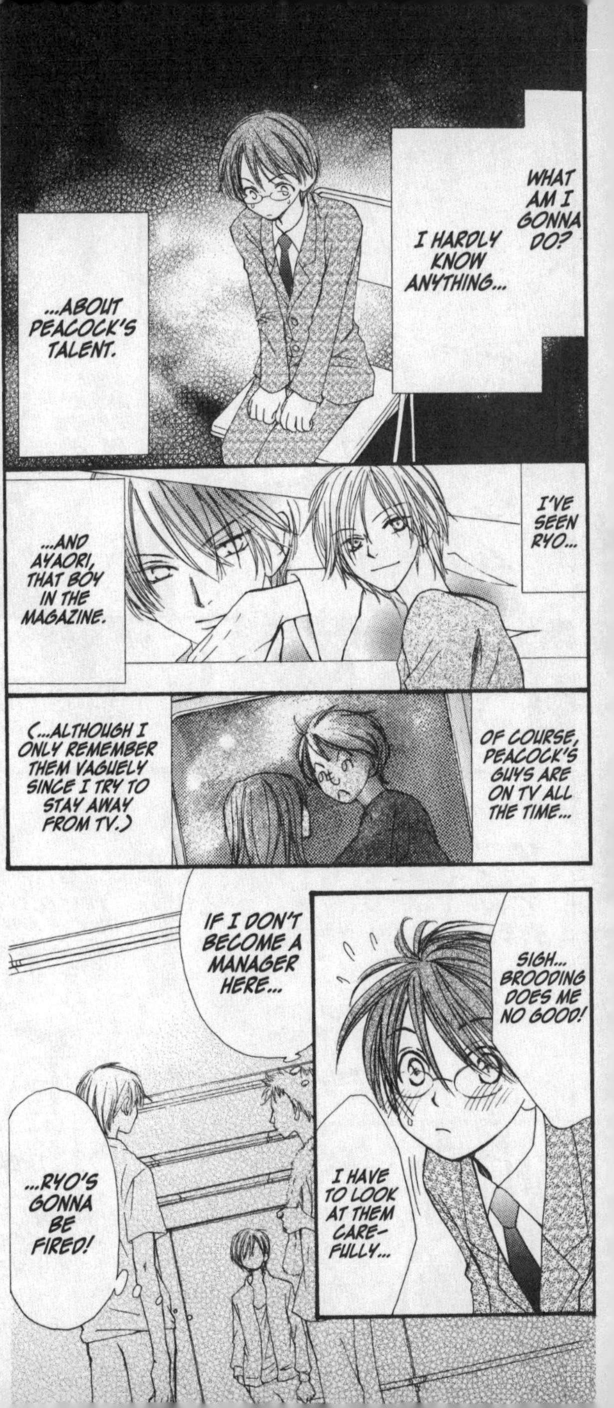
WHAT AM I GONNA DO?
I HARDLY KNOW ANYTHING...
...ABOUT PEACOCK'S TALENT.
I'VE SEEN RYO...
...AND AYAORI, THAT BOY IN THE MAGAZINE.
OF COURSE, PEACOCK'S GUYS ARE ON TV ALL THE TIME...
(...ALTHOUGH I ONLY REMEMBER THEM VAGUELY SINCE I TRY TO STAY AWAY FROM TV.)
SIGH... BROODING DOES ME NO GOOD!
I HAVE TO LOOK AT THEM CARE-FULLY...
IF I DON'T BECOME A MANAGER HERE...
...RYO'S GONNA BE FIRED!

1/4 Sakura Mail

part 2 continued

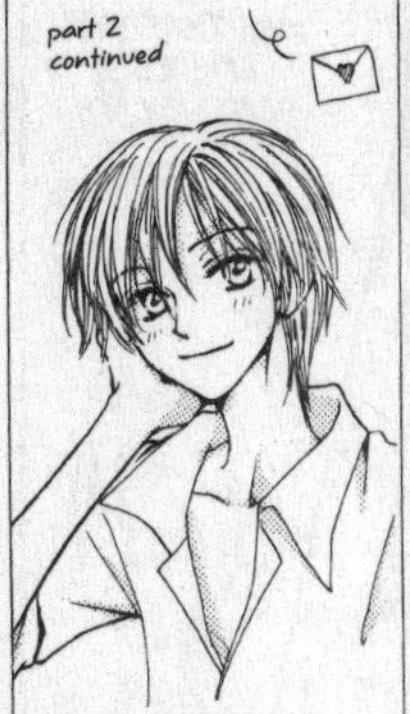

I have to admit that I'm unfamiliar with the world of showbiz and when it comes to teen idols, that was completely new territory to me. But once the idea popped into my head, I couldn't let go of it and couldn't "entertain" the thought of changing it to a different setting or theme. It really is a business of selling "dreams," which makes it extremely compelling! In creating this story, my goal was to include as many dramatic, exciting developments as I could, so I hope all of you enjoy it!!

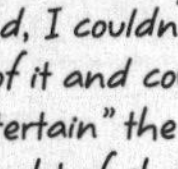

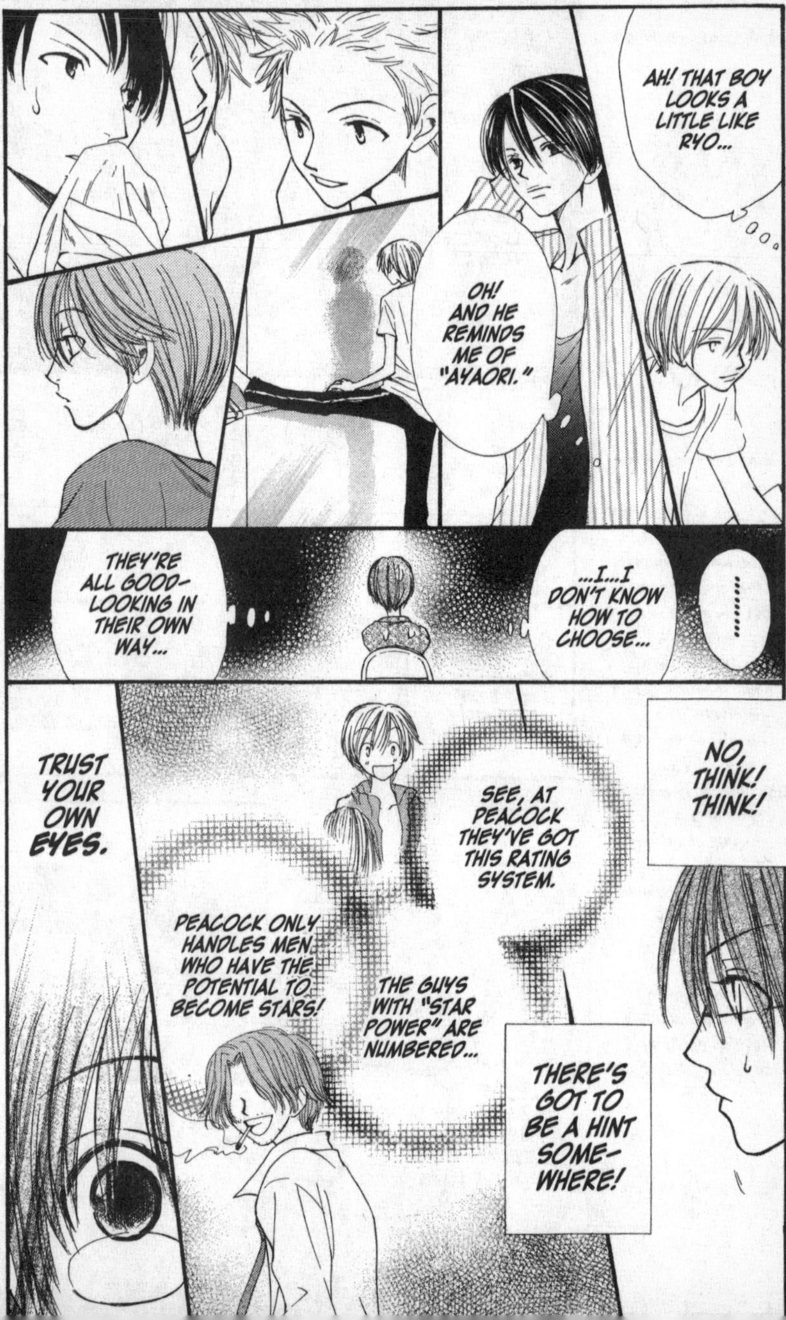
AH! THAT BOY LOOKS A LITTLE LIKE RYO...
OH! AND HE REMINDS ME OF "AYAORI."
......
...I...I DON'T KNOW HOW TO CHOOSE...
THEY'RE ALL GOOD-LOOKING IN THEIR OWN WAY...
NO, THINK! THINK!
THERE'S GOT TO BE A HINT SOME-WHERE!
SEE, AT PEACOCK THEY'VE GOT THIS RATING SYSTEM.
THE GUYS WITH "STAR POWER" ARE NUMBERED...
PEACOCK ONLY HANDLES MEN WHO HAVE THE POTENTIAL TO BECOME STARS!
TRUST YOUR OWN EYES.

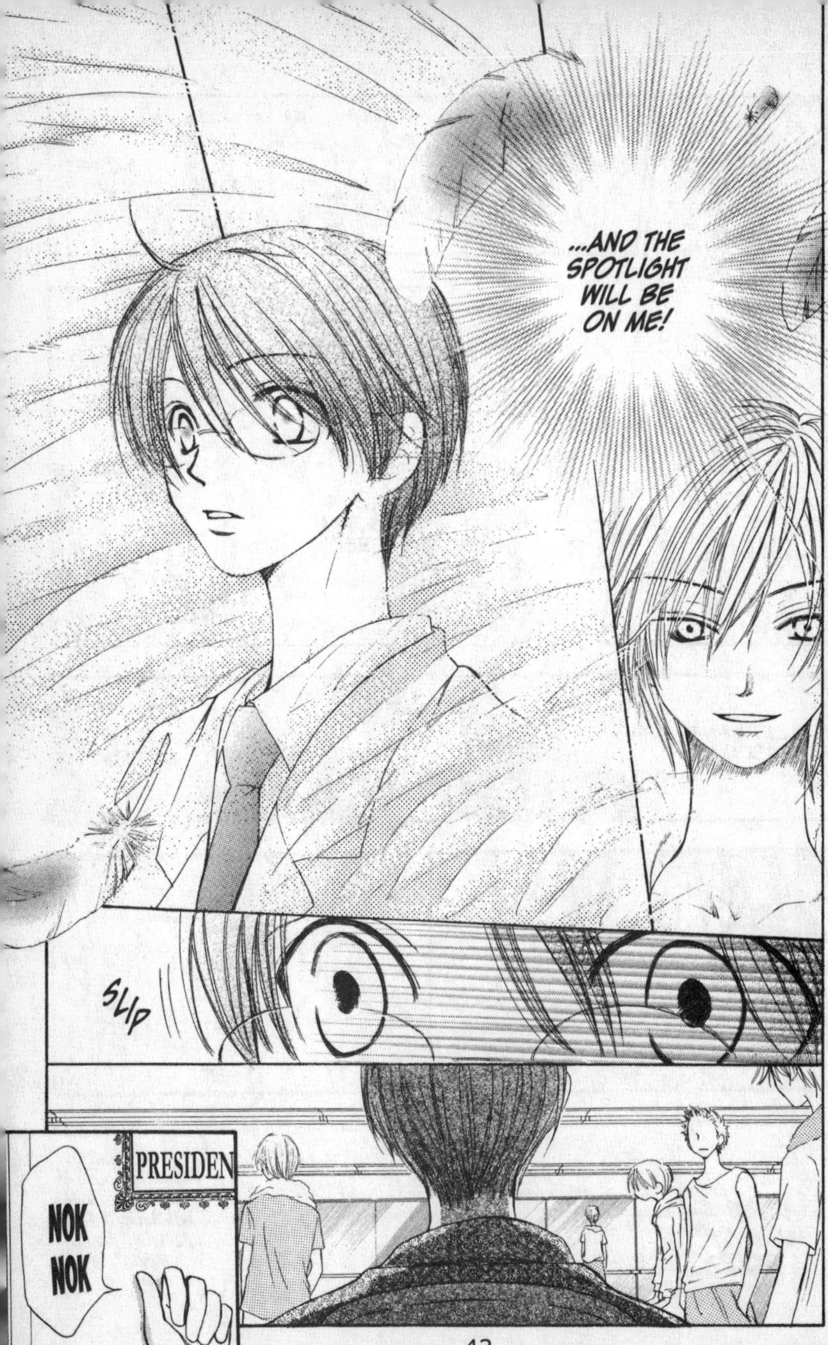
...AND THE SPOTLIGHT WILL BE ON ME!
SLIP
PRESIDEN
NOK NOK

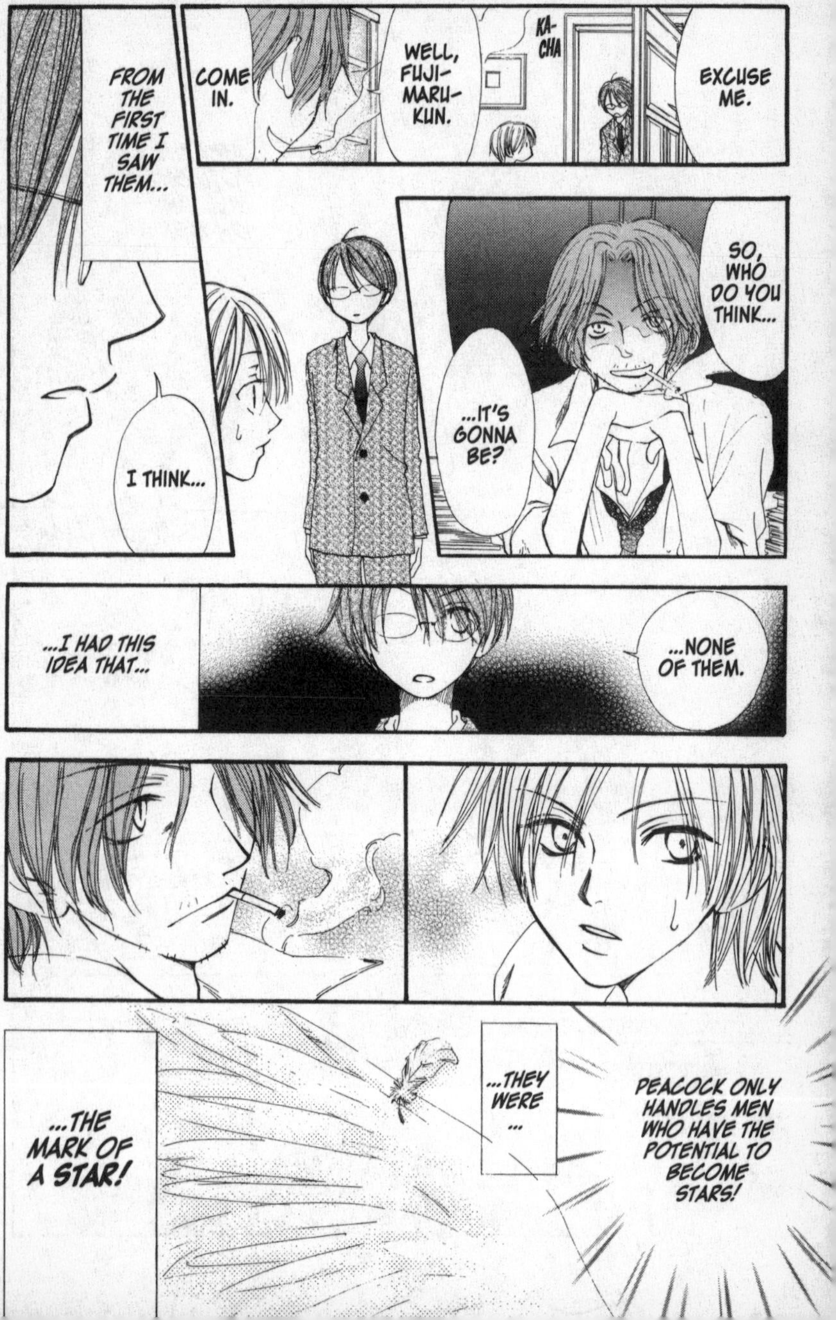
EXCUSE ME.
KA-CHA
WELL, FUJI-MARU-KUN.
COME IN.
SO, WHO DO YOU THINK...
...IT'S GONNA BE?
FROM THE FIRST TIME I SAW THEM...
I THINK...
...NONE OF THEM.
...I HAD THIS IDEA THAT...
PEACOCK ONLY HANDLES MEN WHO HAVE THE POTENTIAL TO BECOME STARS!
...THEY WERE ...
...THE MARK OF A STAR!

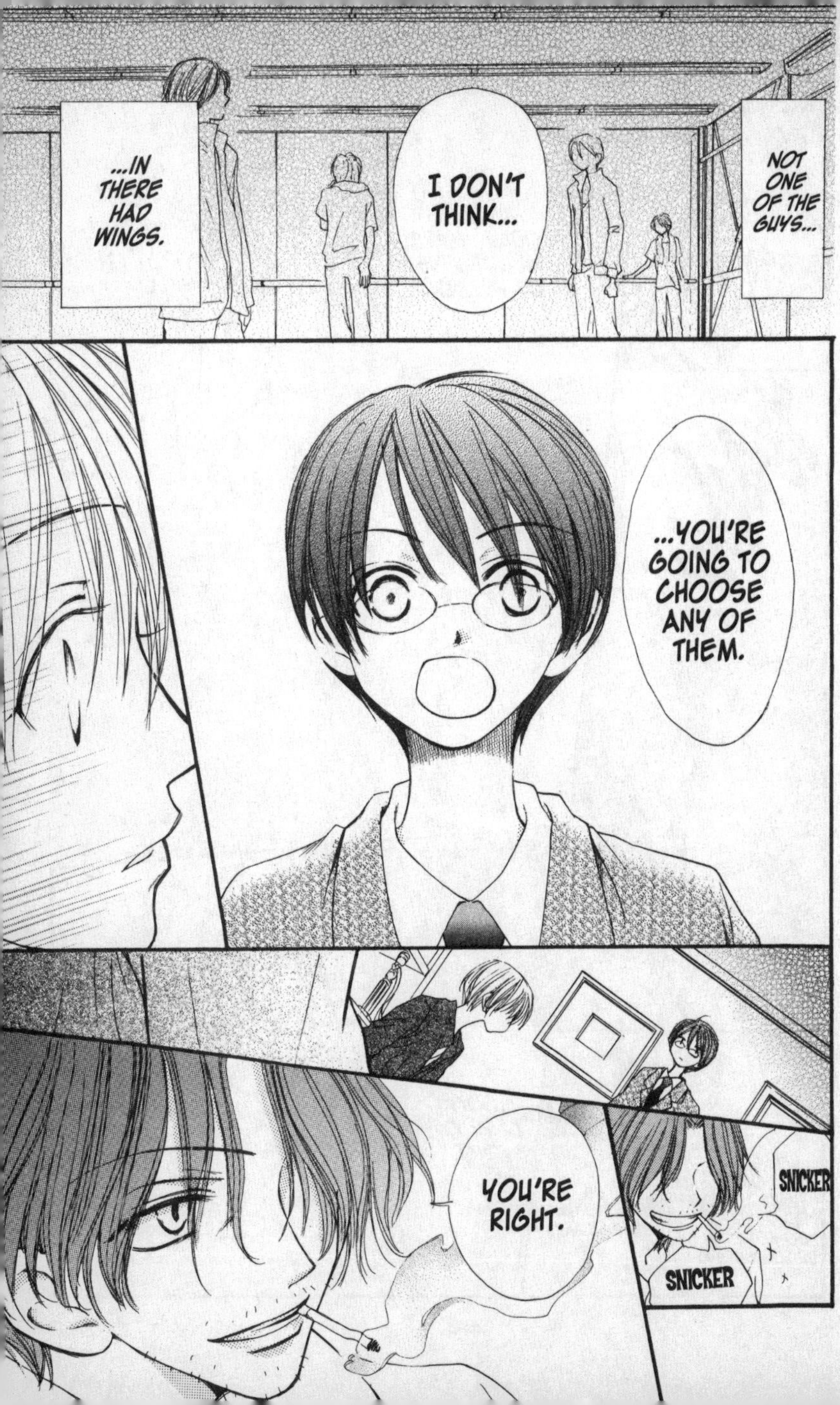
NOT ONE OF THE GUYS...
I DON'T THINK...
...IN THERE HAD WINGS.
...YOU'RE GOING TO CHOOSE ANY OF THEM.
SNICKER
SNICKER
YOU'RE RIGHT.

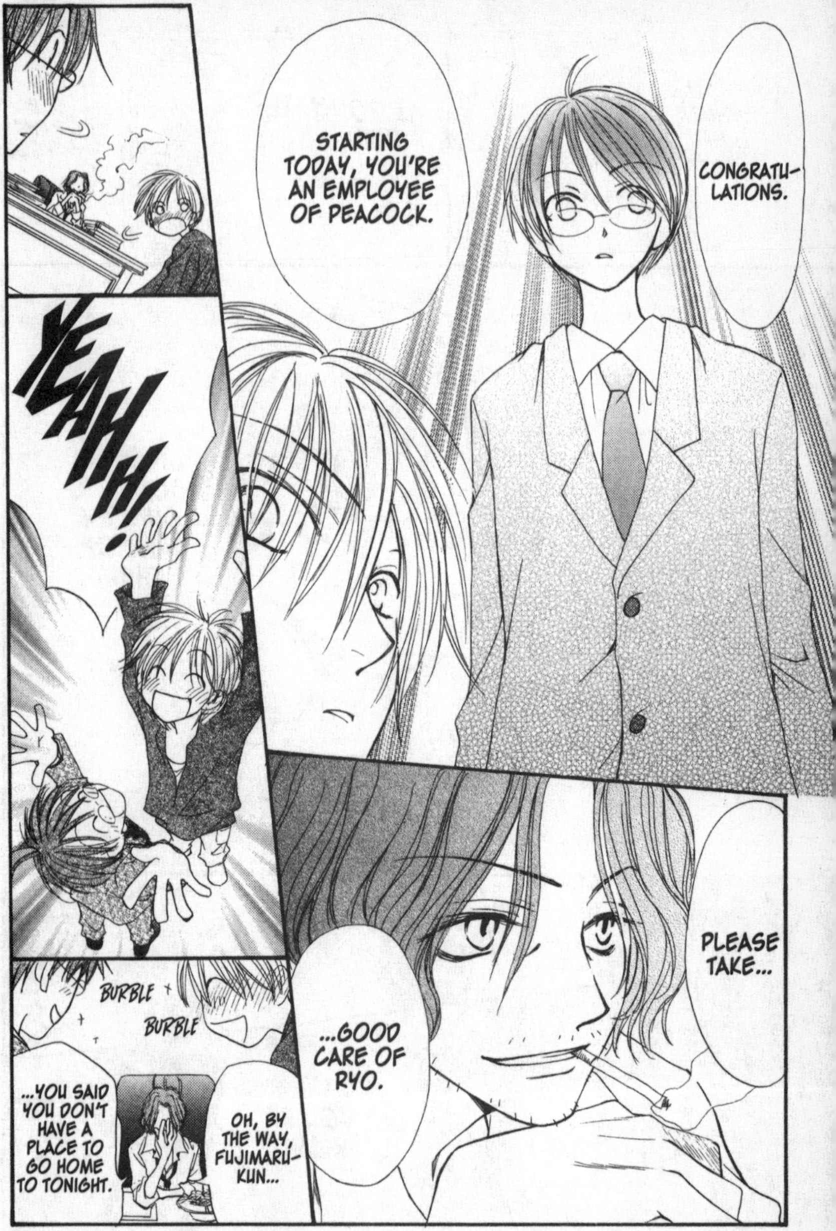
CONGRATU-LATIONS.
STARTING TODAY, YOU'RE AN EMPLOYEE OF PEACOCK.
PLEASE TAKE...
...GOOD CARE OF RYO.
YEAAH!
BURBLE
BURBLE
OH, BY THE WAY, FUJIMARU-KUN...
...YOU SAID YOU DON'T HAVE A PLACE TO GO HOME TO TONIGHT.

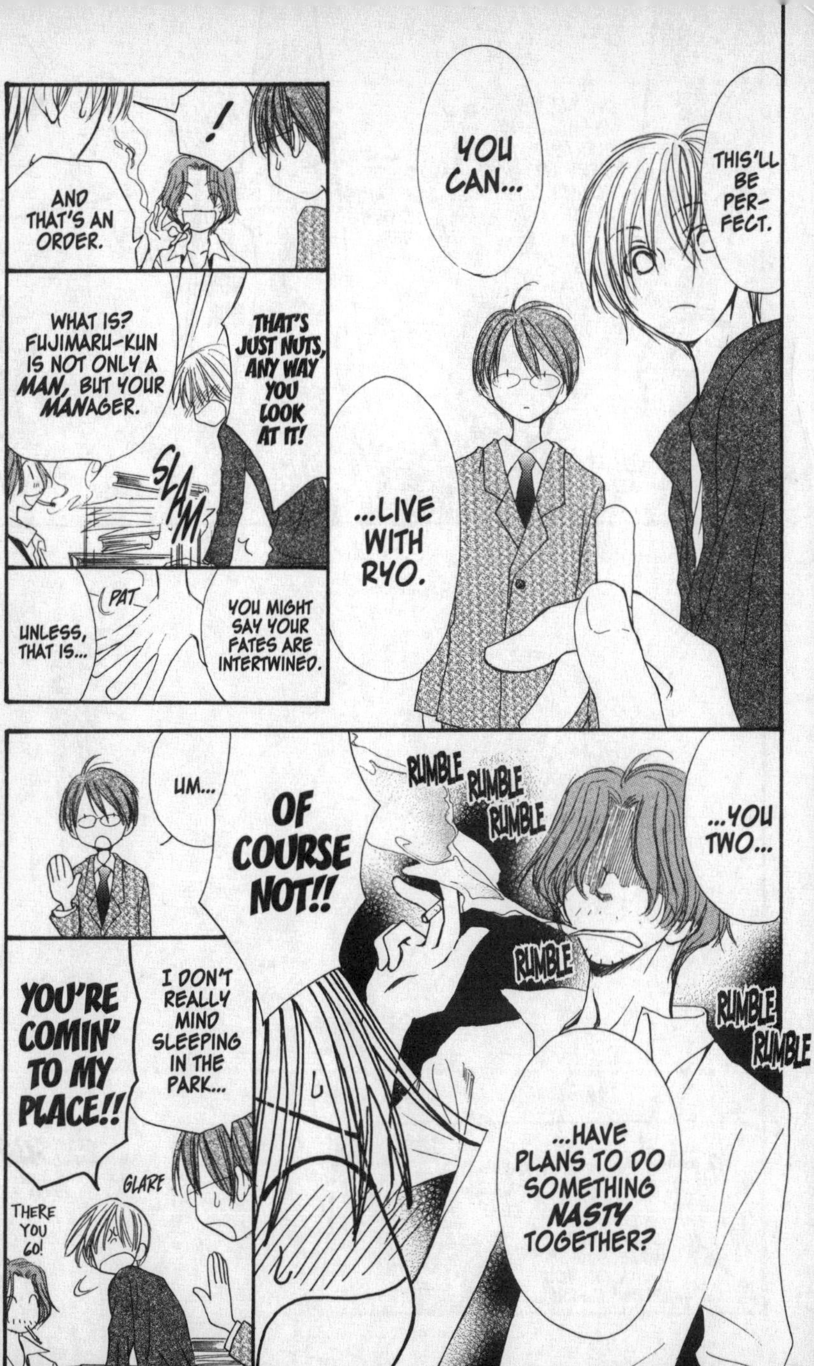
THIS'LL BE PER-FECT.
YOU CAN...
...LIVE WITH RYO.
!
AND THAT'S AN ORDER.
THAT'S JUST NUTS, ANY WAY YOU LOOK AT IT!
WHAT IS? FUJIMARU-KUN IS NOT ONLY A MAN, BUT YOUR MANAGER.
SLAM
YOU MIGHT SAY YOUR FATES ARE INTERTWINED.
PAT
UNLESS, THAT IS...
...YOU TWO...
RUMBLE RUMBLE
RUMBLE RUMBLE RUMBLE
RUMBLE
...HAVE PLANS TO DO SOMETHING NASTY TOGETHER?
OF COURSE NOT!!
UM...
I DON'T REALLY MIND SLEEPING IN THE PARK...
YOU'RE COMIN' TO MY PLACE!!
GLARE
THERE YOU GO!

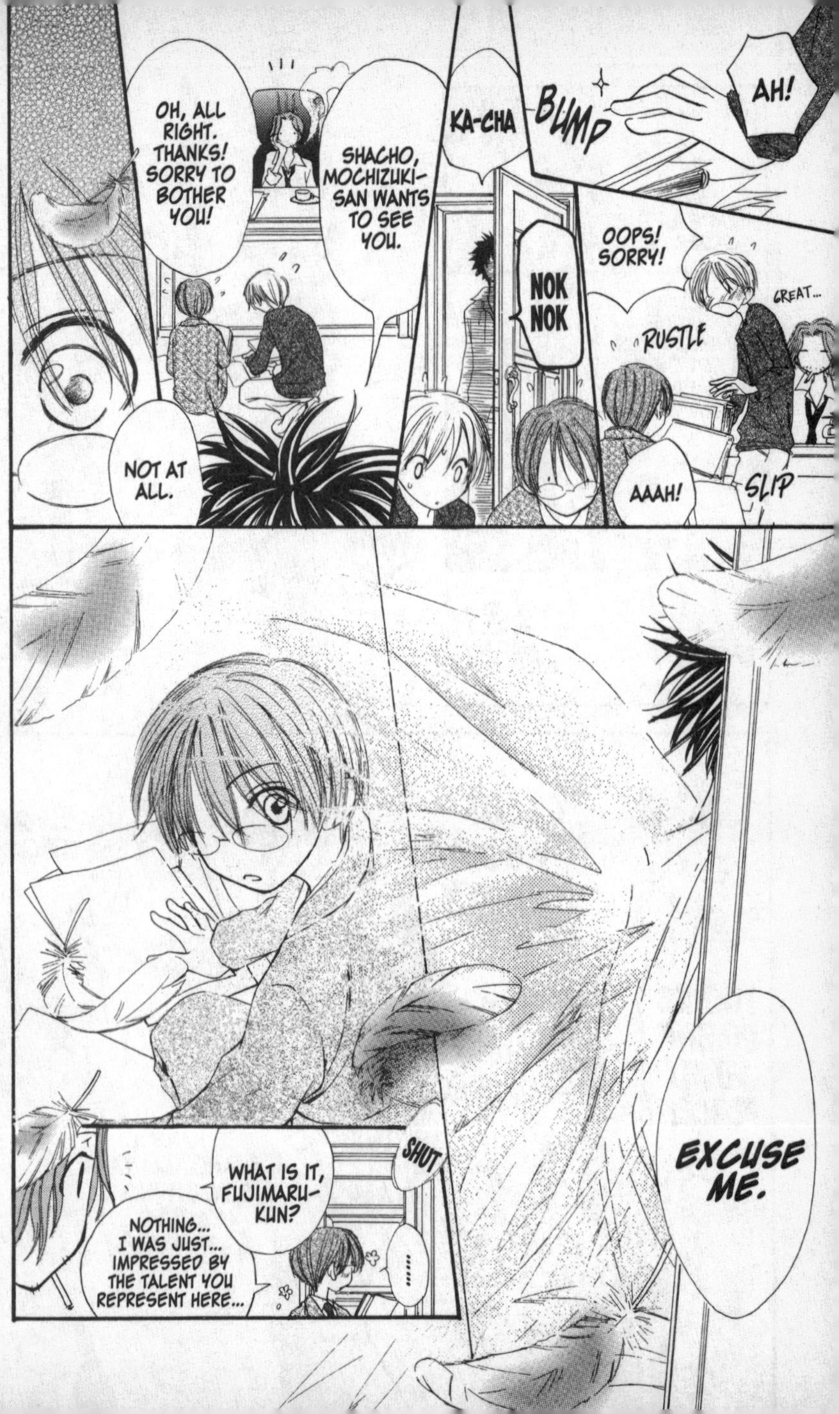
AH!
BUMP
OOPS! SORRY!
GREAT...
RUSTLE
AAAH!
SLIP
KA-CHA
NOK NOK
SHACHO, MOCHIZUKI-SAN WANTS TO SEE YOU.
OH, ALL RIGHT. THANKS! SORRY TO BOTHER YOU!
NOT AT ALL.
EXCUSE ME.
SHUT
WHAT IS IT, FUJIMARU-KUN?
......
NOTHING... I WAS JUST... IMPRESSED BY THE TALENT YOU REPRESENT HERE...

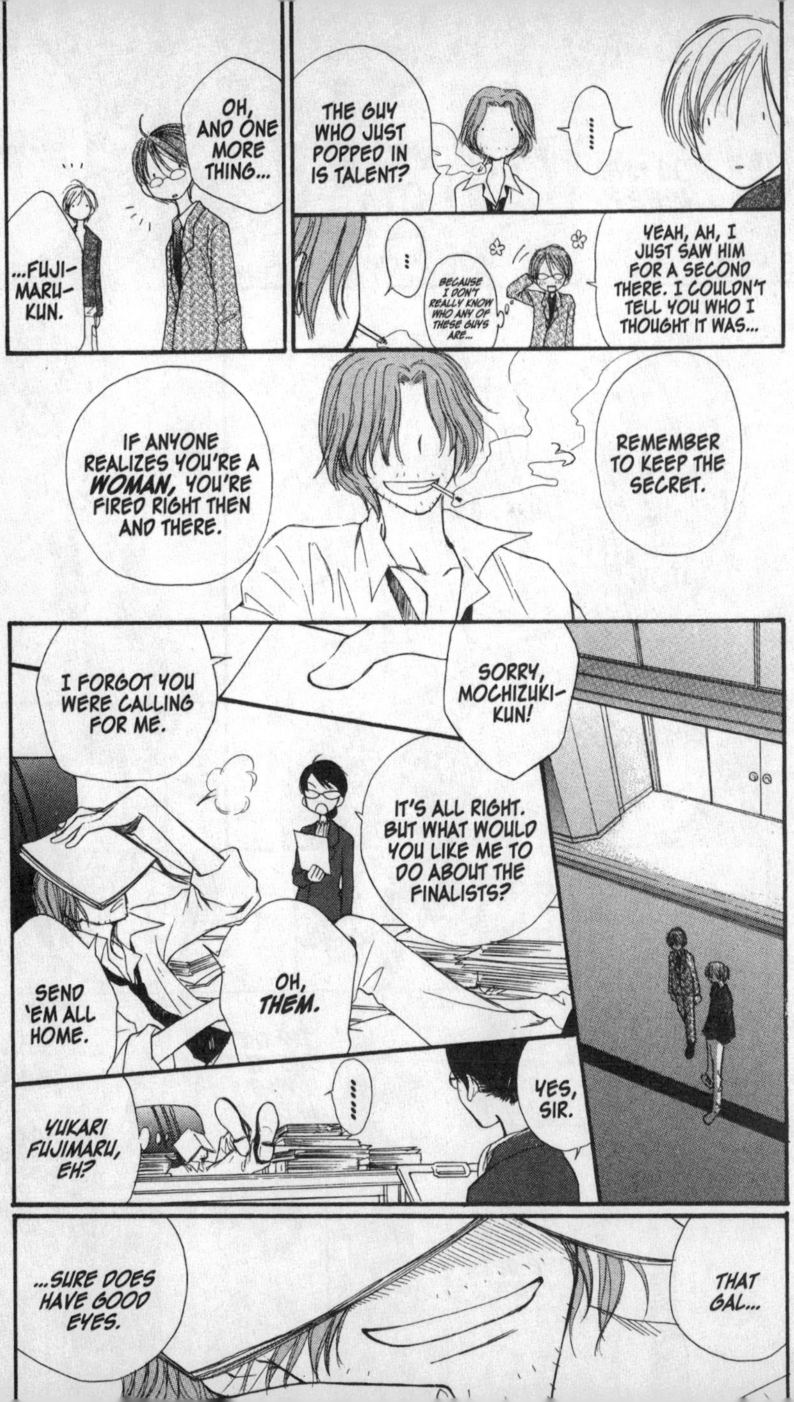
.....
THE GUY WHO JUST POPPED IN IS TALENT?
YEAH, AH, I JUST SAW HIM FOR A SECOND THERE. I COULDN'T TELL YOU WHO I THOUGHT IT WAS...
BECAUSE I DON'T REALLY KNOW WHO ANY OF THESE GUYS ARE...
...
OH, AND ONE MORE THING...
...FUJI-MARU-KUN.
REMEMBER TO KEEP THE SECRET.
IF ANYONE REALIZES YOU'RE A WOMAN, YOU'RE FIRED RIGHT THEN AND THERE.
SORRY, MOCHIZUKI-KUN!
I FORGOT YOU WERE CALLING FOR ME.
IT'S ALL RIGHT. BUT WHAT WOULD YOU LIKE ME TO DO ABOUT THE FINALISTS?
OH, THEM.
SEND 'EM ALL HOME.
YES, SIR.
.....
YUKARI FUJIMARU, EH?
THAT GAL...
...SURE DOES HAVE GOOD EYES.

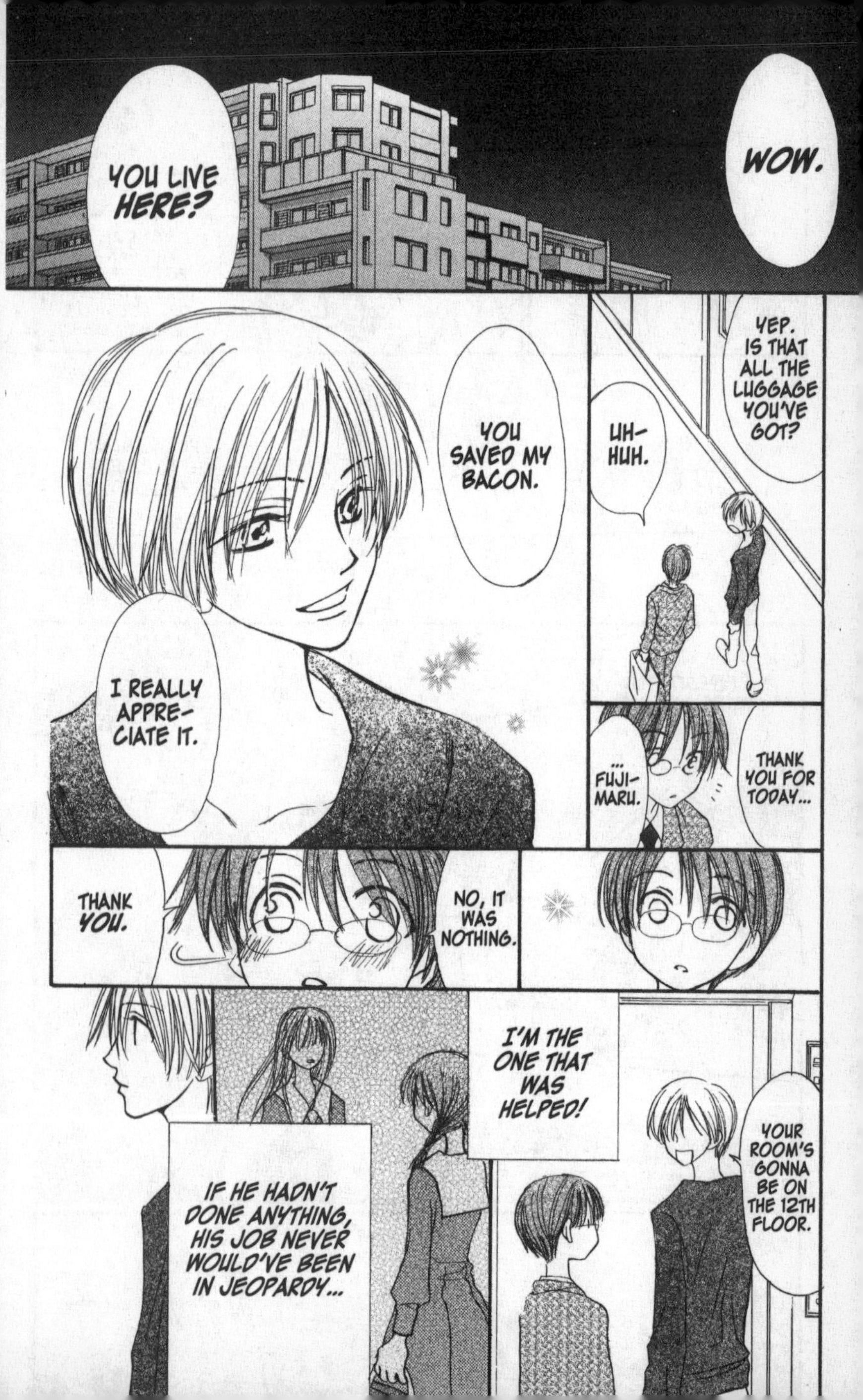
WOW.
YOU LIVE HERE?
YEP. IS THAT ALL THE LUGGAGE YOU'VE GOT?
UH-HUH.
THANK YOU FOR TODAY...
... FUJIMARU.
YOU SAVED MY BACON.
I REALLY APPRECIATE IT.
NO, IT WAS NOTHING.
THANK YOU.
YOUR ROOM'S GONNA BE ON THE 12TH FLOOR.
I'M THE ONE THAT WAS HELPED!
IF HE HADN'T DONE ANYTHING, HIS JOB NEVER WOULD'VE BEEN IN JEOPARDY...

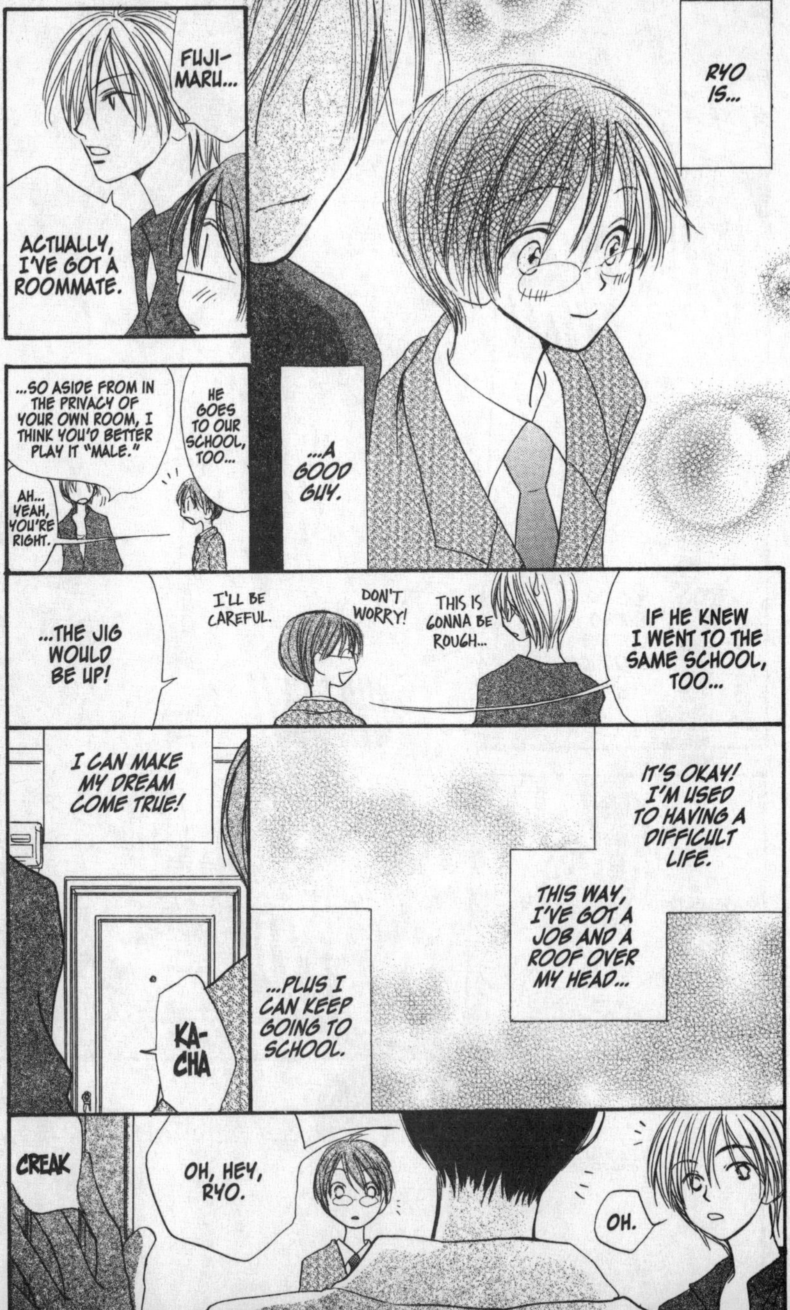
RYO IS...
...A GOOD GUY.
FUJI-MARU...
ACTUALLY, I'VE GOT A ROOMMATE.
HE GOES TO OUR SCHOOL, TOO...
...SO ASIDE FROM IN THE PRIVACY OF YOUR OWN ROOM, I THINK YOU'D BETTER PLAY IT "MALE."
AH... YEAH, YOU'RE RIGHT.
IF HE KNEW I WENT TO THE SAME SCHOOL, TOO...
THIS IS GONNA BE ROUGH...
DON'T WORRY!
I'LL BE CAREFUL.
...THE JIG WOULD BE UP!
IT'S OKAY! I'M USED TO HAVING A DIFFICULT LIFE.
THIS WAY, I'VE GOT A JOB AND A ROOF OVER MY HEAD...
...PLUS I CAN KEEP GOING TO SCHOOL.
I CAN MAKE MY DREAM COME TRUE!
KA-CHA
OH.
OH, HEY, RYO.
CREAK

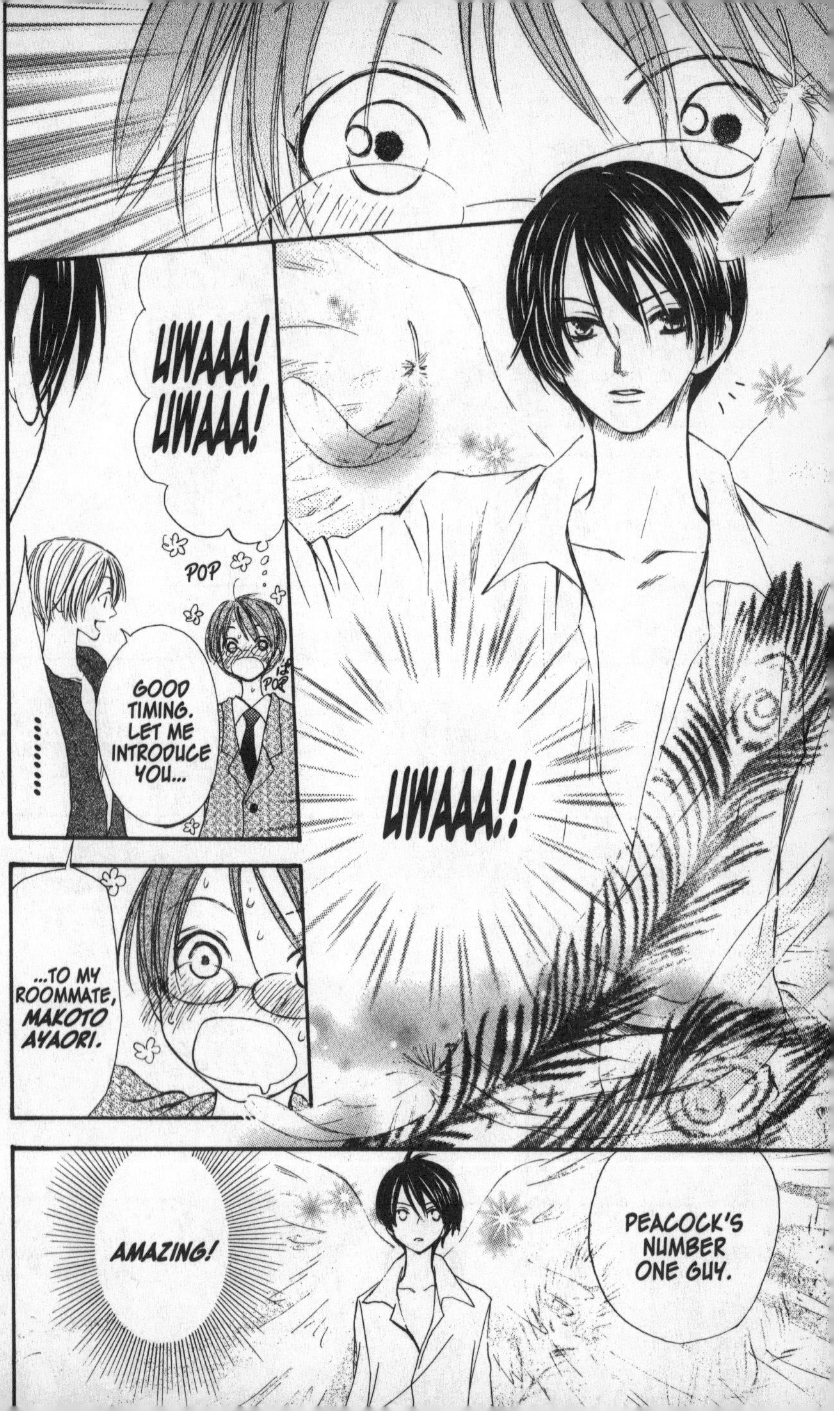
UWAAA!!
UWAAA! UWAAA!
POP
POP
GOOD TIMING. LET ME INTRODUCE YOU...
....
...TO MY ROOMMATE, MAKOTO AYAORI.
PEACOCK'S NUMBER ONE GUY.
AMAZING!

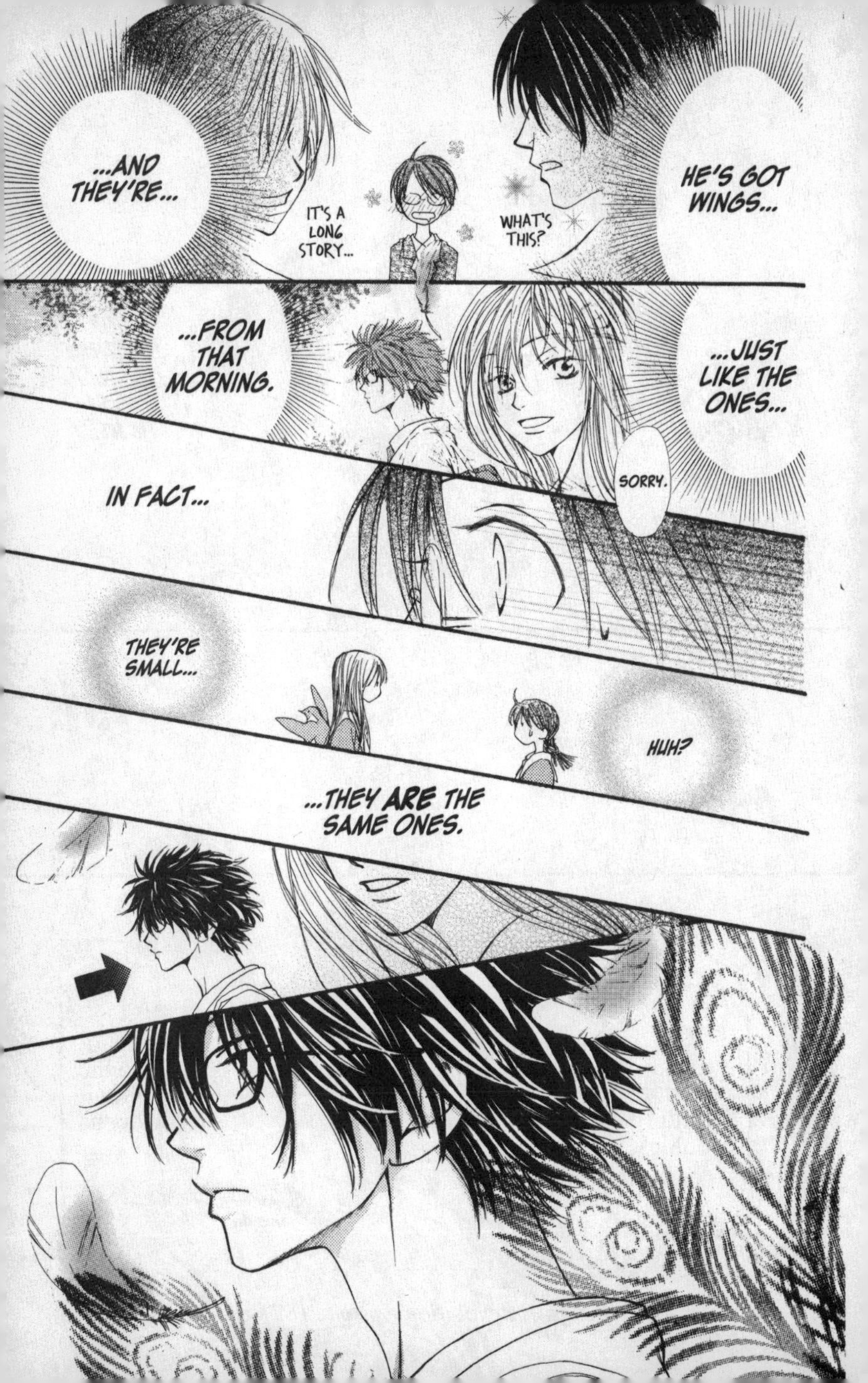
HE'S GOT WINGS...
WHAT'S THIS?
IT'S A LONG STORY...
...AND THEY'RE...
...JUST LIKE THE ONES...
...FROM THAT MORNING.
SORRY.
IN FACT...
THEY'RE SMALL...
HUH?
...THEY ARE THE SAME ONES.

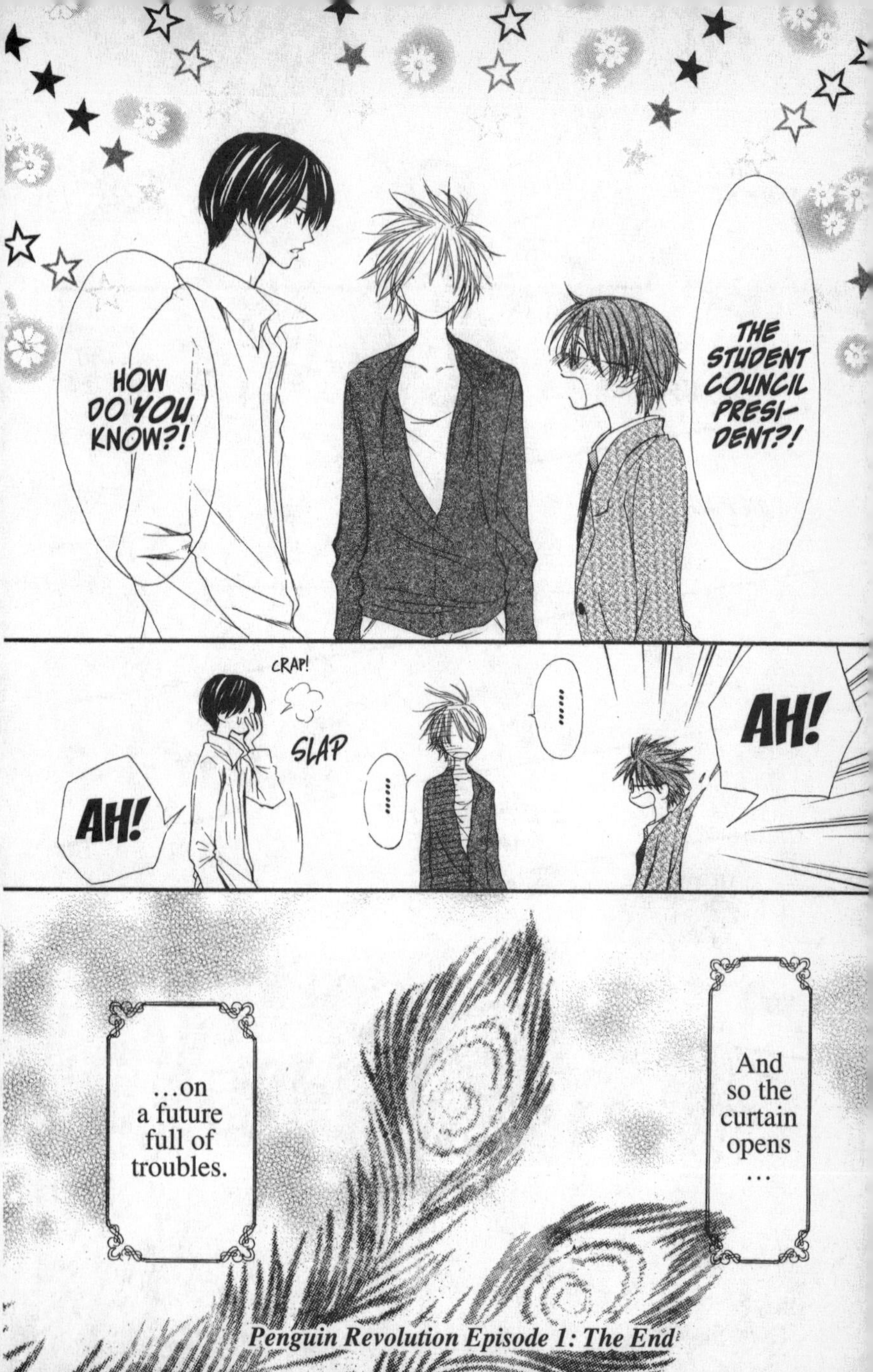
THE STUDENT COUNCIL PRESIDENT?!
HOW DO YOU KNOW?!
AH!
......
CRAP!
SLAP
......
AH!
And so the curtain opens …
…on a future full of troubles.

Penguin Revolution Episode 1: The End

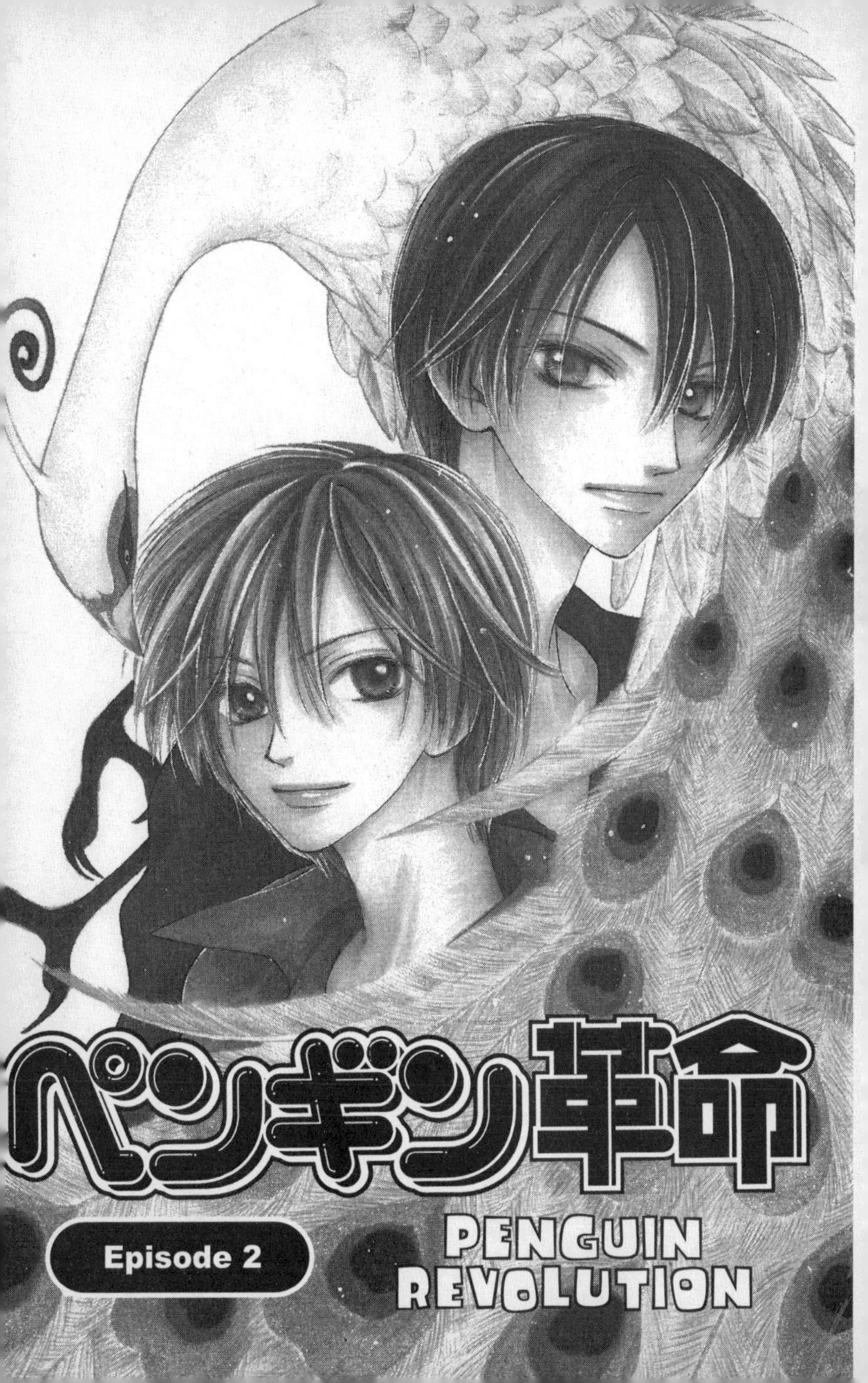
ペンギン革命
PENGUIN REVOLUTION
Episode 2

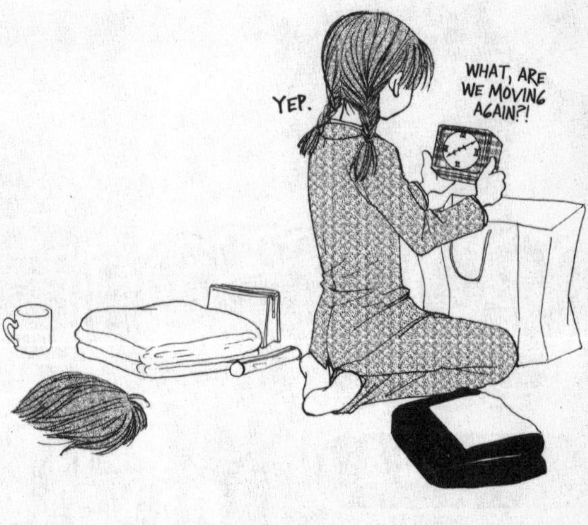
WHAT, ARE WE MOVING AGAIN?!
YEP.

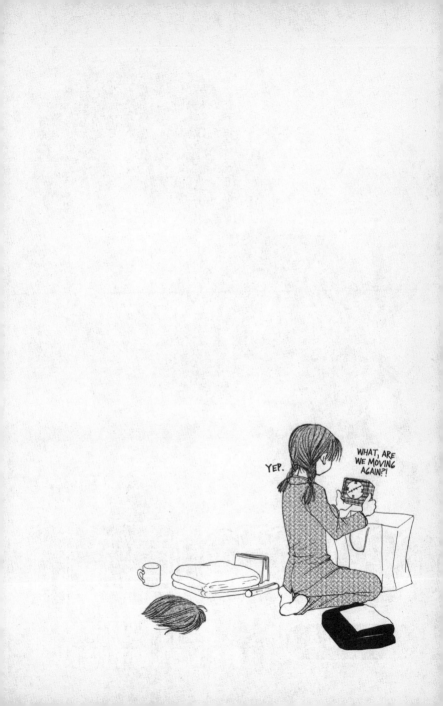

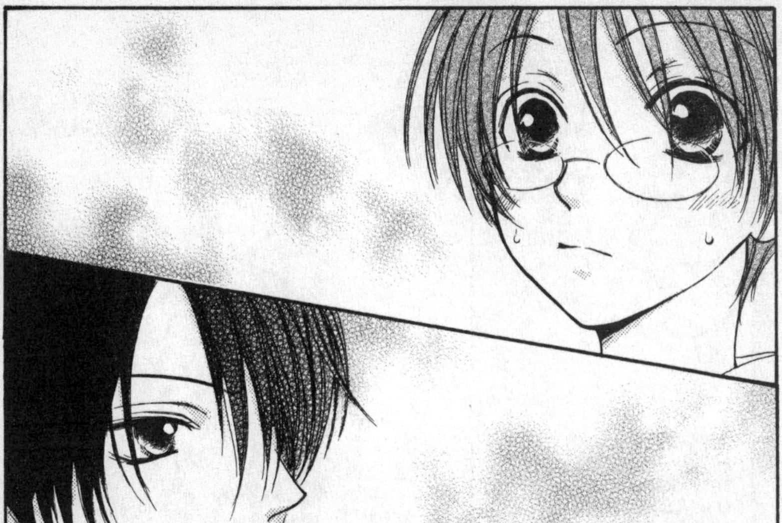
UM...
I WAS GONNA TELL YOU ANYWAY, BUT...

1/4 Sakura Mail

part 3

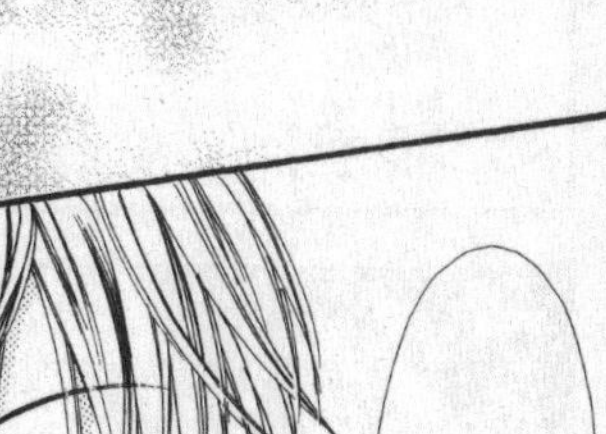

Though I'm clueless about the world of showbiz, I'm wild about plays and convinced myself that sheer force of enthusiasm would be enough to make the material work! The big problem is, I only have experience watching plays. So right now, I'm studying the performance side of things.

My own performance experience is limited to playing a fox in an elementary school play and appearing in a show at a high school festival......

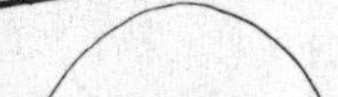
SAKURA TSUKUBA IN 6TH GRADE

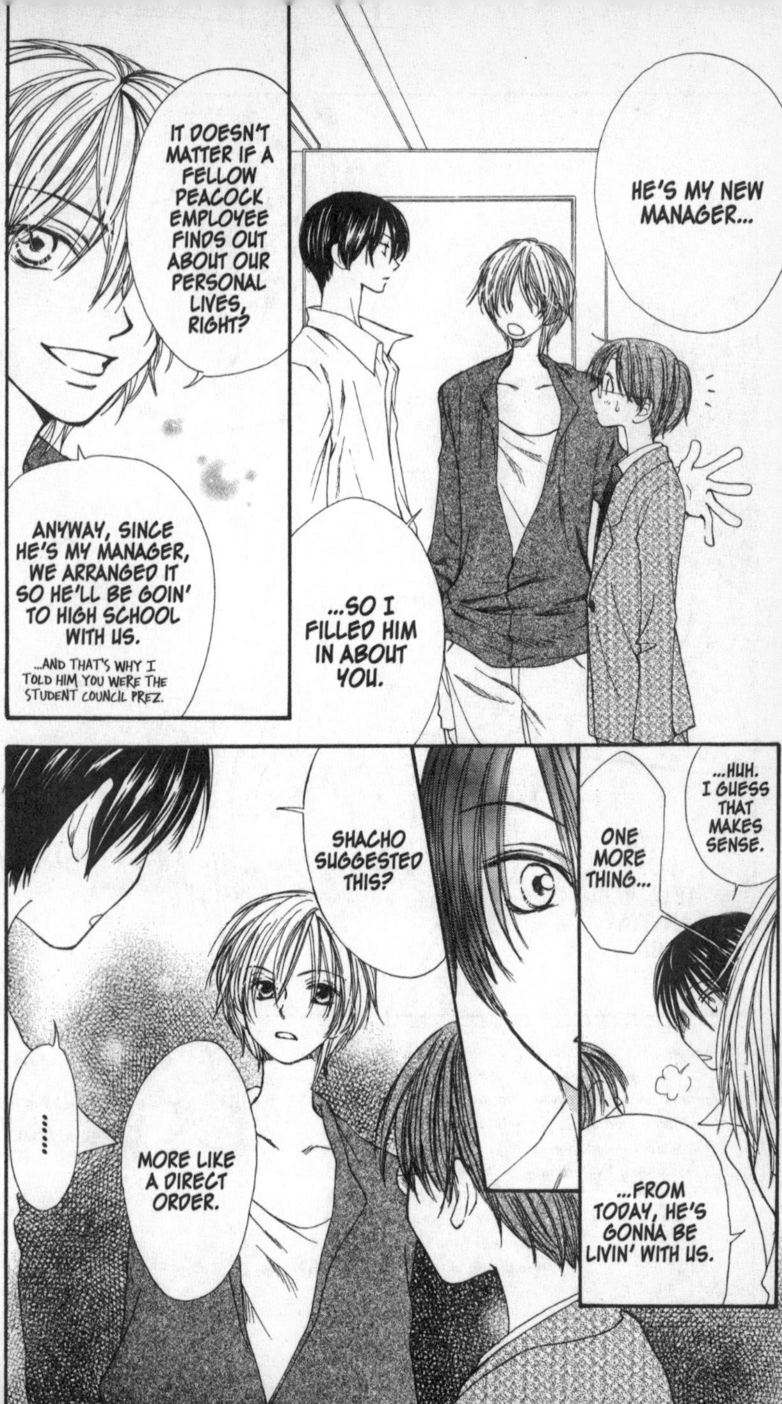
HE'S MY NEW MANAGER...
...SO I FILLED HIM IN ABOUT YOU.
IT DOESN'T MATTER IF A FELLOW PEACOCK EMPLOYEE FINDS OUT ABOUT OUR PERSONAL LIVES, RIGHT?
ANYWAY, SINCE HE'S MY MANAGER, WE ARRANGED IT SO HE'LL BE GOIN' TO HIGH SCHOOL WITH US.
...AND THAT'S WHY I TOLD HIM YOU WERE THE STUDENT COUNCIL PREZ.
...HUH. I GUESS THAT MAKES SENSE.
ONE MORE THING...
...FROM TODAY, HE'S GONNA BE LIVIN' WITH US.
SHACHO SUGGESTED THIS?
MORE LIKE A DIRECT ORDER.
......

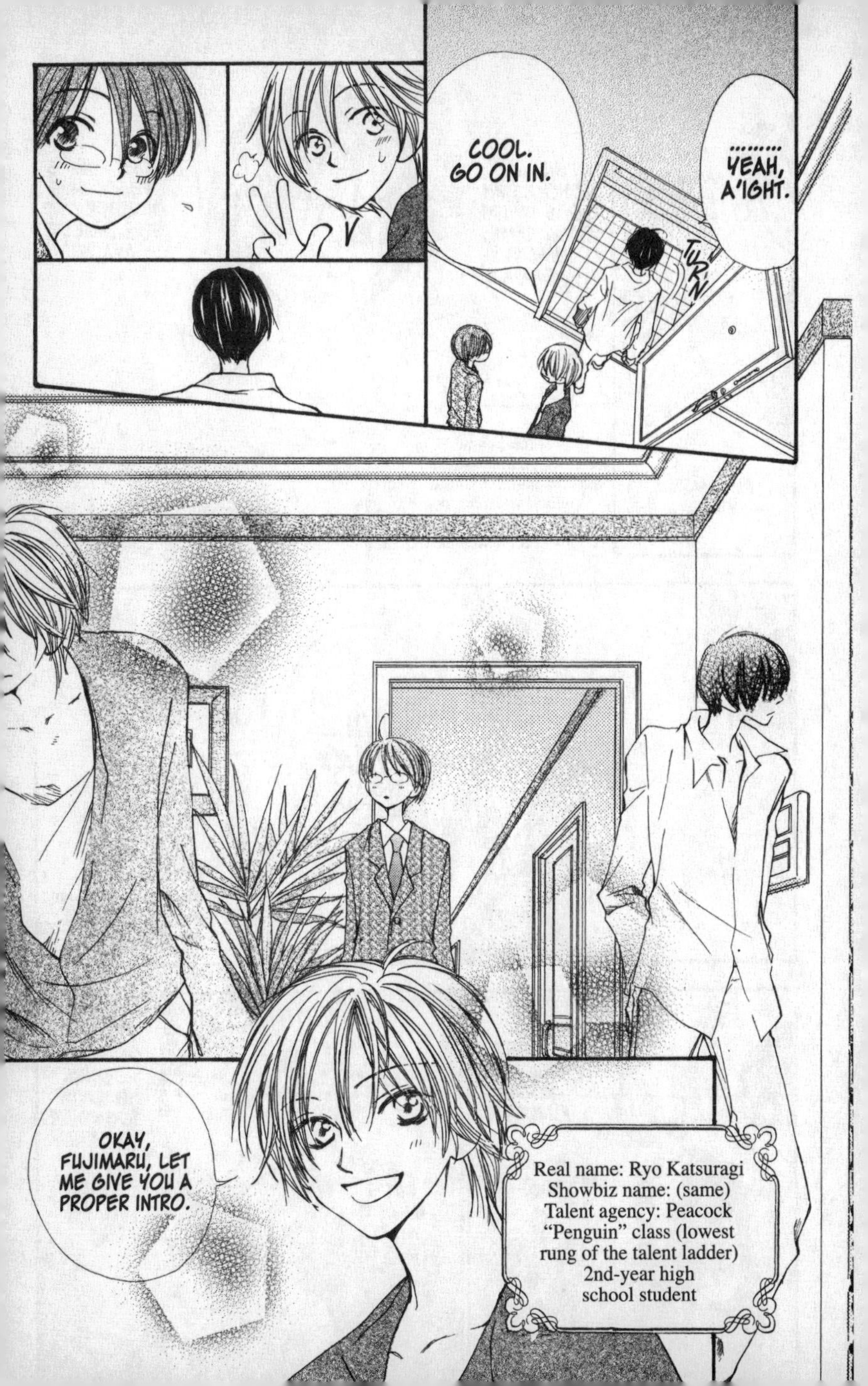
.........YEAH, A'IGHT.
TURN
COOL. GO ON IN.
OKAY, FUJIMARU, LET ME GIVE YOU A PROPER INTRO.
Real name: Ryo Katsuragi
Showbiz name: (same)
Talent agency: Peacock
"Penguin" class (lowest rung of the talent ladder)
2nd-year high school student

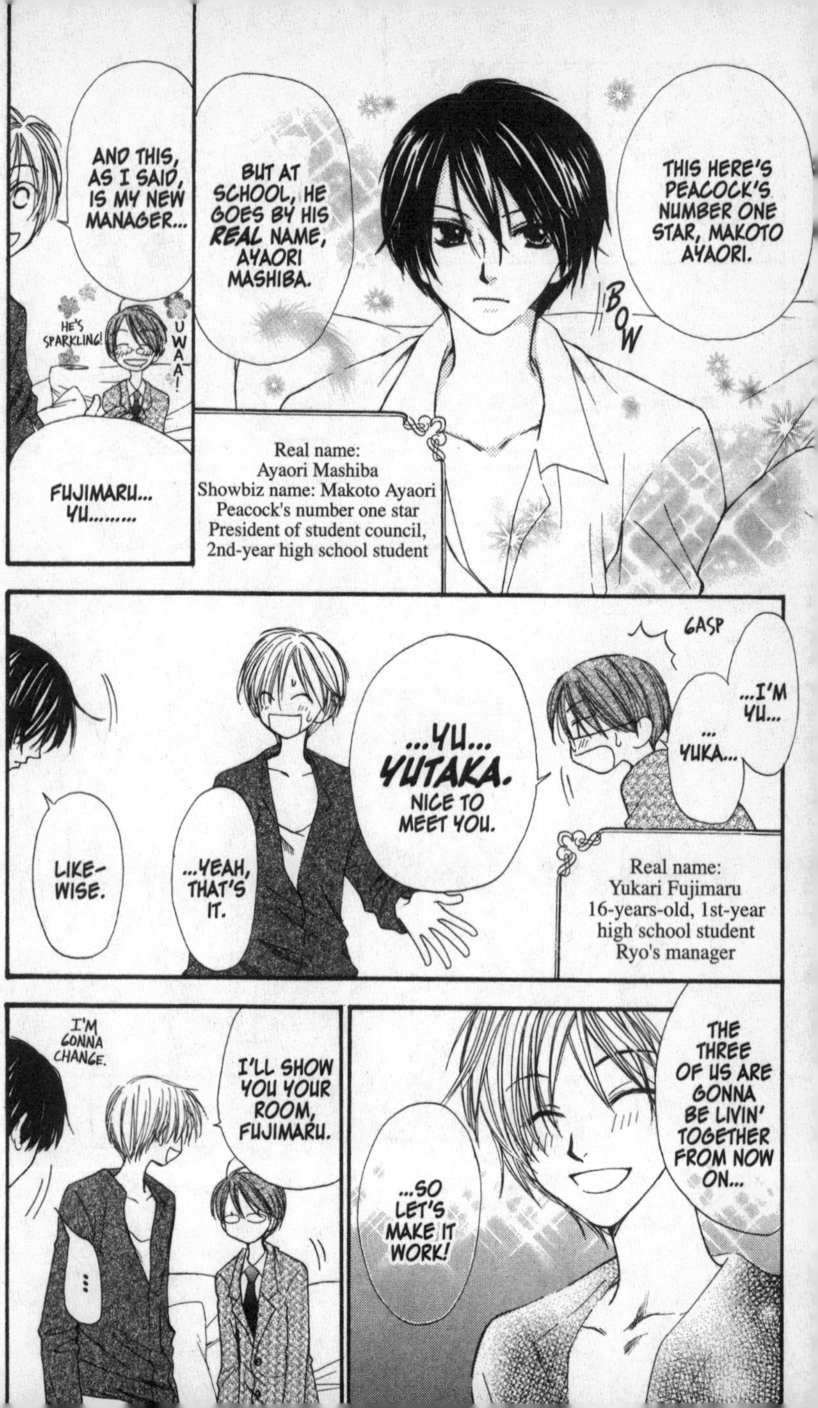
THIS HERE'S PEACOCK'S NUMBER ONE STAR, MAKOTO AYAORI.
BOW
BUT AT SCHOOL, HE GOES BY HIS REAL NAME, AYAORI MASHIBA.
Real name: Ayaori Mashiba
Showbiz name: Makoto Ayaori
Peacock's number one star
President of student council, 2nd-year high school student
AND THIS, AS I SAID, IS MY NEW MANAGER...
HE'S SPARKLING!
UWAA!
FUJIMARU... YU........
GASP
...I'M YU... ... YUKA...
Real name: Yukari Fujimaru
16-years-old, 1st-year high school student
Ryo's manager
...YU... YUTAKA. NICE TO MEET YOU.
...YEAH, THAT'S IT.
LIKE-WISE.
THE THREE OF US ARE GONNA BE LIVIN' TOGETHER FROM NOW ON...
...SO LET'S MAKE IT WORK!
I'M GONNA CHANGE.
I'LL SHOW YOU YOUR ROOM, FUJIMARU.
...

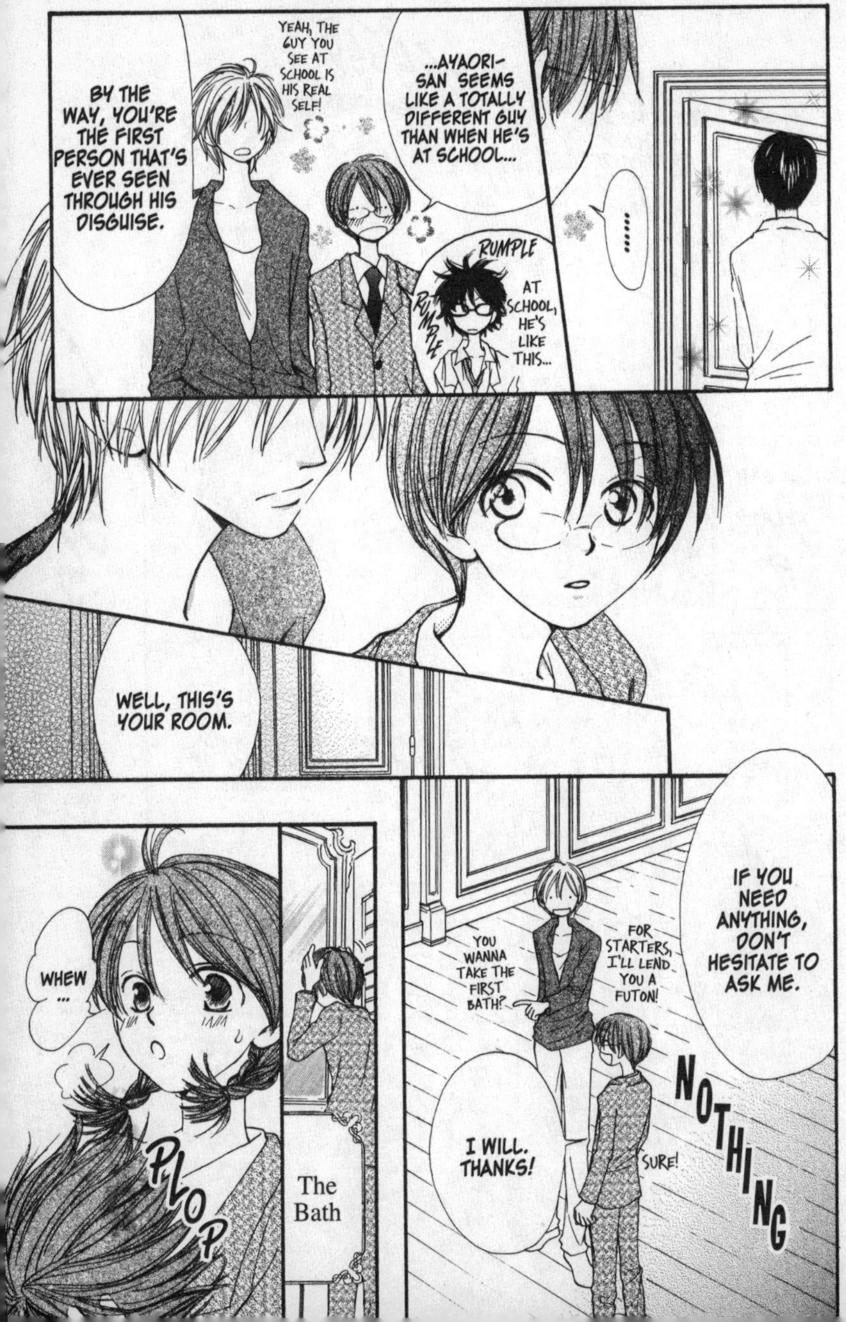
......
...AYAORI-SAN SEEMS LIKE A TOTALLY DIFFERENT GUY THAN WHEN HE'S AT SCHOOL...
RUMPLE
RUMPLE
AT SCHOOL, HE'S LIKE THIS...
YEAH, THE GUY YOU SEE AT SCHOOL IS HIS REAL SELF!
BY THE WAY, YOU'RE THE FIRST PERSON THAT'S EVER SEEN THROUGH HIS DISGUISE.
WELL, THIS'S YOUR ROOM.
IF YOU NEED ANYTHING, DON'T HESITATE TO ASK ME.
FOR STARTERS, I'LL LEND YOU A FUTON!
YOU WANNA TAKE THE FIRST BATH?
NOTHING
SURE!
I WILL. THANKS!
The Bath
WHEW ...
PLOP

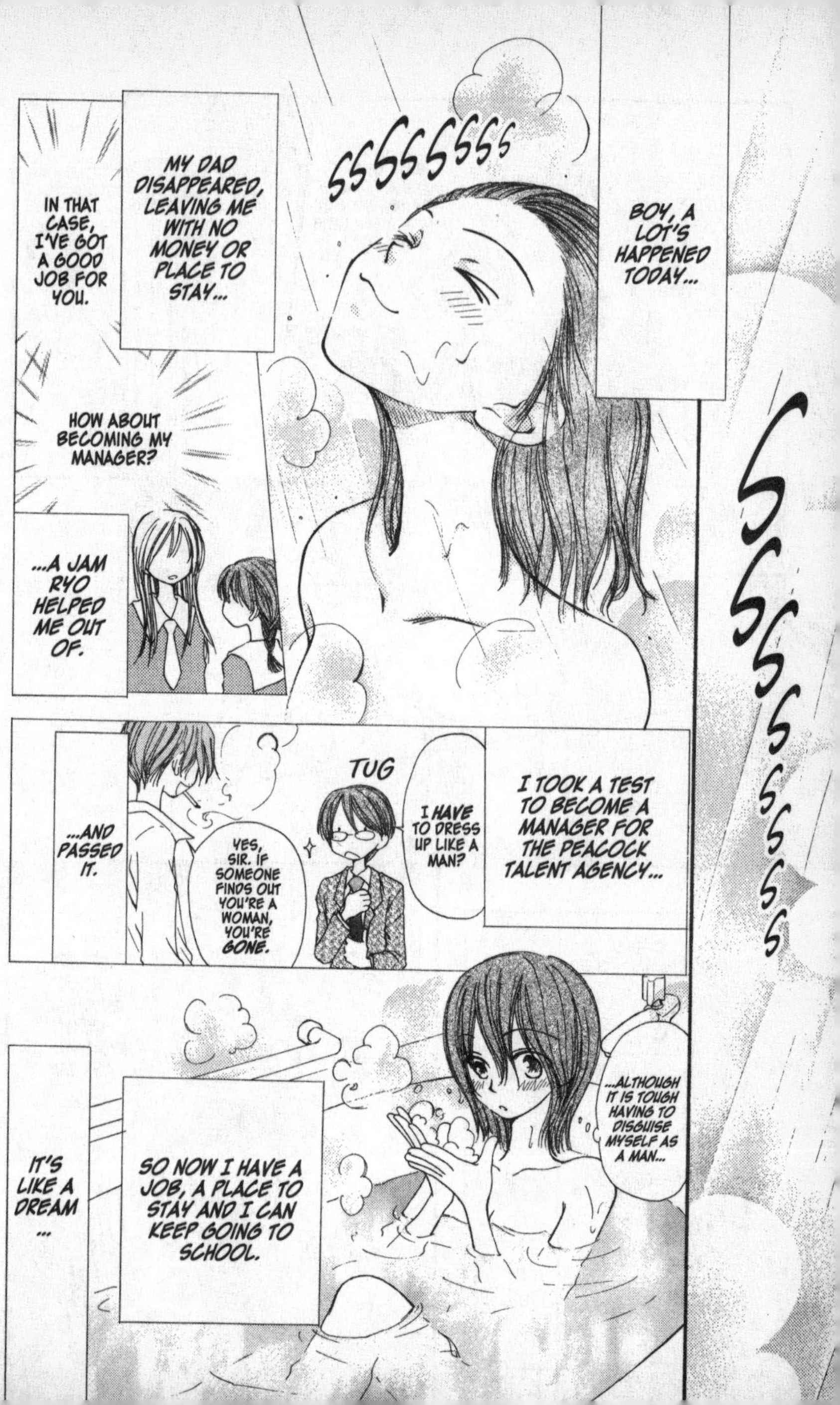
SSSSSSSSS
BOY, A LOT'S HAPPENED TODAY...
SSSSSSSSS
MY DAD DISAPPEARED, LEAVING ME WITH NO MONEY OR PLACE TO STAY...
IN THAT CASE, I'VE GOT A GOOD JOB FOR YOU.
HOW ABOUT BECOMING MY MANAGER?
...A JAM RYO HELPED ME OUT OF.
I TOOK A TEST TO BECOME A MANAGER FOR THE PEACOCK TALENT AGENCY...
I HAVE TO DRESS UP LIKE A MAN?
TUG
YES, SIR. IF SOMEONE FINDS OUT YOU'RE A WOMAN, YOU'RE GONE.
...AND PASSED IT.
...ALTHOUGH IT IS TOUGH HAVING TO DISGUISE MYSELF AS A MAN...
SO NOW I HAVE A JOB, A PLACE TO STAY AND I CAN KEEP GOING TO SCHOOL.
IT'S LIKE A DREAM ...

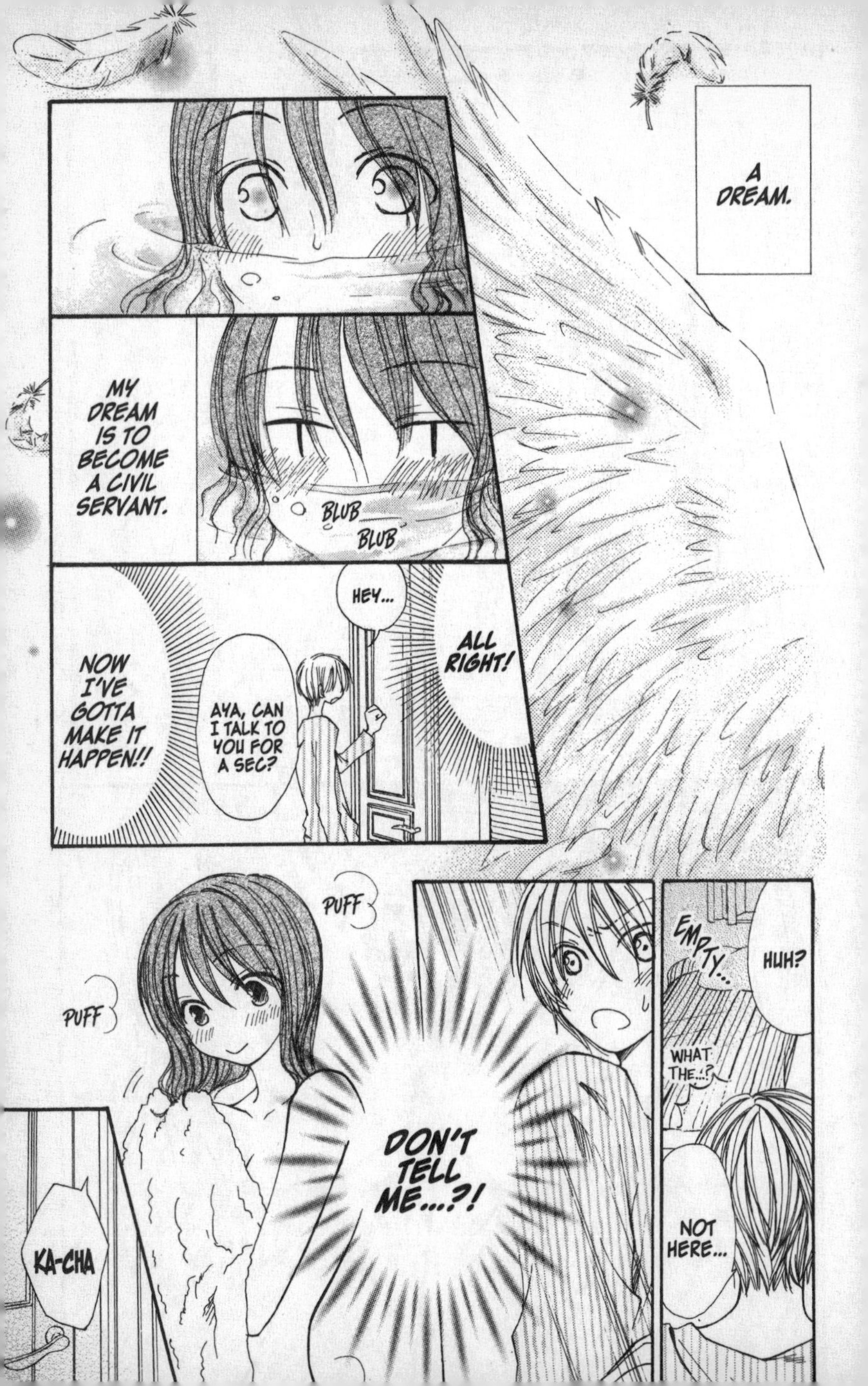
A DREAM.
MY DREAM IS TO BECOME A CIVIL SERVANT.
BLUB BLUB
ALL RIGHT!
HEY...
AYA, CAN I TALK TO YOU FOR A SEC?
NOW I'VE GOTTA MAKE IT HAPPEN!!
HUH?
EMPTY...
WHAT THE...?
NOT HERE...
DON'T TELL ME...?!
PUFF
PUFF
KA-CHA

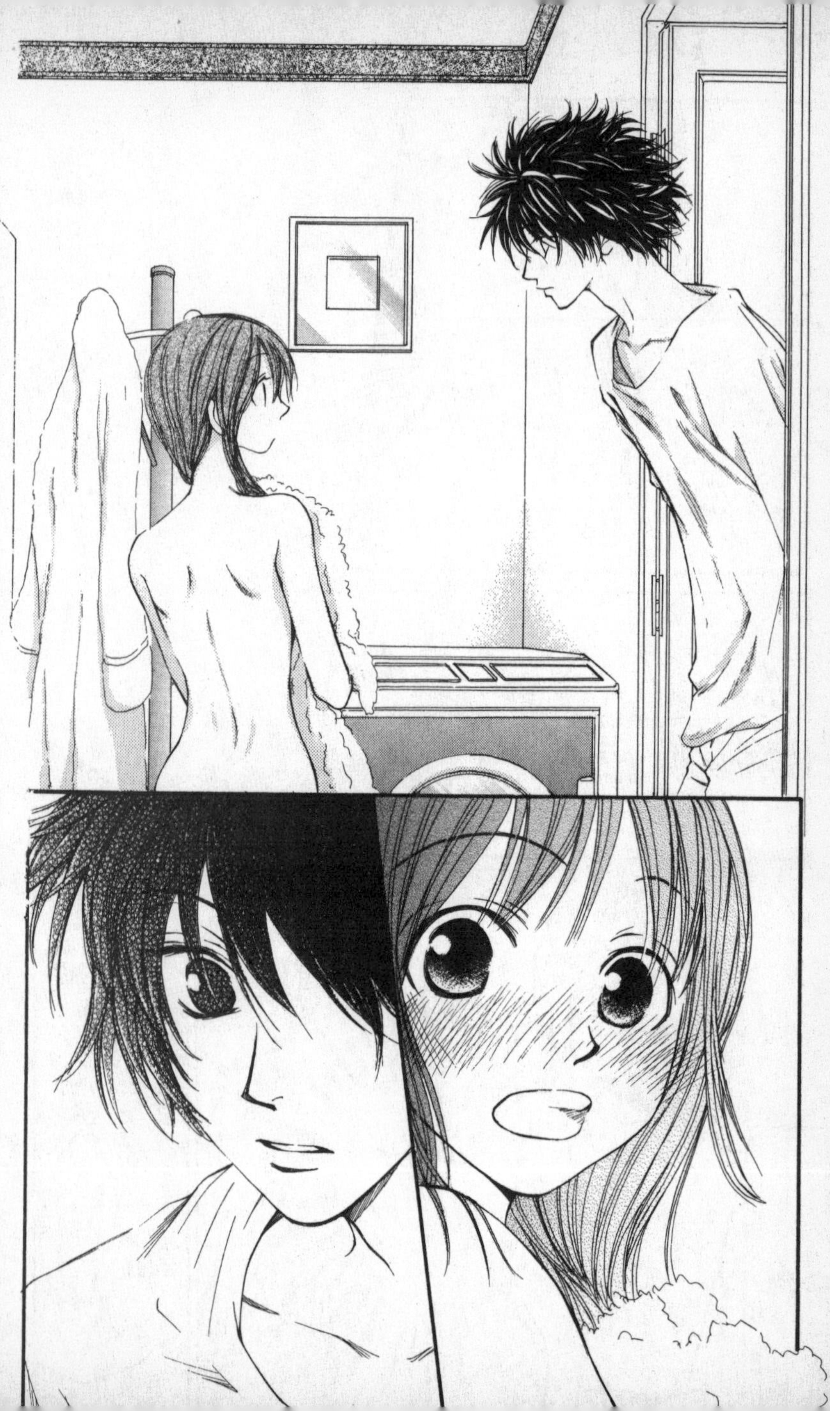

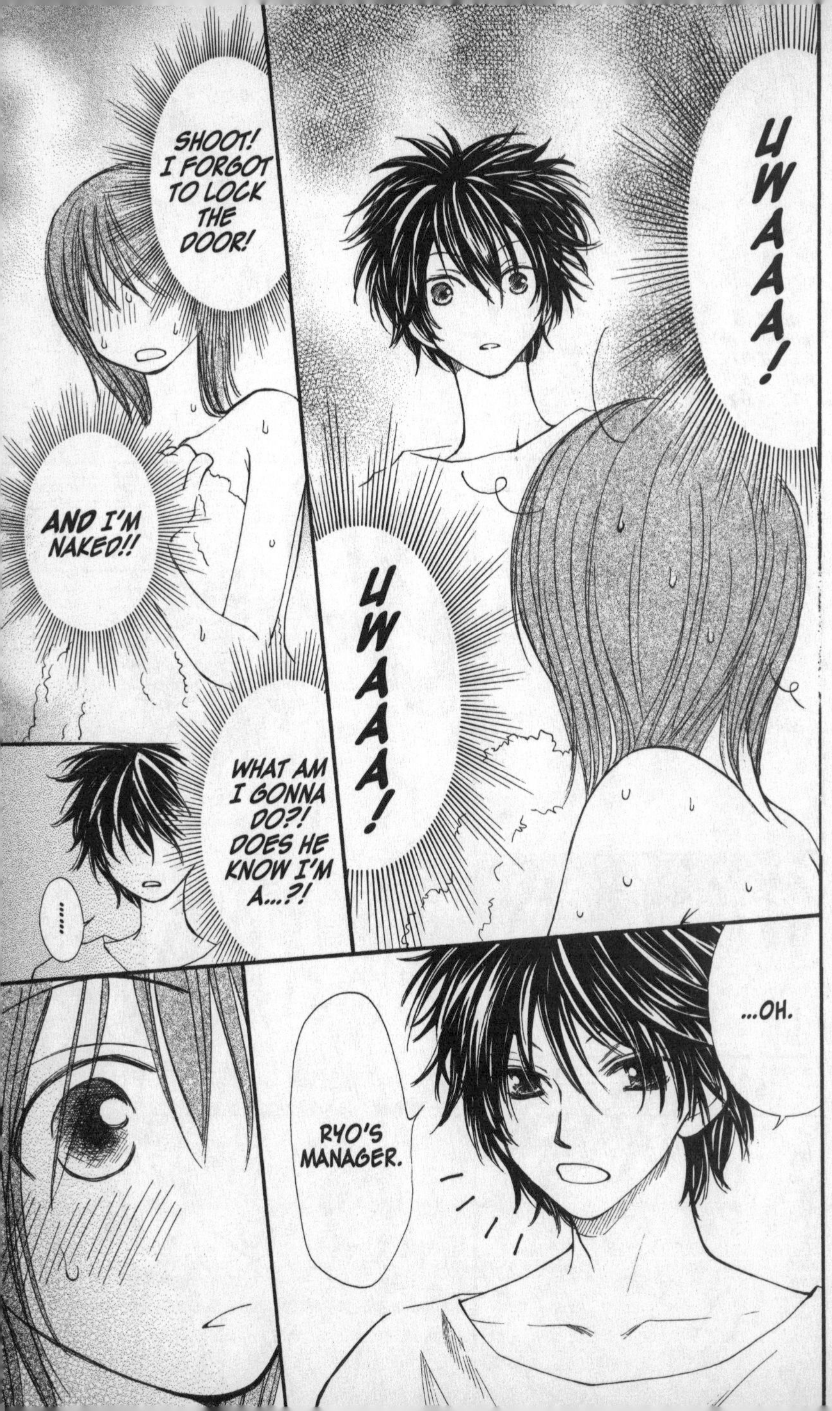

UWAAAA!
UWAAAA!
SHOOT! I FORGOT TO LOCK THE DOOR!
AND I'M NAKED!!
WHAT AM I GONNA DO?! DOES HE KNOW I'M A...?!
......
...OH.
RYO'S MANAGER.

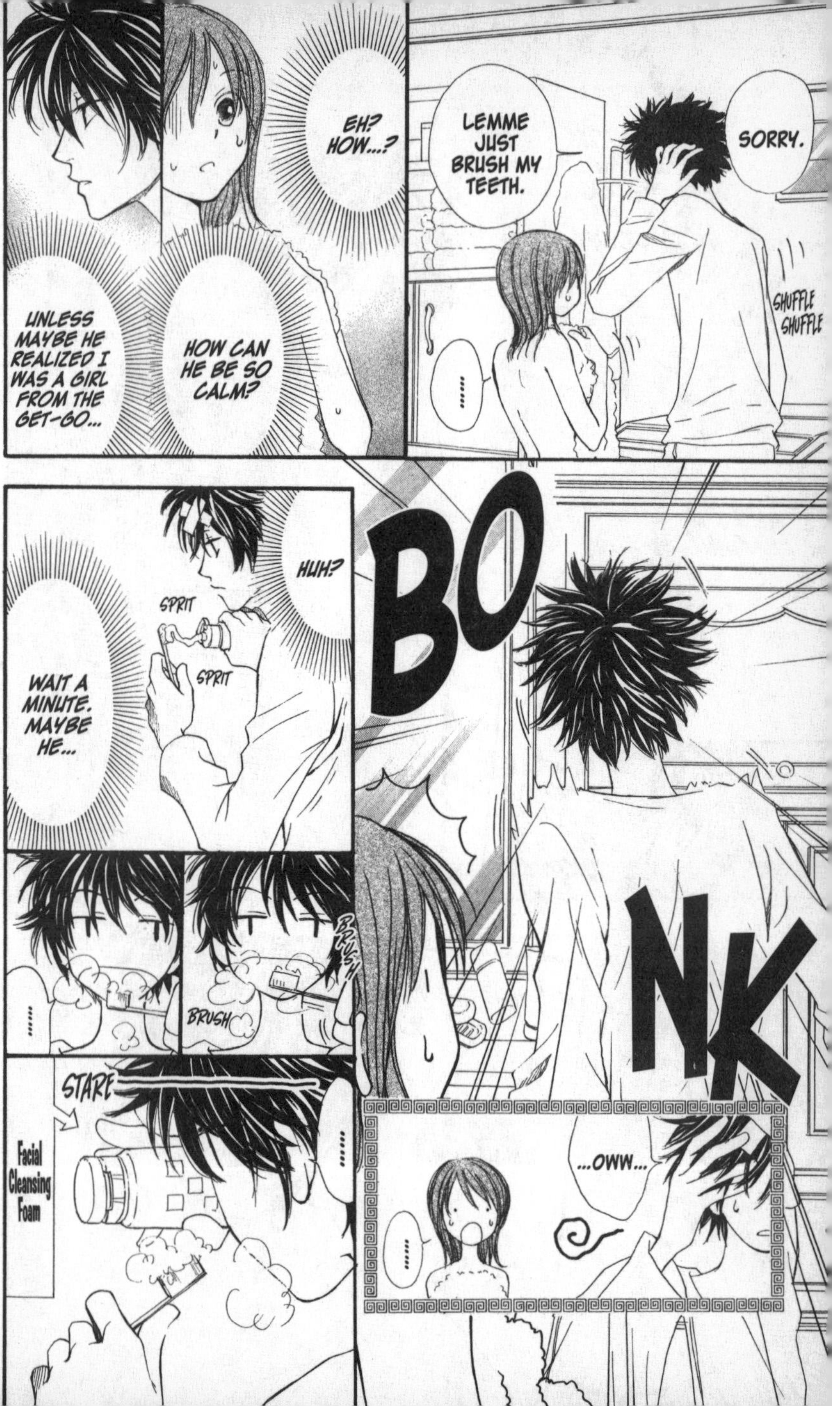
SORRY.
LEMME JUST BRUSH MY TEETH.
SHUFFLE SHUFFLE
......
EH? HOW...?
HOW CAN HE BE SO CALM?
UNLESS MAYBE HE REALIZED I WAS A GIRL FROM THE GET-GO...
BONK
...OWW...
......
HUH?
SPRIT
SPRIT
WAIT A MINUTE. MAYBE HE...
BRUSH
BRUSH
......
......
STARE
Facial Cleansing Foam

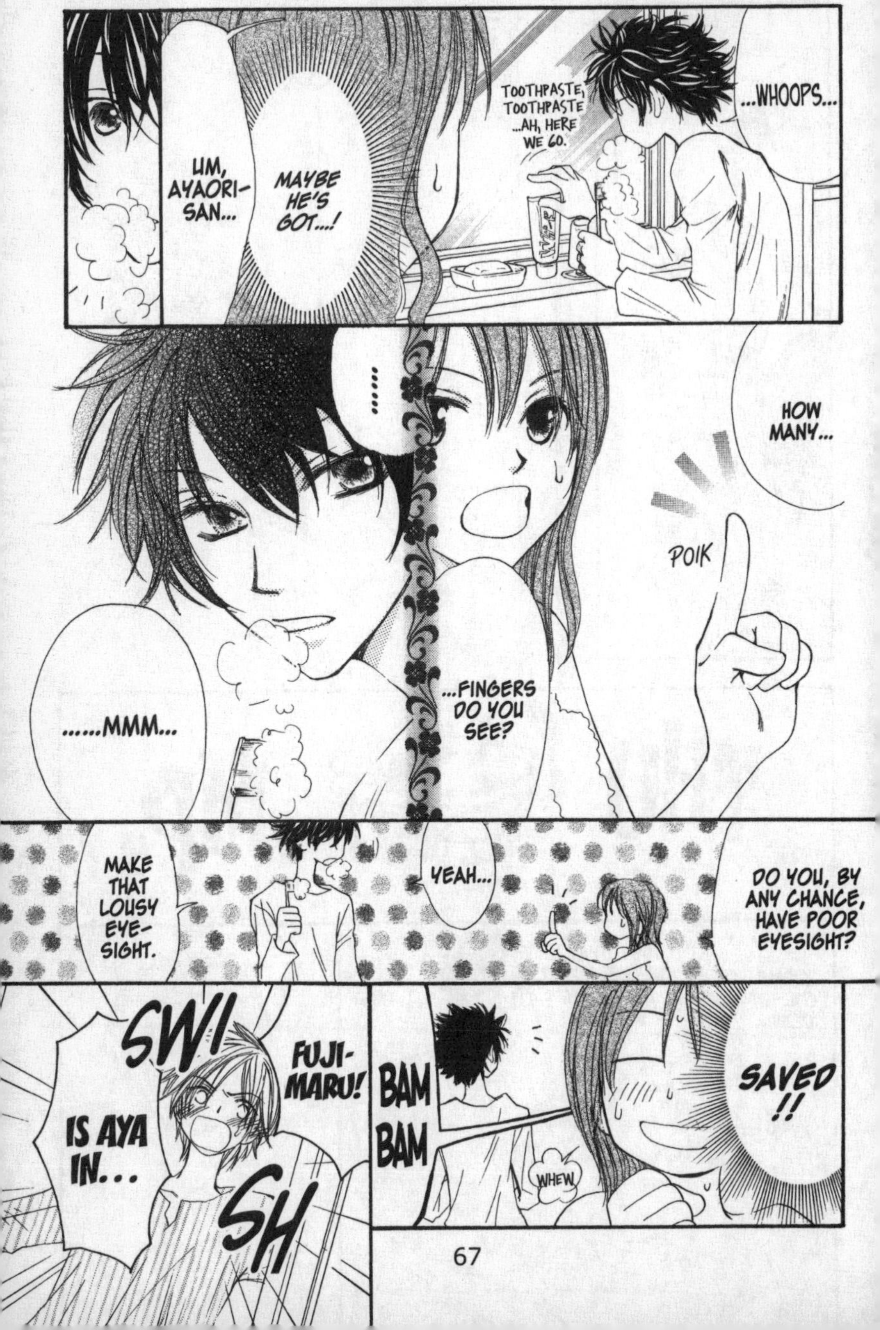
...WHOOPS...
TOOTHPASTE, TOOTHPASTE ...AH, HERE WE GO.
MAYBE HE'S GOT...!
UM, AYAORI-SAN...
HOW MANY...
POIK
......
...FINGERS DO YOU SEE?
......MMM...
DO YOU, BY ANY CHANCE, HAVE POOR EYESIGHT?
YEAH...
MAKE THAT LOUSY EYE-SIGHT.
SAVED!!
WHEW
BAM BAM
FUJI-MARU!
SWI SH
IS AYA IN...

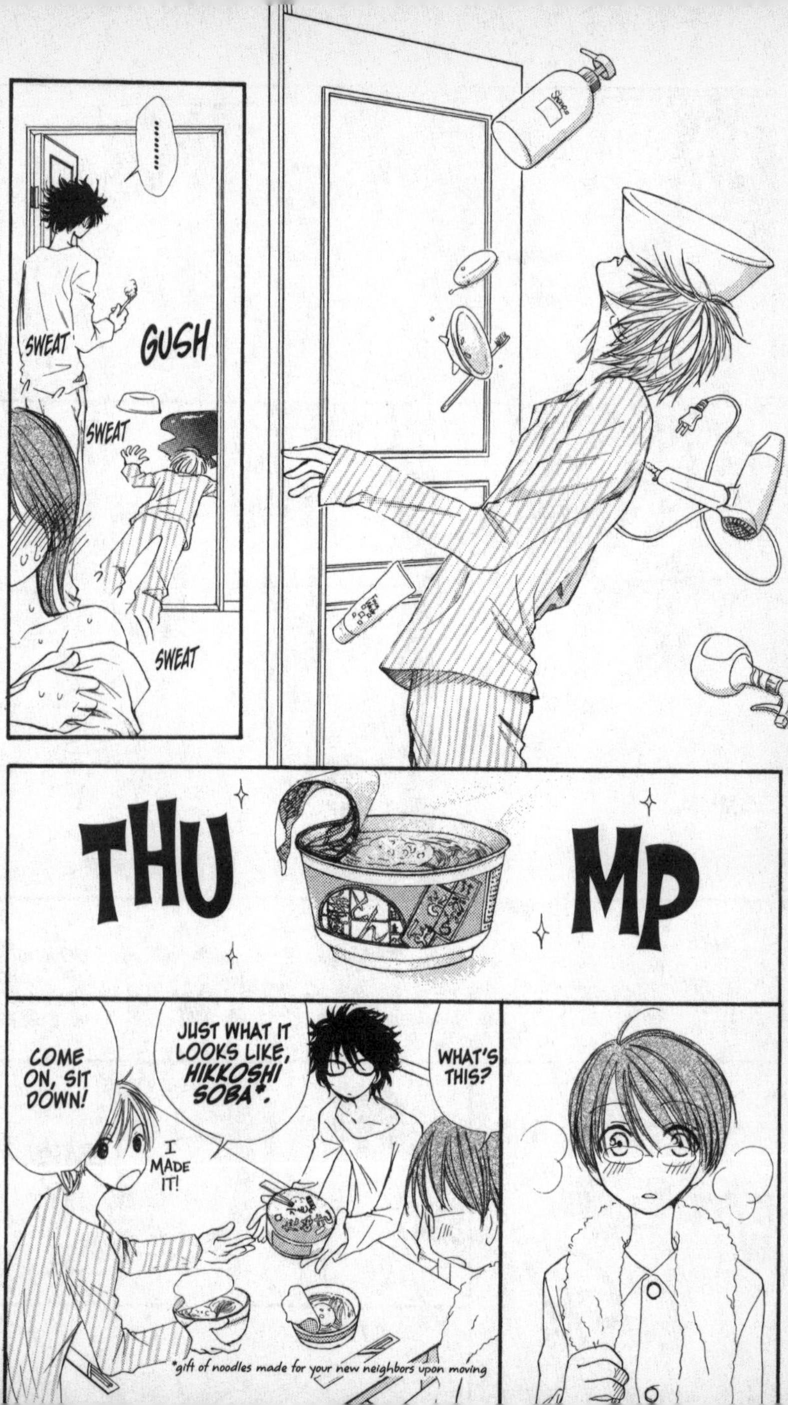
......
GUSH
SWEAT
SWEAT
SWEAT
THUMP
WHAT'S THIS?
JUST WHAT IT LOOKS LIKE, HIKKOSHI SOBA*.
COME ON, SIT DOWN!
I MADE IT!
*gift of noodles made for your new neighbors upon moving

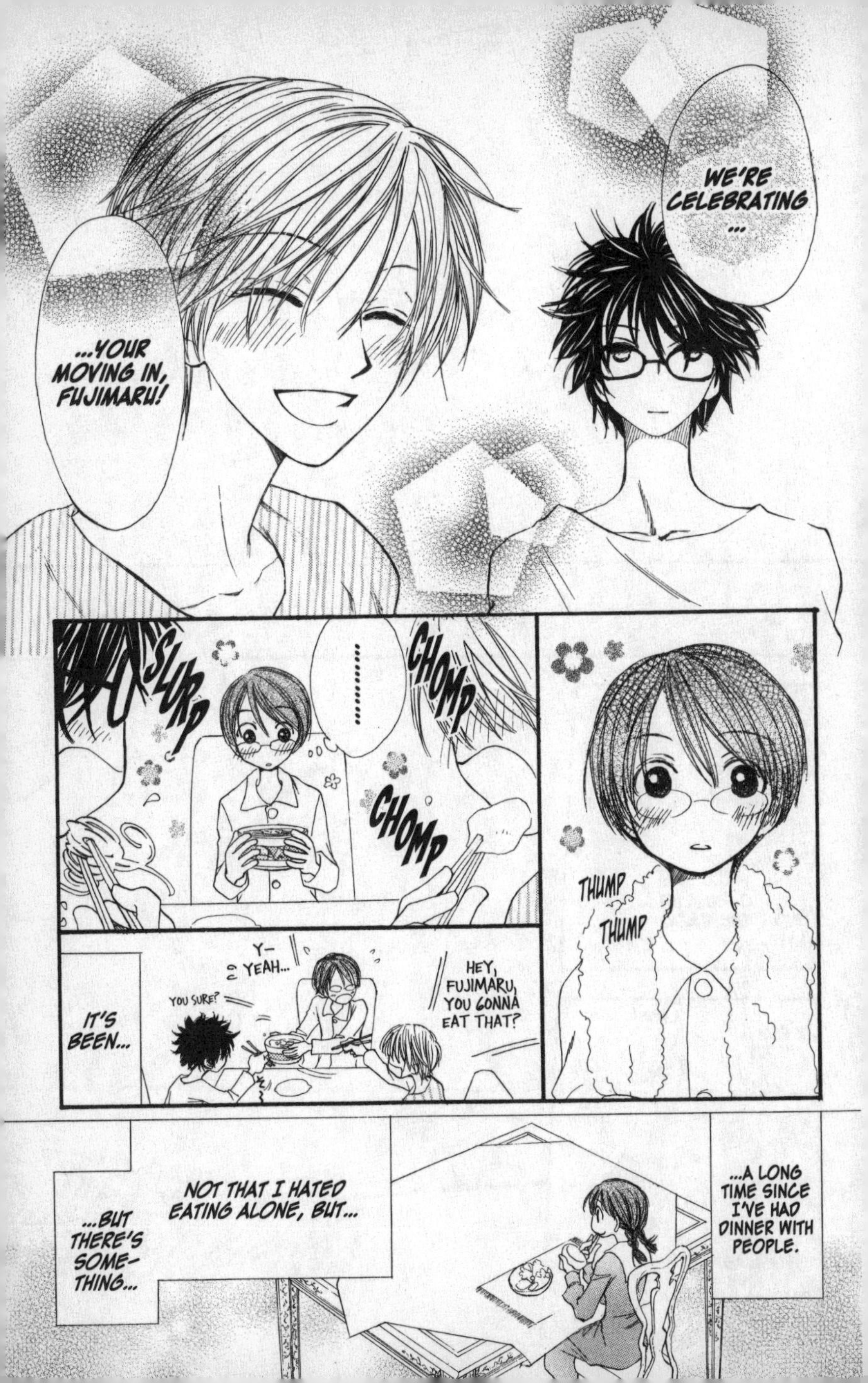
WE'RE CELEBRATING...
...YOUR MOVING IN, FUJIMARU!
THUMP THUMP
CHOMP
......
SLURP
CHOMP
HEY, FUJIMARU, YOU GONNA EAT THAT?
Y- YEAH...
YOU SURE?
IT'S BEEN...
...A LONG TIME SINCE I'VE HAD DINNER WITH PEOPLE.
NOT THAT I HATED EATING ALONE, BUT...
...BUT THERE'S SOME-THING...

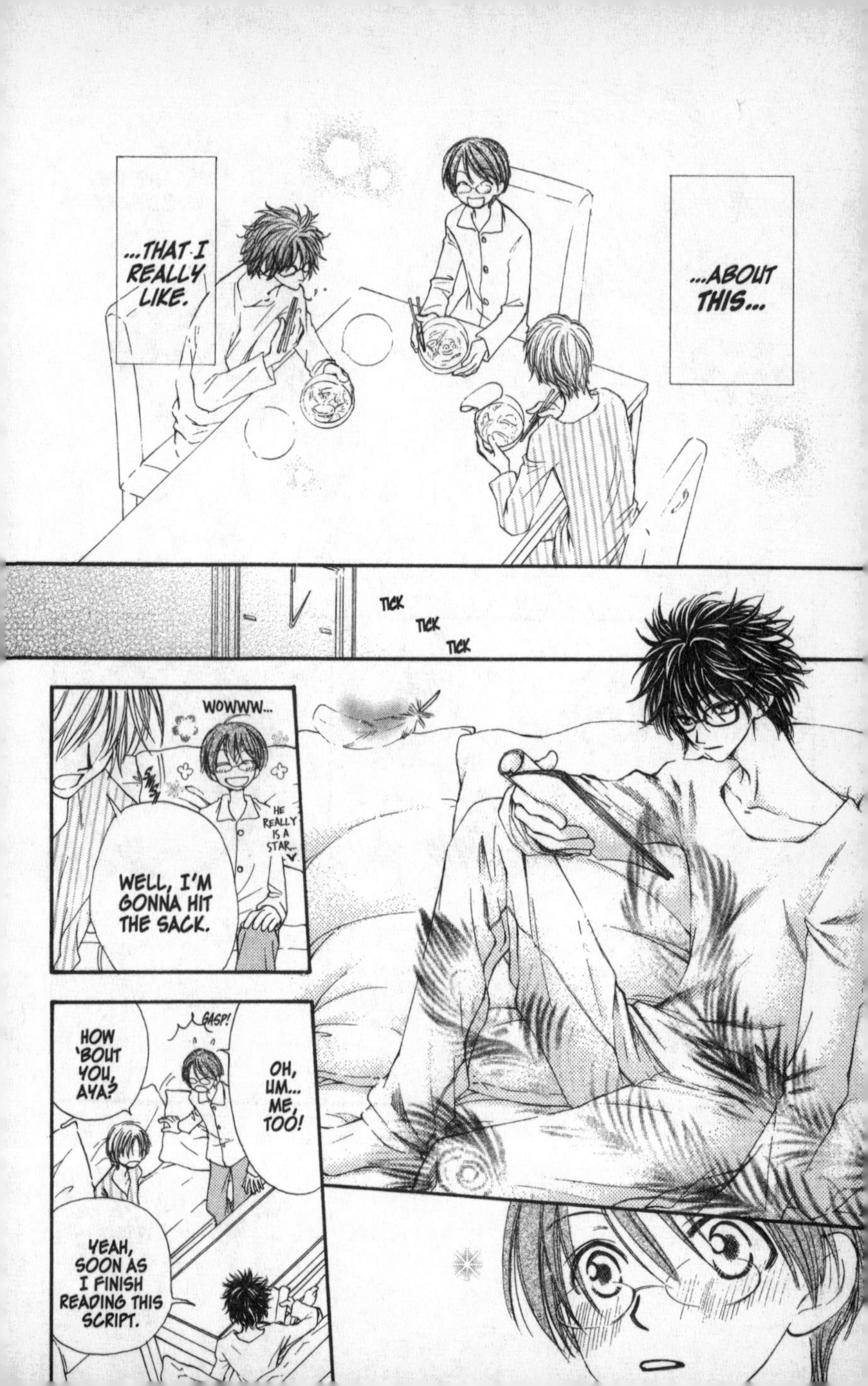
...ABOUT THIS...
...THAT I REALLY LIKE.
TICK
TICK
TICK
WOWWW...
HE REALLY IS A STAR...
WELL, I'M GONNA HIT THE SACK.
HOW 'BOUT YOU, AYA?
GASP!
OH, UM... ME, TOO!
YEAH, SOON AS I FINISH READING THIS SCRIPT.

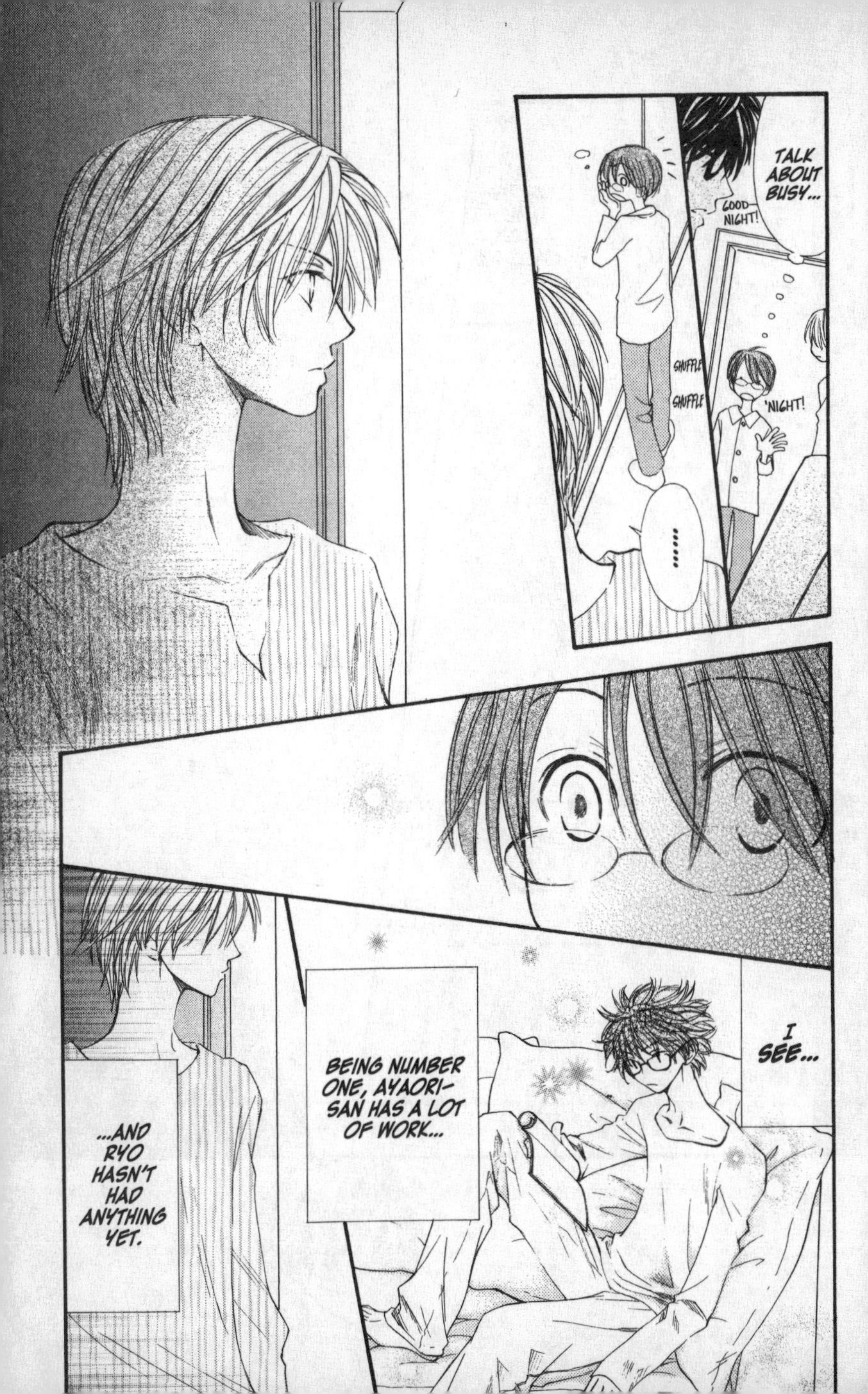
TALK ABOUT BUSY...
GOOD NIGHT!
'NIGHT!
SHUFFLE
SHUFFLE
......
I SEE...
BEING NUMBER ONE, AYAORI-SAN HAS A LOT OF WORK...
...AND RYO HASN'T HAD ANYTHING YET.

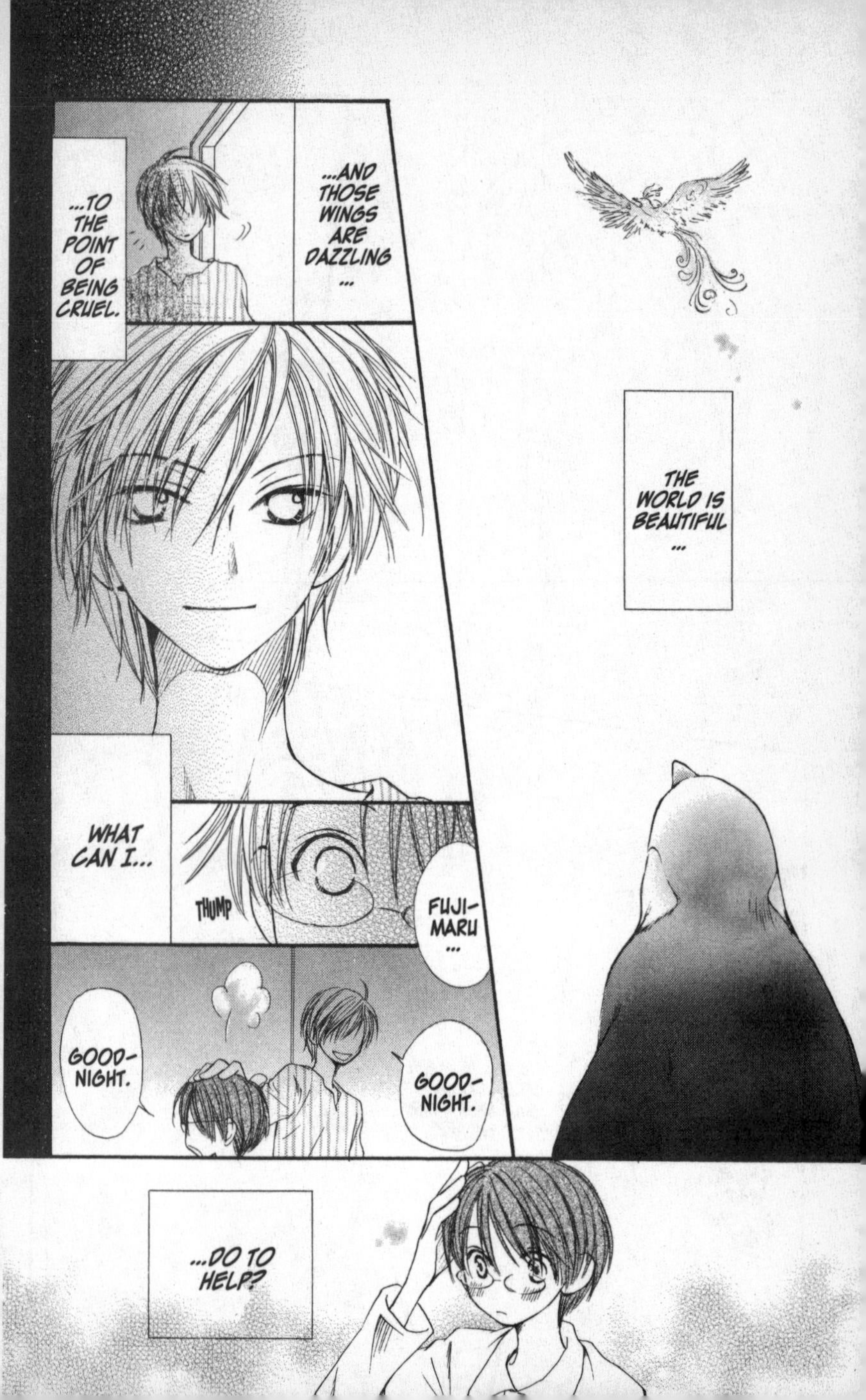
THE WORLD IS BEAUTIFUL...
...AND THOSE WINGS ARE DAZZLING...
...TO THE POINT OF BEING CRUEL.
FUJI-MARU...
THUMP
WHAT CAN I...
GOOD-NIGHT.
GOOD-NIGHT.
...DO TO HELP?

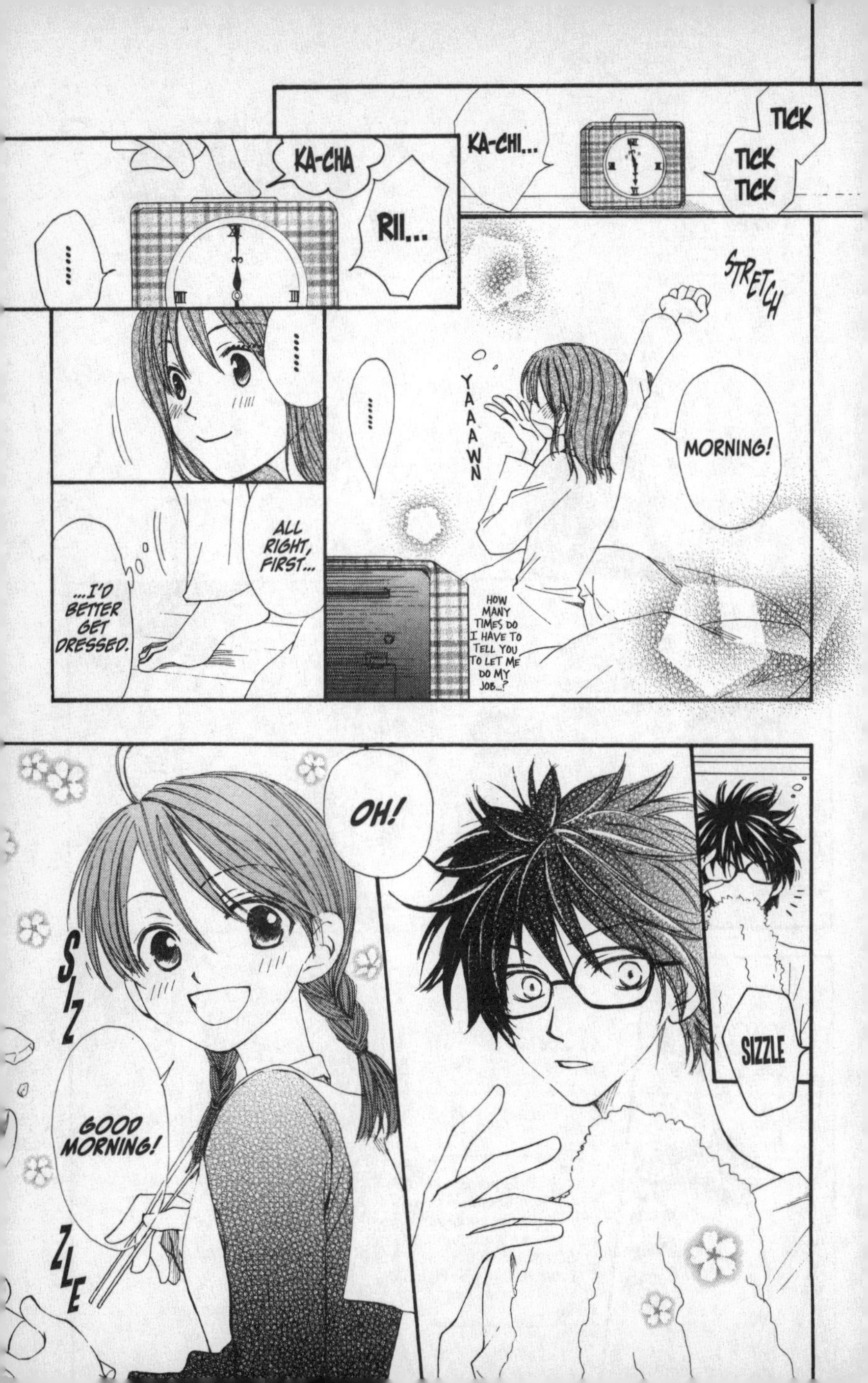

TICK
TICK
TICK
KA-CHI...
KA-CHA
RII...
......
STRETCH
MORNING!
YAAAAWN
......
HOW MANY TIMES DO I HAVE TO TELL YOU TO LET ME DO MY JOB...?
......
ALL RIGHT, FIRST...
...I'D BETTER GET DRESSED.
SIZZLE
OH!
SIZZLE
GOOD MORNING!

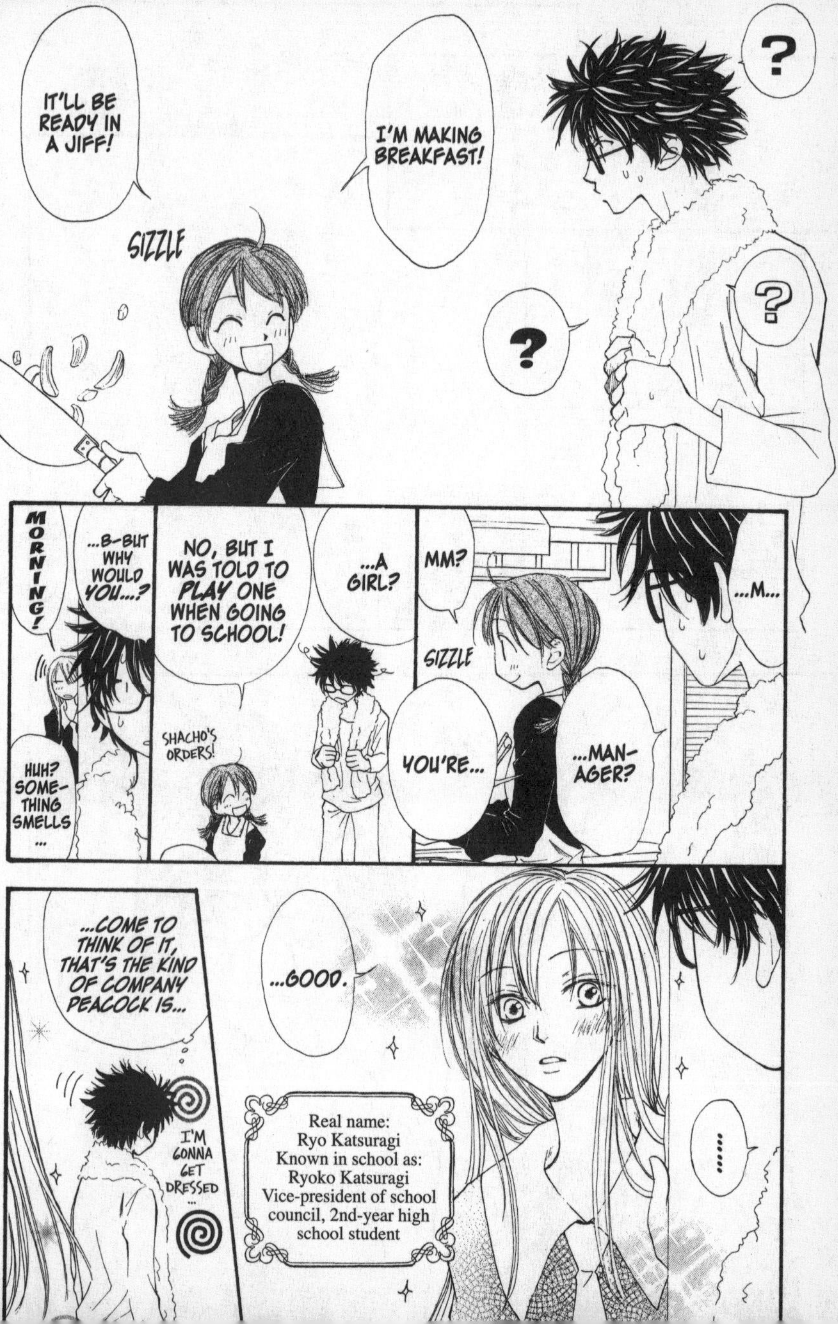
?
?
?
I'M MAKING BREAKFAST!
IT'LL BE READY IN A JIFF!
SIZZLE
...M...
...MAN-AGER?
YOU'RE...
MM?
SIZZLE
...A GIRL?
NO, BUT I WAS TOLD TO PLAY ONE WHEN GOING TO SCHOOL!
SHACHO'S ORDERS!
...B-BUT WHY WOULD YOU...?
MORNING!
HUH? SOME-THING SMELLS ...
......
...GOOD.
Real name: Ryo Katsuragi Known in school as: Ryoko Katsuragi Vice-president of school council, 2nd-year high school student
...COME TO THINK OF IT, THAT'S THE KIND OF COMPANY PEACOCK IS...
I'M GONNA GET DRESSED ...

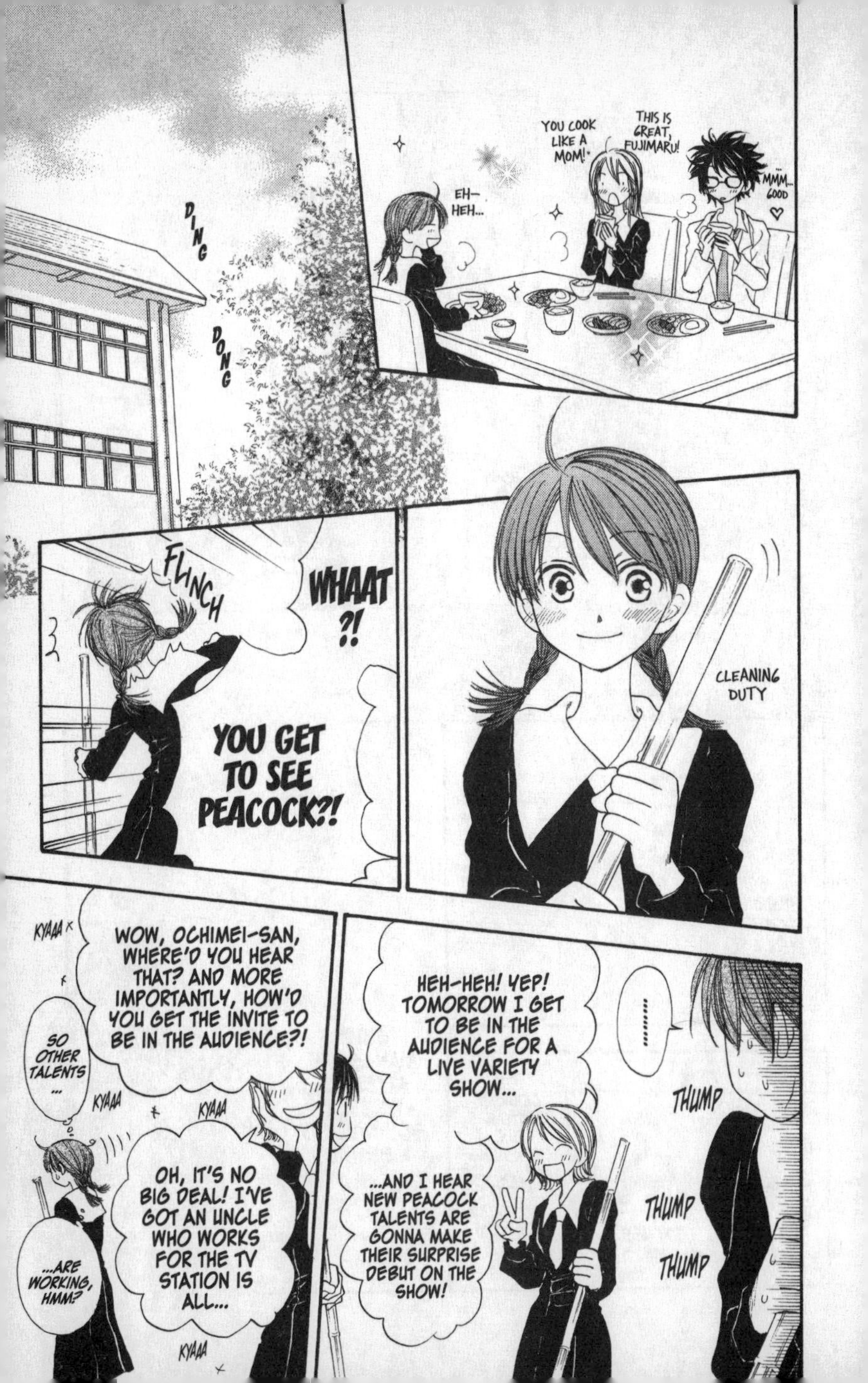
THIS IS GREAT, FUJIMARU!
...MMM... GOOD
YOU COOK LIKE A MOM!
EH-HEH...
DING
DONG
CLEANING DUTY
WHAAT?!
FLINCH
YOU GET TO SEE PEACOCK?!
......
THUMP
THUMP
THUMP
HEH-HEH! YEP! TOMORROW I GET TO BE IN THE AUDIENCE FOR A LIVE VARIETY SHOW...
...AND I HEAR NEW PEACOCK TALENTS ARE GONNA MAKE THEIR SURPRISE DEBUT ON THE SHOW!
WOW, OCHIMEI-SAN, WHERE'D YOU HEAR THAT? AND MORE IMPORTANTLY, HOW'D YOU GET THE INVITE TO BE IN THE AUDIENCE?!
KYAAA
KYAAA
KYAAA
OH, IT'S NO BIG DEAL! I'VE GOT AN UNCLE WHO WORKS FOR THE TV STATION IS ALL...
KYAAA
SO OTHER TALENTS...
...ARE WORKING, HMM?

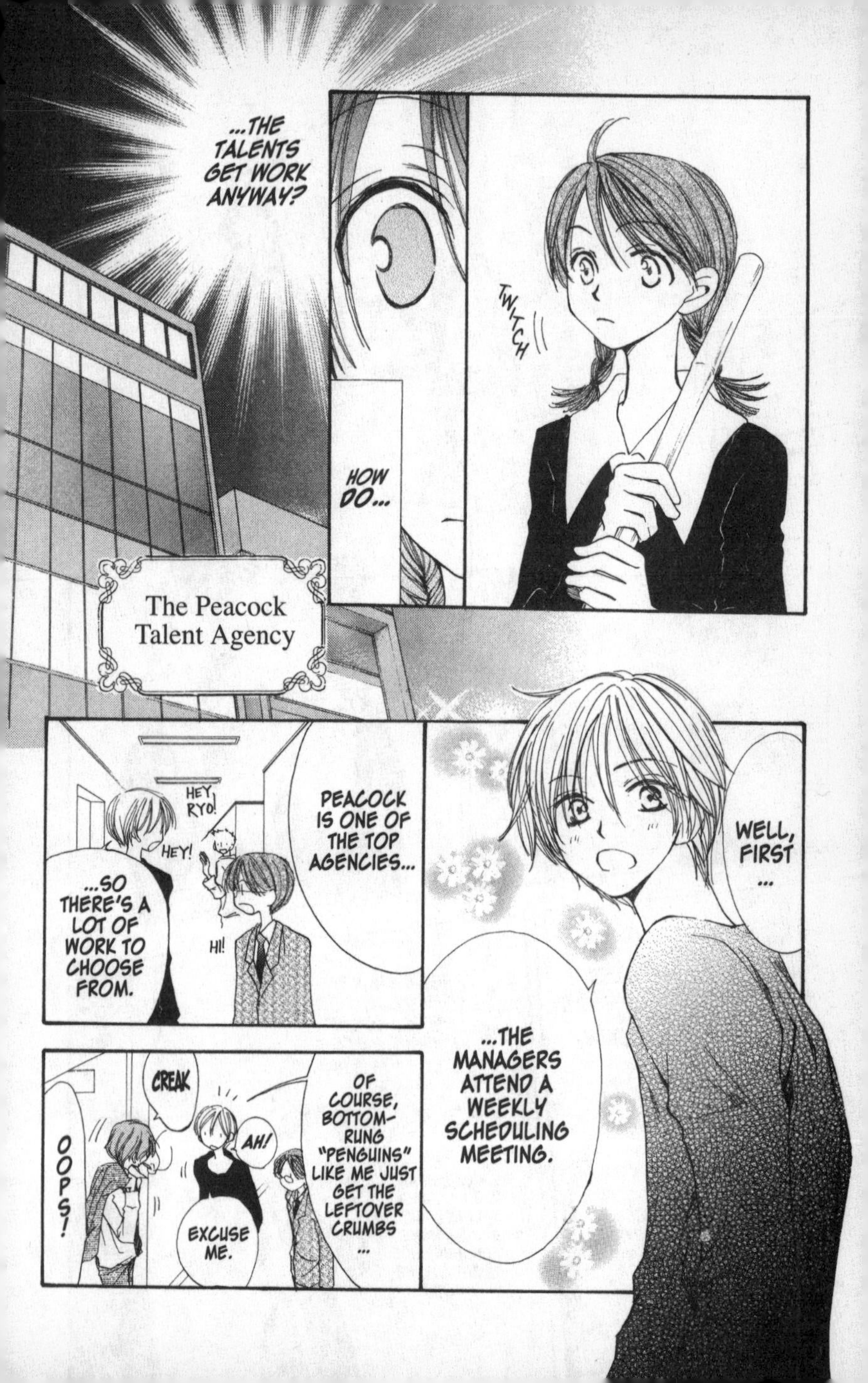
TWITCH
HOW DO...
...THE TALENTS GET WORK ANYWAY?
The Peacock Talent Agency
WELL, FIRST...
...THE MANAGERS ATTEND A WEEKLY SCHEDULING MEETING.
PEACOCK IS ONE OF THE TOP AGENCIES...
HEY RYO!
HEY!
HI!
...SO THERE'S A LOT OF WORK TO CHOOSE FROM.
OF COURSE, BOTTOM-RUNG "PENGUINS" LIKE ME JUST GET THE LEFTOVER CRUMBS...
CREAK
AH!
EXCUSE ME.
OOPS!

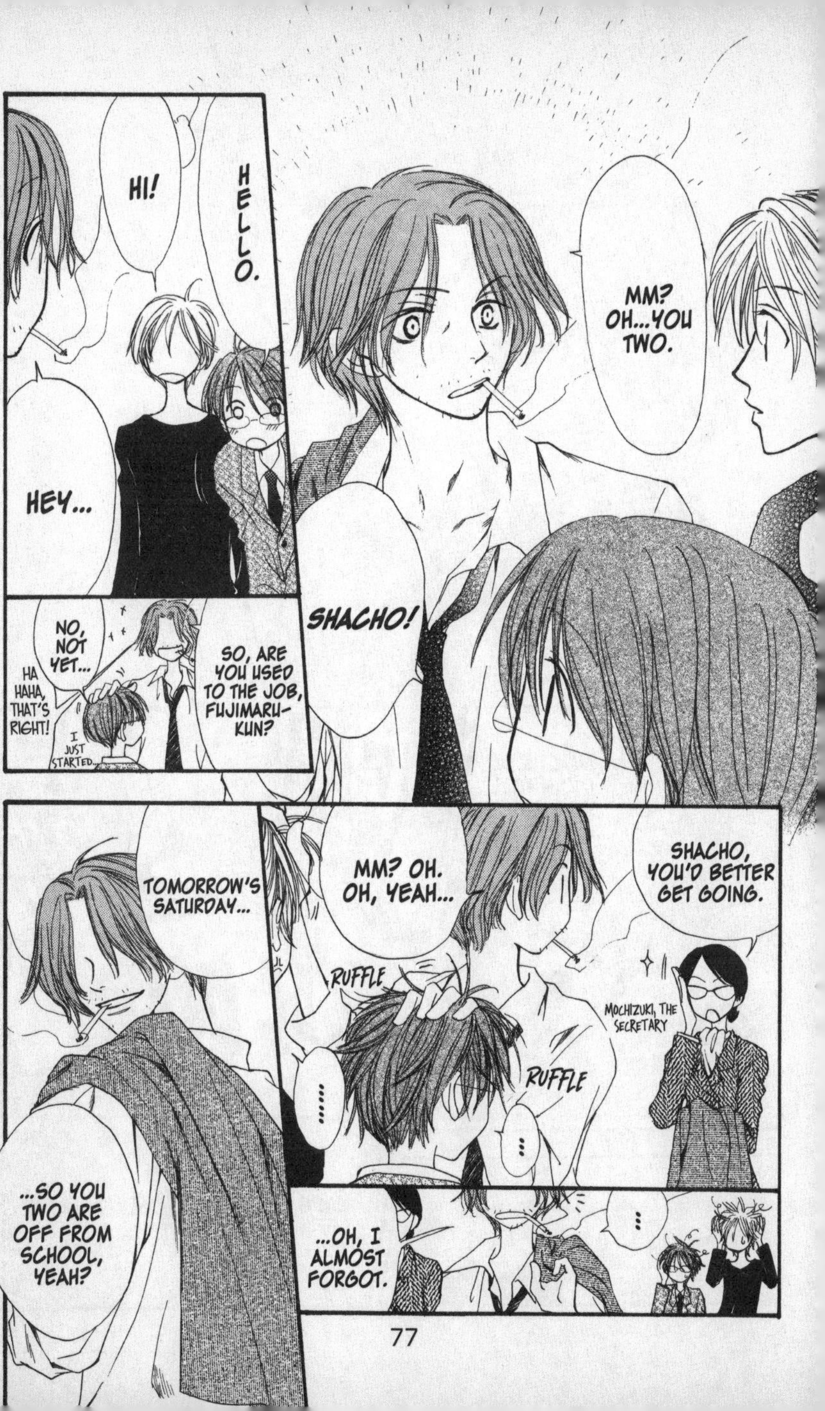
MM? OH...YOU TWO.
SHACHO!
HELLO.
HI!
HEY...
SO, ARE YOU USED TO THE JOB, FUJIMARU-KUN?
NO, NOT YET...
HA HAHA, THAT'S RIGHT!
I JUST STARTED...
SHACHO, YOU'D BETTER GET GOING.
MOCHIZUKI, THE SECRETARY
MM? OH. OH, YEAH...
RUFFLE
......
RUFFLE
...
...
...OH, I ALMOST FORGOT.
TOMORROW'S SATURDAY...
...SO YOU TWO ARE OFF FROM SCHOOL, YEAH?

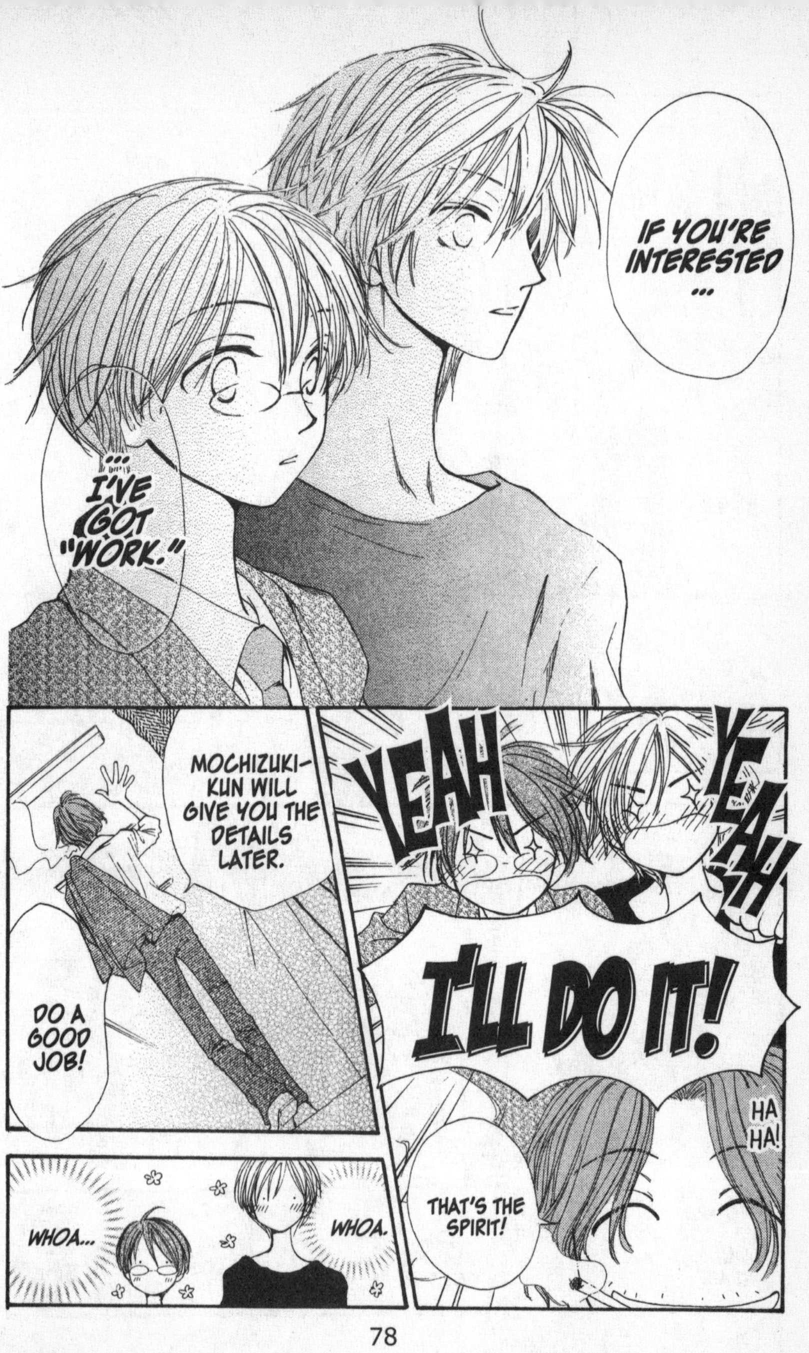
IF YOU'RE INTERESTED ...
... I'VE GOT "WORK."
YEAH
YEAH
I'LL DO IT!
HA HA!
THAT'S THE SPIRIT!
MOCHIZUKI-KUN WILL GIVE YOU THE DETAILS LATER.
DO A GOOD JOB!
WHOA.
WHOA...

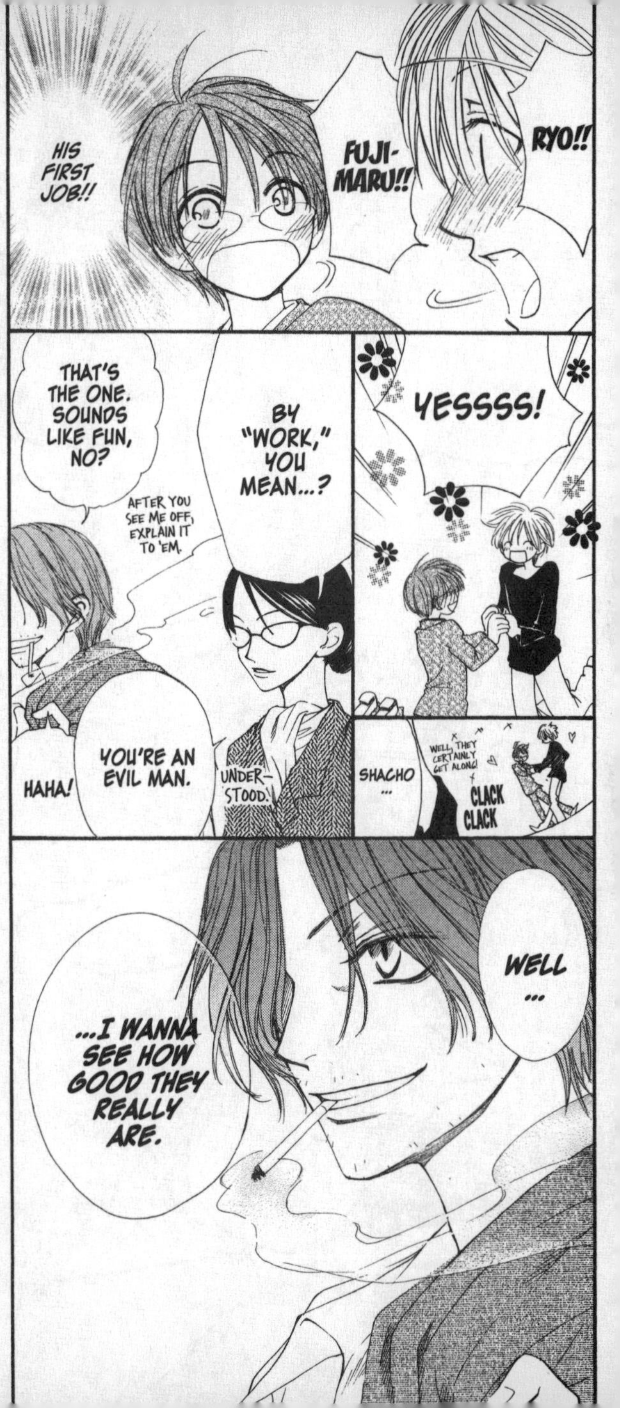
RYO!!
FUJI-MARU!!
HIS FIRST JOB!!
YESSSS!
SHACHO ...
WELL, THEY CERTAINLY GET ALONG!
CLACK CLACK
BY "WORK," YOU MEAN...?
THAT'S THE ONE. SOUNDS LIKE FUN, NO?
AFTER YOU SEE ME OFF, EXPLAIN IT TO 'EM.
UNDER-STOOD.
YOU'RE AN EVIL MAN.
HAHA!
WELL ...
...I WANNA SEE HOW GOOD THEY REALLY ARE.

1/4 Sakura Mail

part 4

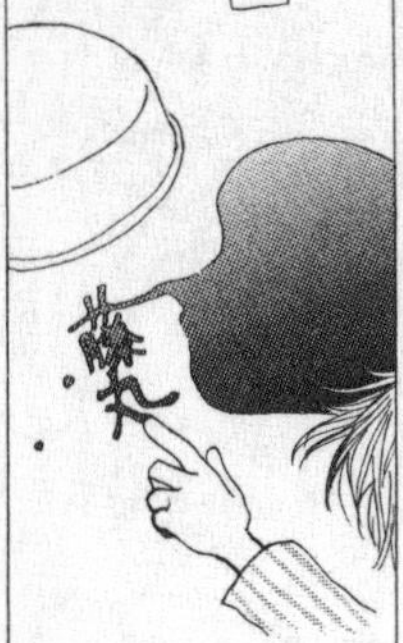

In this second episode, Yuka-chan, Ryo and Aya begin cohabiting. That's one of the things I wanted to accomplish here, life in a co-ed apartment (albeit a very odd one...). In this ep, Ryo spurts blood. In the past, in a one-shot story I did, I had a scene where a girl spurts blood, but drawing it didn't disturb me. Even my assistant pleaded for me to go with a light tone for the blood because she said it looked painful and felt sorry for the character!

To be continued...

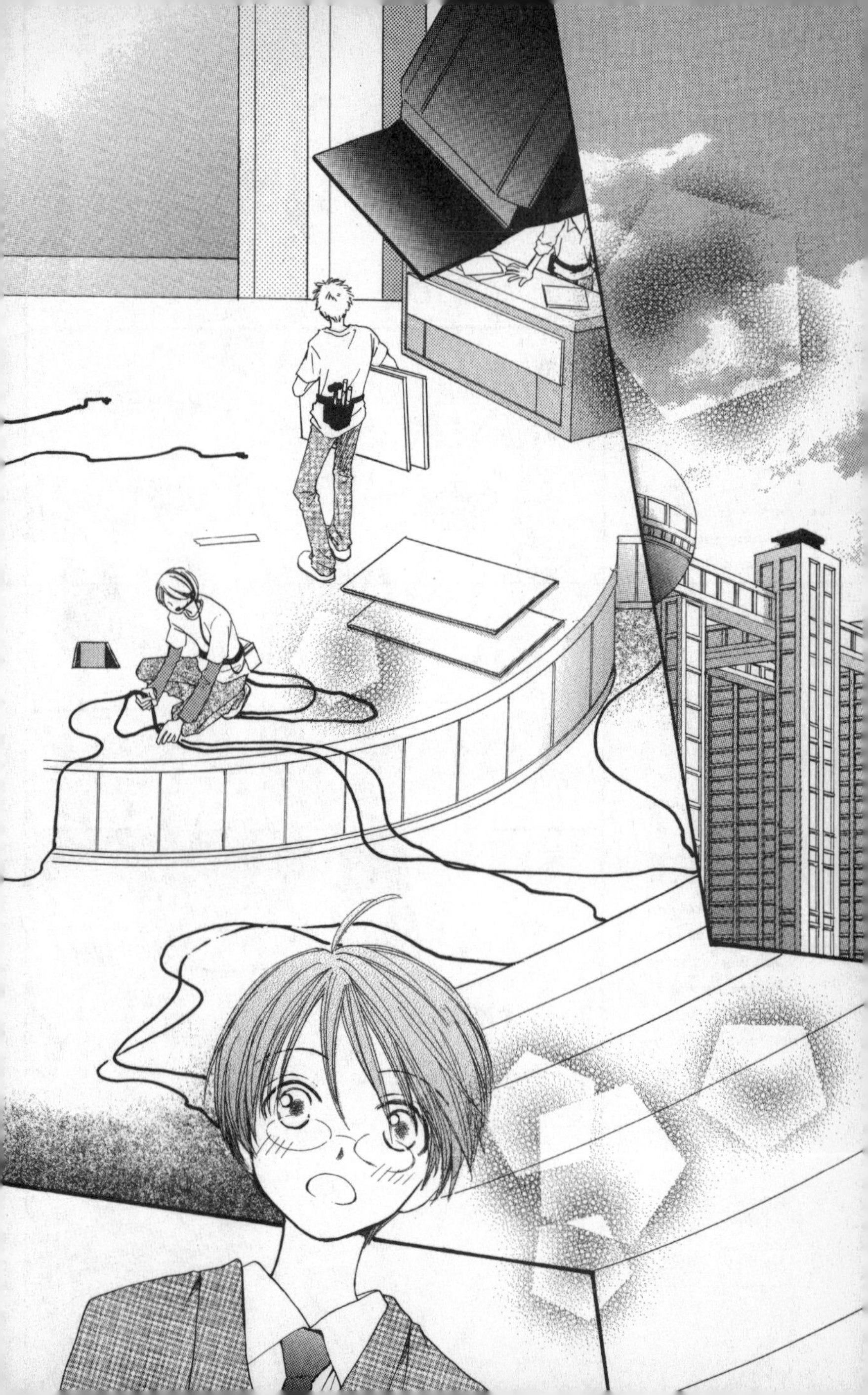

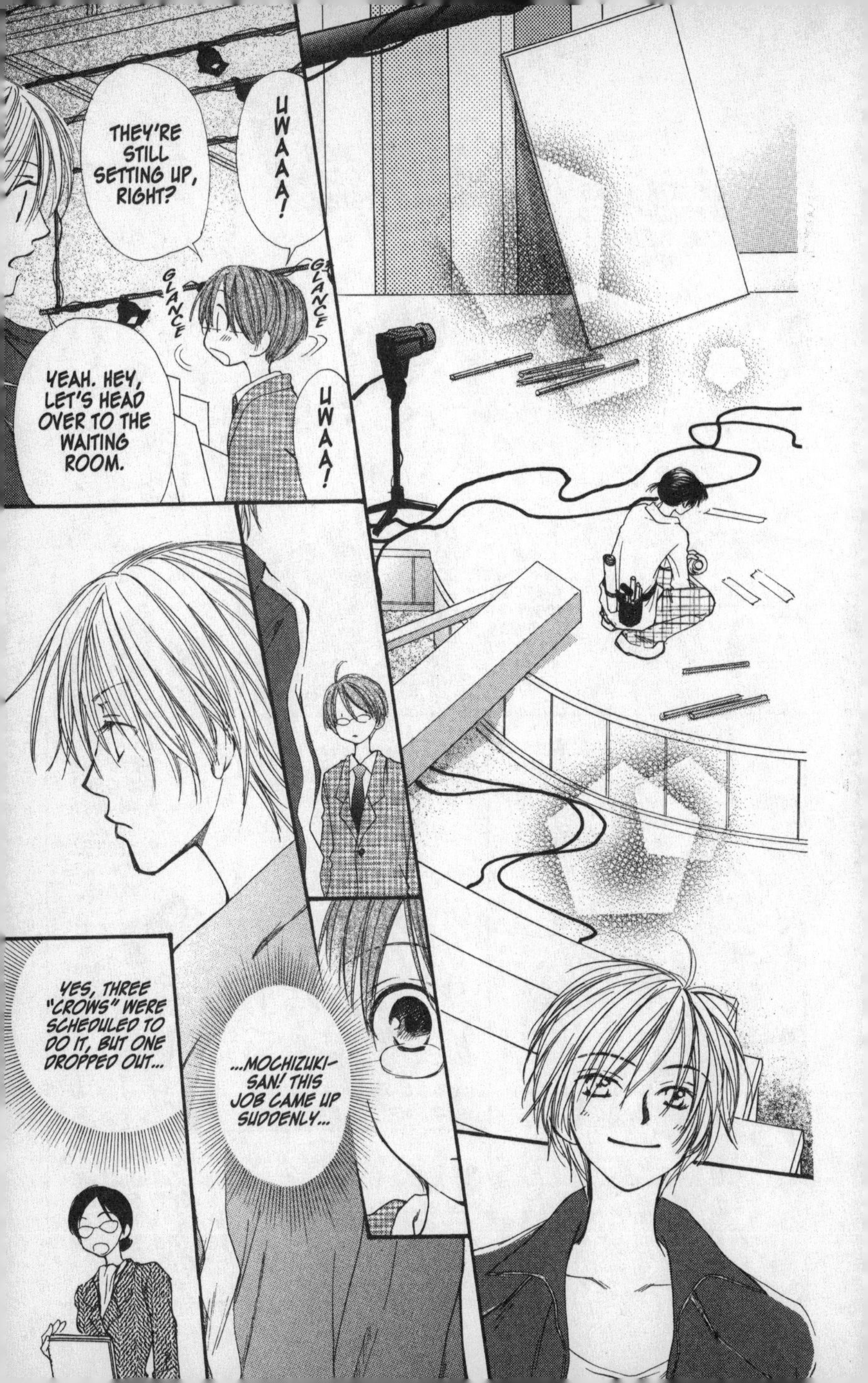
UWAAAA!
THEY'RE STILL SETTING UP, RIGHT?
GLANCE
GLANCE
UWAAA!
YEAH. HEY, LET'S HEAD OVER TO THE WAITING ROOM.
...MOCHIZUKI-SAN! THIS JOB CAME UP SUDDENLY...
YES, THREE "CROWS" WERE SCHEDULED TO DO IT, BUT ONE DROPPED OUT...

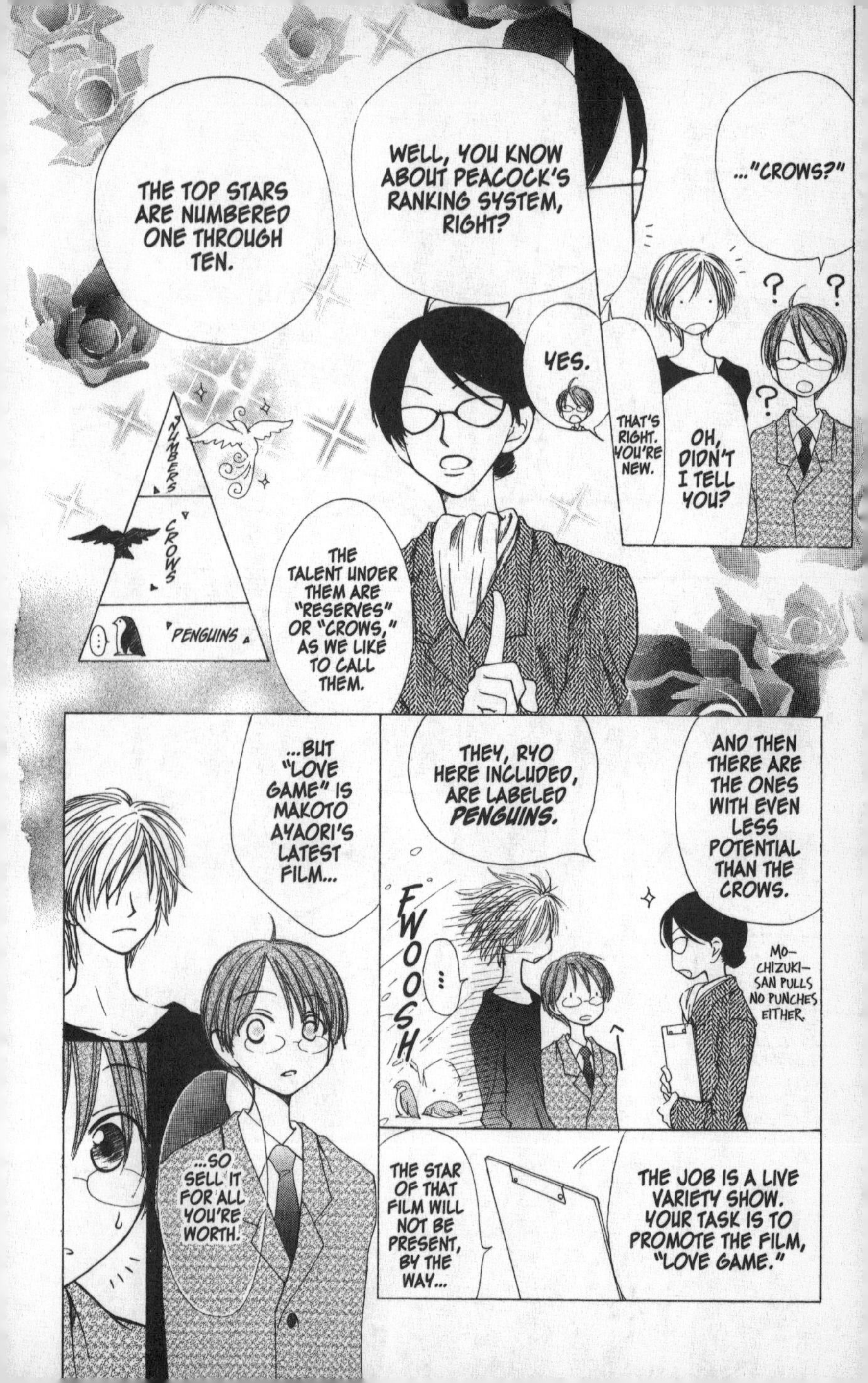
..."CROWS?"
OH, DIDN'T I TELL YOU?
THAT'S RIGHT. YOU'RE NEW.
WELL, YOU KNOW ABOUT PEACOCK'S RANKING SYSTEM, RIGHT?
YES.
THE TOP STARS ARE NUMBERED ONE THROUGH TEN.
THE TALENT UNDER THEM ARE "RESERVES" OR "CROWS," AS WE LIKE TO CALL THEM.
NUMBERS
CROWS
PENGUINS
AND THEN THERE ARE THE ONES WITH EVEN LESS POTENTIAL THAN THE CROWS.
THEY, RYO HERE INCLUDED, ARE LABELED *PENGUINS.*
FWOOSH
MO-CHIZUKI-SAN PULLS NO PUNCHES EITHER.
THE JOB IS A LIVE VARIETY SHOW. YOUR TASK IS TO PROMOTE THE FILM, "LOVE GAME."
THE STAR OF THAT FILM WILL NOT BE PRESENT, BY THE WAY...
...BUT "LOVE GAME" IS MAKOTO AYAORI'S LATEST FILM...
...SO SELL IT FOR ALL YOU'RE WORTH.

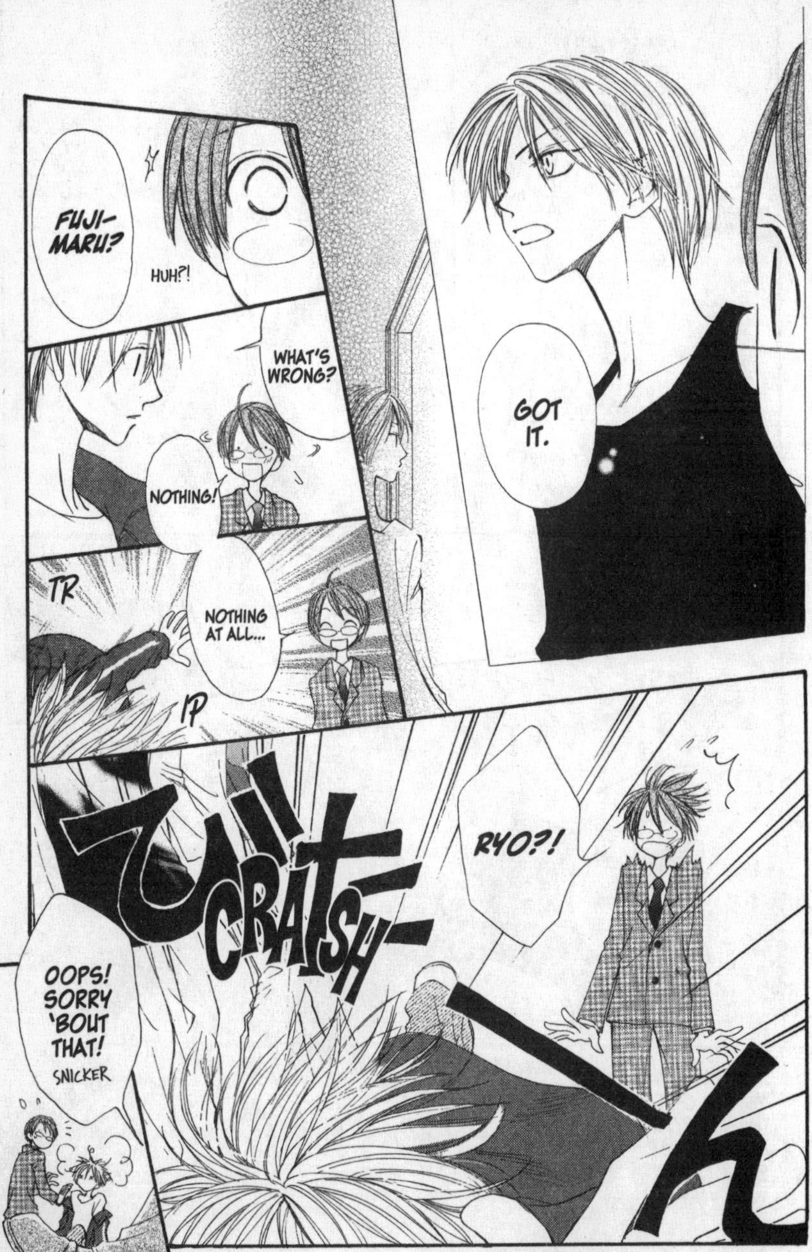
GOT IT.
FUJI-MARU?
HUH?!
WHAT'S WRONG?
NOTHING!
NOTHING AT ALL...
TR
IP
RYO?!
CRATSH
OOPS! SORRY 'BOUT THAT!
SNICKER

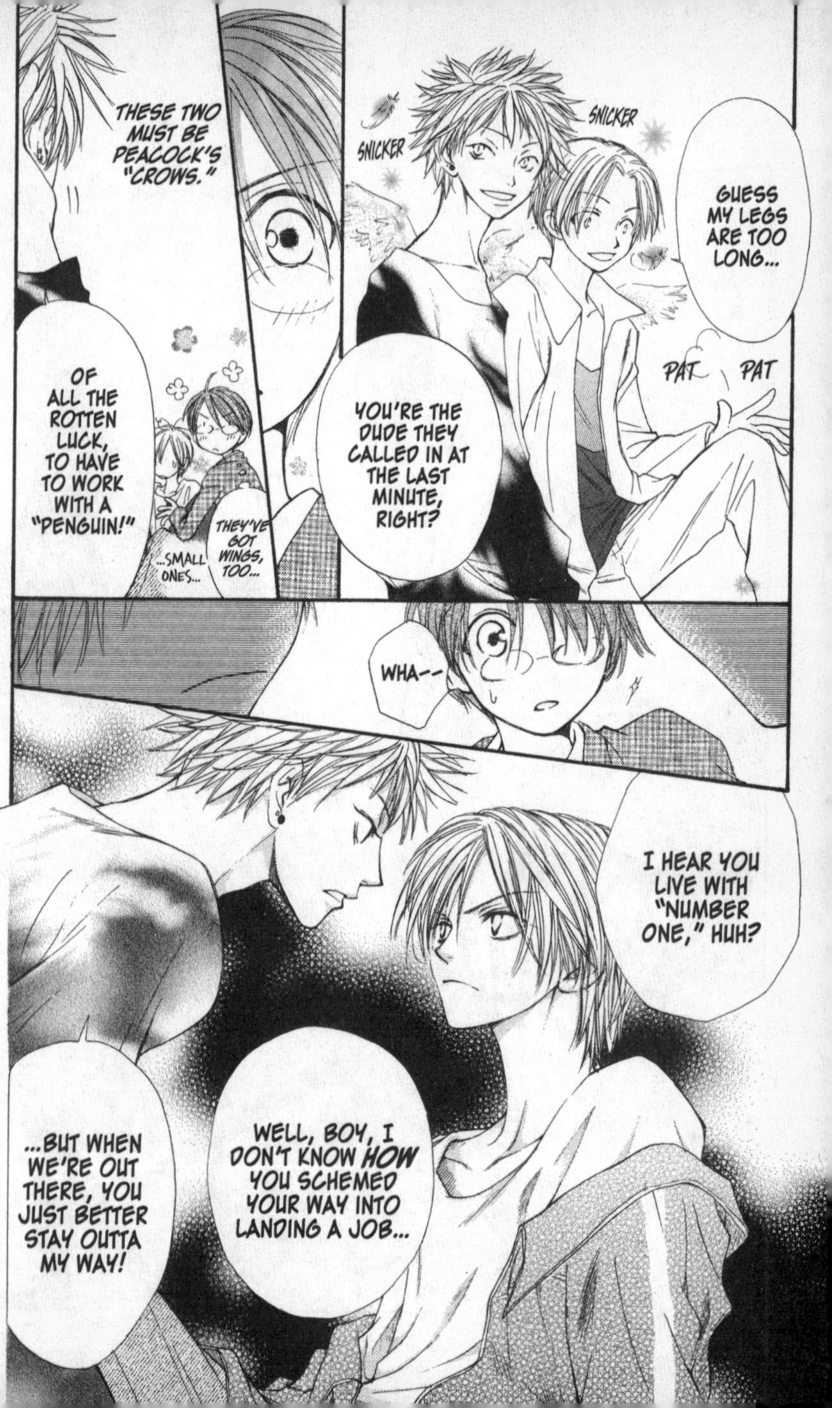
GUESS MY LEGS ARE TOO LONG...
SNICKER
SNICKER
PAT PAT
YOU'RE THE DUDE THEY CALLED IN AT THE LAST MINUTE, RIGHT?
THESE TWO MUST BE PEACOCK'S "CROWS."
OF ALL THE ROTTEN LUCK, TO HAVE TO WORK WITH A "PENGUIN!"
THEY'VE GOT WINGS, TOO...
...SMALL ONES...
WHA--
I HEAR YOU LIVE WITH "NUMBER ONE," HUH?
WELL, BOY, I DON'T KNOW ***HOW*** YOU SCHEMED YOUR WAY INTO LANDING A JOB...
...BUT WHEN WE'RE OUT THERE, YOU JUST BETTER STAY OUTTA MY WAY!

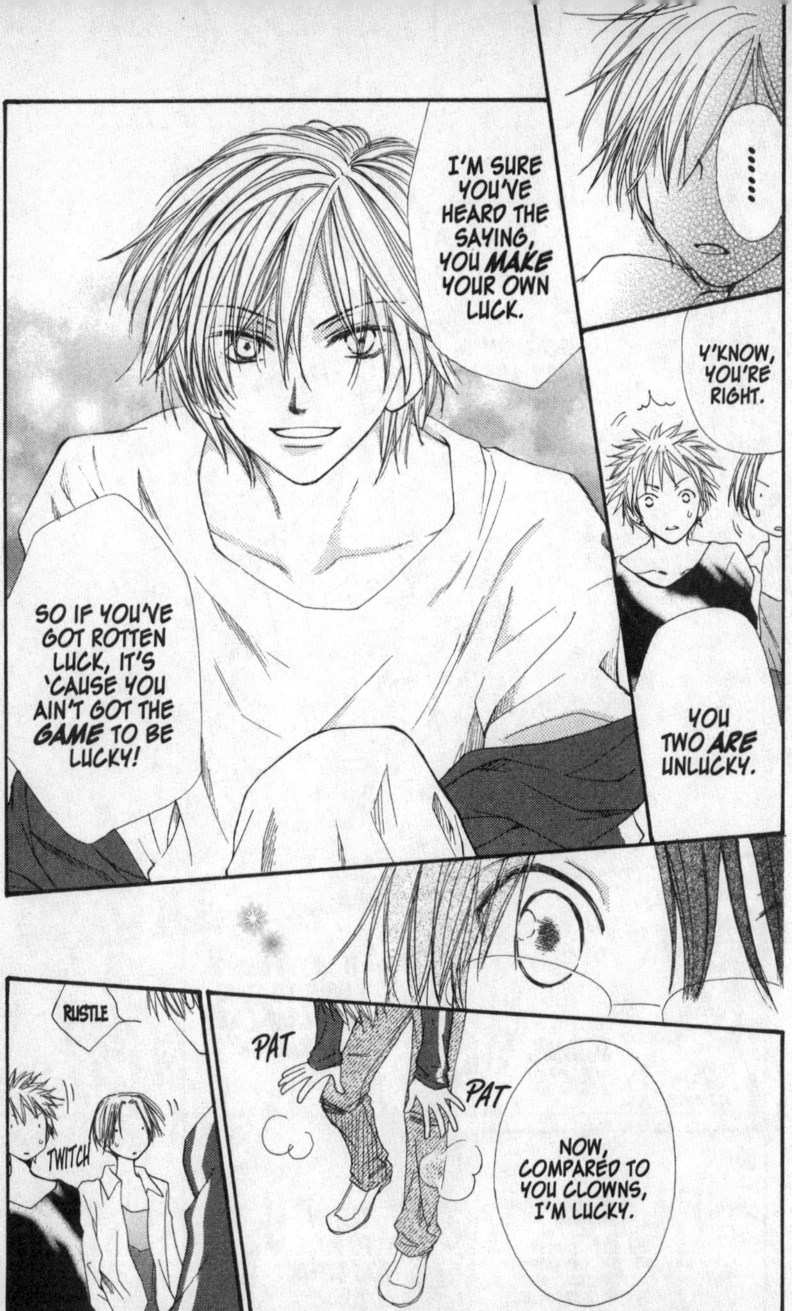
……
Y'KNOW, YOU'RE RIGHT.
YOU TWO ARE UNLUCKY.
I'M SURE YOU'VE HEARD THE SAYING, YOU MAKE YOUR OWN LUCK.
SO IF YOU'VE GOT ROTTEN LUCK, IT'S 'CAUSE YOU AIN'T GOT THE GAME TO BE LUCKY!
PAT
PAT
NOW, COMPARED TO YOU CLOWNS, I'M LUCKY.
RUSTLE
TWITCH

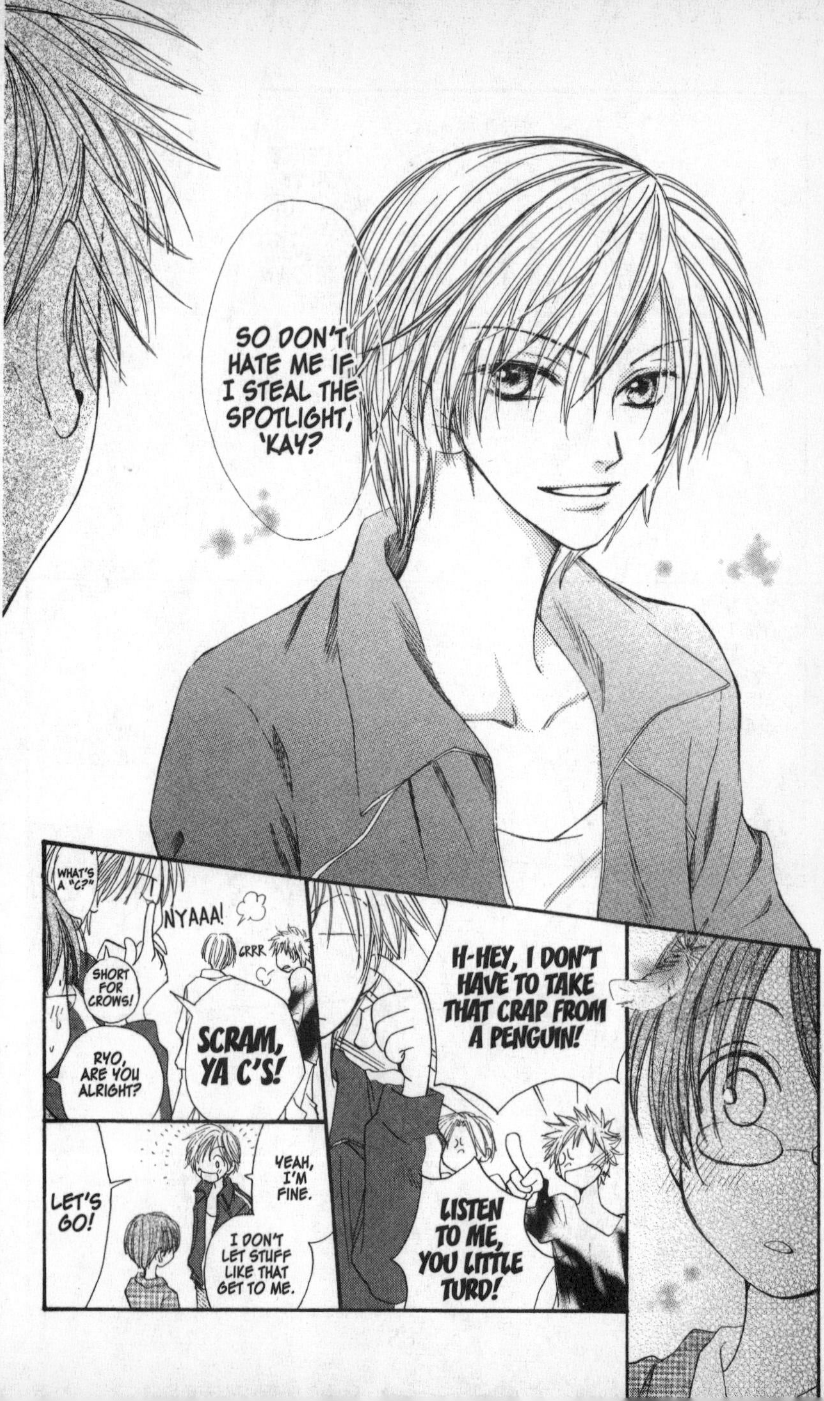
SO DON'T HATE ME IF I STEAL THE SPOTLIGHT, 'KAY?
H-HEY, I DON'T HAVE TO TAKE THAT CRAP FROM A PENGUIN!
LISTEN TO ME, YOU LITTLE TURD!
NYAAA!
GRRR
SCRAM, YA C'S!
WHAT'S A "C?"
SHORT FOR CROWS!
RYO, ARE YOU ALRIGHT?
YEAH, I'M FINE.
I DON'T LET STUFF LIKE THAT GET TO ME.
LET'S GO!

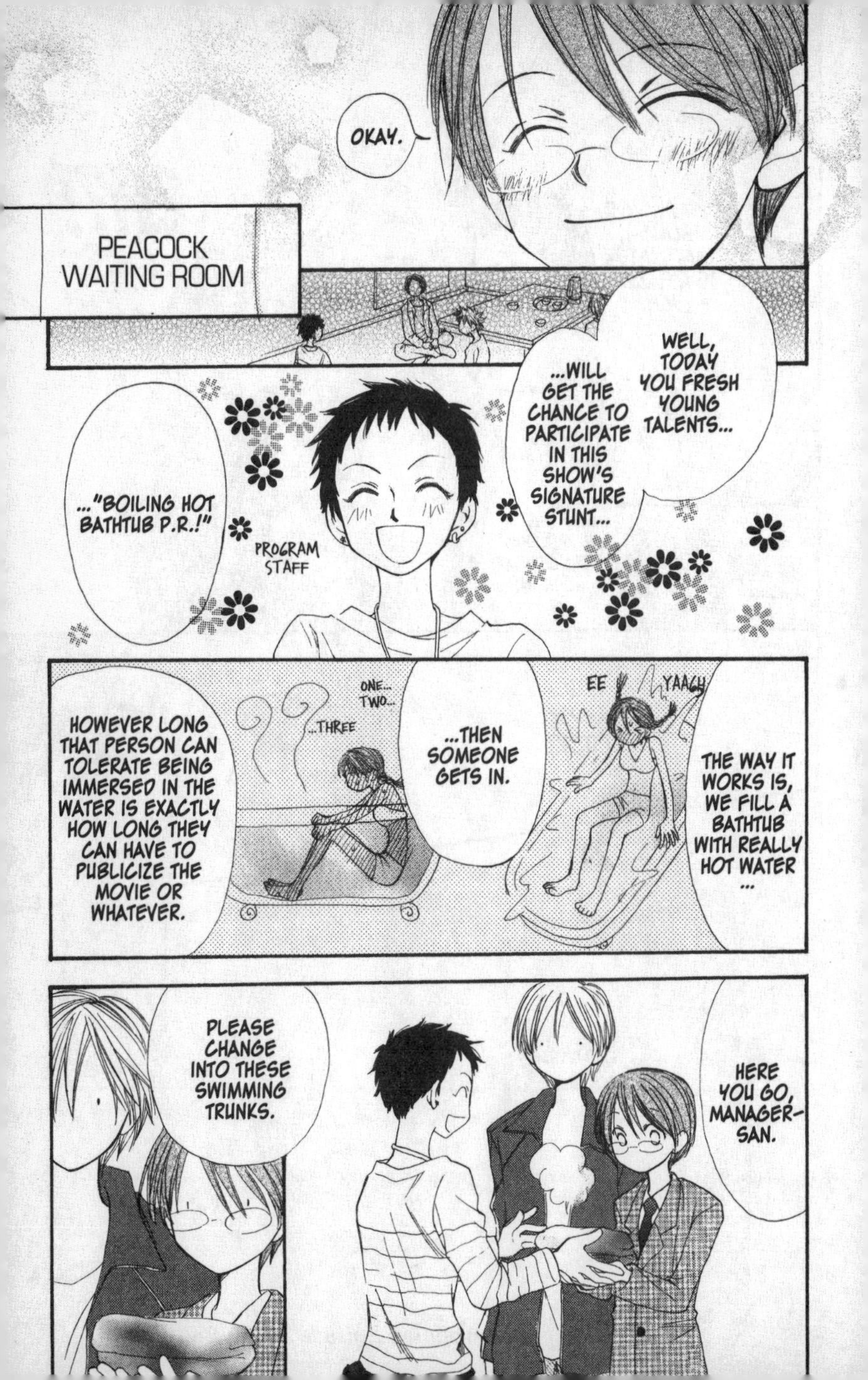
OKAY.
PEACOCK WAITING ROOM
WELL, TODAY YOU FRESH YOUNG TALENTS...
...WILL GET THE CHANCE TO PARTICIPATE IN THIS SHOW'S SIGNATURE STUNT...
..."BOILING HOT BATHTUB P.R.!"
PROGRAM STAFF
THE WAY IT WORKS IS, WE FILL A BATHTUB WITH REALLY HOT WATER ...
EE
YAAGH
...THEN SOMEONE GETS IN.
ONE... TWO...
...THREE
HOWEVER LONG THAT PERSON CAN TOLERATE BEING IMMERSED IN THE WATER IS EXACTLY HOW LONG THEY CAN HAVE TO PUBLICIZE THE MOVIE OR WHATEVER.
HERE YOU GO, MANAGER-SAN.
PLEASE CHANGE INTO THESE SWIMMING TRUNKS.

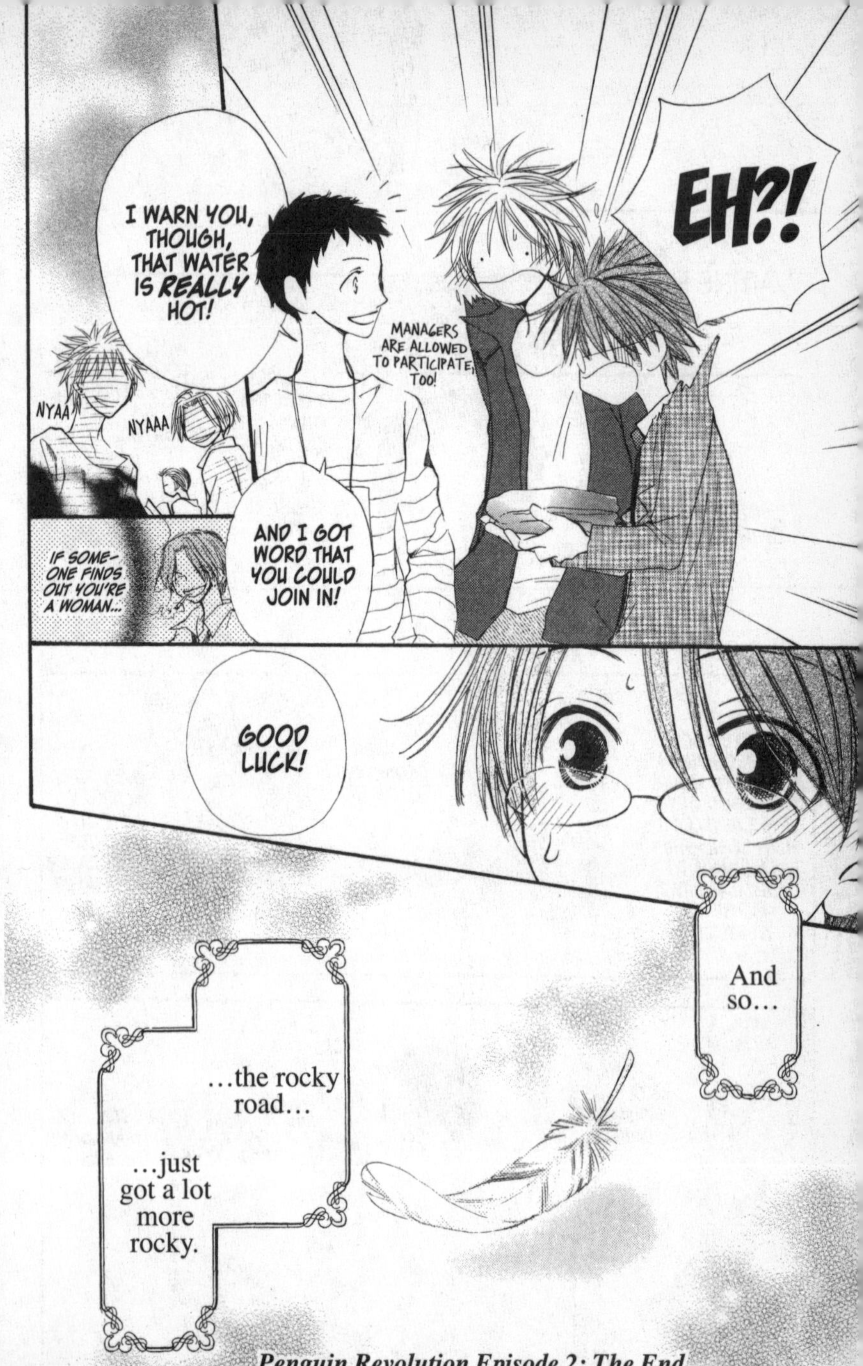

EH?!
MANAGERS ARE ALLOWED TO PARTICIPATE, TOO!
I WARN YOU, THOUGH, THAT WATER IS REALLY HOT!
NYAA
NYAAA
AND I GOT WORD THAT YOU COULD JOIN IN!
IF SOME-ONE FINDS OUT YOU'RE A WOMAN...
GOOD LUCK!
And so…
…the rocky road…
…just got a lot more rocky.

Penguin Revolution Episode 2: The End

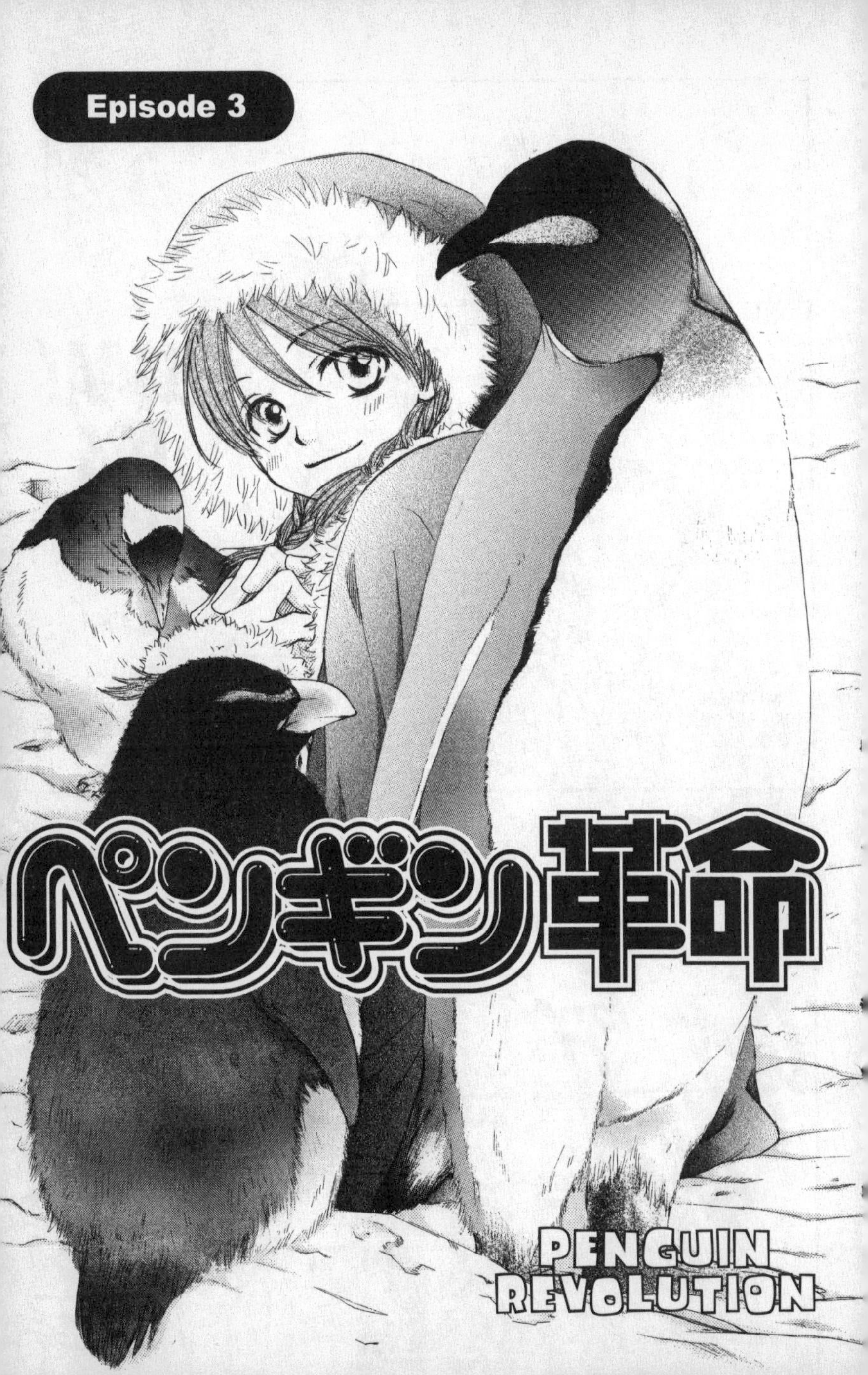
Episode 3
ペンギン革命
PENGUIN
REVOLUTION

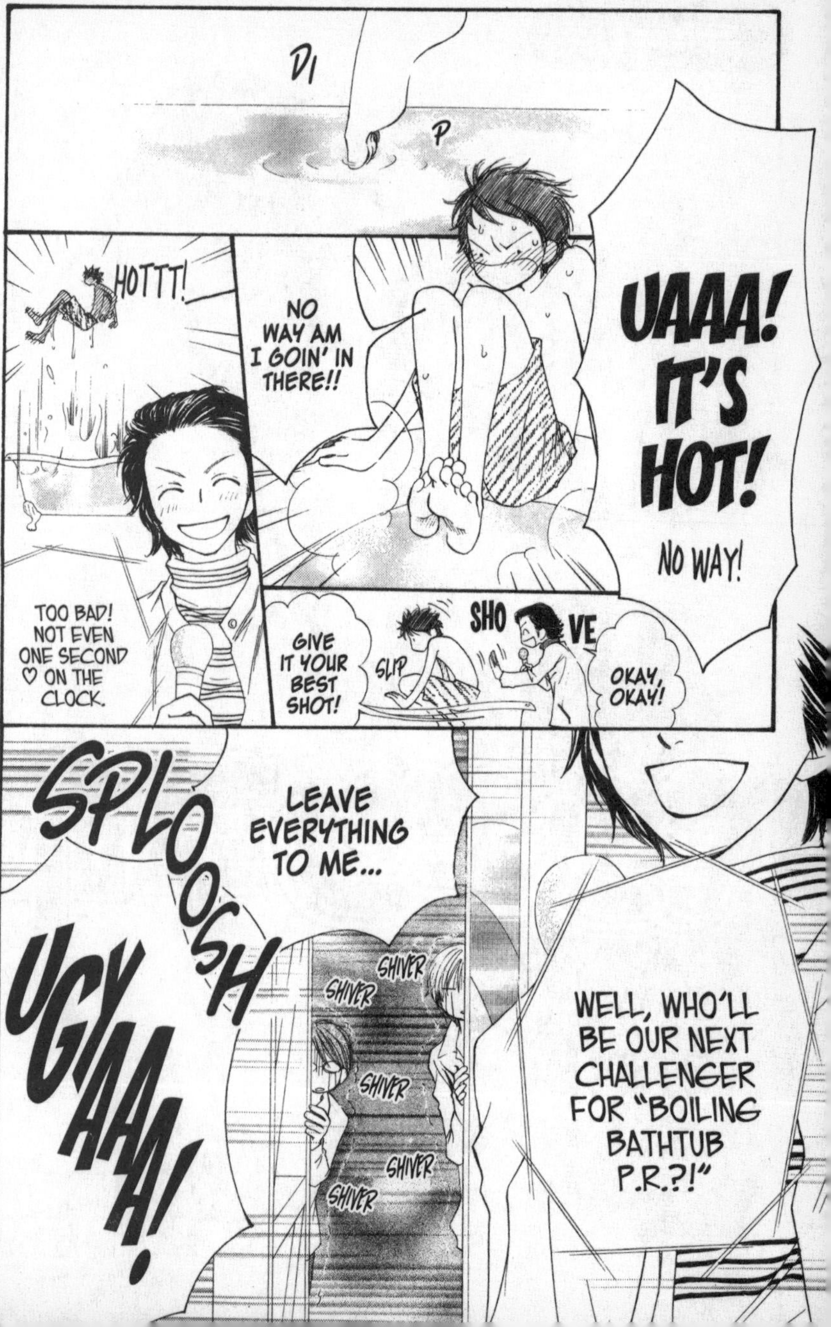
DI
P
UAAA! IT'S HOT!
NO WAY!
NO WAY AM I GOIN' IN THERE!!
OKAY, OKAY!
SHO VE
SLIP
GIVE IT YOUR BEST SHOT!
HOTTT!
TOO BAD! NOT EVEN ONE SECOND ♡ ON THE CLOCK.
WELL, WHO'LL BE OUR NEXT CHALLENGER FOR "BOILING BATHTUB P.R.?!"
SHIVER
SHIVER
SHIVER
SHIVER
SHIVER
LEAVE EVERYTHING TO ME...
SPLOOSH
UGYAAAA!

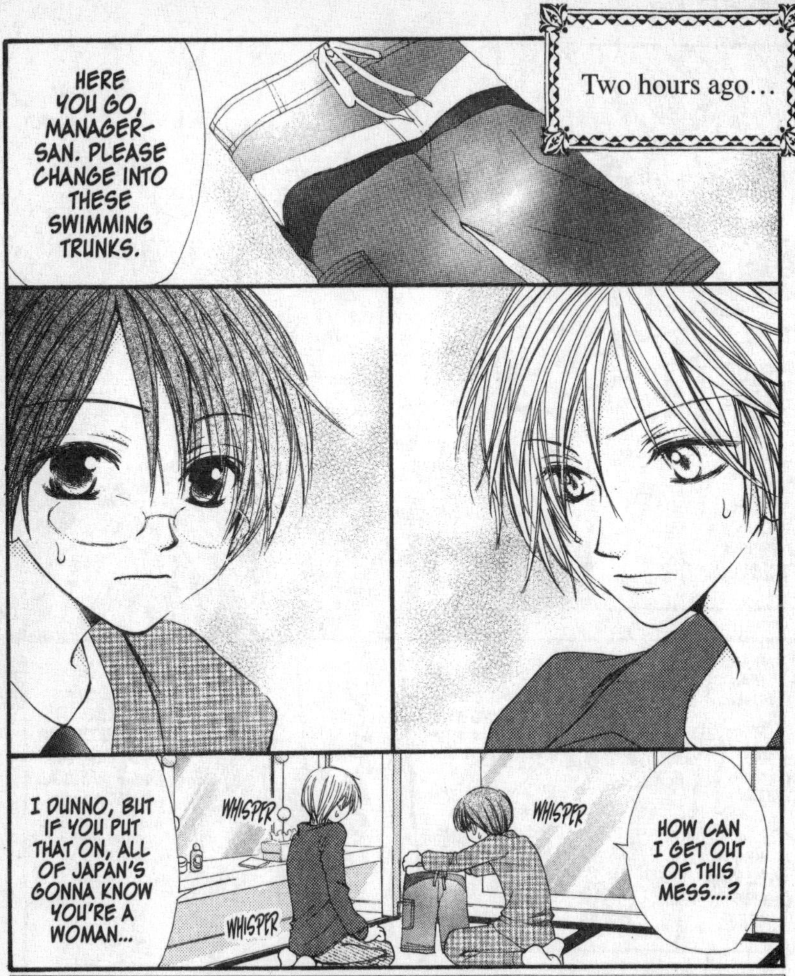
Two hours ago…
HERE YOU GO, MANAGER-SAN. PLEASE CHANGE INTO THESE SWIMMING TRUNKS.
HOW CAN I GET OUT OF THIS MESS...?
WHISPER
WHISPER
I DUNNO, BUT IF YOU PUT THAT ON, ALL OF JAPAN'S GONNA KNOW YOU'RE A WOMAN...
WHISPER

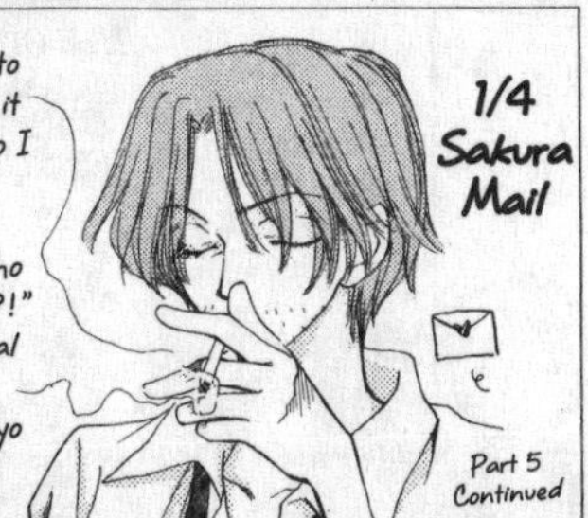

1/4 Sakura Mail

But this time around, I threw myself into it and as for the blood, "Let it flow! Let it flow! Let it flow!" was the key phrase, so I had buckets spilling out of Ryo's head. Ryo, lucky guy that he is, got an outpouring of sympathy from readers who generally commented, "But he's an idol?!" From me, his creator, Ryo receives equal time being bullied and comforted. One thing I realized, though, is that Ryo is taking a beating every time out. But that's okay, it's good for him!

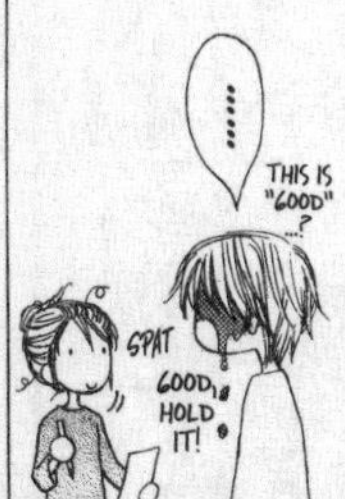
......
THIS IS "GOOD"...?
SPAT
GOOD, HOLD IT!

Part 5 Continued

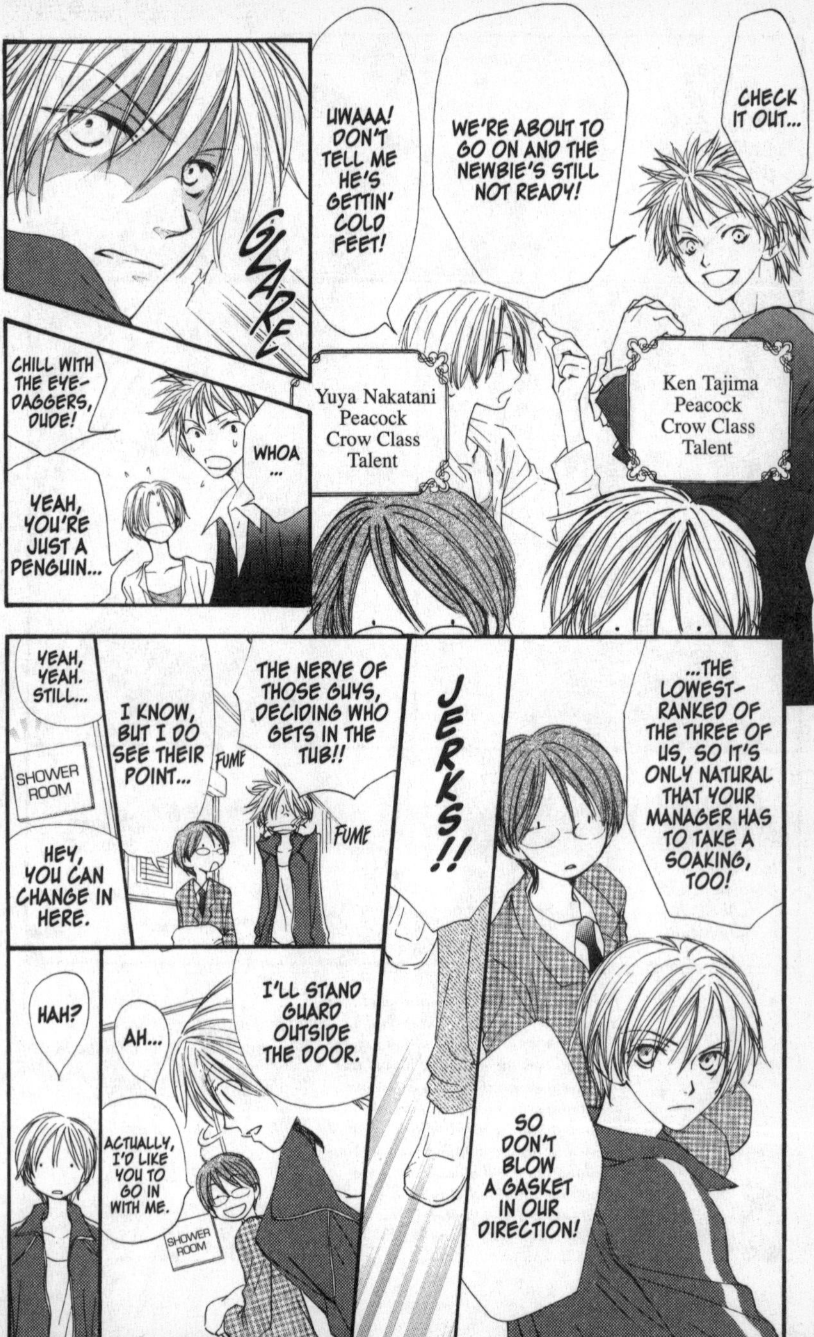
CHECK IT OUT...
Ken Tajima Peacock Crow Class Talent
WE'RE ABOUT TO GO ON AND THE NEWBIE'S STILL NOT READY!
UWAAA! DON'T TELL ME HE'S GETTIN' COLD FEET!
Yuya Nakatani Peacock Crow Class Talent
GLARE
WHOA ...
CHILL WITH THE EYE-DAGGERS, DUDE!
YEAH, YOU'RE JUST A PENGUIN...
...THE LOWEST-RANKED OF THE THREE OF US, SO IT'S ONLY NATURAL THAT YOUR MANAGER HAS TO TAKE A SOAKING, TOO!
SO DON'T BLOW A GASKET IN OUR DIRECTION!
JERKS!!
THE NERVE OF THOSE GUYS, DECIDING WHO GETS IN THE TUB!!
FUME
FUME
I KNOW, BUT I DO SEE THEIR POINT...
YEAH, YEAH. STILL...
SHOWER ROOM
HEY, YOU CAN CHANGE IN HERE.
I'LL STAND GUARD OUTSIDE THE DOOR.
AH...
HAH?
ACTUALLY, I'D LIKE YOU TO GO IN WITH ME.
SHOWER ROOM

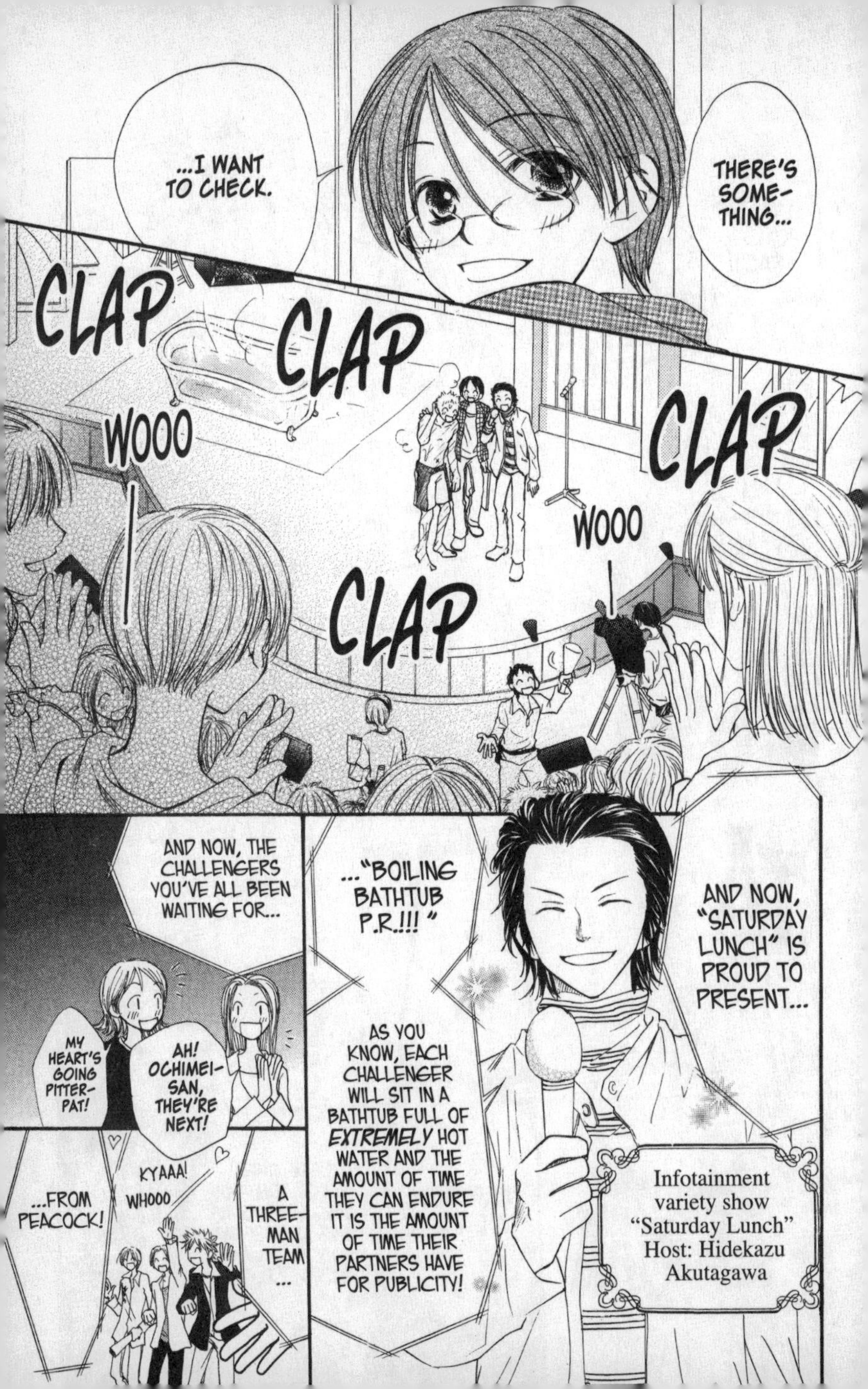
THERE'S SOME-THING...
...I WANT TO CHECK.
CLAP
CLAP
WOOO
CLAP
CLAP
WOOO
CLAP
AND NOW, "SATURDAY LUNCH" IS PROUD TO PRESENT...
..."BOILING BATHTUB P.R.!!!"
AS YOU KNOW, EACH CHALLENGER WILL SIT IN A BATHTUB FULL OF *EXTREMELY* HOT WATER AND THE AMOUNT OF TIME THEY CAN ENDURE IT IS THE AMOUNT OF TIME THEIR PARTNERS HAVE FOR PUBLICITY!
Infotainment variety show "Saturday Lunch" Host: Hidekazu Akutagawa
AND NOW, THE CHALLENGERS YOU'VE ALL BEEN WAITING FOR...
AH! OCHIMEI-SAN, THEY'RE NEXT!
MY HEART'S GOING PITTER-PAT!
A THREE-MAN TEAM ...
KYAAA!
WHOOO
...FROM PEACOCK!

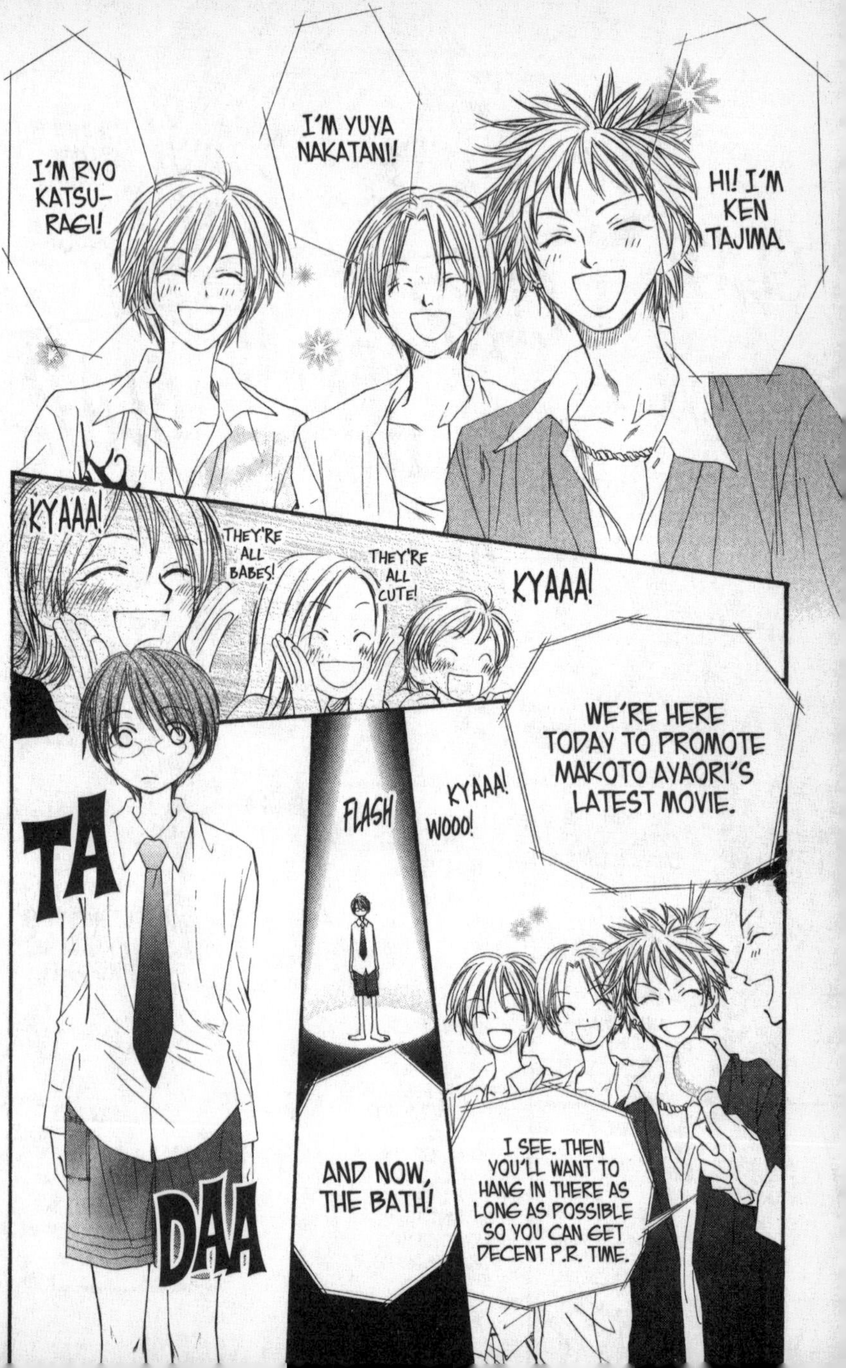
HI! I'M KEN TAJIMA.
I'M YUYA NAKATANI!
I'M RYO KATSURAGI!
KYAAA!
THEY'RE ALL CUTE!
THEY'RE ALL BABES!
KYAAA!
WE'RE HERE TODAY TO PROMOTE MAKOTO AYAORI'S LATEST MOVIE.
I SEE. THEN YOU'LL WANT TO HANG IN THERE AS LONG AS POSSIBLE SO YOU CAN GET DECENT P.R. TIME.
KYAAA!
WOOO!
FLASH
AND NOW, THE BATH!
TA
DAA

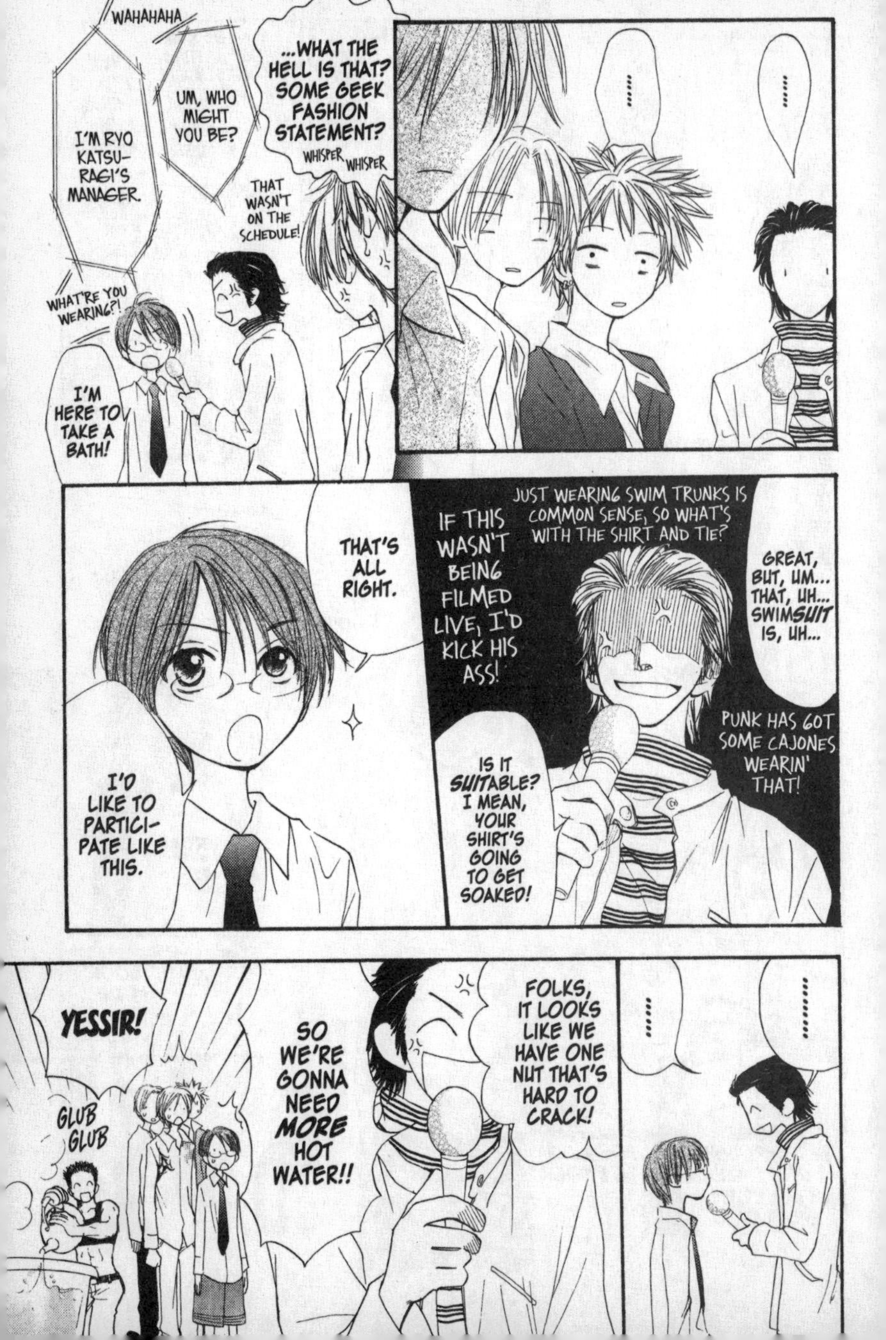
……
……
...WHAT THE HELL IS THAT? SOME GEEK FASHION STATEMENT?
WHISPER WHISPER
THAT WASN'T ON THE SCHEDULE!
WAHAHAHA
UM, WHO MIGHT YOU BE?
I'M RYO KATSURAGI'S MANAGER.
WHAT'RE YOU WEARING?!
I'M HERE TO TAKE A BATH!
GREAT, BUT, UM... THAT, UH... SWIMSUIT IS, UH...
JUST WEARING SWIM TRUNKS IS COMMON SENSE, SO WHAT'S WITH THE SHIRT AND TIE?
IF THIS WASN'T BEING FILMED LIVE, I'D KICK HIS ASS!
PUNK HAS GOT SOME CAJONES WEARIN' THAT!
IS IT SUITABLE? I MEAN, YOUR SHIRT'S GOING TO GET SOAKED!
THAT'S ALL RIGHT.
I'D LIKE TO PARTICIPATE LIKE THIS.
……
……
FOLKS, IT LOOKS LIKE WE HAVE ONE NUT THAT'S HARD TO CRACK!
SO WE'RE GONNA NEED MORE HOT WATER!!
YESSIR!
GLUB GLUB

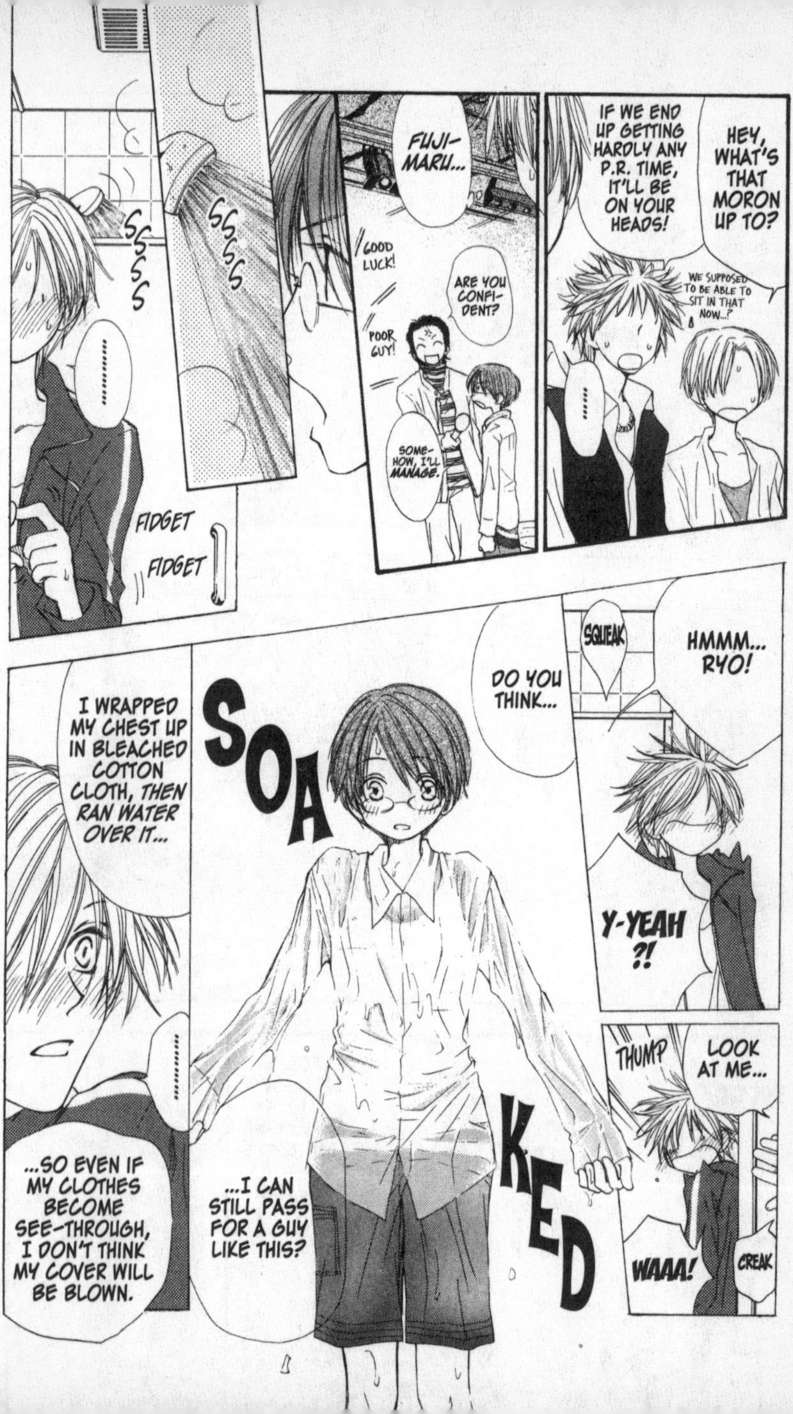
HEY, WHAT'S THAT MORON UP TO?
IF WE END UP GETTING HARDLY ANY P.R. TIME, IT'LL BE ON YOUR HEADS!
WE SUPPOSED TO BE ABLE TO SIT IN THAT NOW...?
......
FUJI-MARU...
ARE YOU CONFI-DENT?
GOOD LUCK!
POOR GUY!
SOME-HOW, I'LL MANAGE.
SSSS
SSSS
......
FIDGET
FIDGET
HMMM... RYO!
SQUEAK
Y-YEAH ?!
LOOK AT ME...
THUMP
CREAK
WAAA!
DO YOU THINK...
SOAKED
...I CAN STILL PASS FOR A GUY LIKE THIS?
I WRAPPED MY CHEST UP IN BLEACHED COTTON CLOTH, THEN RAN WATER OVER IT...
......
...SO EVEN IF MY CLOTHES BECOME SEE-THROUGH, I DON'T THINK MY COVER WILL BE BLOWN.

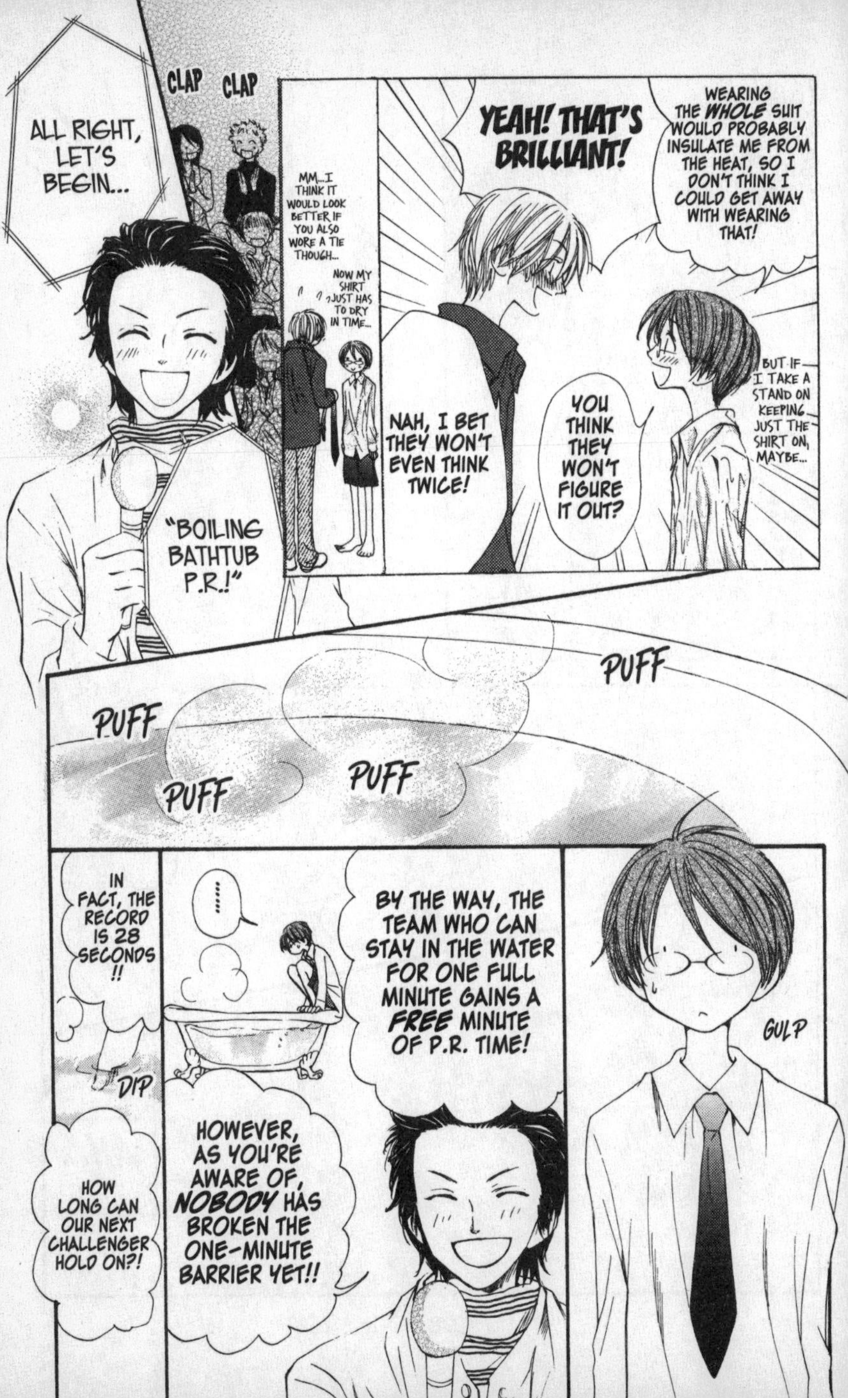
WEARING THE WHOLE SUIT WOULD PROBABLY INSULATE ME FROM THE HEAT, SO I DON'T THINK I COULD GET AWAY WITH WEARING THAT!
BUT IF I TAKE A STAND ON KEEPING JUST THE SHIRT ON, MAYBE...
YEAH! THAT'S BRILLIANT!
YOU THINK THEY WON'T FIGURE IT OUT?
NAH, I BET THEY WON'T EVEN THINK TWICE!
MM...I THINK IT WOULD LOOK BETTER IF YOU ALSO WORE A TIE THOUGH...
NOW MY SHIRT JUST HAS TO DRY IN TIME...
CLAP
CLAP
ALL RIGHT, LET'S BEGIN...
"BOILING BATHTUB P.R.!"
PUFF
PUFF
PUFF
PUFF
GULP
BY THE WAY, THE TEAM WHO CAN STAY IN THE WATER FOR ONE FULL MINUTE GAINS A FREE MINUTE OF P.R. TIME!
......
HOWEVER, AS YOU'RE AWARE OF, NOBODY HAS BROKEN THE ONE-MINUTE BARRIER YET!!
IN FACT, THE RECORD IS 28 SECONDS!!
DIP
HOW LONG CAN OUR NEXT CHALLENGER HOLD ON?!

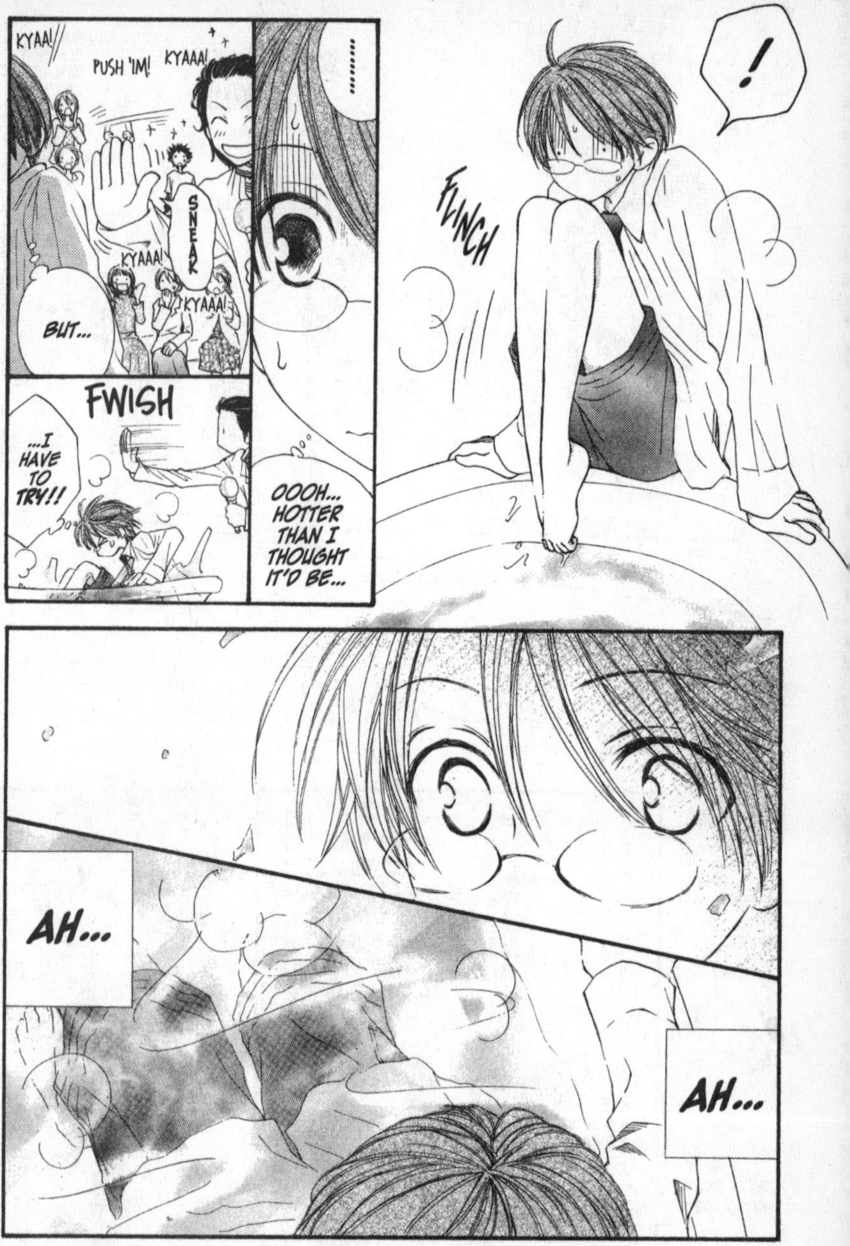
!
FLINCH
....
OOOH... HOTTER THAN I THOUGHT IT'D BE...
KYAA!
PUSH 'IM!
KYAAA!
SNEAK
KYAAA!
KYAAA!
BUT...
FWISH
...I HAVE TO TRY!!
AH...
AH...

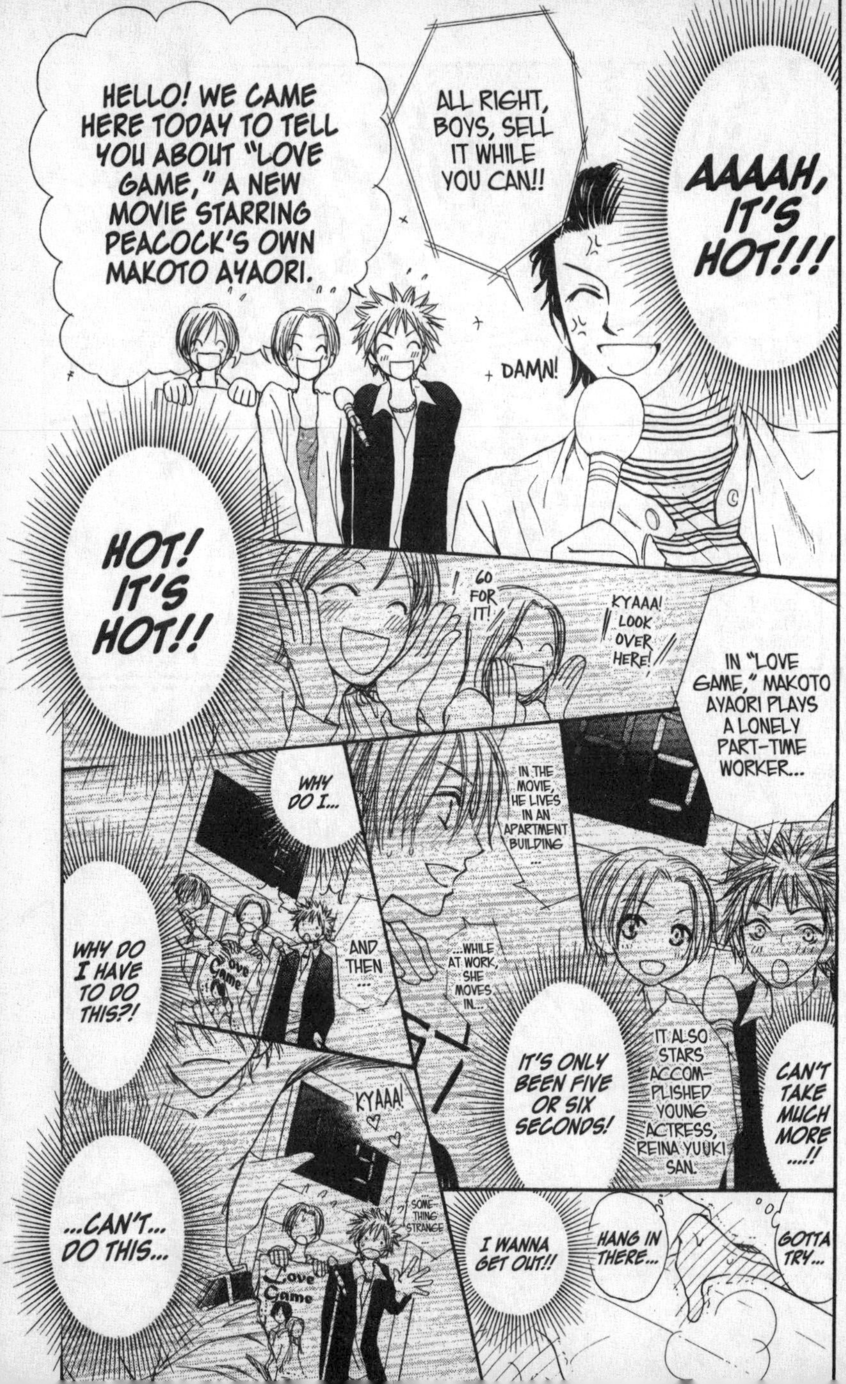
AAAAH, IT'S HOT!!!
ALL RIGHT, BOYS, SELL IT WHILE YOU CAN!!
HELLO! WE CAME HERE TODAY TO TELL YOU ABOUT "LOVE GAME," A NEW MOVIE STARRING PEACOCK'S OWN MAKOTO AYAORI.
DAMN!
HOT! IT'S HOT!!
KYAAA! LOOK OVER HERE!
GO FOR IT!
IN "LOVE GAME," MAKOTO AYAORI PLAYS A LONELY PART-TIME WORKER...
IN THE MOVIE, HE LIVES IN AN APARTMENT BUILDING...
WHY DO I...
...WHILE AT WORK, SHE MOVES IN...
AND THEN...
WHY DO I HAVE TO DO THIS?!
Love Game
CAN'T TAKE MUCH MORE.....!!
IT ALSO STARS ACCOM-PLISHED YOUNG ACTRESS, REINA YUUKI SAN.
IT'S ONLY BEEN FIVE OR SIX SECONDS!
KYAAA!
SOME-THING STRANGE...
...CAN'T... DO THIS...
Love Game
GOTTA TRY...
HANG IN THERE...
I WANNA GET OUT!!

...ANY-MORE!
KERSPLASH
HUH?
SLOSH
SLOSH
SVOSH
AAAH!
When hot water is stirred, its heat rises.
SVOSH
SLOSH
THAT'S HOT! IT'S HOT!
CUT IT OUT!
DON'T MAKE THE WATER...
FUJI-MARU...

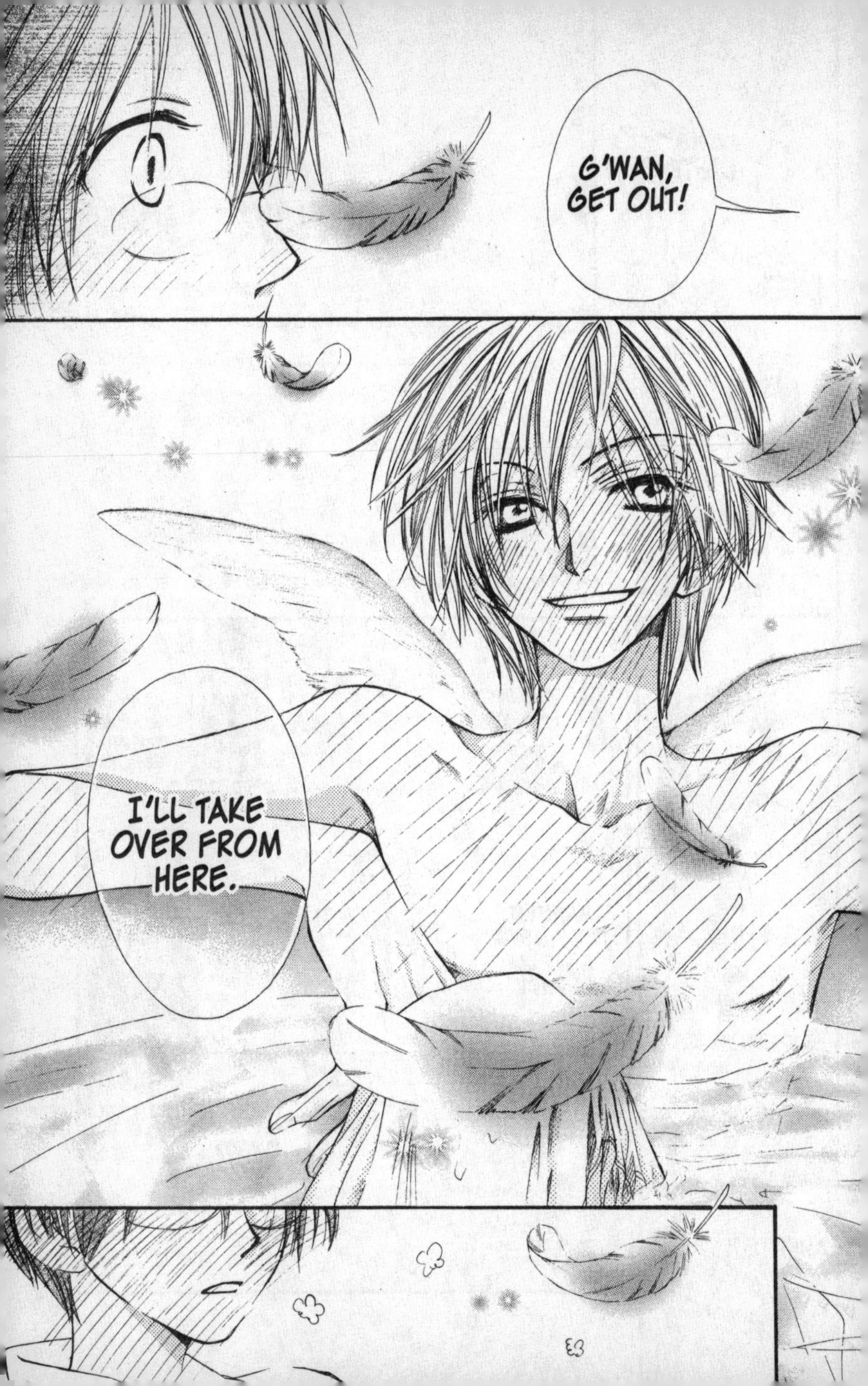
G'WAN, GET OUT!
I'LL TAKE OVER FROM HERE.

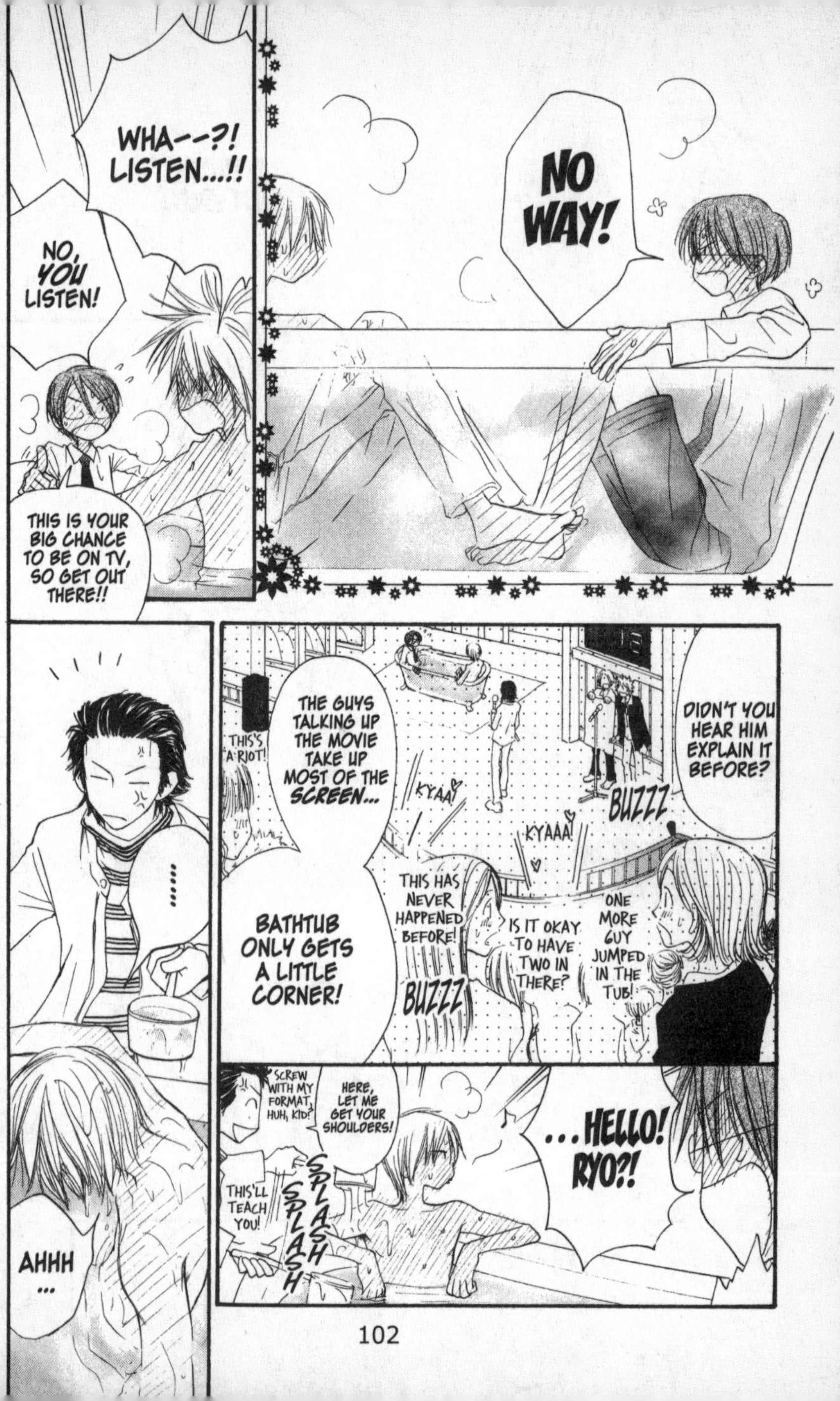

NO WAY!
WHA--?! LISTEN...!!
NO, YOU LISTEN!
THIS IS YOUR BIG CHANCE TO BE ON TV, SO GET OUT THERE!!
DIDN'T YOU HEAR HIM EXPLAIN IT BEFORE?
BUZZZ
KYAAA!
ONE MORE GUY JUMPED IN THE TUB!
IS IT OKAY TO HAVE TWO IN THERE?
THIS HAS NEVER HAPPENED BEFORE!
BUZZZ
KYAA!
THE GUYS TALKING UP THE MOVIE TAKE UP MOST OF THE SCREEN...
BATHTUB ONLY GETS A LITTLE CORNER!
THIS'S A RIOT!
...HELLO! RYO?!
HERE, LET ME GET YOUR SHOULDERS!
SCREW WITH MY FORMAT, HUH, KID?
SPLASH
SPLASH
THIS'LL TEACH YOU!
.....
AHHH...

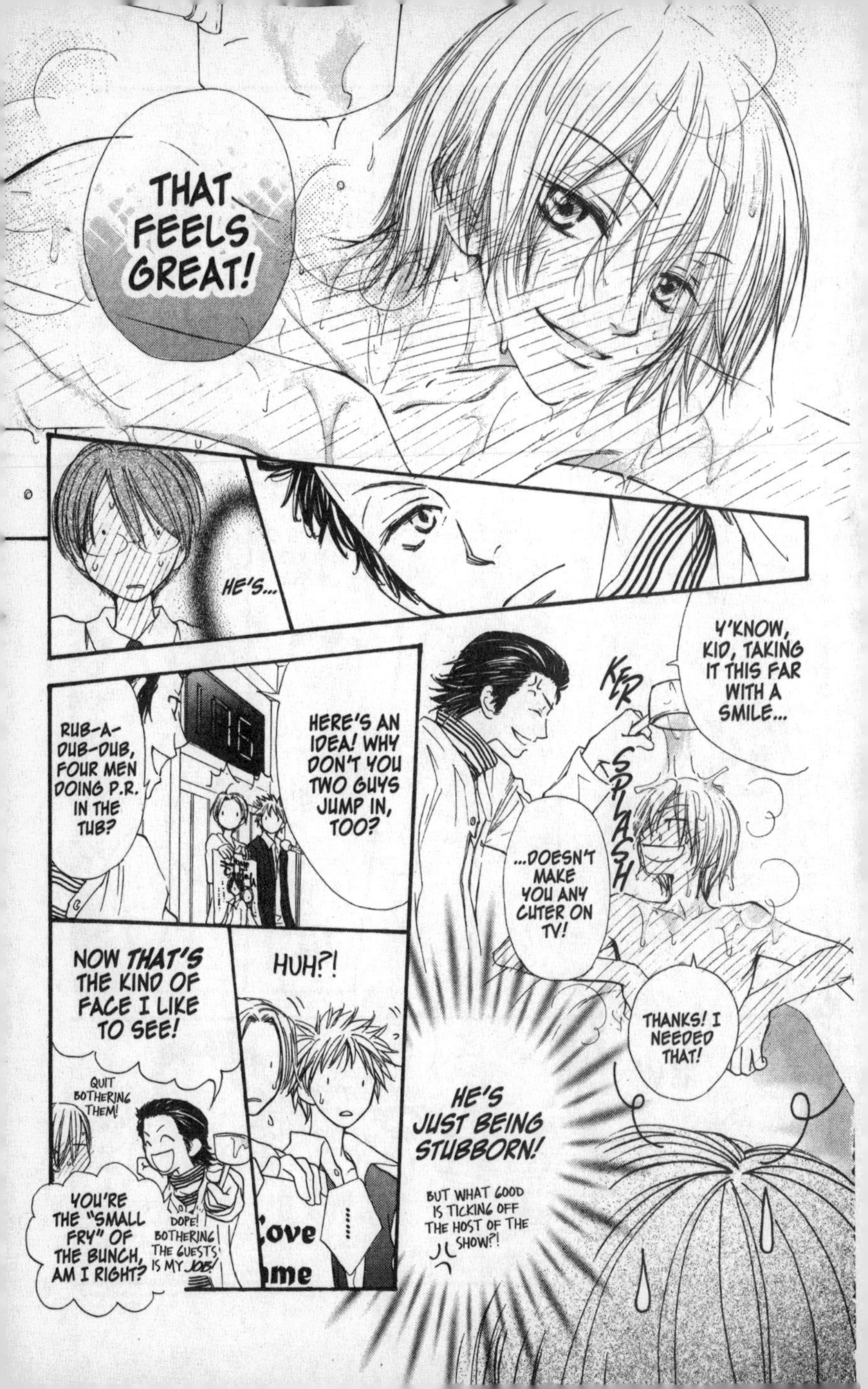
THAT FEELS GREAT!
HE'S...
Y'KNOW, KID, TAKING IT THIS FAR WITH A SMILE...
KER SPLASH
...DOESN'T MAKE YOU ANY CUTER ON TV!
THANKS! I NEEDED THAT!
HE'S JUST BEING STUBBORN!
BUT WHAT GOOD IS TICKING OFF THE HOST OF THE SHOW?!
HERE'S AN IDEA! WHY DON'T YOU TWO GUYS JUMP IN, TOO?
RUB-A-DUB-DUB, FOUR MEN DOING P.R. IN THE TUB?
HUH?!
......
NOW THAT'S THE KIND OF FACE I LIKE TO SEE!
QUIT BOTHERING THEM!
YOU'RE THE "SMALL FRY" OF THE BUNCH, AM I RIGHT?
DOPE! BOTHERING THE GUESTS IS MY JOB!

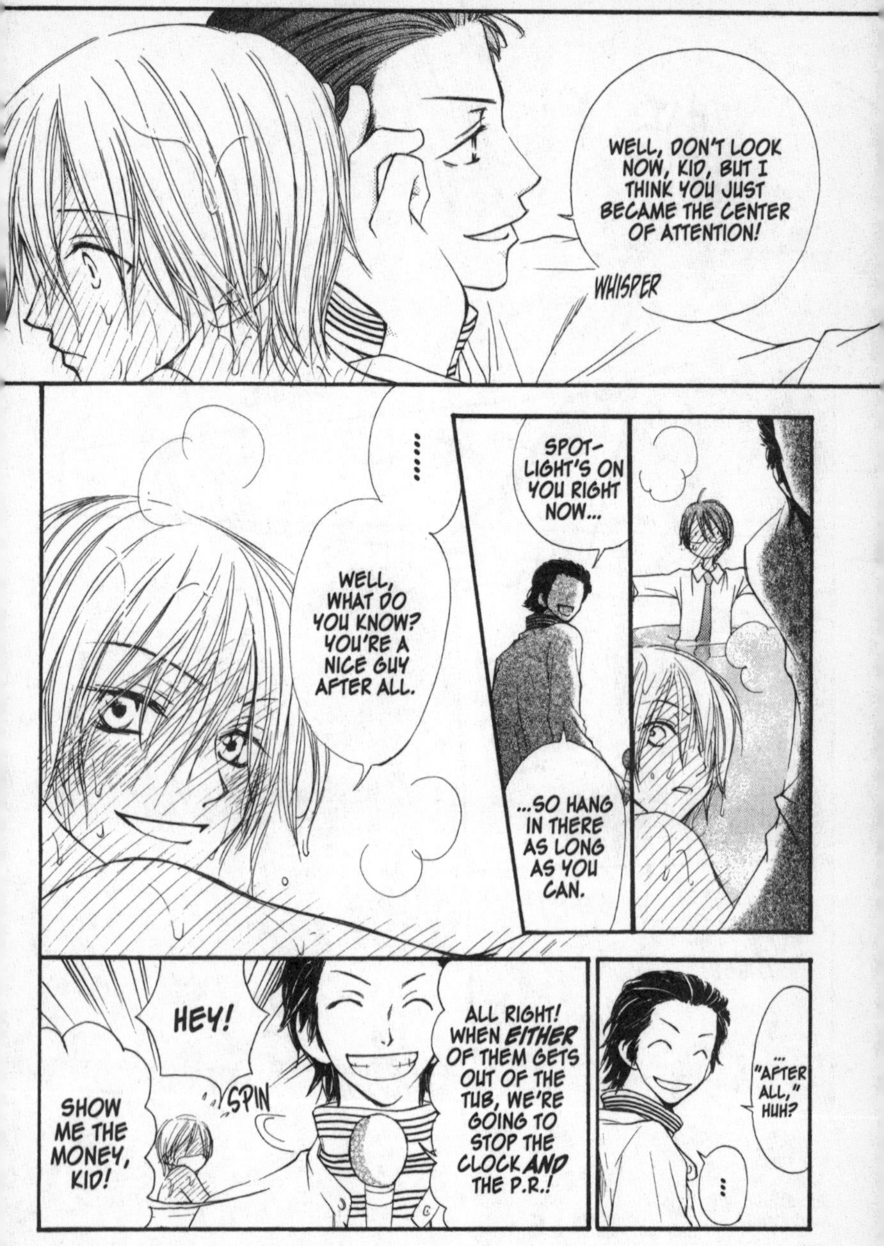
WELL, DON'T LOOK NOW, KID, BUT I THINK YOU JUST BECAME THE CENTER OF ATTENTION!
WHISPER
SPOT-LIGHT'S ON YOU RIGHT NOW...
...SO HANG IN THERE AS LONG AS YOU CAN.
......
WELL, WHAT DO YOU KNOW? YOU'RE A NICE GUY AFTER ALL.
... "AFTER ALL," HUH?
...
ALL RIGHT! WHEN *EITHER* OF THEM GETS OUT OF THE TUB, WE'RE GOING TO STOP THE CLOCK *AND* THE P.R.!
HEY!
SPIN
SHOW ME THE MONEY, KID!

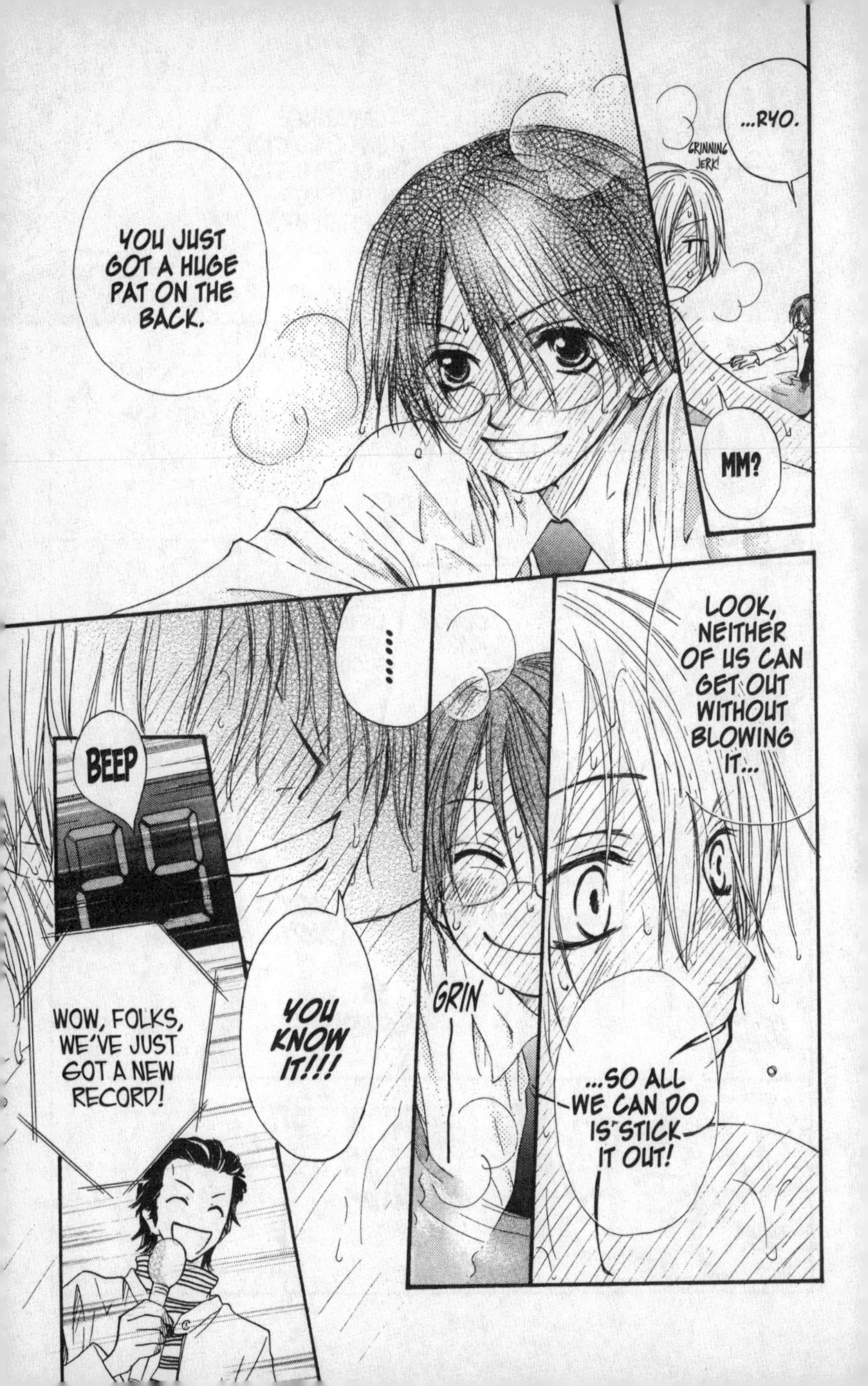
...RYO.
GRINNING JERK!
MM?
YOU JUST GOT A HUGE PAT ON THE BACK.
LOOK, NEITHER OF US CAN GET OUT WITHOUT BLOWING IT...
...SO ALL WE CAN DO IS STICK IT OUT!
......
GRIN
YOU KNOW IT!!!
BEEP
WOW, FOLKS, WE'VE JUST GOT A NEW RECORD!

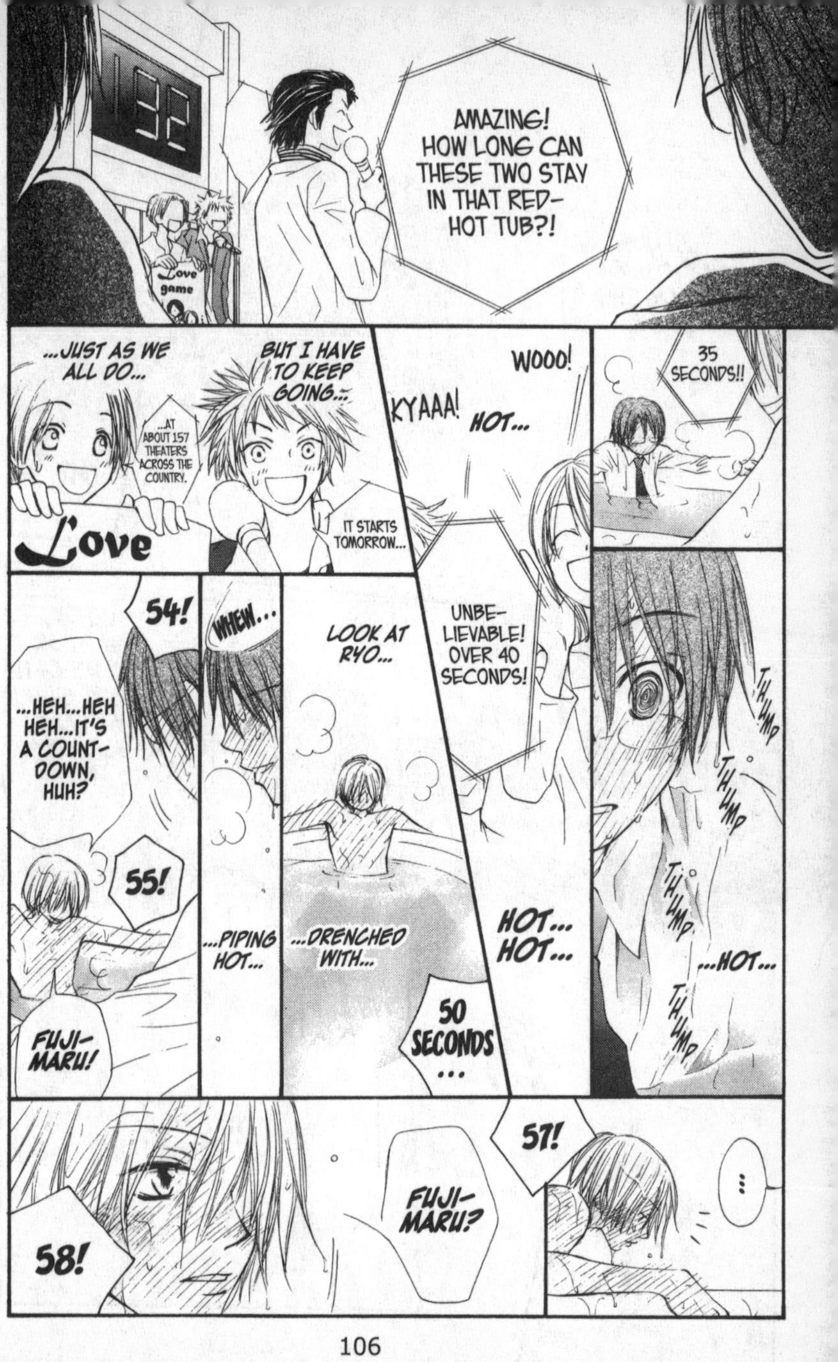

AMAZING! HOW LONG CAN THESE TWO STAY IN THAT RED-HOT TUB?!
Love game
35 SECONDS!!
WOOO!
KYAAA!
HOT...
BUT I HAVE TO KEEP GOING...
IT STARTS TOMORROW...
...AT ABOUT 157 THEATERS ACROSS THE COUNTRY.
...JUST AS WE ALL DO...
Love
THUMP
THUMP
THUMP
THUMP
...HOT...
UNBE-LIEVABLE! OVER 40 SECONDS!
HOT... HOT...
50 SECONDS...
LOOK AT RYO...
...DRENCHED WITH...
WHEW...
...PIPING HOT...
54!
...HEH...HEH HEH...IT'S A COUNT-DOWN, HUH?
55!
FUJI-MARU!
57!
...
FUJI-MARU?
58!

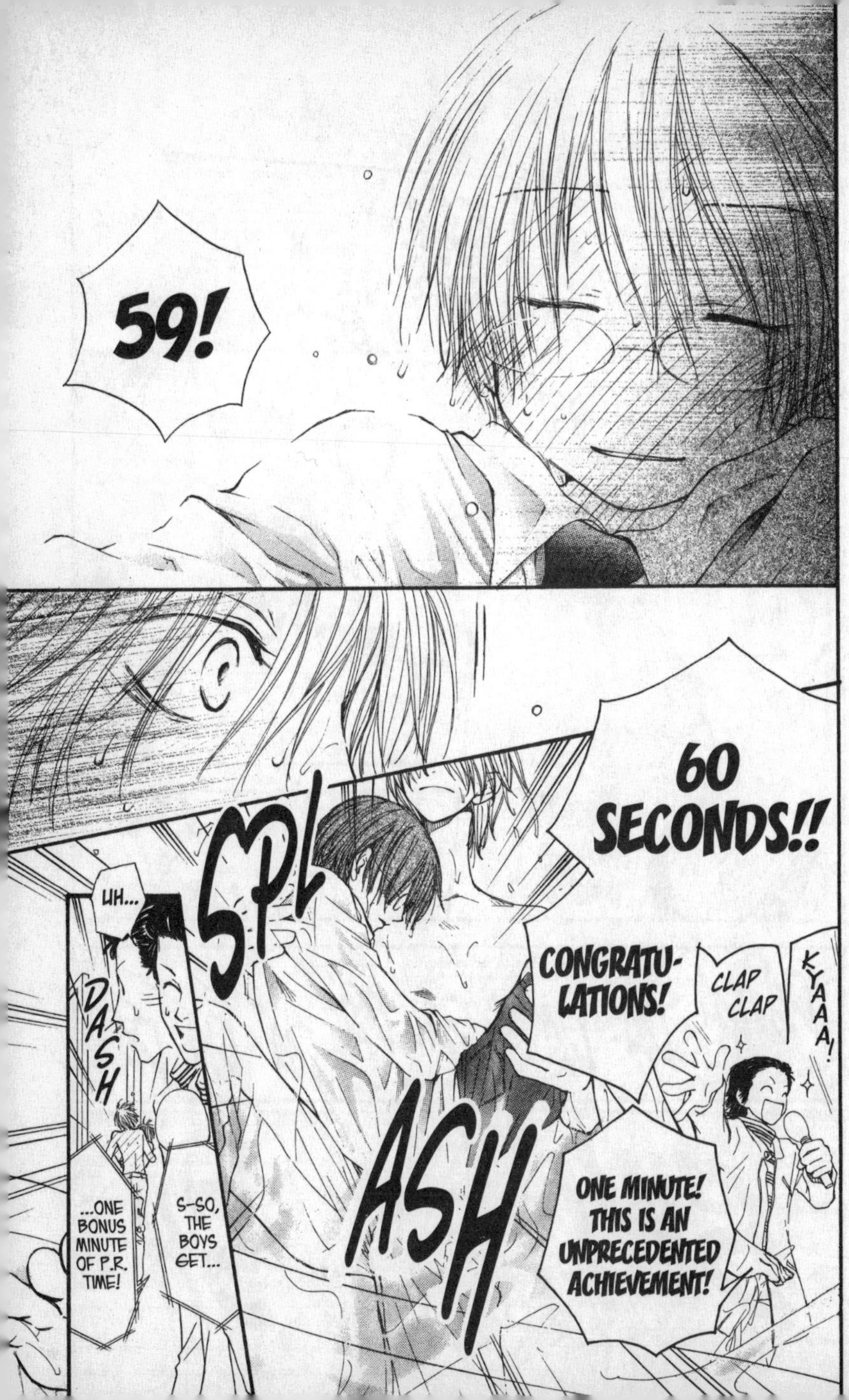
59!
60 SECONDS!!
KYAAAA!
CLAP CLAP
CONGRATU-LATIONS!
SPLASH
UH...
DASH
ONE MINUTE! THIS IS AN UNPRECEDENTED ACHIEVEMENT!
S-SO, THE BOYS GET...
...ONE BONUS MINUTE OF P.R. TIME!

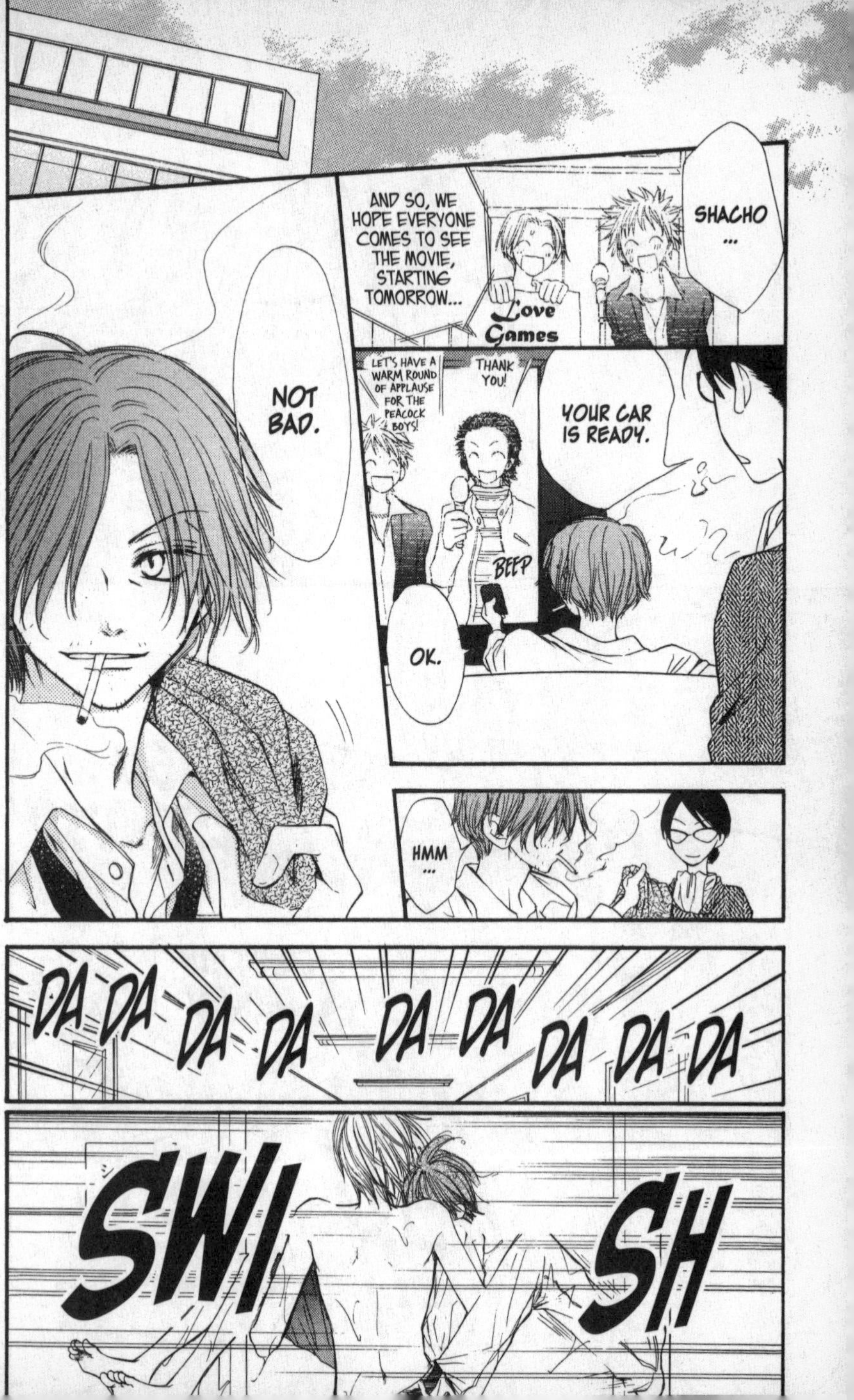
SHACHO ...
AND SO, WE HOPE EVERYONE COMES TO SEE THE MOVIE, STARTING TOMORROW...
Love Games
YOUR CAR IS READY.
THANK YOU!
LET'S HAVE A WARM ROUND OF APPLAUSE FOR THE PEACOCK BOYS!
BEEP
OK.
HMM ...
NOT BAD.
DA DA DA DA DA DA DA DA DA
SWI SH

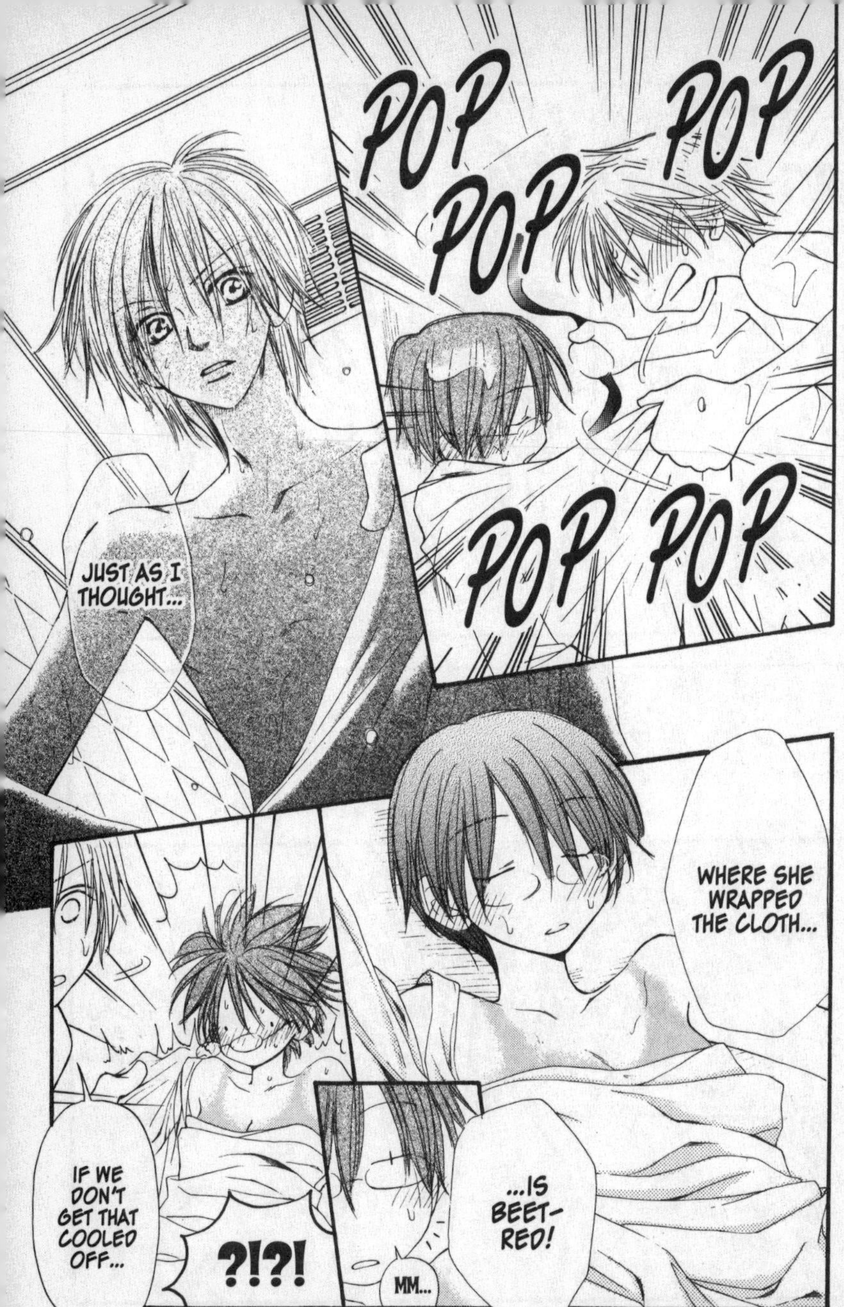
POP
POP
POP
POP
POP POP
JUST AS I THOUGHT...
WHERE SHE WRAPPED THE CLOTH...
...IS BEET-RED!
MM...
?!?!
IF WE DON'T GET THAT COOLED OFF...

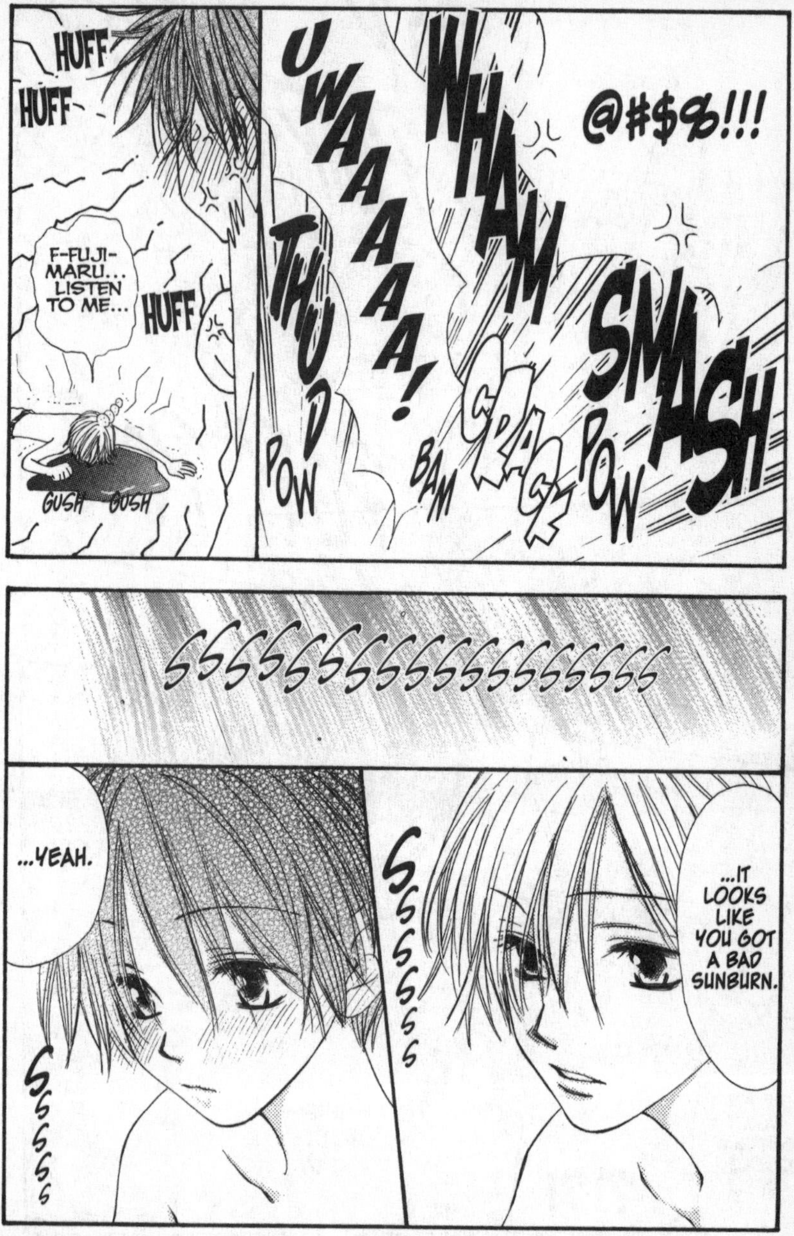
@#$%!!!
WHAM
SMASH
CRACK
POW
BAM
UWAAAAAAA!
THUD
POW
HUFF
HUFF
F-FUJI-MARU... LISTEN TO ME...
HUFF
GUSH GUSH
SSSSSSSSSSSSSSSSSSSSSSS
...IT LOOKS LIKE YOU GOT A BAD SUNBURN.
SSSSSS
...YEAH.
SSSSS

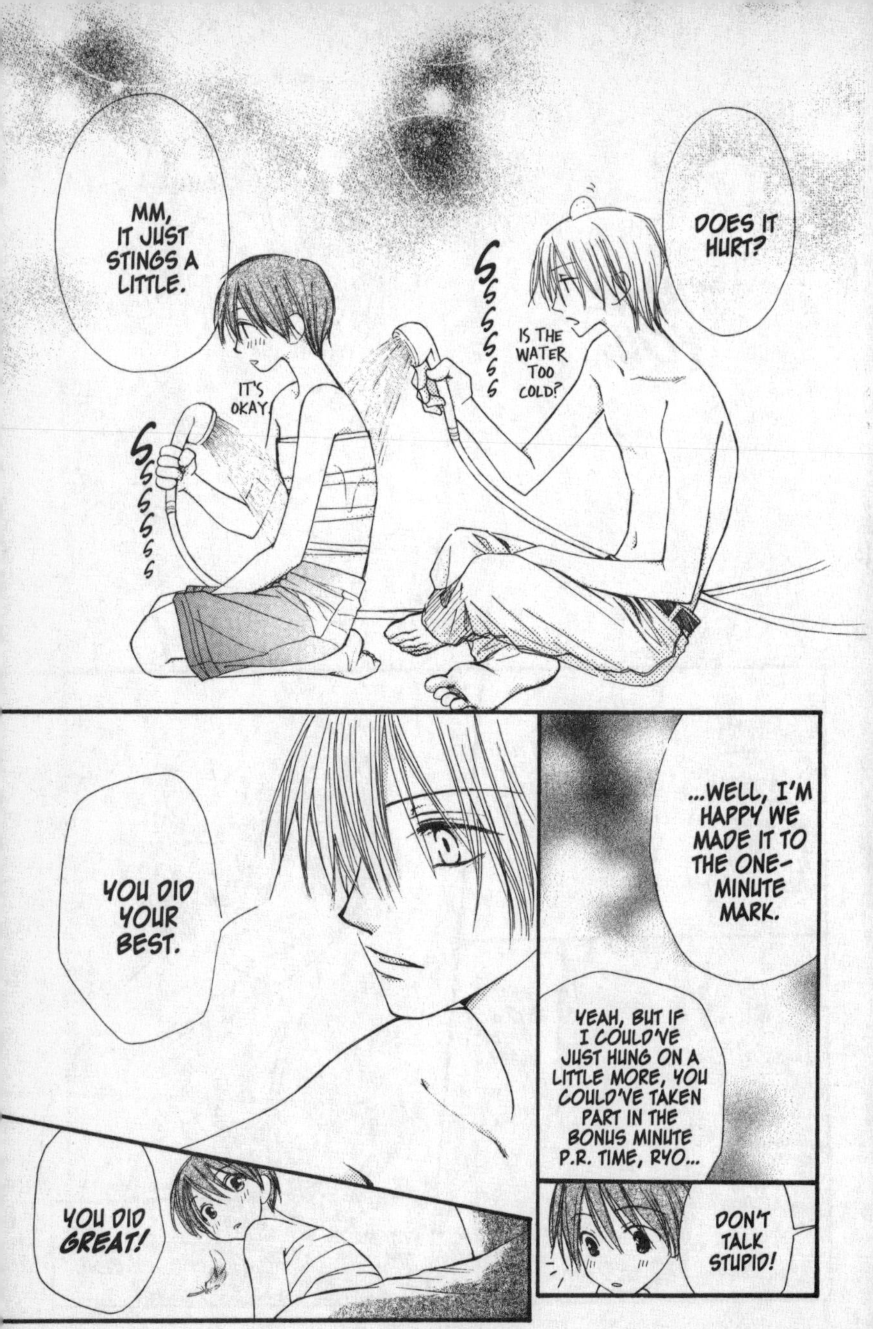
DOES IT HURT?
IS THE WATER TOO COLD?
SSSSSS
MM, IT JUST STINGS A LITTLE.
IT'S OKAY.
SSSSSS
...WELL, I'M HAPPY WE MADE IT TO THE ONE-MINUTE MARK.
YEAH, BUT IF I COULD'VE JUST HUNG ON A LITTLE MORE, YOU COULD'VE TAKEN PART IN THE BONUS MINUTE P.R. TIME, RYO...
DON'T TALK STUPID!
YOU DID YOUR BEST.
YOU DID GREAT!

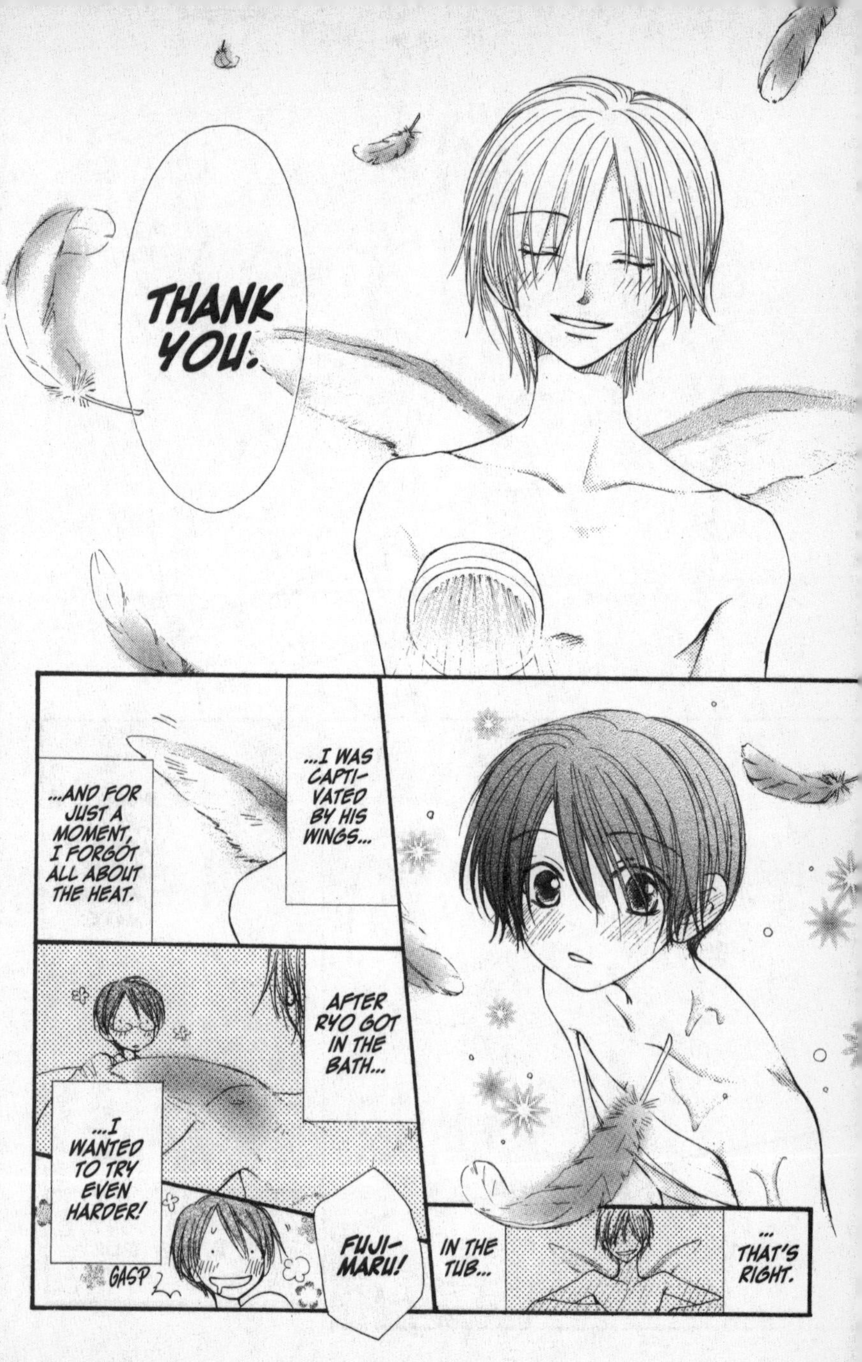
THANK YOU.
...THAT'S RIGHT.
IN THE TUB...
...I WAS CAPTIVATED BY HIS WINGS...
...AND FOR JUST A MOMENT, I FORGOT ALL ABOUT THE HEAT.
AFTER RYO GOT IN THE BATH...
...I WANTED TO TRY EVEN HARDER!
FUJI-MARU!
GASP

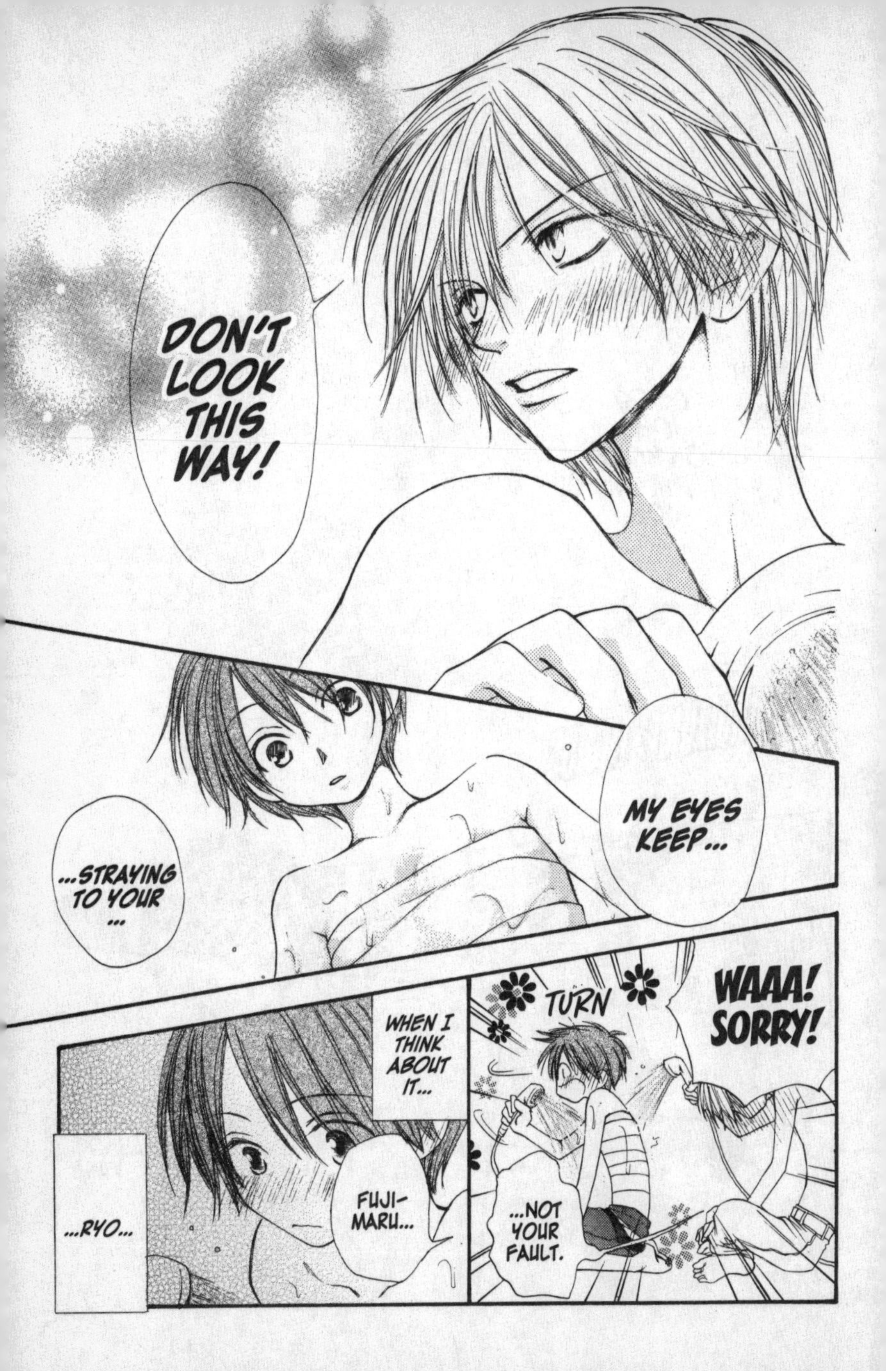
DON'T LOOK THIS WAY!
MY EYES KEEP...
...STRAYING TO YOUR ...
WAAA! SORRY!
TURN
...NOT YOUR FAULT.
WHEN I THINK ABOUT IT...
FUJI-MARU...
...RYO...

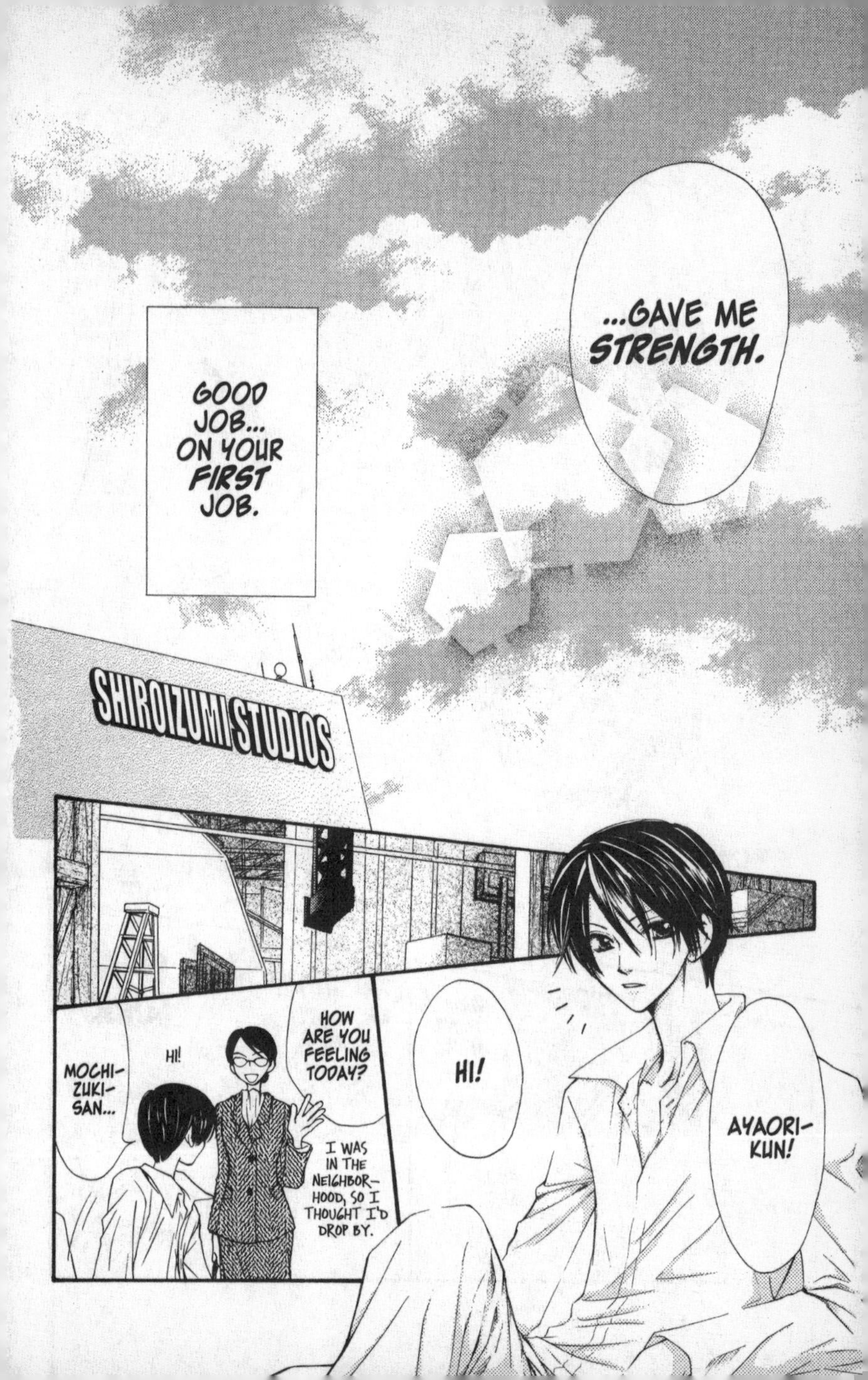
...GAVE ME STRENGTH.
GOOD JOB... ON YOUR FIRST JOB.
SHIROIZUMI STUDIOS
AYAORI-KUN!
HI!
HOW ARE YOU FEELING TODAY?
HI!
MOCHIZUKI-SAN...
I WAS IN THE NEIGHBOR-HOOD, SO I THOUGHT I'D DROP BY.

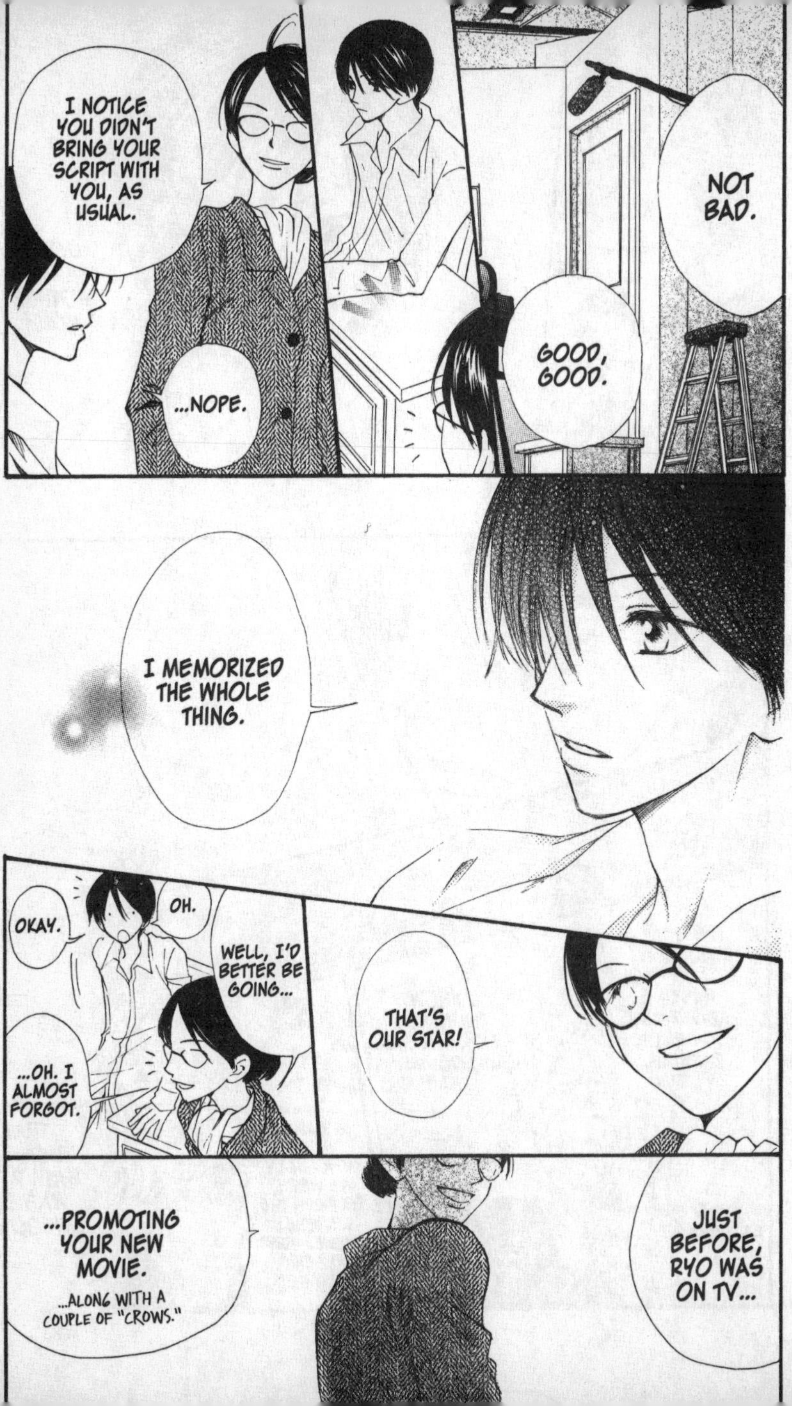
NOT BAD.
GOOD, GOOD.
I NOTICE YOU DIDN'T BRING YOUR SCRIPT WITH YOU, AS USUAL.
...NOPE.
I MEMORIZED THE WHOLE THING.
THAT'S OUR STAR!
WELL, I'D BETTER BE GOING...
OH.
OKAY.
...OH. I ALMOST FORGOT.
JUST BEFORE, RYO WAS ON TV...
...PROMOTING YOUR NEW MOVIE.
...ALONG WITH A COUPLE OF "CROWS."

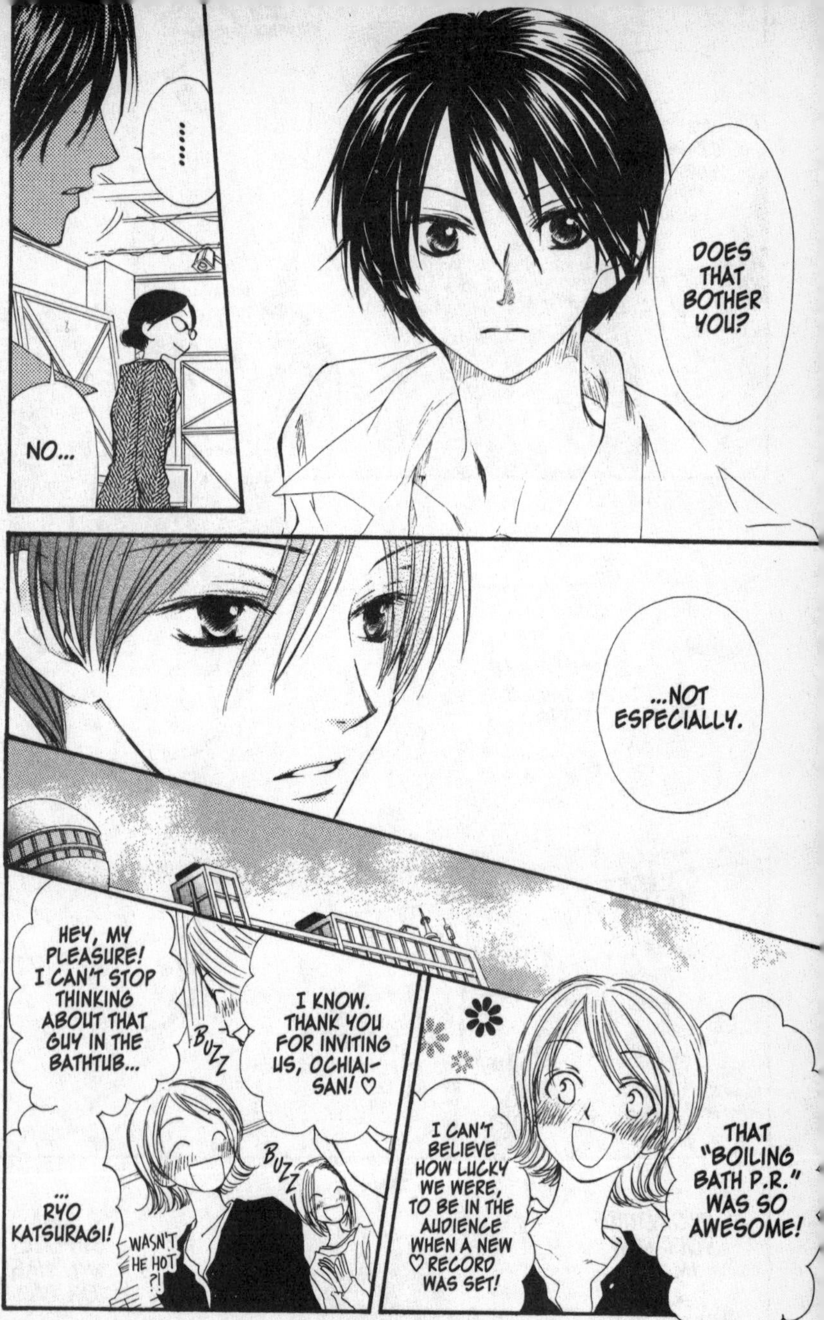
DOES THAT BOTHER YOU?
......
NO...
...NOT ESPECIALLY.
THAT "BOILING BATH P.R." WAS SO AWESOME!
I CAN'T BELIEVE HOW LUCKY WE WERE, TO BE IN THE AUDIENCE WHEN A NEW ♡ RECORD WAS SET!
I KNOW. THANK YOU FOR INVITING US, OCHIAI-SAN! ♡
BUZZ
HEY, MY PLEASURE! I CAN'T STOP THINKING ABOUT THAT GUY IN THE BATHTUB...
BUZZ
... RYO KATSURAGI!
WASN'T HE HOT ?!

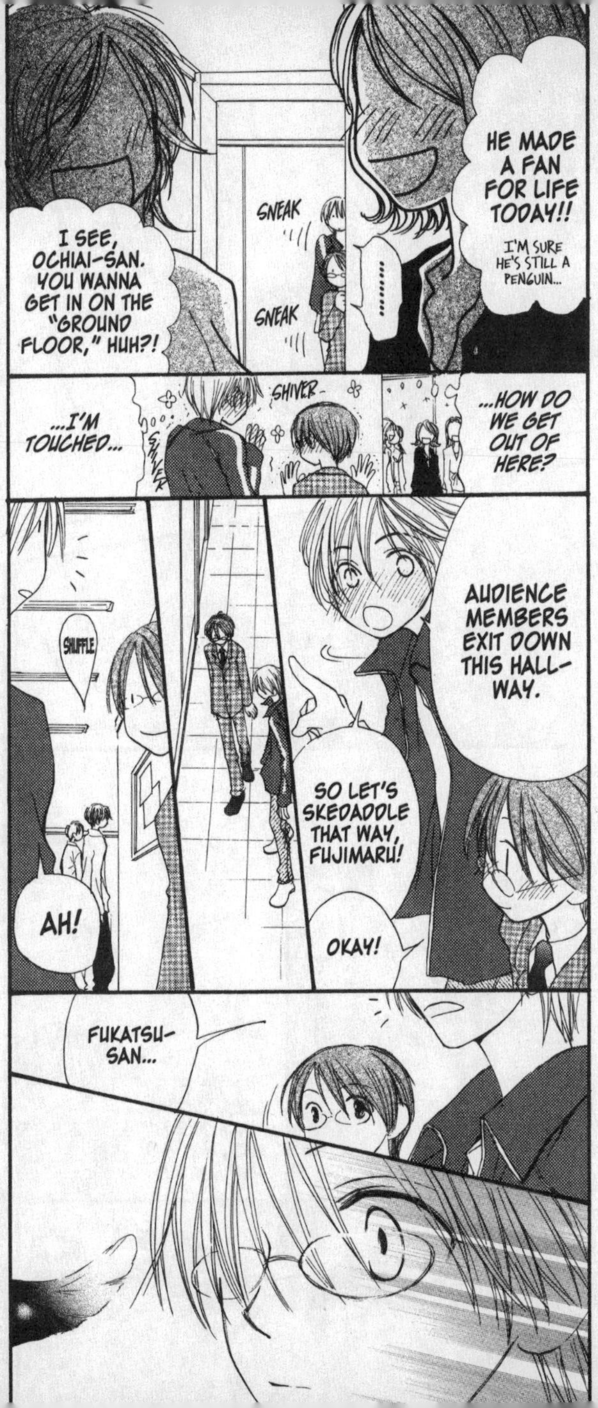
HE MADE A FAN FOR LIFE TODAY!!
I'M SURE HE'S STILL A PENGUIN...
......
SNEAK
SNEAK
I SEE, OCHIAI-SAN. YOU WANNA GET IN ON THE "GROUND FLOOR," HUH?!
...HOW DO WE GET OUT OF HERE?
SHIVER
SHIVER
...I'M TOUCHED...
AUDIENCE MEMBERS EXIT DOWN THIS HALL-WAY.
SO LET'S SKEDADDLE THAT WAY, FUJIMARU!
OKAY!
SHUFFLE
AH!
FUKATSU-SAN...

1/4 Sakura Mail

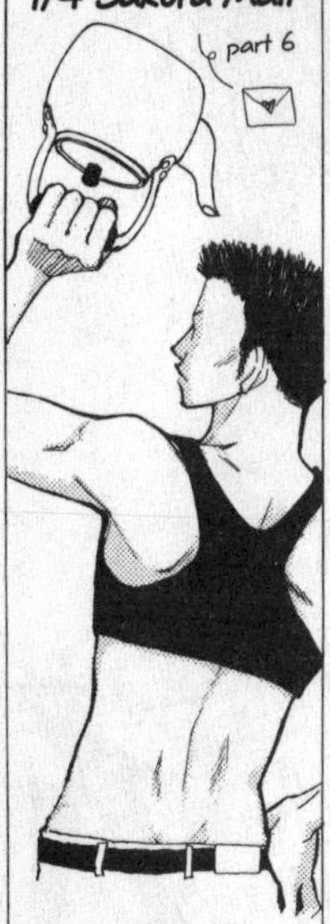
part 6

And so that was "Boiling Bathtub P.R.," which my editor has wanted to subject Ryo to ("All idols have to go through this!") ever since the beginning of the series. (As it turns out, though, Yuka-chan became the focal point of the story when she got in the tub...) Whoever originally came up with the idea for this kind of televised torture is a genius! It makes for great TV and I had a great time drawing it... ♡

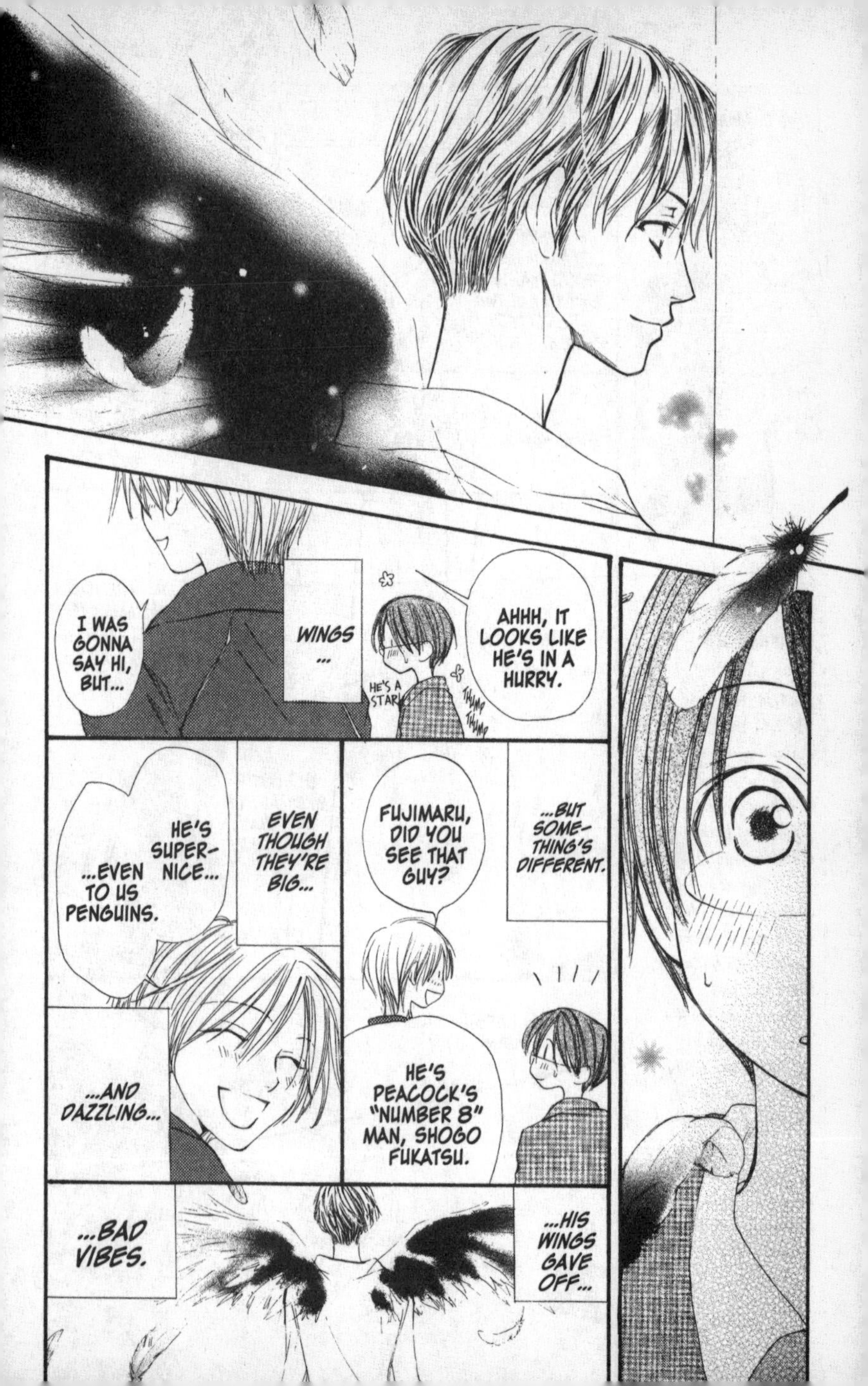
AHHH, IT LOOKS LIKE HE'S IN A HURRY.
WINGS...
HE'S A STAR!
THUMP THUMP
I WAS GONNA SAY HI, BUT...
...BUT SOMETHING'S DIFFERENT.
FUJIMARU, DID YOU SEE THAT GUY?
HE'S PEACOCK'S "NUMBER 8" MAN, SHOGO FUKATSU.
EVEN THOUGH THEY'RE BIG...
HE'S SUPER-NICE...
...EVEN TO US PENGUINS.
...AND DAZZLING...
...HIS WINGS GAVE OFF...
...BAD VIBES.

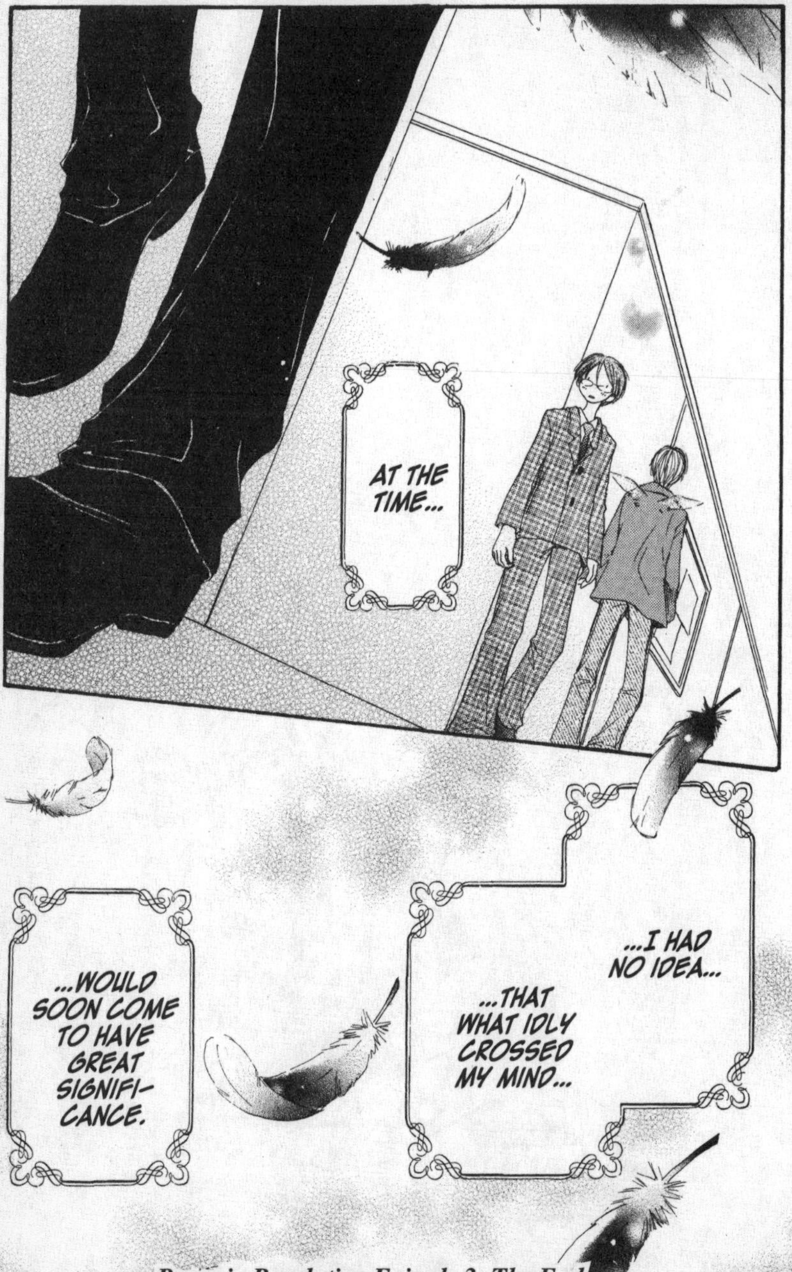
AT THE TIME...
...I HAD NO IDEA...
...THAT WHAT IDLY CROSSED MY MIND...
...WOULD SOON COME TO HAVE GREAT SIGNIFI-CANCE.

Penguin Revolution Episode 3: The End

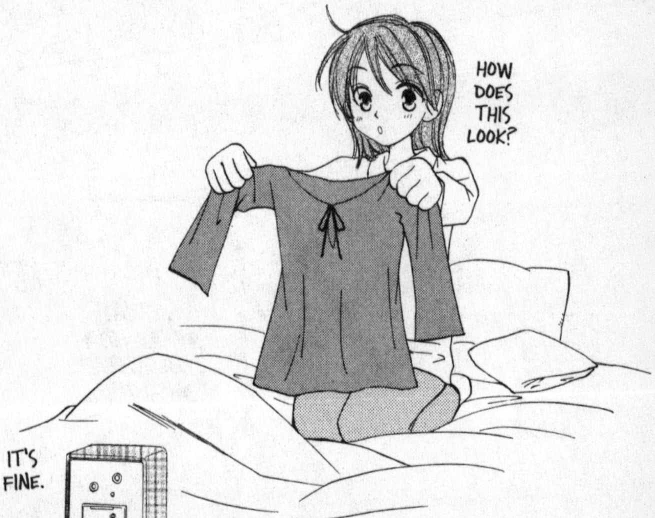
HOW DOES THIS LOOK?
IT'S FINE.

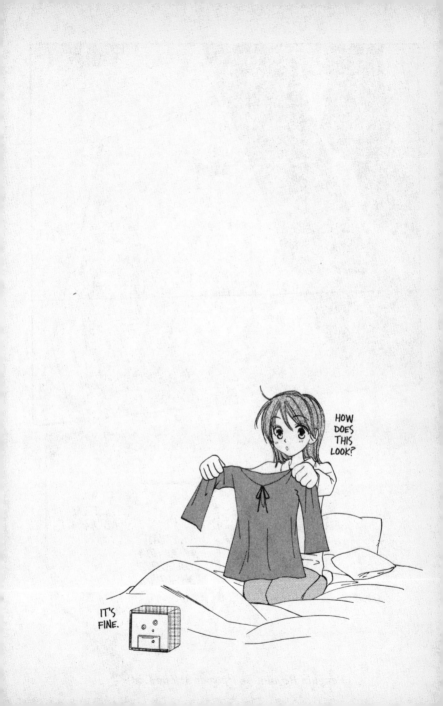

Episode 4

ペンギン革命

PENGUIN REVOLUTION

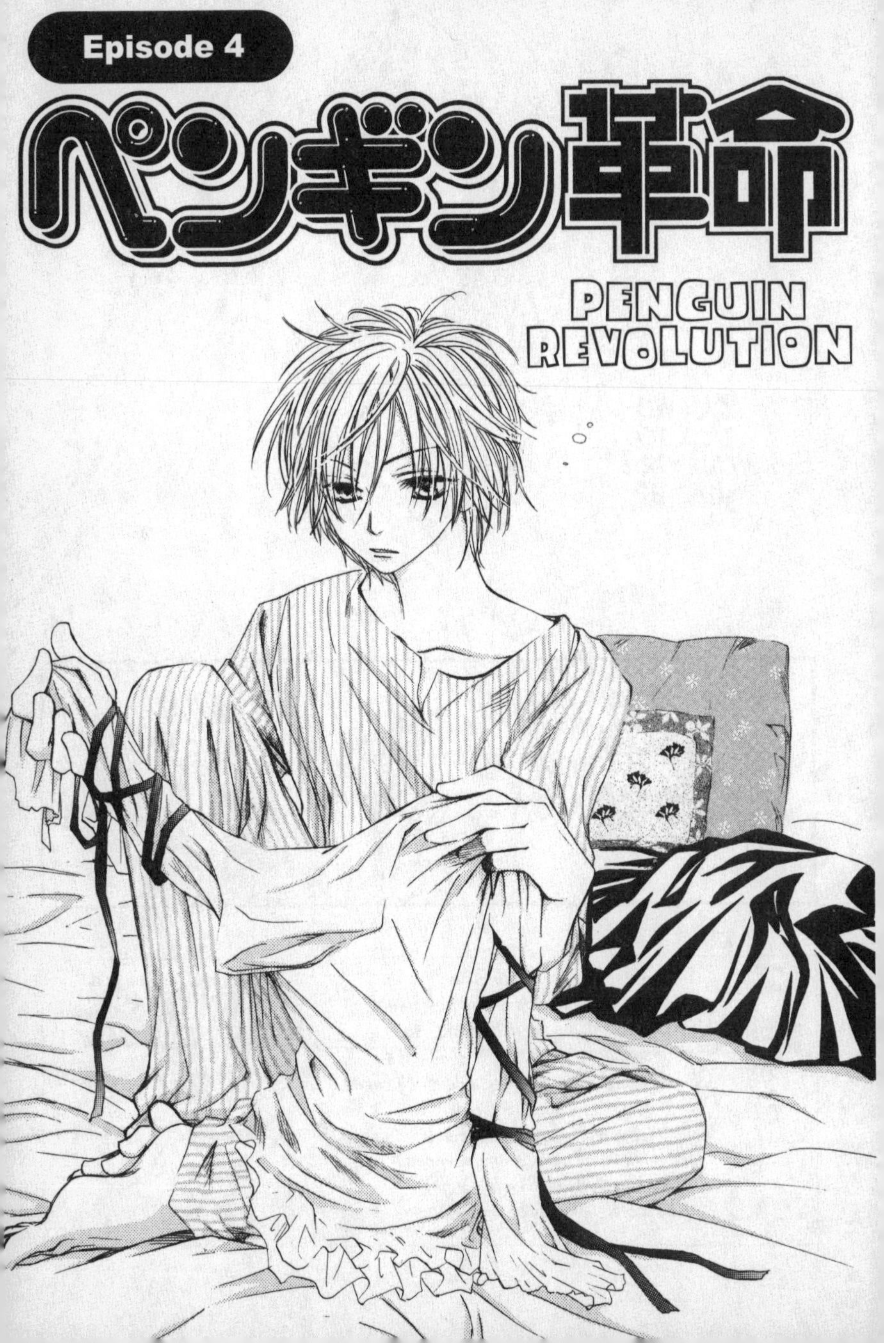

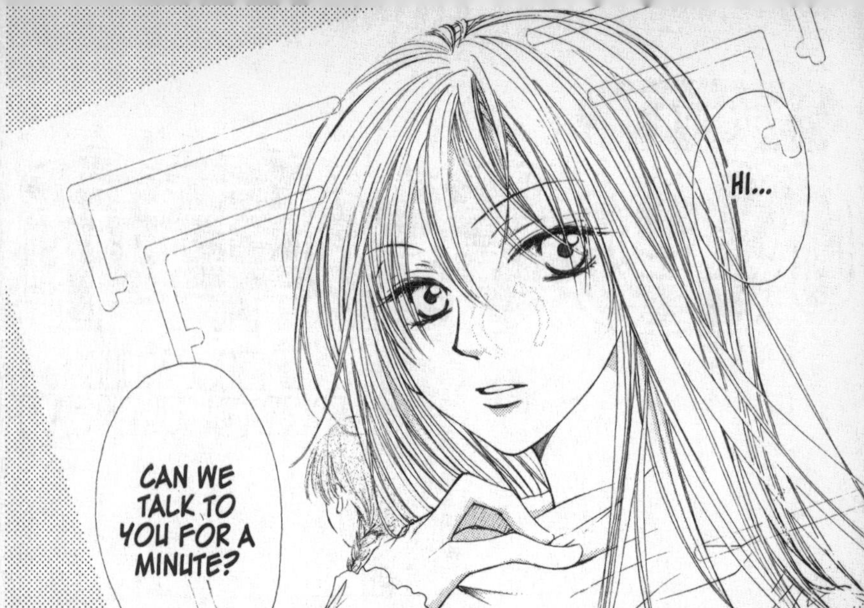
HI...
CAN WE TALK TO YOU FOR A MINUTE?
YOU'RE REALLY CUTE. ARE YOU ALONE?
A BEAUTY!
WE'RE SHOOTING FOOTAGE FOR A SHOW, "IN SEARCH OF BEAUTIFUL GIRLS." AND HERE WE'VE FOUND ONE! WHAT DO YOU SAY?
......

1/4 Sakura Mail

part 7

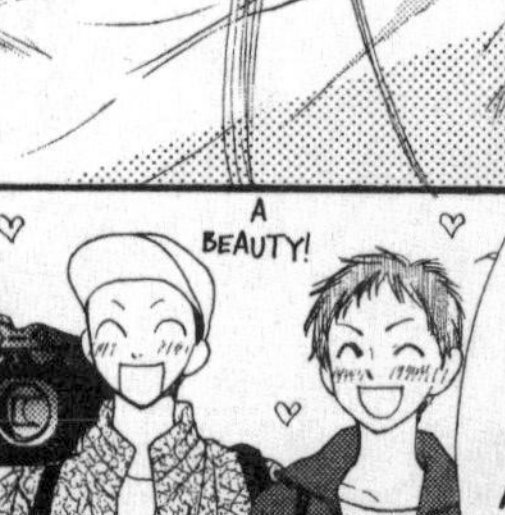

This episode, Fukatsu-san makes his debut, the first of the Peacock "numbered talents" to appear since Aya. And since it's been established there are only ten of those, it makes me want to draw them. Of course, there are also a lot of "Cs" and more "Penguins" that I hope I get a chance to introduce as well...

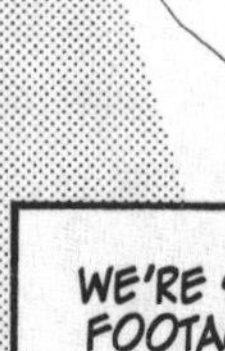
I'M NOT A CROW!

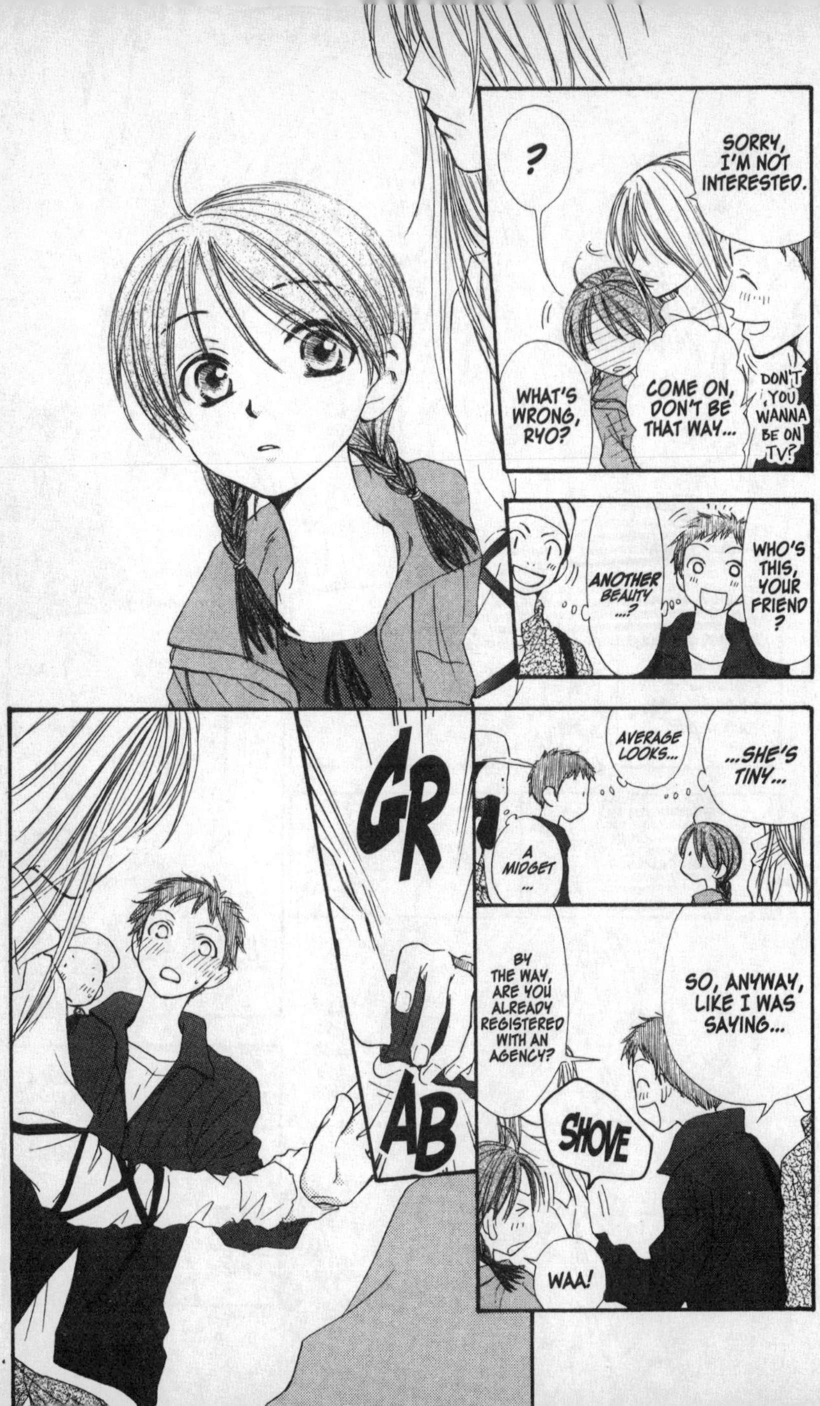
SORRY, I'M NOT INTERESTED.
?
DON'T YOU WANNA BE ON TV?
COME ON, DON'T BE THAT WAY...
WHAT'S WRONG, RYO?
WHO'S THIS, YOUR FRIEND?
ANOTHER BEAUTY...?
...SHE'S TINY...
AVERAGE LOOKS...
A MIDGET...
SO, ANYWAY, LIKE I WAS SAYING...
BY THE WAY, ARE YOU ALREADY REGISTERED WITH AN AGENCY?
SHOVE
WAA!
GRAB

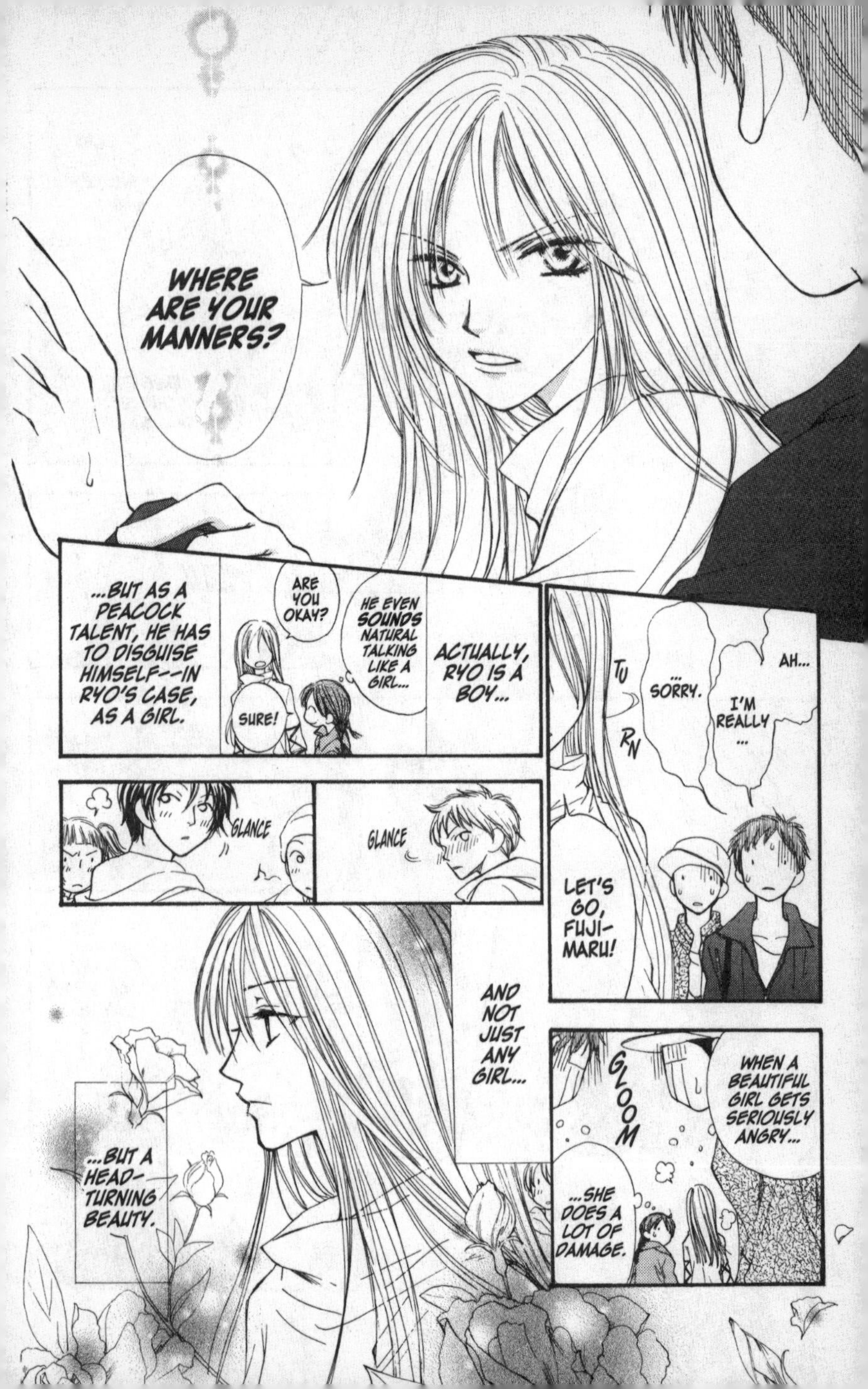
WHERE ARE YOUR MANNERS?
AH... I'M REALLY ...
... SORRY.
TURN
LET'S GO, FUJI-MARU!
ACTUALLY, RYO IS A BOY...
HE EVEN SOUNDS NATURAL TALKING LIKE A GIRL...
ARE YOU OKAY?
SURE!
...BUT AS A PEACOCK TALENT, HE HAS TO DISGUISE HIMSELF--IN RYO'S CASE, AS A GIRL.
GLANCE
GLANCE
WHEN A BEAUTIFUL GIRL GETS SERIOUSLY ANGRY...
GLOOM
...SHE DOES A LOT OF DAMAGE.
AND NOT JUST ANY GIRL...
...BUT A HEAD-TURNING BEAUTY.

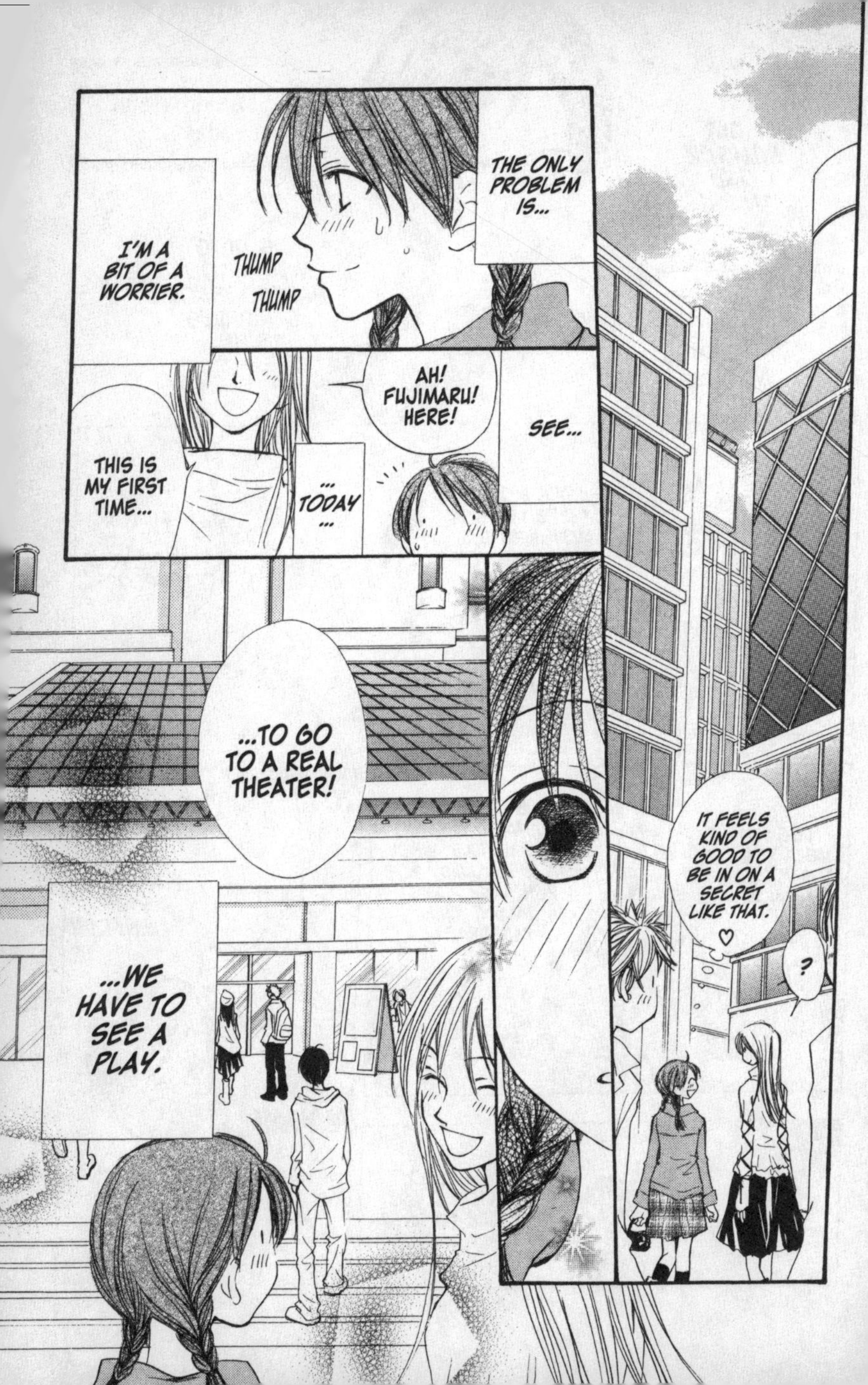
IT FEELS KIND OF GOOD TO BE IN ON A SECRET LIKE THAT. ♡
?
THE ONLY PROBLEM IS...
THUMP
THUMP
I'M A BIT OF A WORRIER.
SEE...
AH! FUJIMARU! HERE!
...TODAY...
THIS IS MY FIRST TIME...
...TO GO TO A REAL THEATER!
...WE HAVE TO SEE A PLAY.

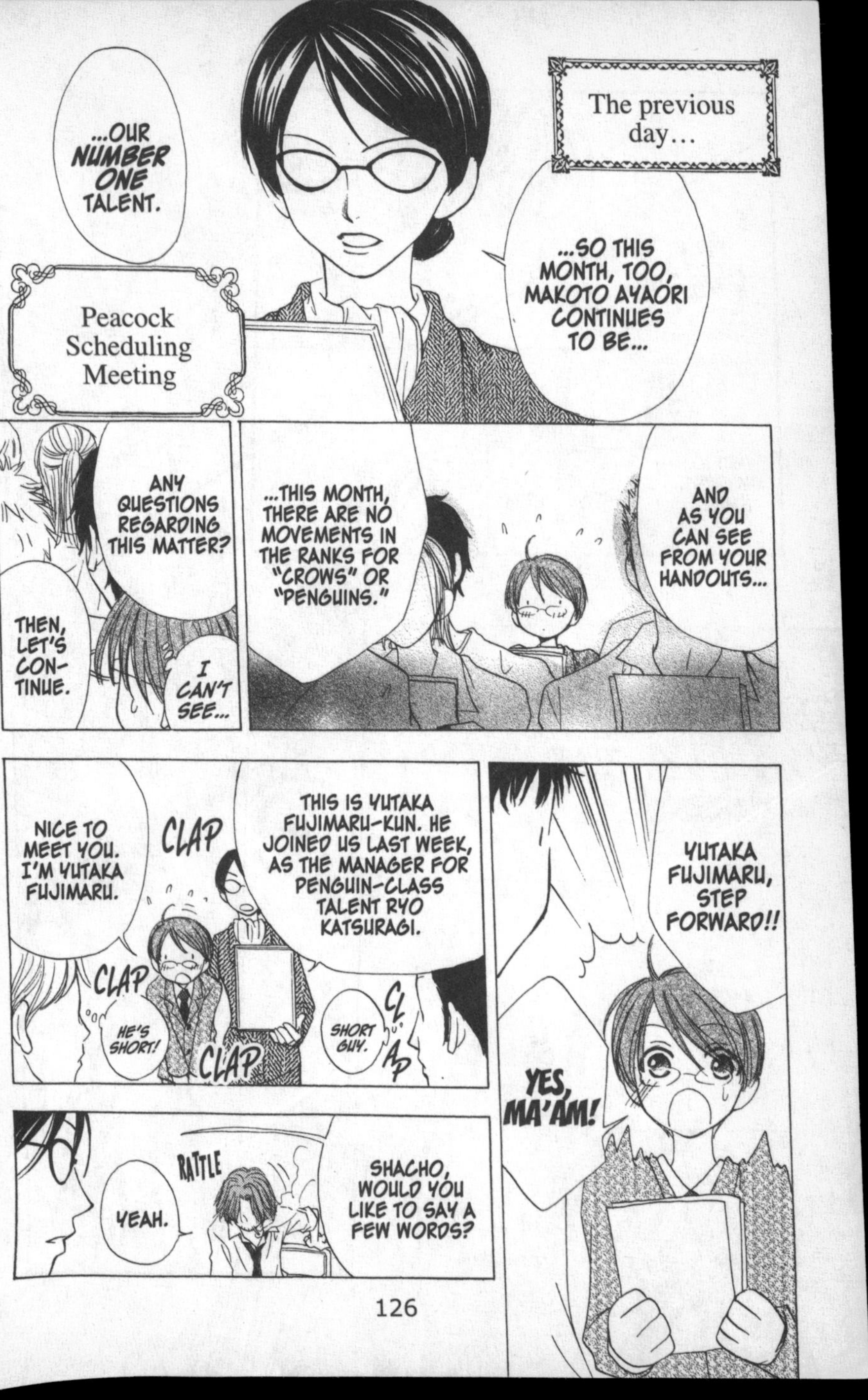
The previous day…
...SO THIS MONTH, TOO, MAKOTO AYAORI CONTINUES TO BE...
...OUR NUMBER ONE TALENT.
Peacock Scheduling Meeting
AND AS YOU CAN SEE FROM YOUR HANDOUTS...
...THIS MONTH, THERE ARE NO MOVEMENTS IN THE RANKS FOR "CROWS" OR "PENGUINS."
ANY QUESTIONS REGARDING THIS MATTER?
I CAN'T SEE...
THEN, LET'S CONTINUE.
YUTAKA FUJIMARU, STEP FORWARD!!
YES, MA'AM!
THIS IS YUTAKA FUJIMARU-KUN. HE JOINED US LAST WEEK, AS THE MANAGER FOR PENGUIN-CLASS TALENT RYO KATSURAGI.
CLAP
NICE TO MEET YOU. I'M YUTAKA FUJIMARU.
CLAP
SHORT GUY.
CLAP
CLAP
HE'S SHORT!
SHACHO, WOULD YOU LIKE TO SAY A FEW WORDS?
RATTLE
YEAH.

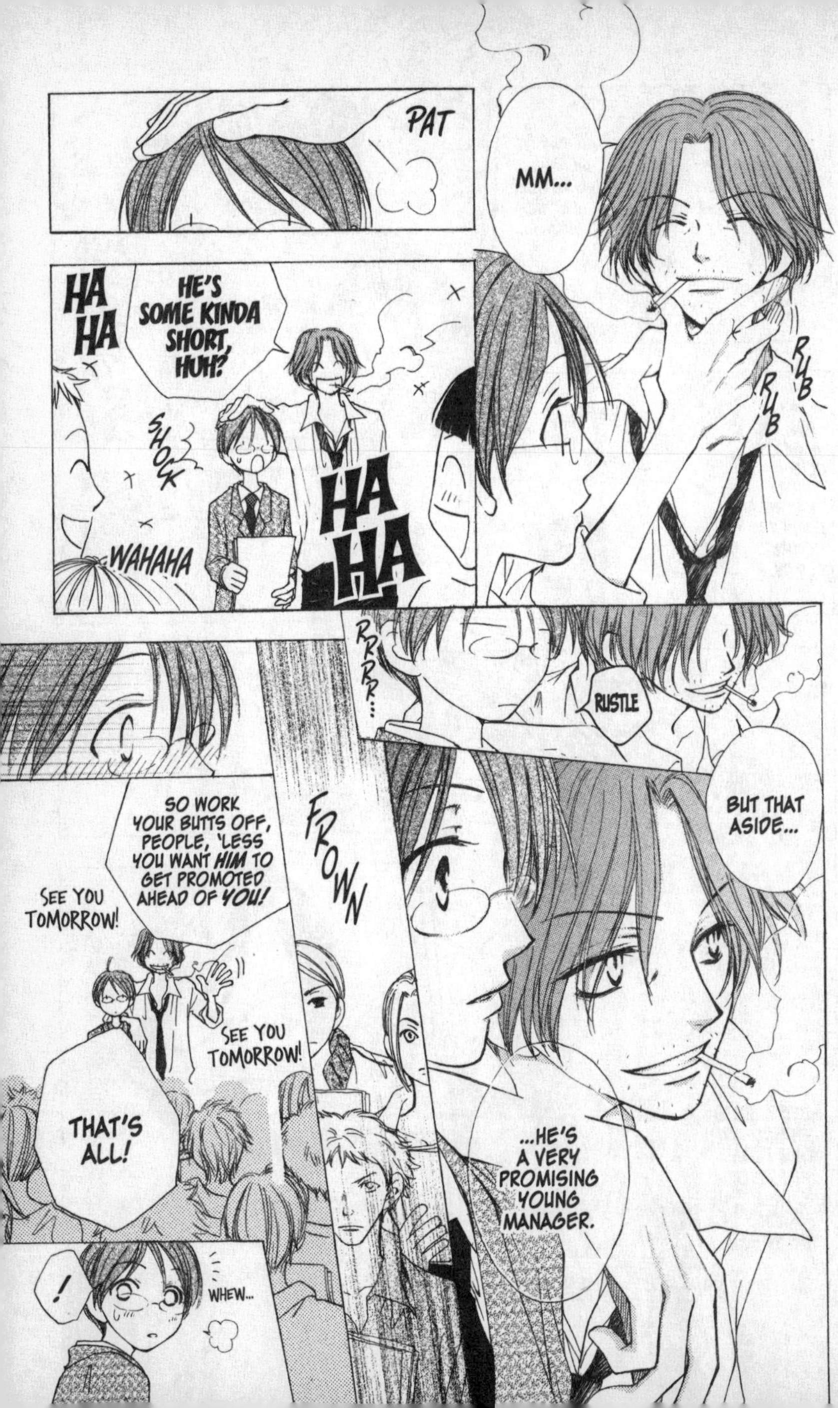
MM...
RUB
RUB
PAT
HA HA
HE'S SOME KINDA SHORT, HUH?
SHOCK
HA HA
WAHAHA
RRRR...
RUSTLE
BUT THAT ASIDE...
...HE'S A VERY PROMISING YOUNG MANAGER.
FROWN
SO WORK YOUR BUTTS OFF, PEOPLE, 'LESS YOU WANT *HIM* TO GET PROMOTED AHEAD OF *YOU*!
SEE YOU TOMORROW!
SEE YOU TOMORROW!
THAT'S ALL!
!
WHEW...

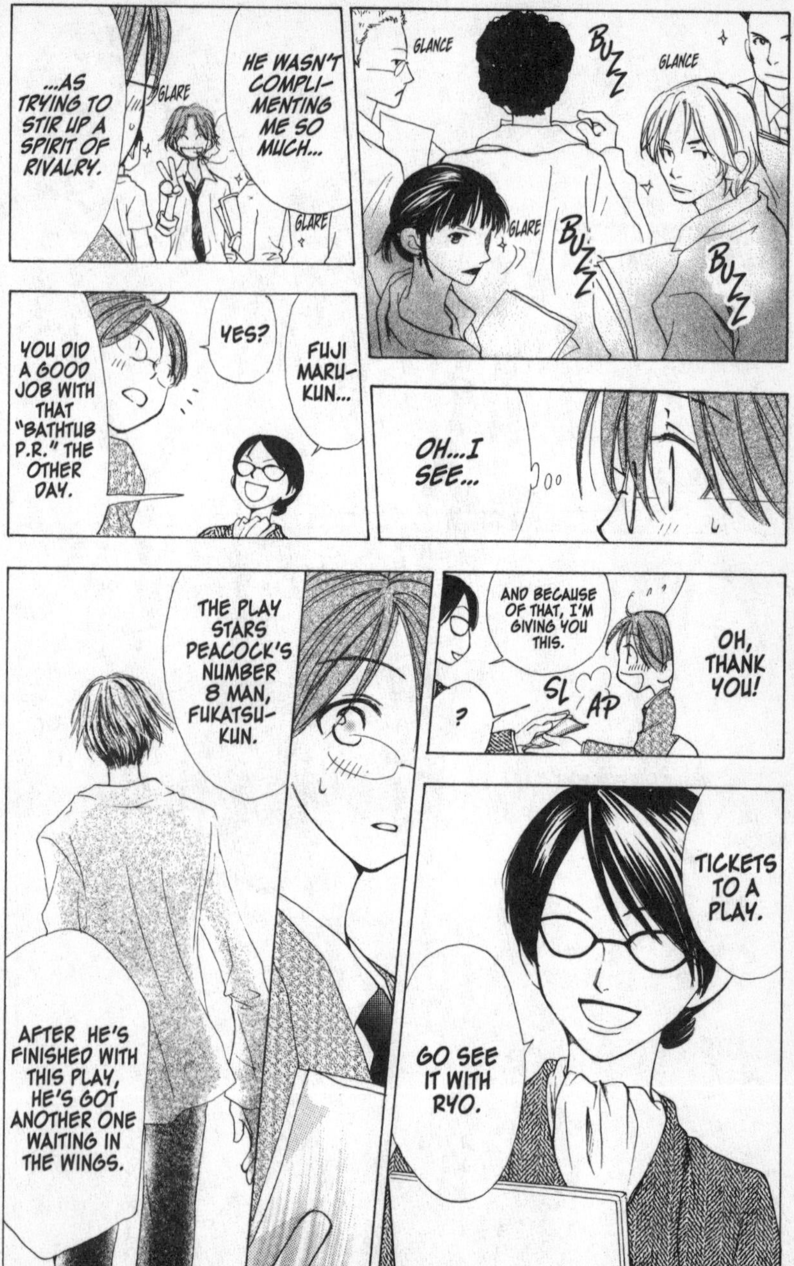
GLANCE
BUZZ
GLANCE
GLARE
BUZZ
BUZZ
HE WASN'T COMPLIMENTING ME SO MUCH...
...AS TRYING TO STIR UP A SPIRIT OF RIVALRY.
GLARE
GLARE
FUJI MARU-KUN...
YES?
YOU DID A GOOD JOB WITH THAT "BATHTUB P.R." THE OTHER DAY.
OH...I SEE...
AND BECAUSE OF THAT, I'M GIVING YOU THIS.
OH, THANK YOU!
SLAP
?
TICKETS TO A PLAY.
GO SEE IT WITH RYO.
THE PLAY STARS PEACOCK'S NUMBER 8 MAN, FUKATSU-KUN.
AFTER HE'S FINISHED WITH THIS PLAY, HE'S GOT ANOTHER ONE WAITING IN THE WINGS.

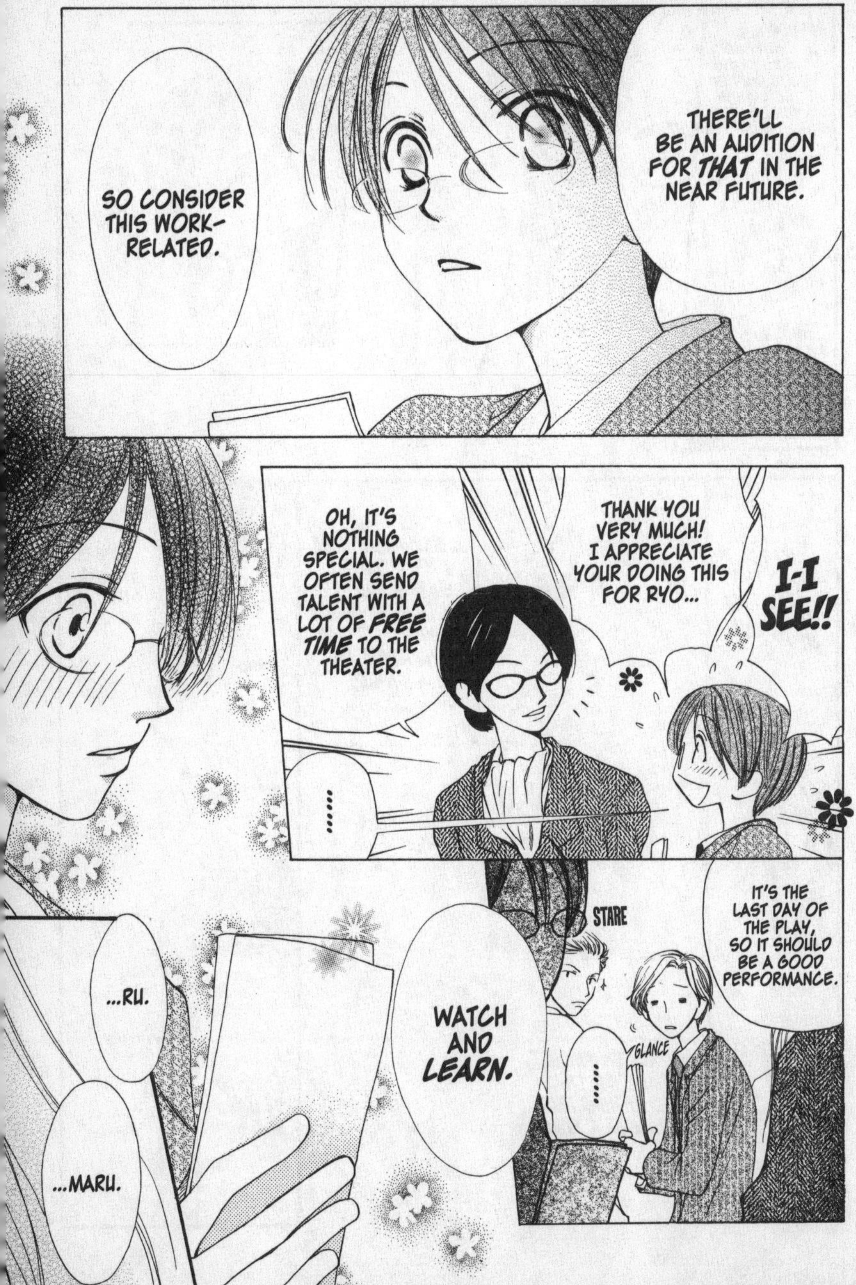
THERE'LL BE AN AUDITION FOR *THAT* IN THE NEAR FUTURE.
SO CONSIDER THIS WORK-RELATED.
I-I SEE!!
THANK YOU VERY MUCH! I APPRECIATE YOUR DOING THIS FOR RYO...
OH, IT'S NOTHING SPECIAL. WE OFTEN SEND TALENT WITH A LOT OF *FREE TIME* TO THE THEATER.
......
IT'S THE LAST DAY OF THE PLAY, SO IT SHOULD BE A GOOD PERFORMANCE.
STARE
GLANCE
......
WATCH AND *LEARN.*
...RU.
...MARU.

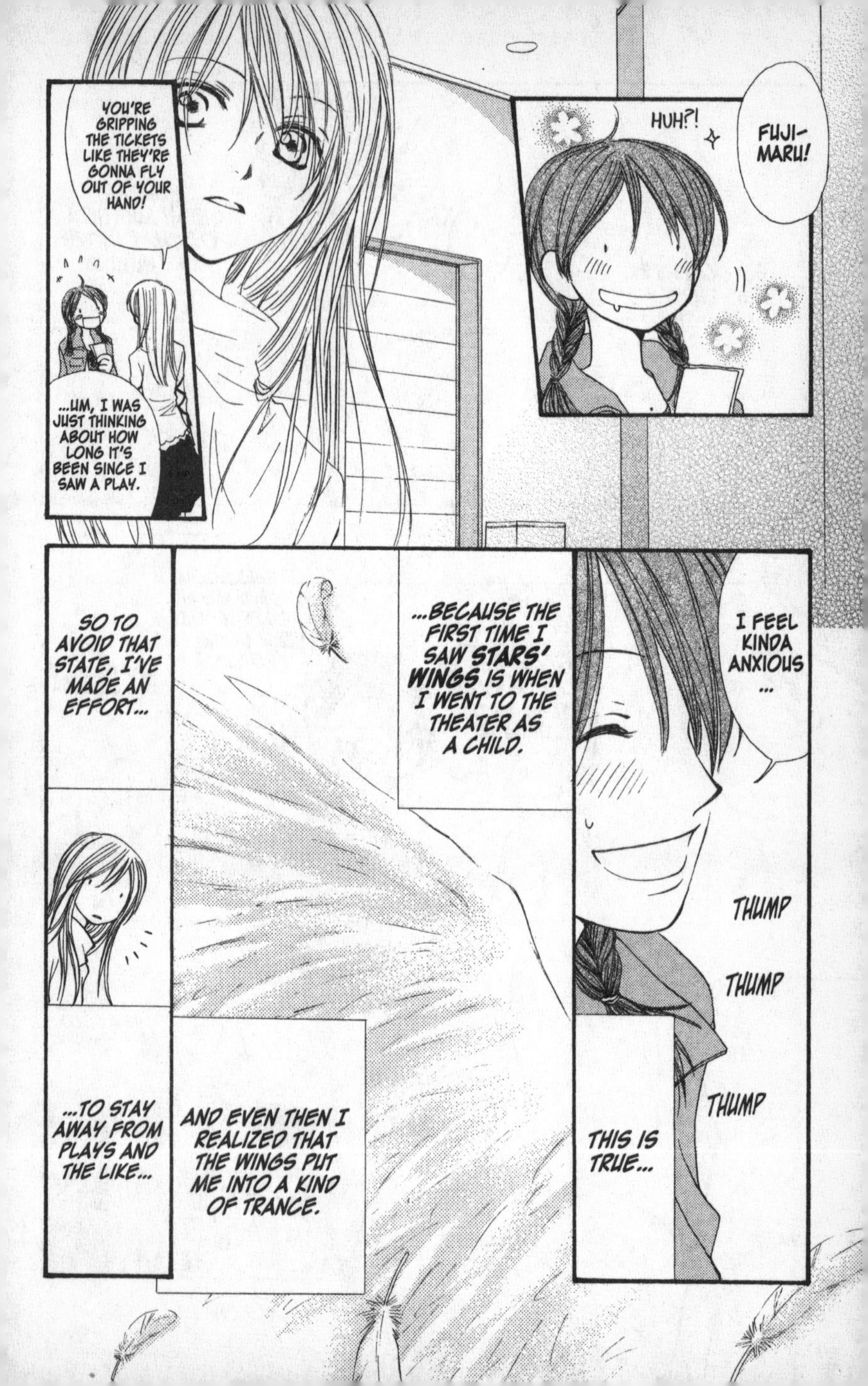
FUJI-MARU!
HUH?!
YOU'RE GRIPPING THE TICKETS LIKE THEY'RE GONNA FLY OUT OF YOUR HAND!
...UM, I WAS JUST THINKING ABOUT HOW LONG IT'S BEEN SINCE I SAW A PLAY.
I FEEL KINDA ANXIOUS...
THUMP
THUMP
THUMP
THIS IS TRUE...
...BECAUSE THE FIRST TIME I SAW STARS' WINGS IS WHEN I WENT TO THE THEATER AS A CHILD.
AND EVEN THEN I REALIZED THAT THE WINGS PUT ME INTO A KIND OF TRANCE.
SO TO AVOID THAT STATE, I'VE MADE AN EFFORT...
...TO STAY AWAY FROM PLAYS AND THE LIKE...

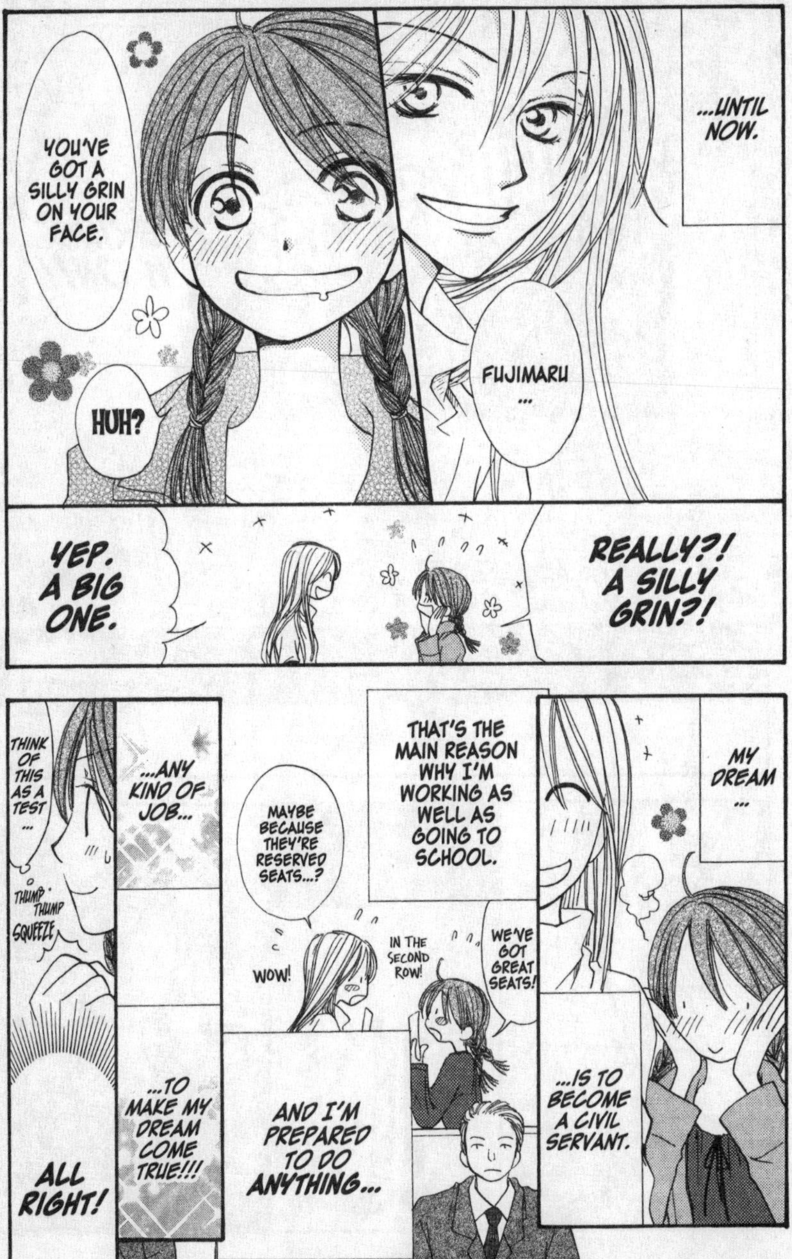
...UNTIL NOW.
FUJIMARU ...
YOU'VE GOT A SILLY GRIN ON YOUR FACE.
HUH?
REALLY?! A SILLY GRIN?!
YEP. A BIG ONE.
MY DREAM ...
...IS TO BECOME A CIVIL SERVANT.
THAT'S THE MAIN REASON WHY I'M WORKING AS WELL AS GOING TO SCHOOL.
WE'VE GOT GREAT SEATS!
IN THE SECOND ROW!
MAYBE BECAUSE THEY'RE RESERVED SEATS...?
WOW!
AND I'M PREPARED TO DO ANYTHING...
...ANY KIND OF JOB...
...TO MAKE MY DREAM COME TRUE!!!
THINK OF THIS AS A TEST ...
THUMP THUMP
SQUEEZE
ALL RIGHT!

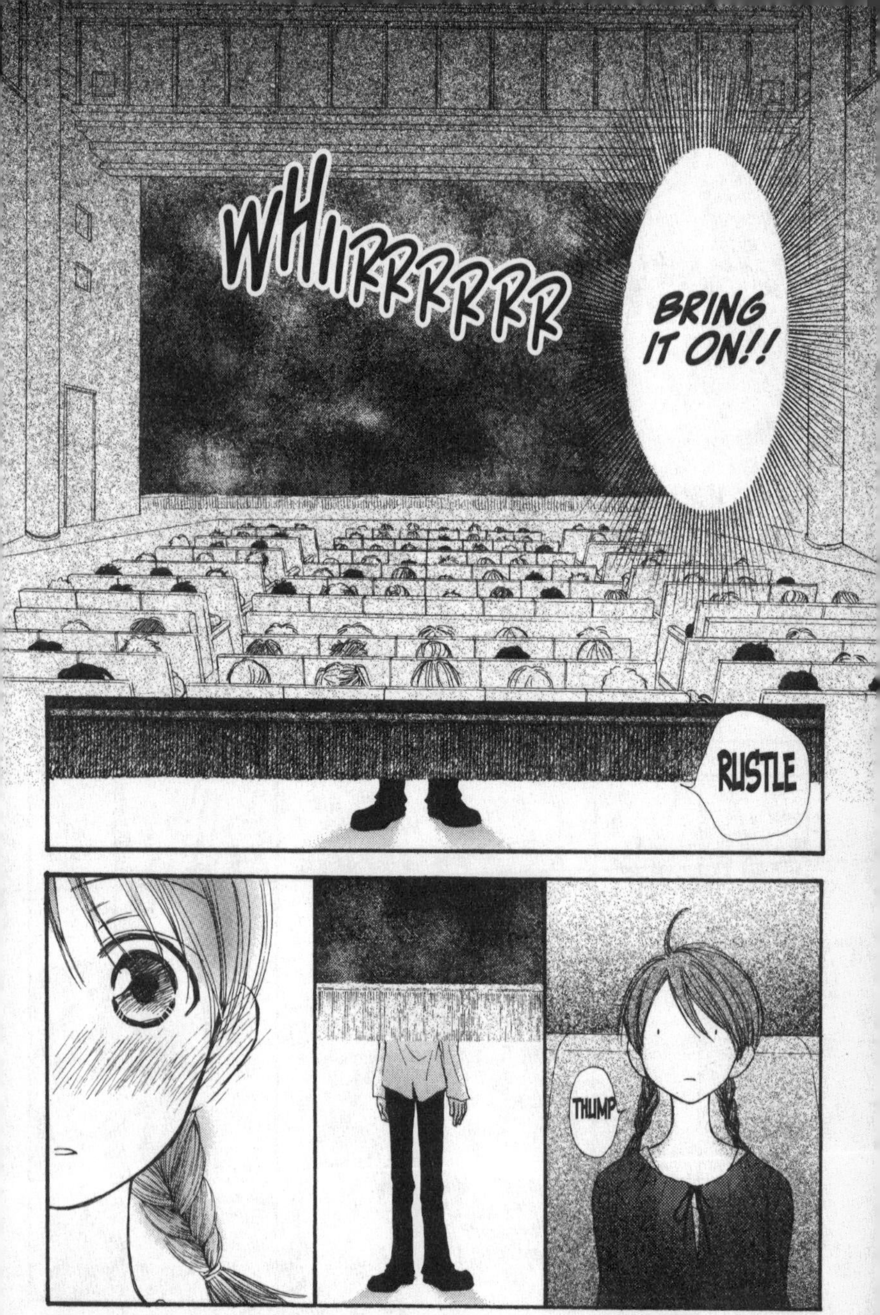
BRING IT ON!!
WHIRRRRRR
RUSTLE
THUMP

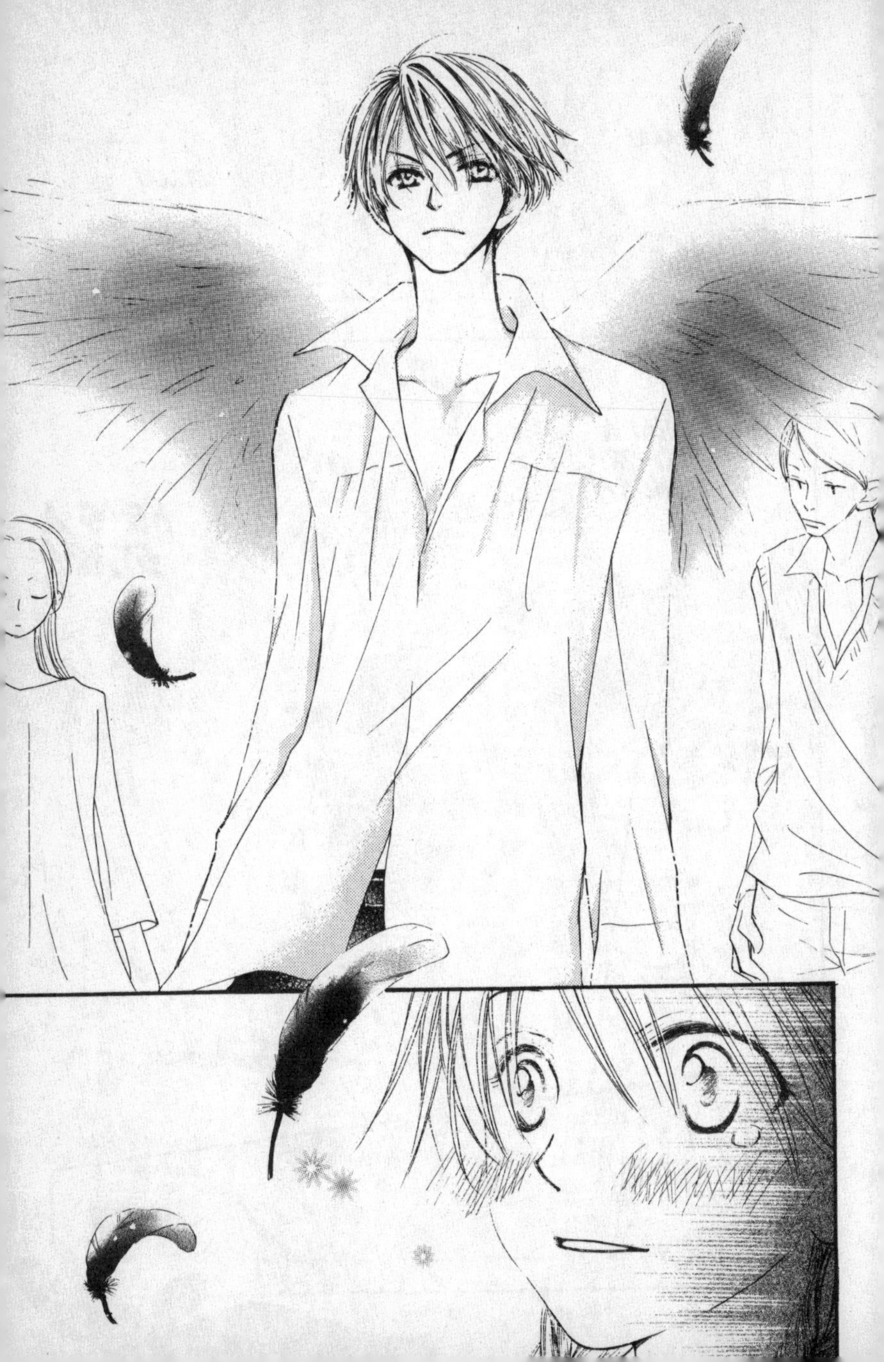

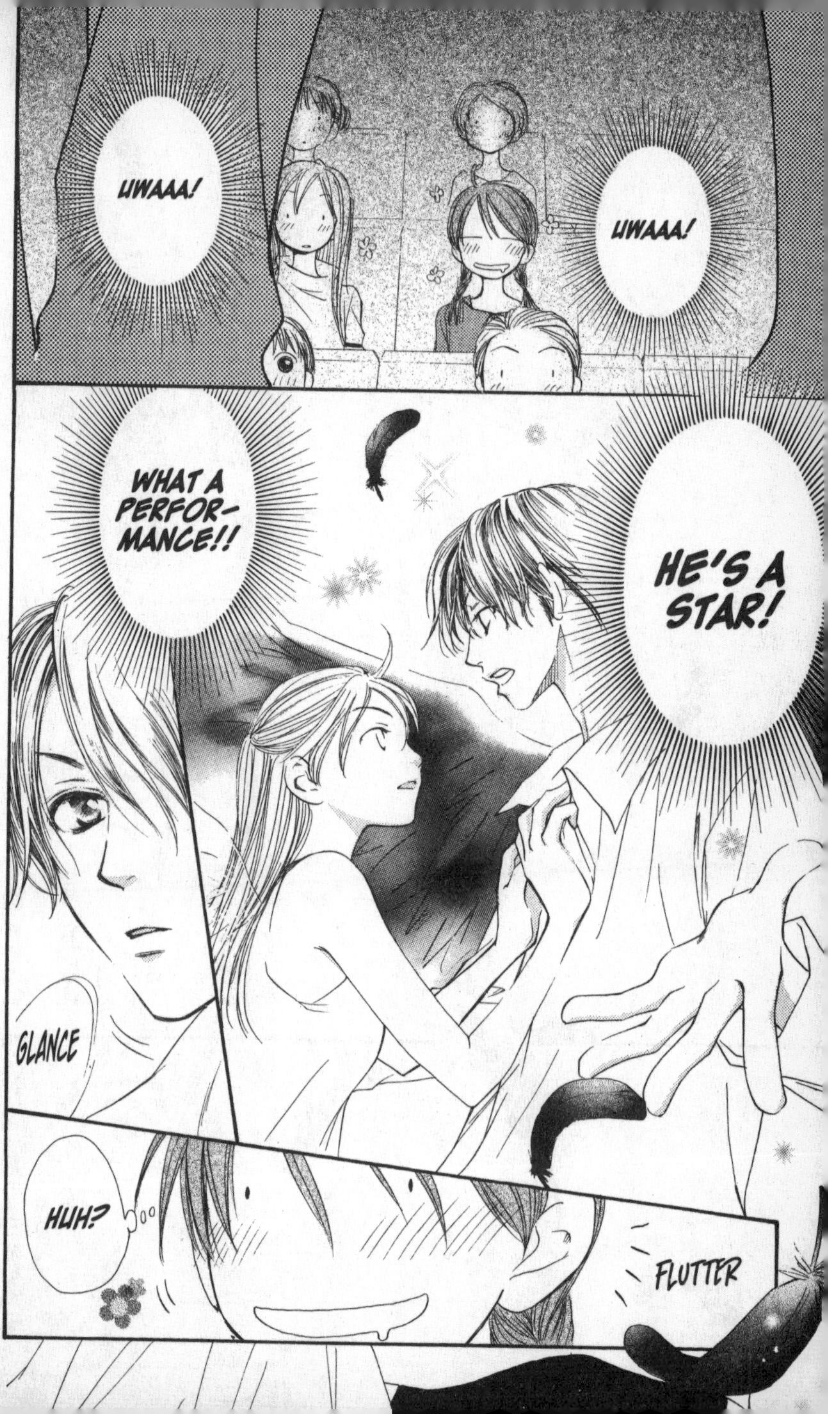
UWAAA!
UWAAA!
HE'S A STAR!
WHAT A PERFORMANCE!!
GLANCE
FLUTTER
HUH?

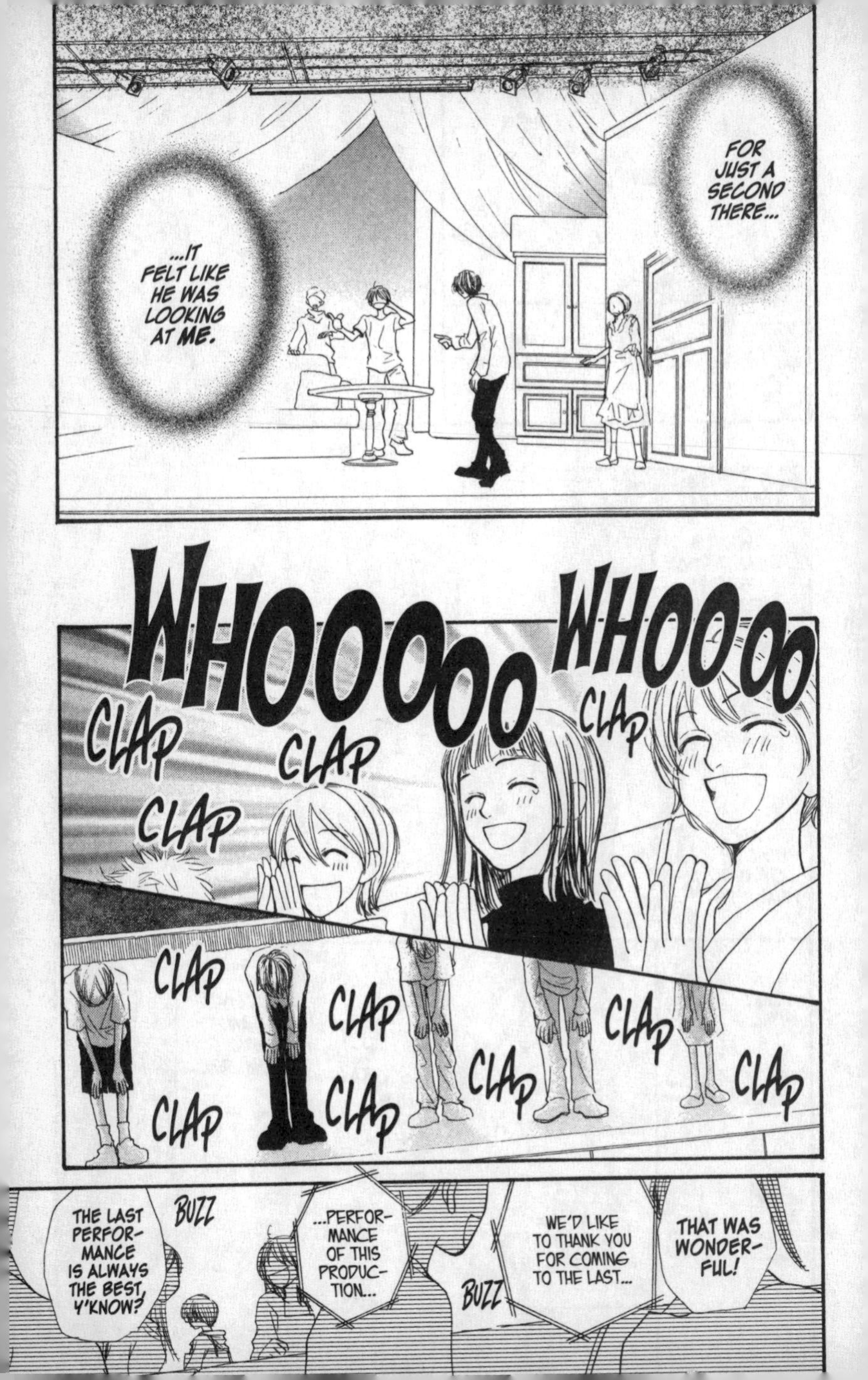
FOR JUST A SECOND THERE...
...IT FELT LIKE HE WAS LOOKING AT ME.
WHOOOO
WHOOOOO
CLAP
CLAP
CLAP
CLAP
CLAP
CLAP
CLAP
CLAP
CLAP
CLAP
CLAP
THAT WAS WONDERFUL!
WE'D LIKE TO THANK YOU FOR COMING TO THE LAST...
BUZZ
...PERFORMANCE OF THIS PRODUCTION...
BUZZ
THE LAST PERFORMANCE IS ALWAYS THE BEST, Y'KNOW?

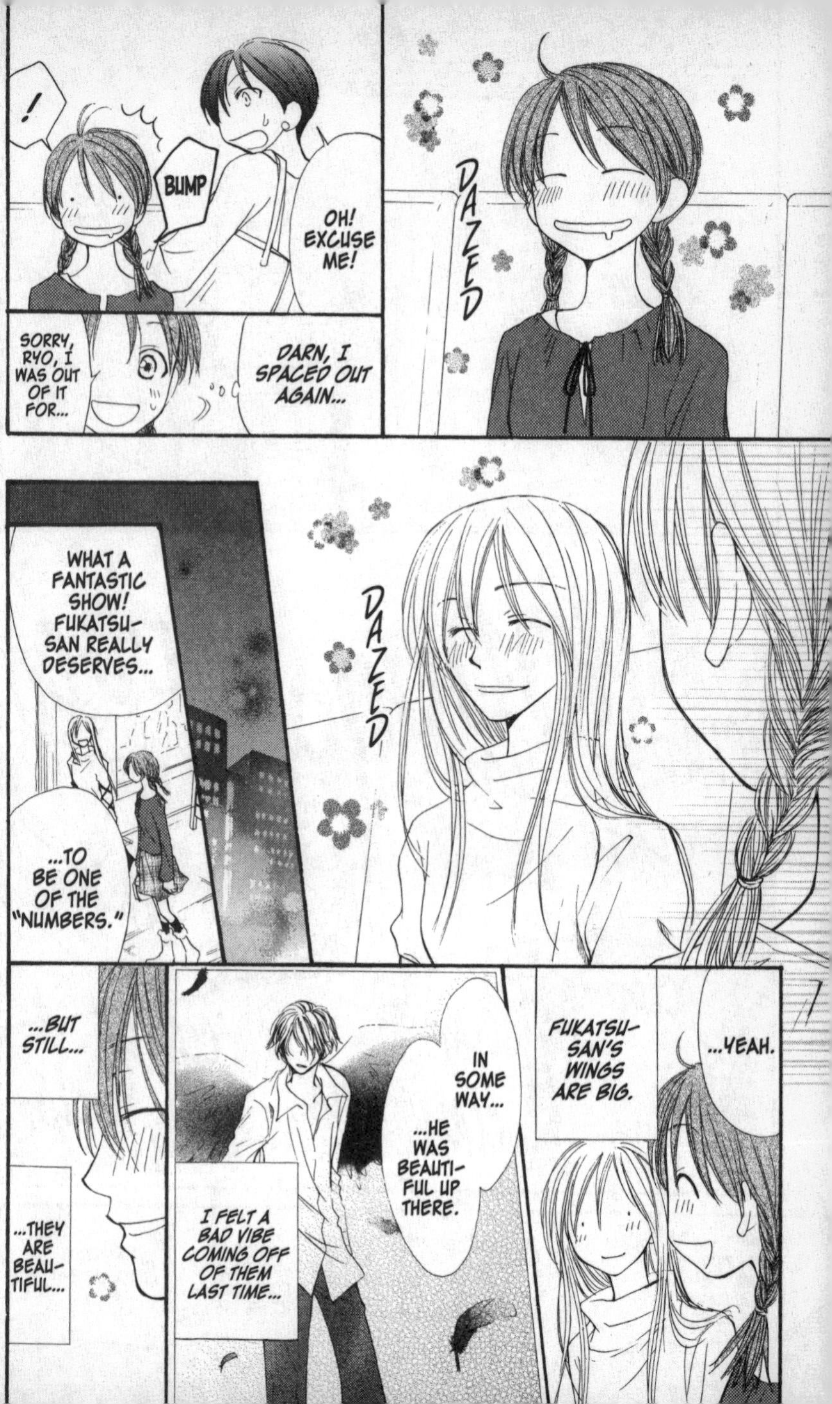
DAZED
!
BUMP
OH! EXCUSE ME!
DARN, I SPACED OUT AGAIN...
SORRY, RYO, I WAS OUT OF IT FOR...
DAZED
WHAT A FANTASTIC SHOW! FUKATSU-SAN REALLY DESERVES...
...TO BE ONE OF THE "NUMBERS."
...YEAH.
FUKATSU-SAN'S WINGS ARE BIG.
IN SOME WAY...
...HE WAS BEAUTIFUL UP THERE.
I FELT A BAD VIBE COMING OFF OF THEM LAST TIME...
...BUT STILL...
...THEY ARE BEAUTIFUL...

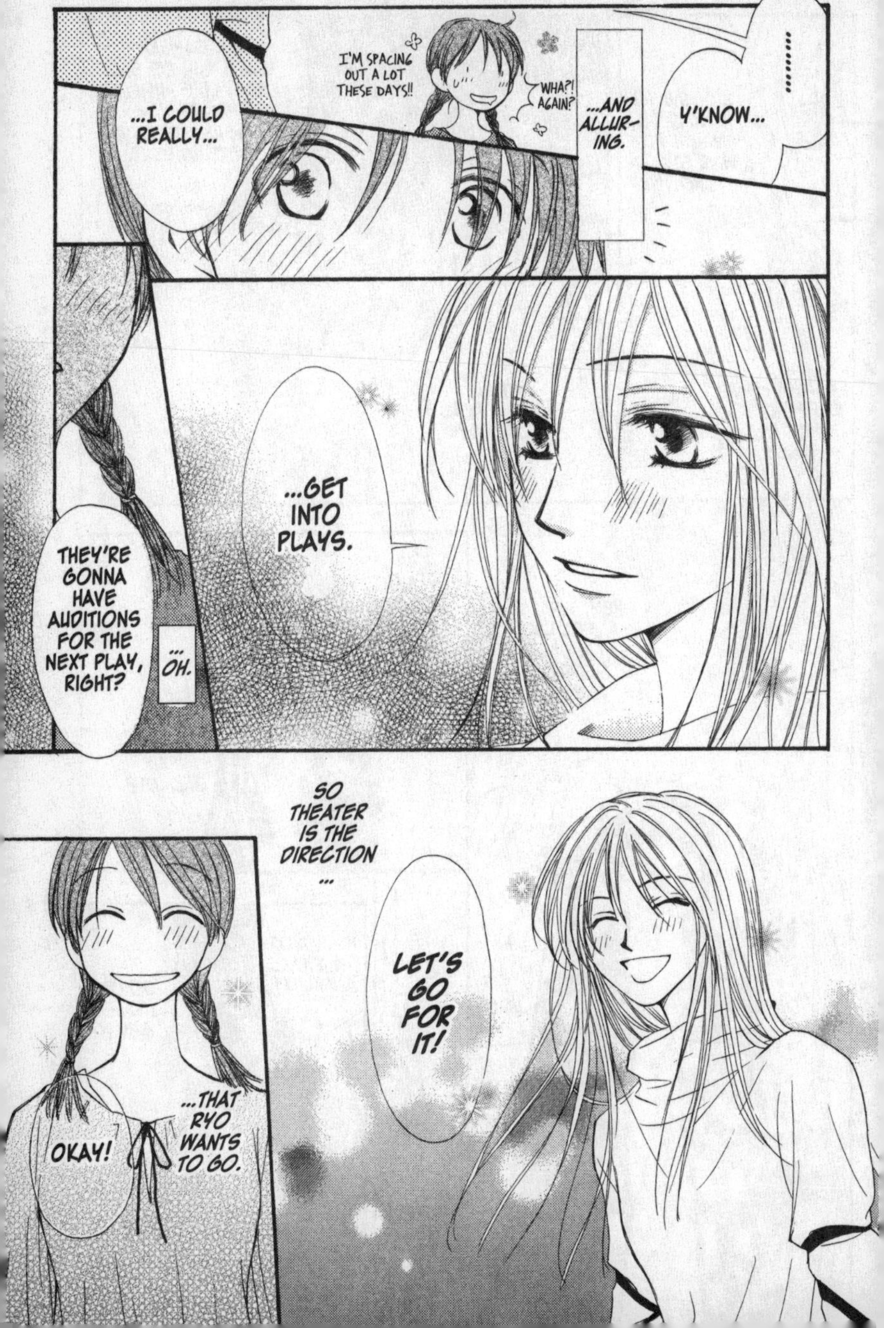

......
Y'KNOW...
...AND ALLURING.
WHA?! AGAIN?
I'M SPACING OUT A LOT THESE DAYS!!
...I COULD REALLY...
...GET INTO PLAYS.
...OH.
THEY'RE GONNA HAVE AUDITIONS FOR THE NEXT PLAY, RIGHT?
LET'S GO FOR IT!
SO THEATER IS THE DIRECTION...
...THAT RYO WANTS TO GO.
OKAY!

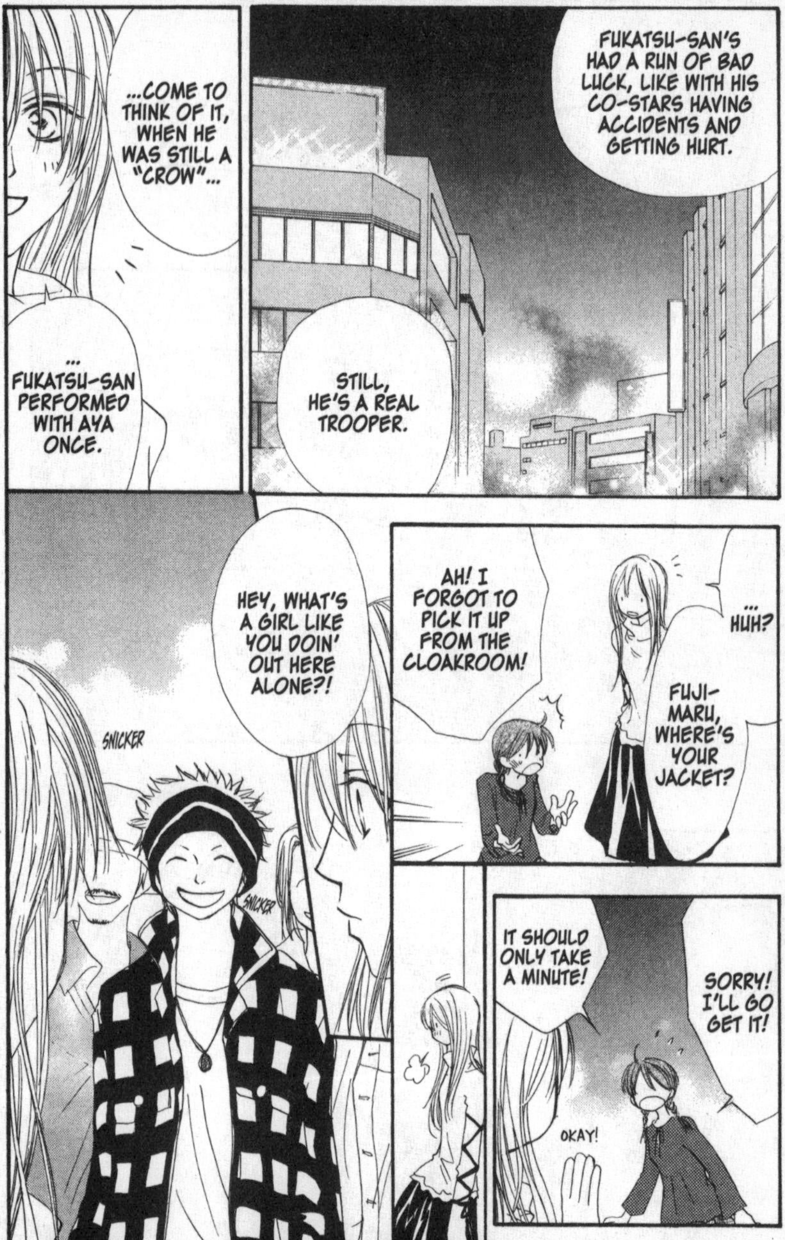
FUKATSU-SAN'S HAD A RUN OF BAD LUCK, LIKE WITH HIS CO-STARS HAVING ACCIDENTS AND GETTING HURT.
STILL, HE'S A REAL TROOPER.
...COME TO THINK OF IT, WHEN HE WAS STILL A "CROW"...
... FUKATSU-SAN PERFORMED WITH AYA ONCE.
... HUH?
FUJI-MARU, WHERE'S YOUR JACKET?
AH! I FORGOT TO PICK IT UP FROM THE CLOAKROOM!
SORRY! I'LL GO GET IT!
IT SHOULD ONLY TAKE A MINUTE!
OKAY!
HEY, WHAT'S A GIRL LIKE YOU DOIN' OUT HERE ALONE?!
SNICKER
SNICKER

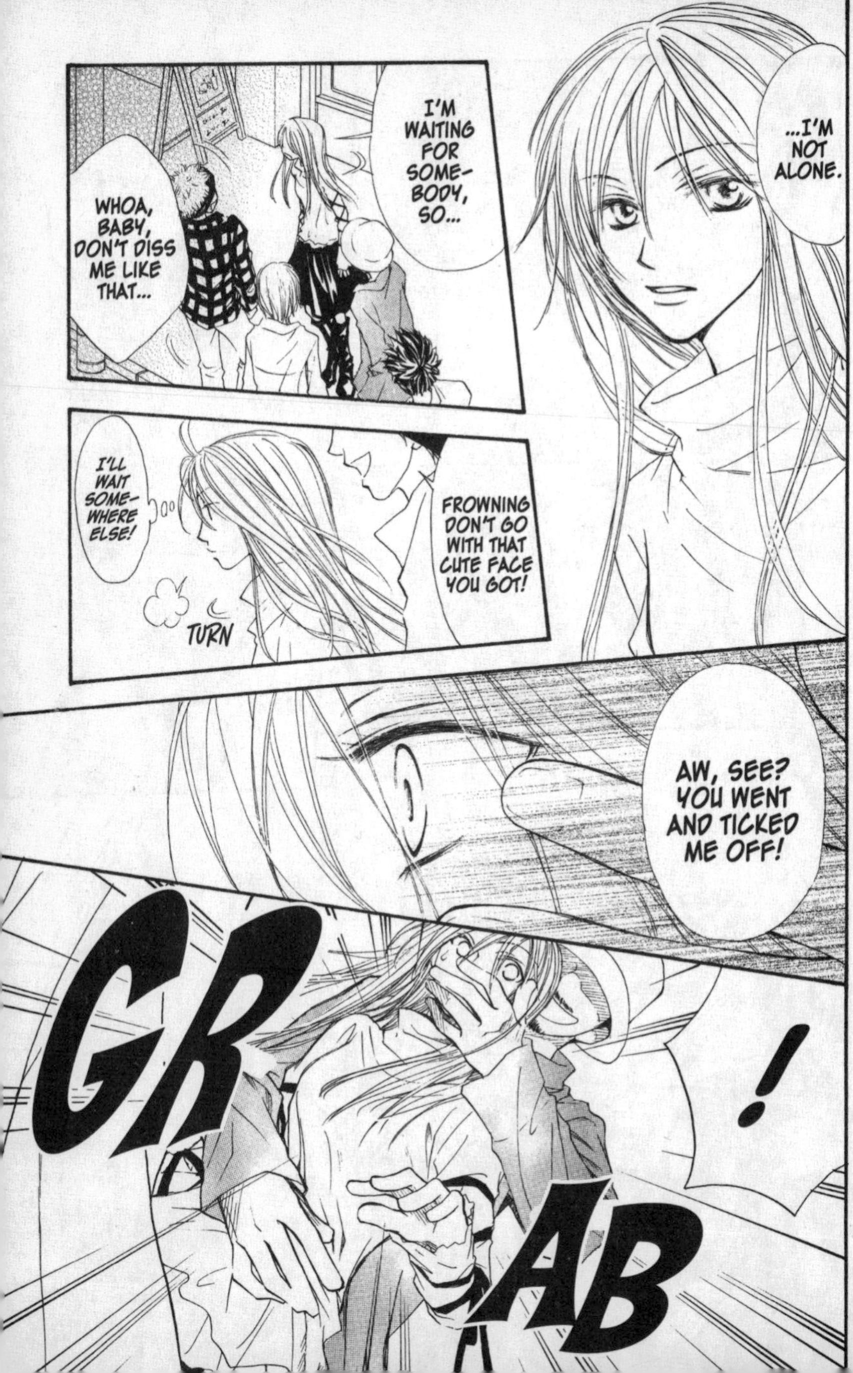
...I'M NOT ALONE.
I'M WAITING FOR SOMEBODY, SO...
WHOA, BABY, DON'T DISS ME LIKE THAT...
FROWNING DON'T GO WITH THAT CUTE FACE YOU GOT!
I'LL WAIT SOMEWHERE ELSE!
TURN
AW, SEE? YOU WENT AND TICKED ME OFF!
!
GRAB

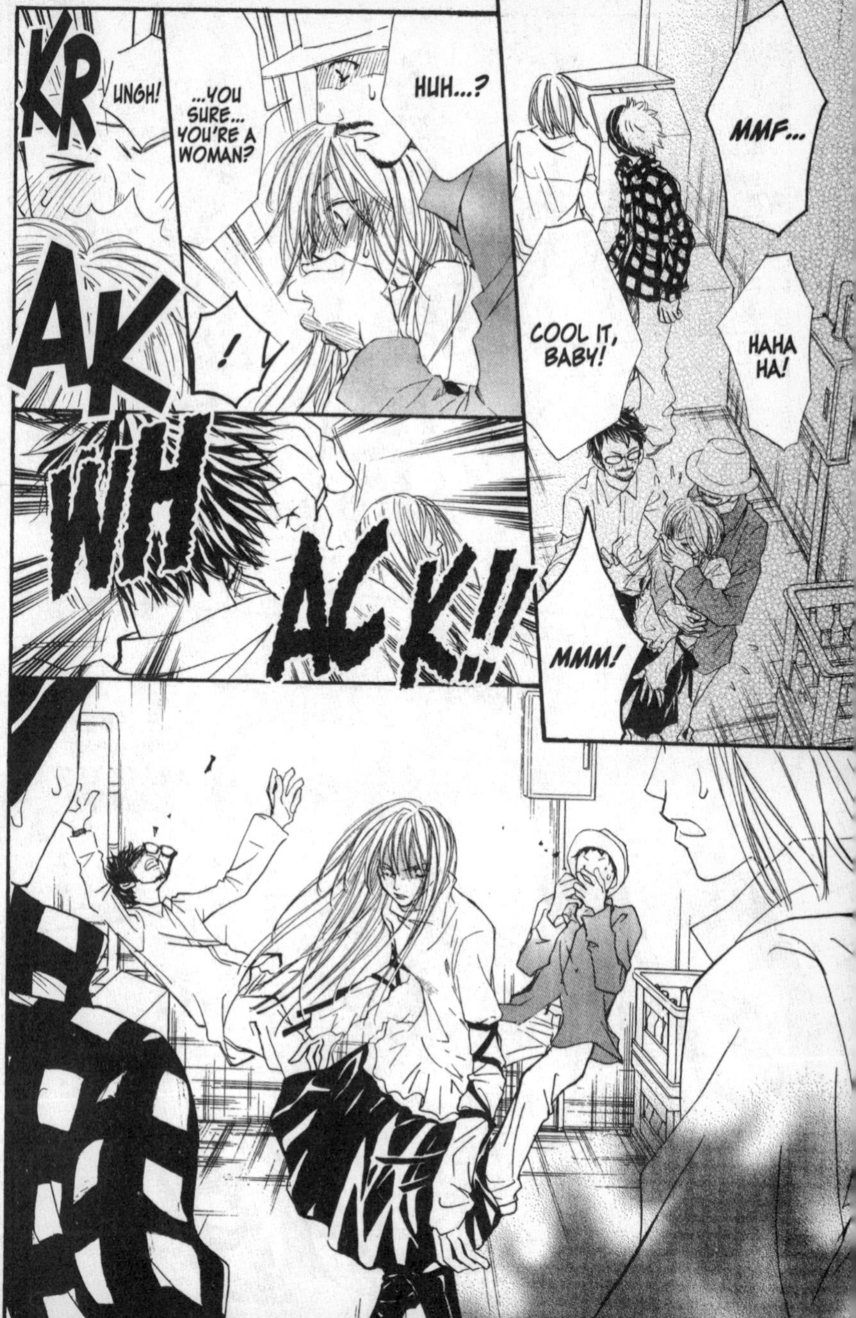
MMF...
HAHA HA!
COOL IT, BABY!
MMM!
HUH...?
...YOU SURE... YOU'RE A WOMAN?
!
UNGH!
KRAK
WHACK!!

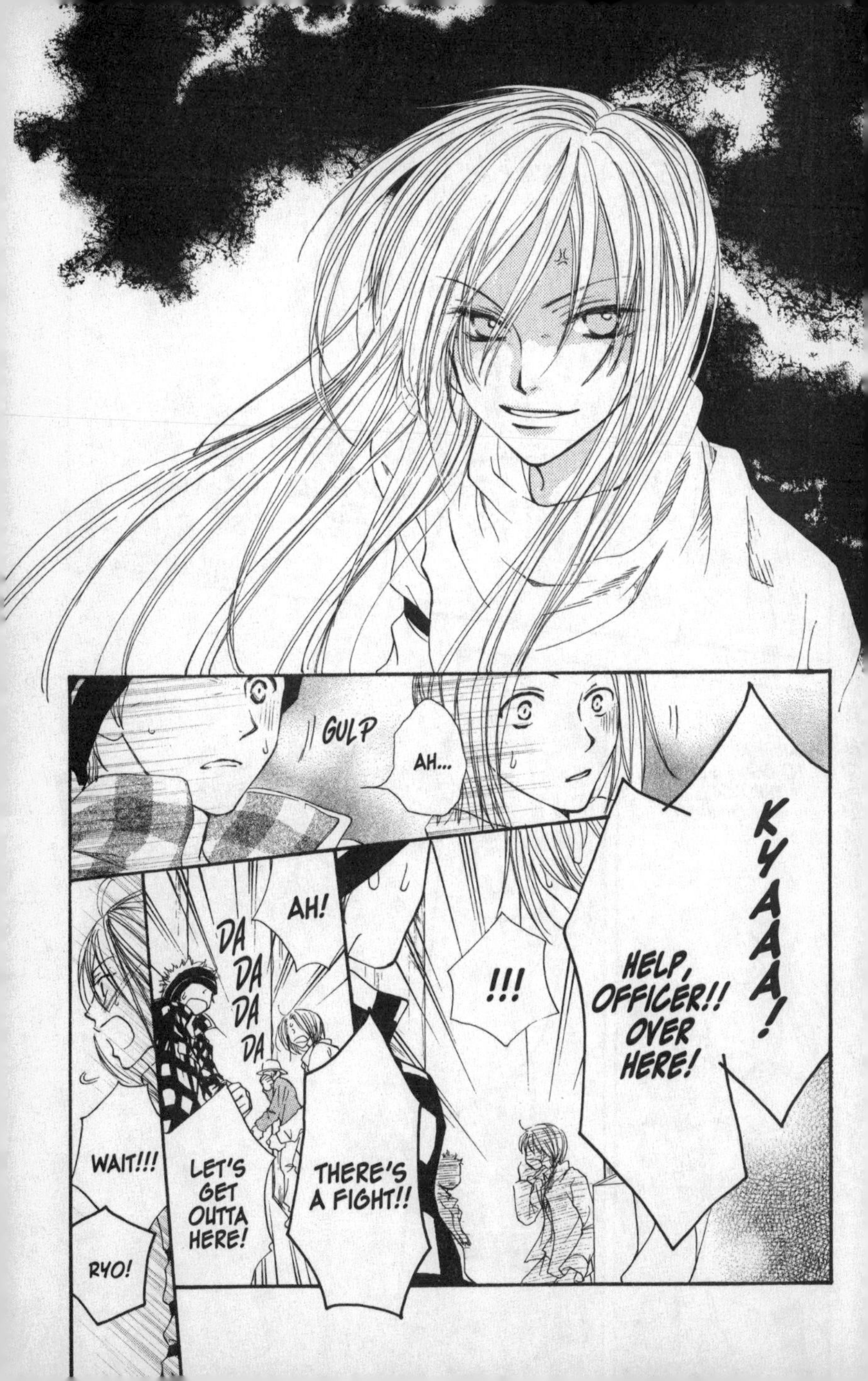
AH...
GULP
KYAAA!
HELP, OFFICER!! OVER HERE!
!!!
AH!
DA DA DA DA DA
THERE'S A FIGHT!!
LET'S GET OUTTA HERE!
WAIT!!!
RYO!

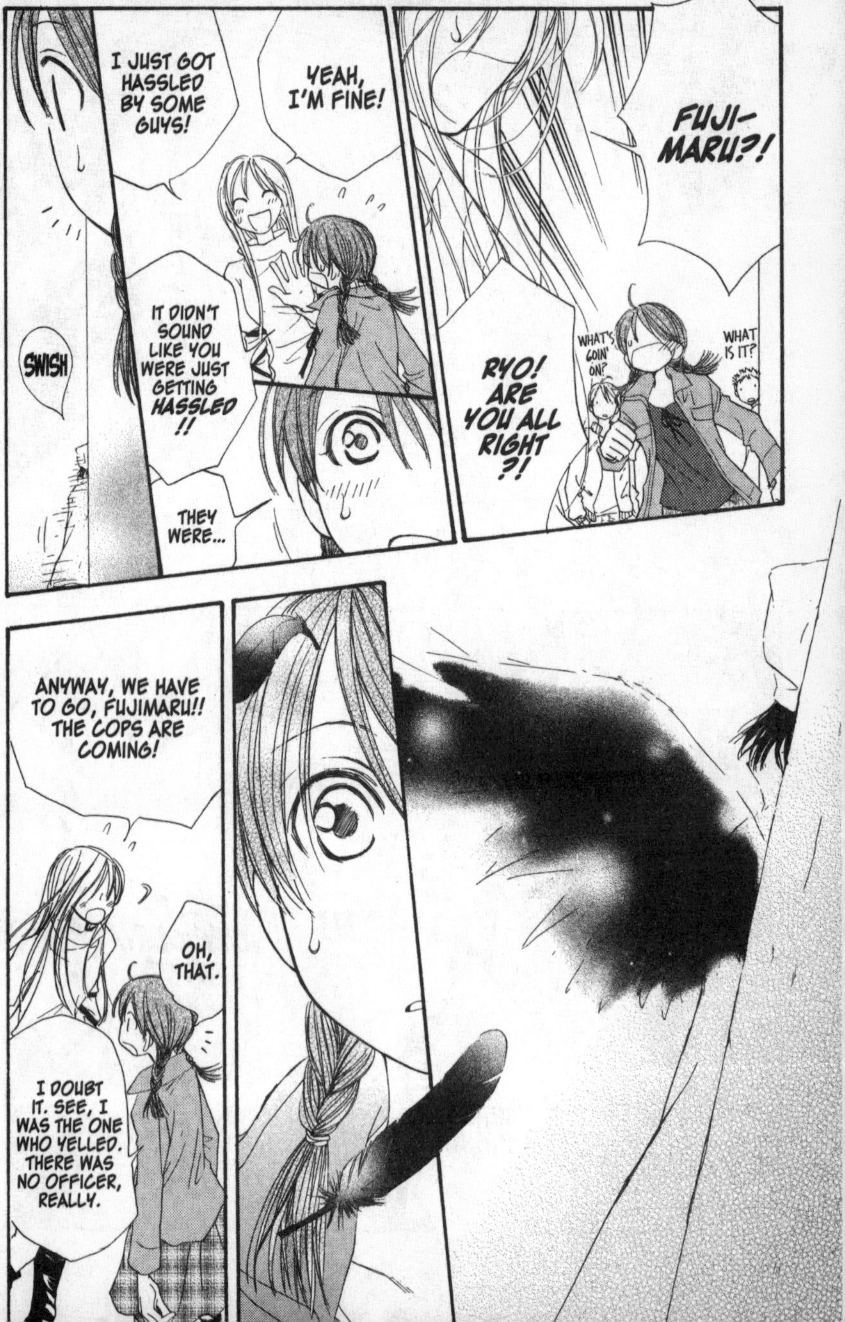
FUJI-MARU?!
RYO! ARE YOU ALL RIGHT?!
WHAT IS IT?
WHAT'S GOIN' ON?
YEAH, I'M FINE!
I JUST GOT HASSLED BY SOME GUYS!
IT DIDN'T SOUND LIKE YOU WERE JUST GETTING HASSLED!!
THEY WERE...
SWISH
ANYWAY, WE HAVE TO GO, FUJIMARU!! THE COPS ARE COMING!
OH, THAT.
I DOUBT IT. SEE, I WAS THE ONE WHO YELLED. THERE WAS NO OFFICER, REALLY.

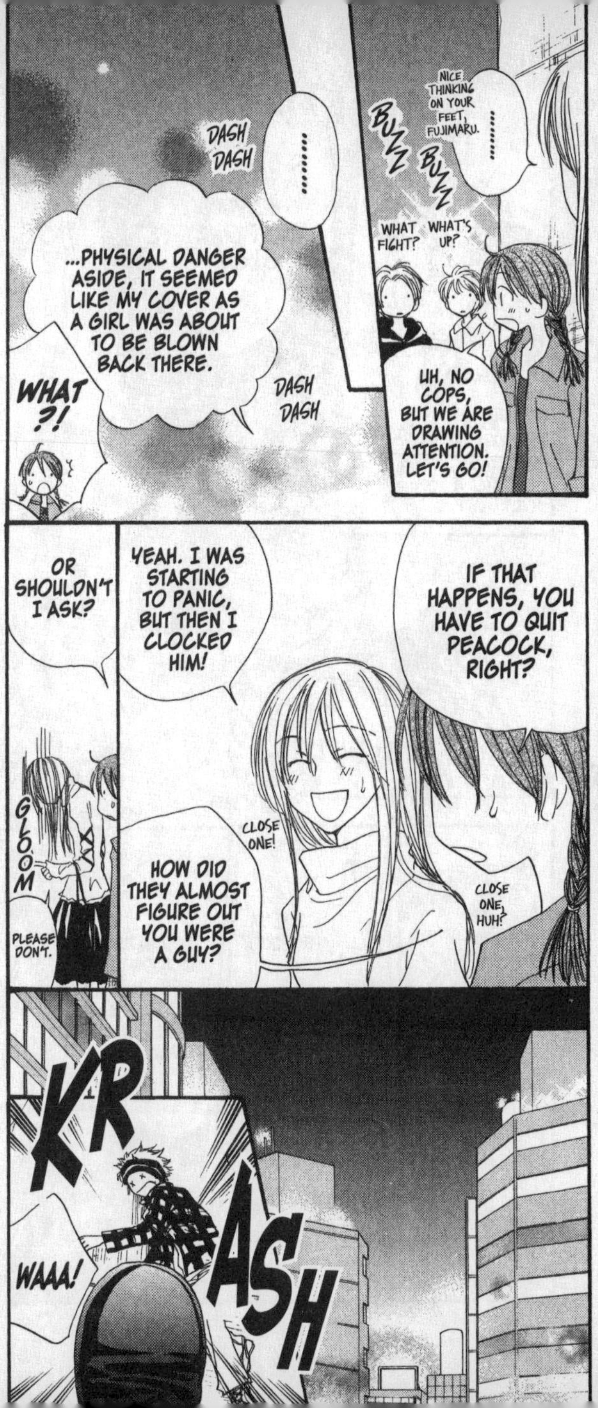
......
NICE THINKING ON YOUR FEET, FUJIMARU.
BUZZ BUZZ
WHAT'S UP?
WHAT FIGHT?
UH, NO COPS, BUT WE ARE DRAWING ATTENTION. LET'S GO!
......
DASH DASH
...PHYSICAL DANGER ASIDE, IT SEEMED LIKE MY COVER AS A GIRL WAS ABOUT TO BE BLOWN BACK THERE.
DASH DASH
WHAT?!
IF THAT HAPPENS, YOU HAVE TO QUIT PEACOCK, RIGHT?
YEAH. I WAS STARTING TO PANIC, BUT THEN I CLOCKED HIM!
CLOSE ONE, HUH?
CLOSE ONE!
HOW DID THEY ALMOST FIGURE OUT YOU WERE A GUY?
OR SHOULDN'T I ASK?
GLOOM
PLEASE DON'T.
KRASH
WAAA!

1/4 Sakura Mail

part 8

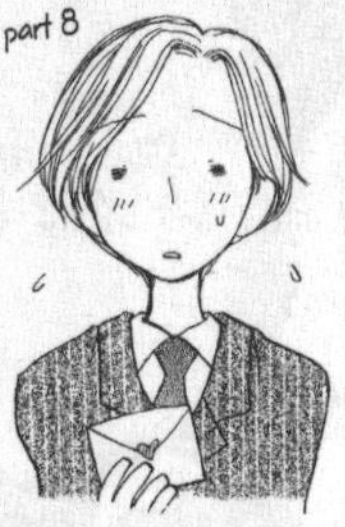

I've said it before, but I love plays. Since starting work on this series, I've been going to lots of plays, concerts and other live events. You know, it just isn't the same thing if you don't see them live; you would miss out on the live **atmosphere.** For me, I like going to these live events for the content as well as that extra feeling. And I hope that amorphous feeling successfully translates into this series here. ...Aw, who am I fooling? Okay, researching for this series has been more pleasure than research...still, I learned a lot, like seeing shows **live** is a powerful experience...

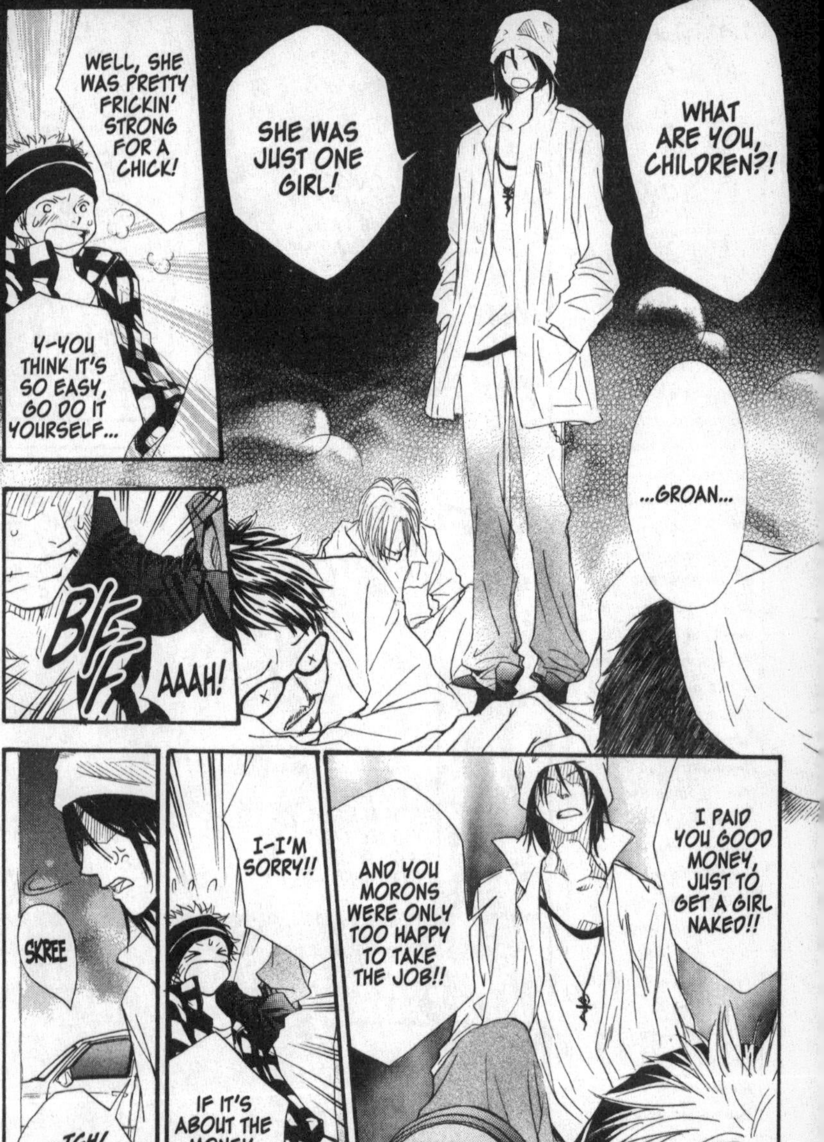
WHAT ARE YOU, CHILDREN?!
SHE WAS JUST ONE GIRL!
...GROAN...
WELL, SHE WAS PRETTY FRICKIN' STRONG FOR A CHICK!
Y-YOU THINK IT'S SO EASY, GO DO IT YOURSELF...
BIFF
AAAH!
I PAID YOU GOOD MONEY, JUST TO GET A GIRL NAKED!!
AND YOU MORONS WERE ONLY TOO HAPPY TO TAKE THE JOB!!
I-I'M SORRY!!
IF IT'S ABOUT THE MONEY, WE'LL GIVE IT BACK...
SKREE
...TCH! YOU'RE ALL WORTHLESS!

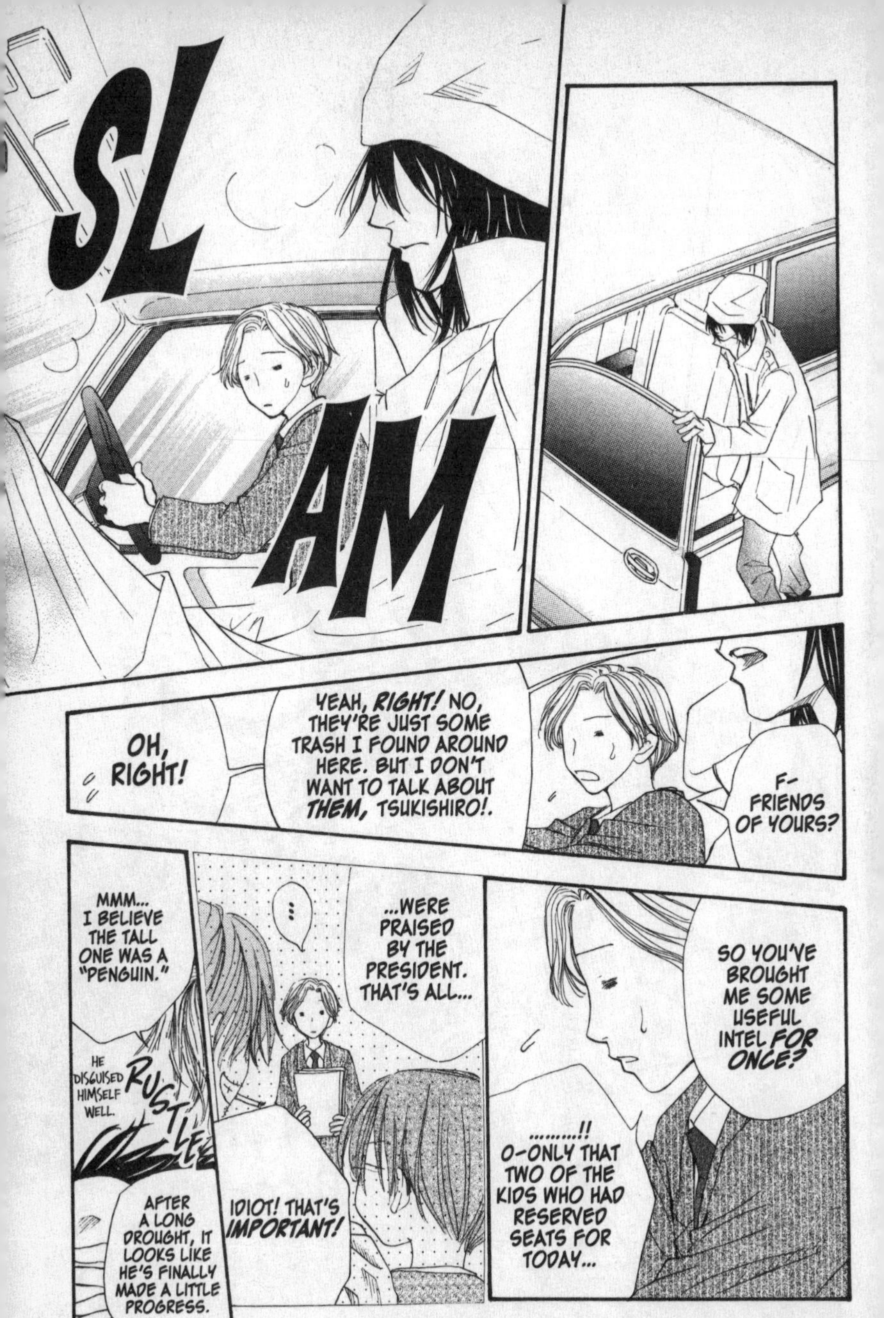
SLAM
F-FRIENDS OF YOURS?
YEAH, RIGHT! NO, THEY'RE JUST SOME TRASH I FOUND AROUND HERE. BUT I DON'T WANT TO TALK ABOUT THEM, TSUKISHIRO!.
OH, RIGHT!
SO YOU'VE BROUGHT ME SOME USEFUL INTEL FOR ONCE?
.........!! O-ONLY THAT TWO OF THE KIDS WHO HAD RESERVED SEATS FOR TODAY...
...WERE PRAISED BY THE PRESIDENT. THAT'S ALL...
...
IDIOT! THAT'S IMPORTANT!
MMM... I BELIEVE THE TALL ONE WAS A "PENGUIN."
HE DISGUISED HIMSELF WELL.
RUSTLE
AFTER A LONG DROUGHT, IT LOOKS LIKE HE'S FINALLY MADE A LITTLE PROGRESS.

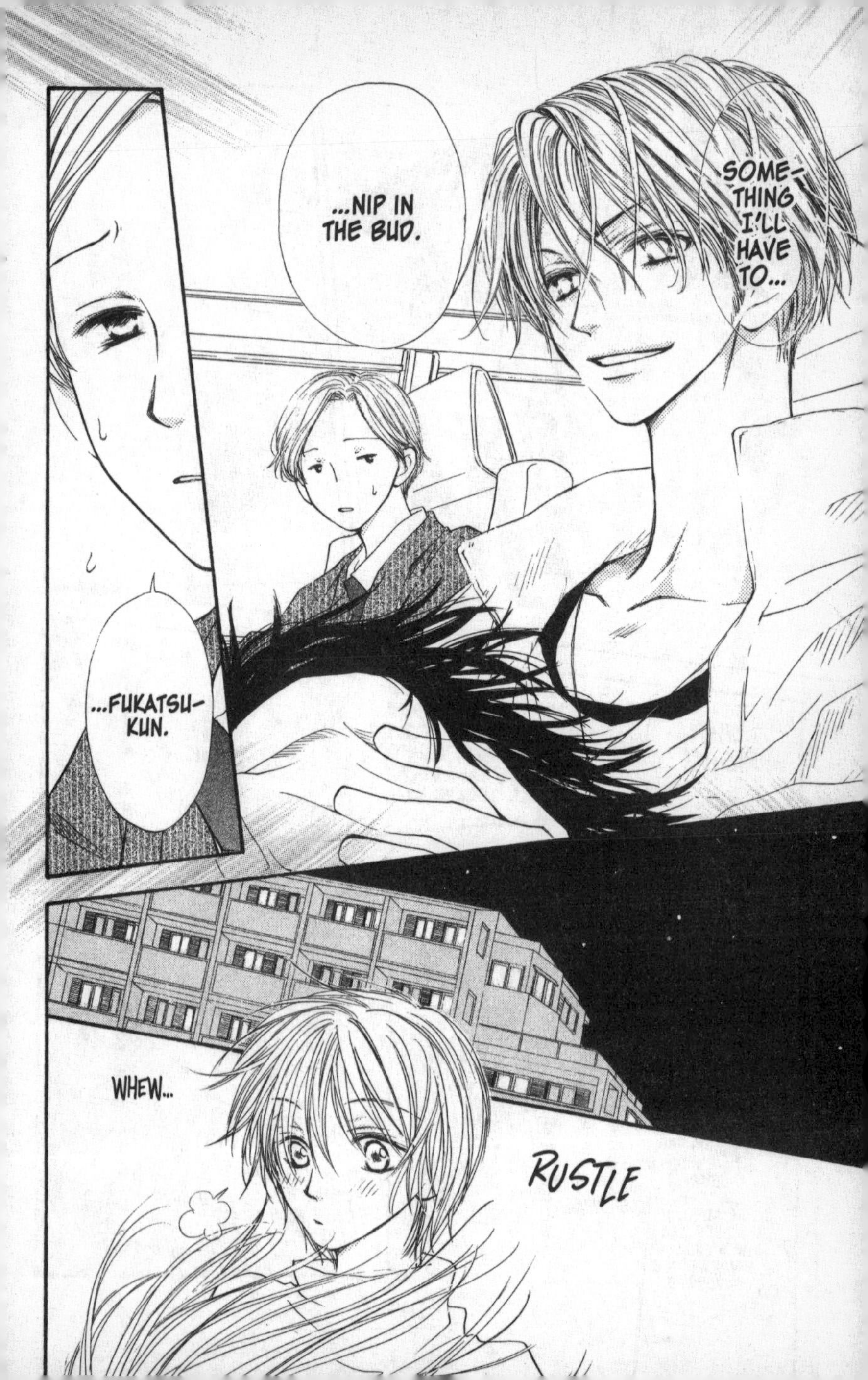
SOME-THING I'LL HAVE TO...
...NIP IN THE BUD.
...FUKATSU-KUN.
WHEW...
RUSTLE

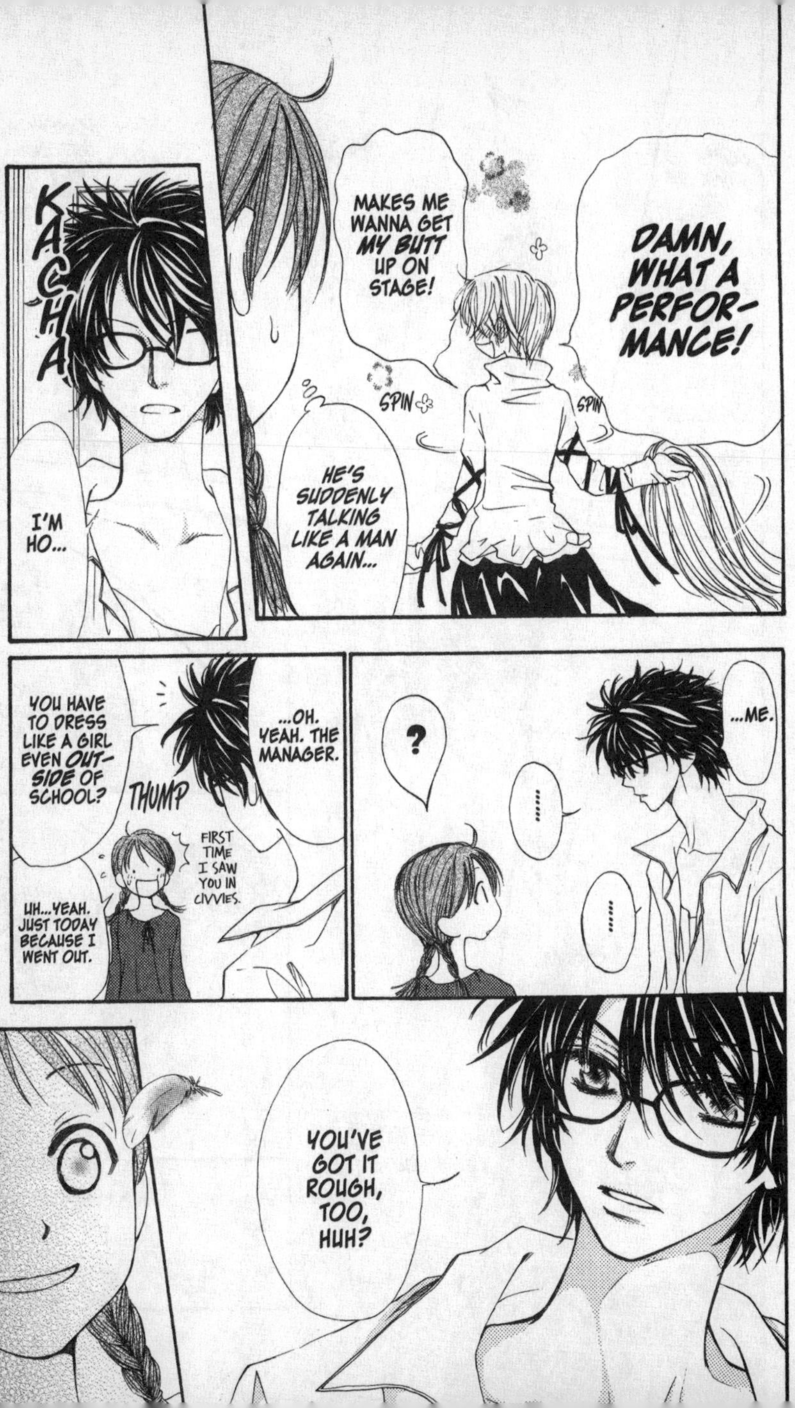
DAMN, WHAT A PERFORMANCE!
MAKES ME WANNA GET MY BUTT UP ON STAGE!
SPIN
SPIN
HE'S SUDDENLY TALKING LIKE A MAN AGAIN...
KACHA
I'M HO...
...ME.
......
?
......
...OH. YEAH. THE MANAGER.
YOU HAVE TO DRESS LIKE A GIRL EVEN OUTSIDE OF SCHOOL?
THUMP
FIRST TIME I SAW YOU IN CIVVIES.
UH...YEAH. JUST TODAY BECAUSE I WENT OUT.
YOU'VE GOT IT ROUGH, TOO, HUH?

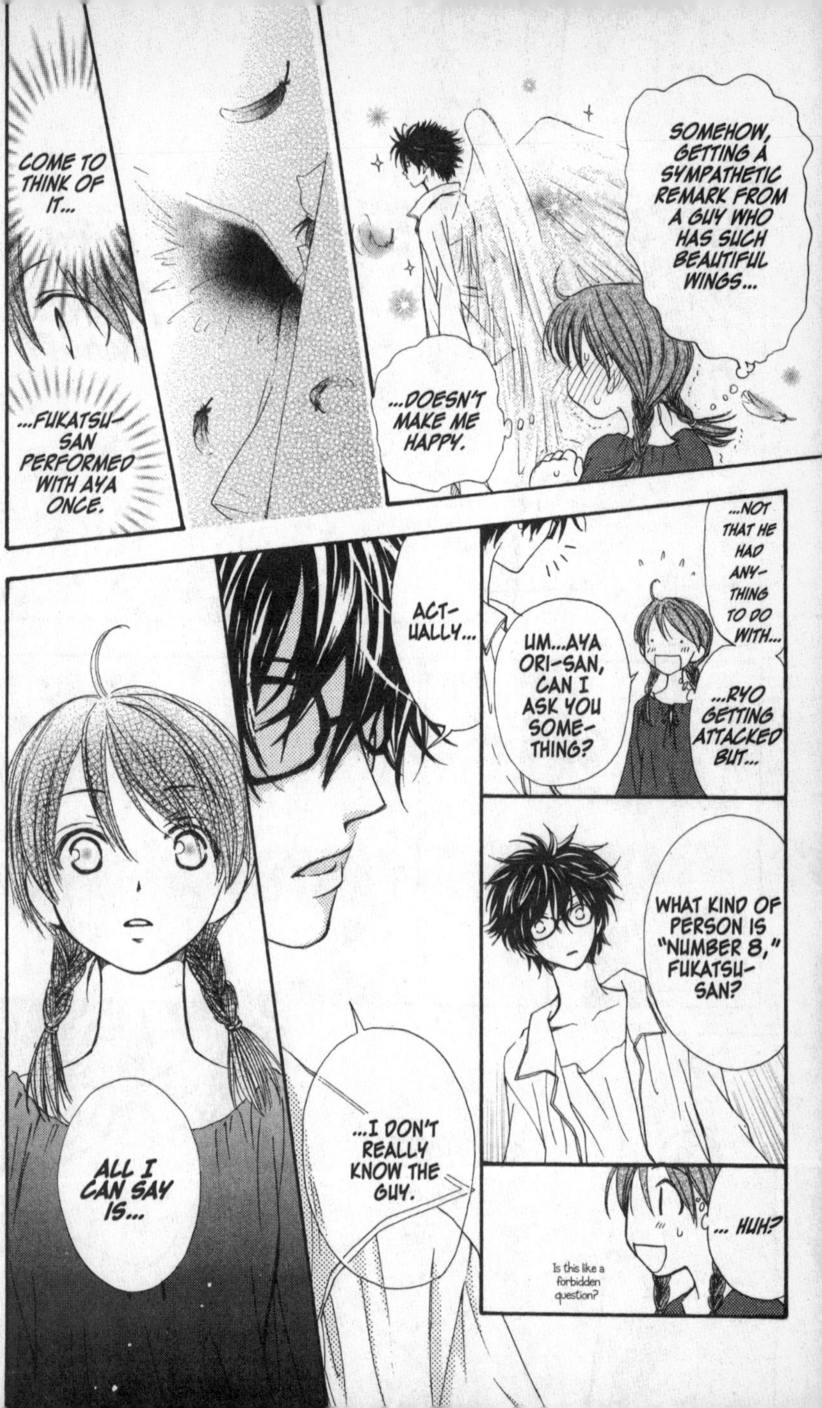
SOMEHOW, GETTING A SYMPATHETIC REMARK FROM A GUY WHO HAS SUCH BEAUTIFUL WINGS...
...DOESN'T MAKE ME HAPPY.
COME TO THINK OF IT...
...FUKATSU-SAN PERFORMED WITH AYA ONCE.
...NOT THAT HE HAD ANYTHING TO DO WITH...
...RYO GETTING ATTACKED BUT...
UM...AYA ORI-SAN, CAN I ASK YOU SOMETHING?
WHAT KIND OF PERSON IS "NUMBER 8," FUKATSU-SAN?
... HUH?
Is this like a forbidden question?
ACTUALLY...
...I DON'T REALLY KNOW THE GUY.
ALL I CAN SAY IS...

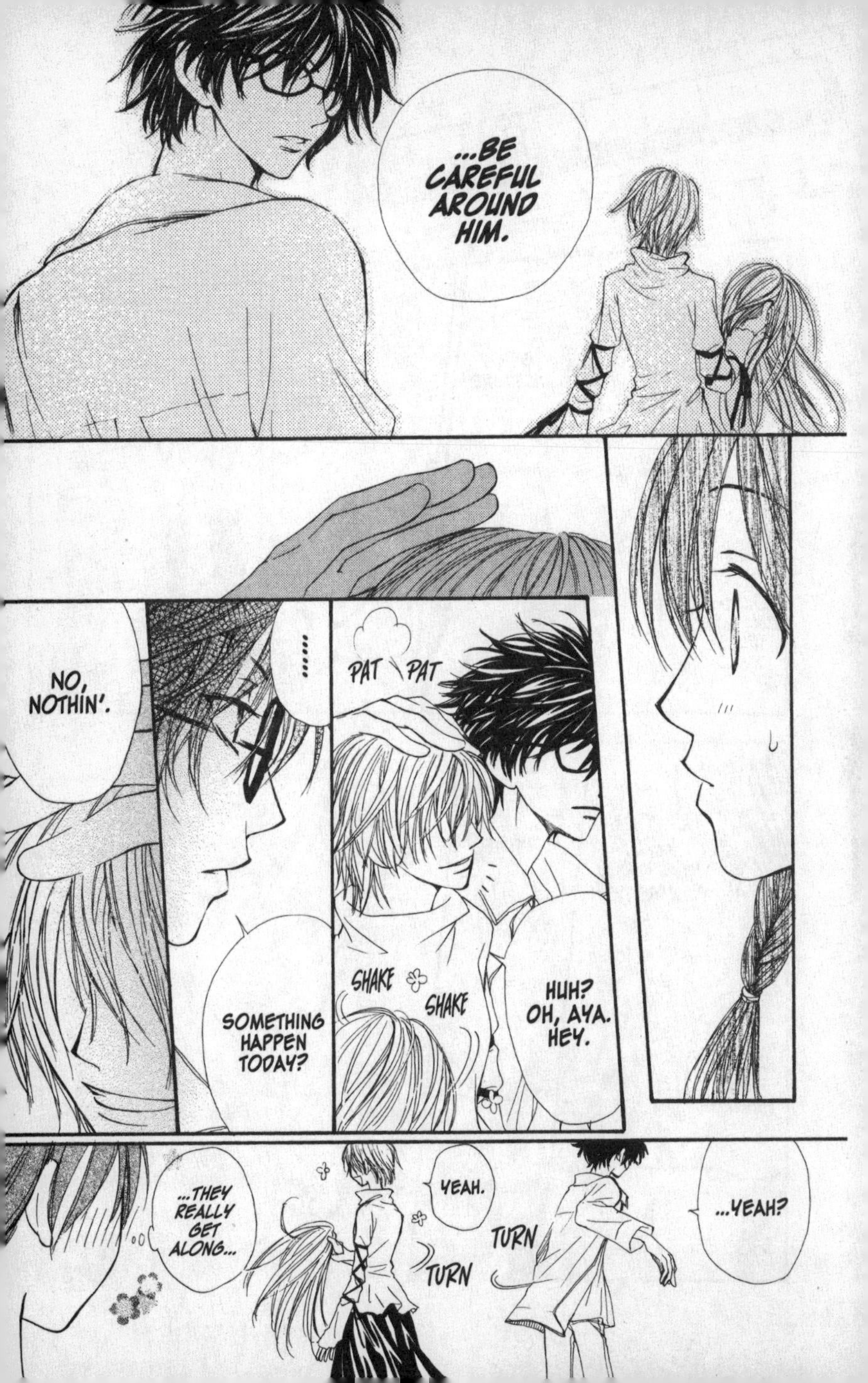
...BE CAREFUL AROUND HIM.
PAT PAT
HUH? OH, AYA. HEY.
SHAKE SHAKE
......
SOMETHING HAPPEN TODAY?
NO, NOTHIN'.
...YEAH?
TURN
TURN
YEAH.
...THEY REALLY GET ALONG...

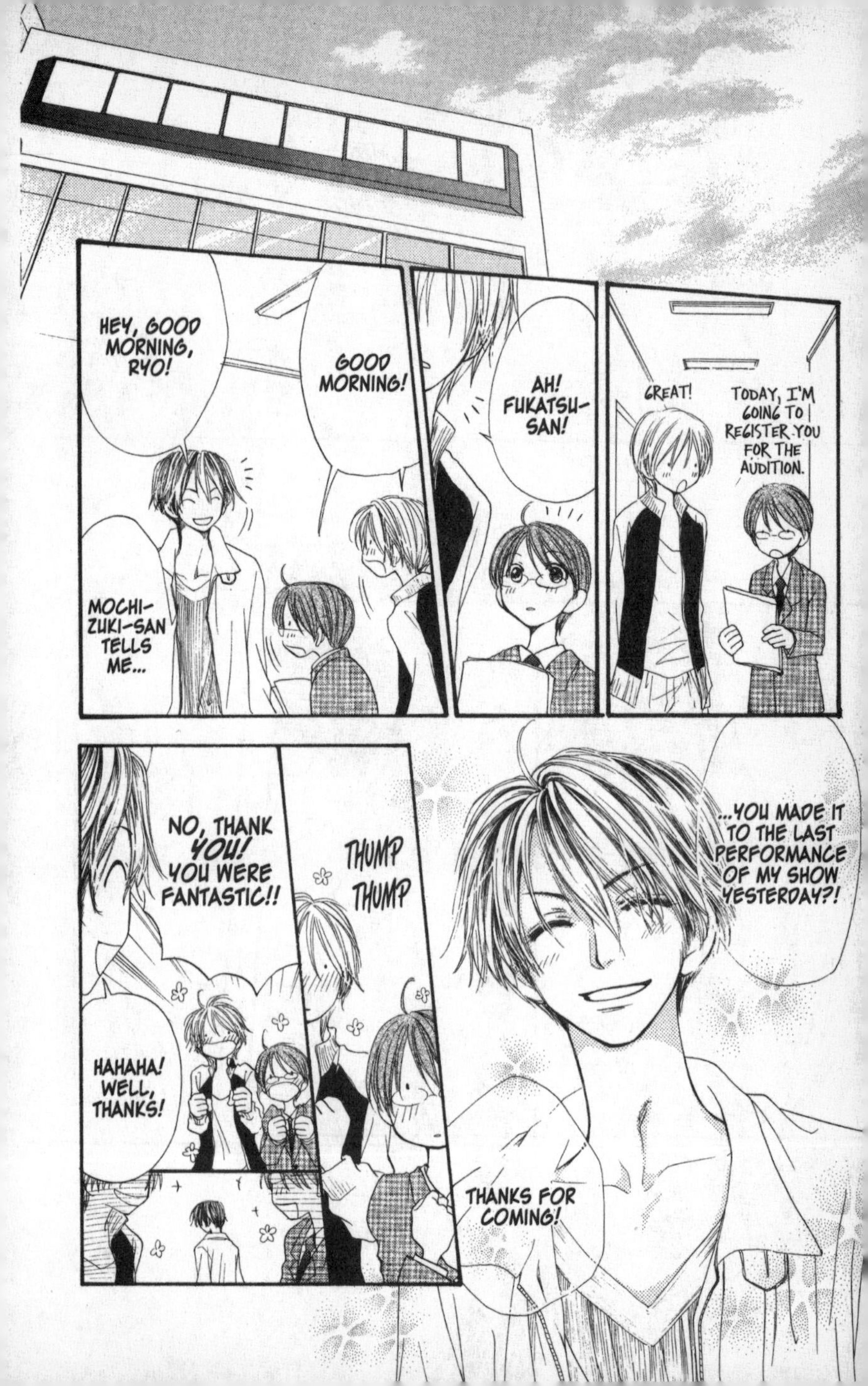
TODAY, I'M GOING TO REGISTER YOU FOR THE AUDITION.
GREAT!
AH! FUKATSU-SAN!
GOOD MORNING!
HEY, GOOD MORNING, RYO!
MOCHIZUKI-SAN TELLS ME...
...YOU MADE IT TO THE LAST PERFORMANCE OF MY SHOW YESTERDAY?!
THANKS FOR COMING!
THUMP THUMP
NO, THANK *YOU!* YOU WERE FANTASTIC!!
HAHAHA! WELL, THANKS!

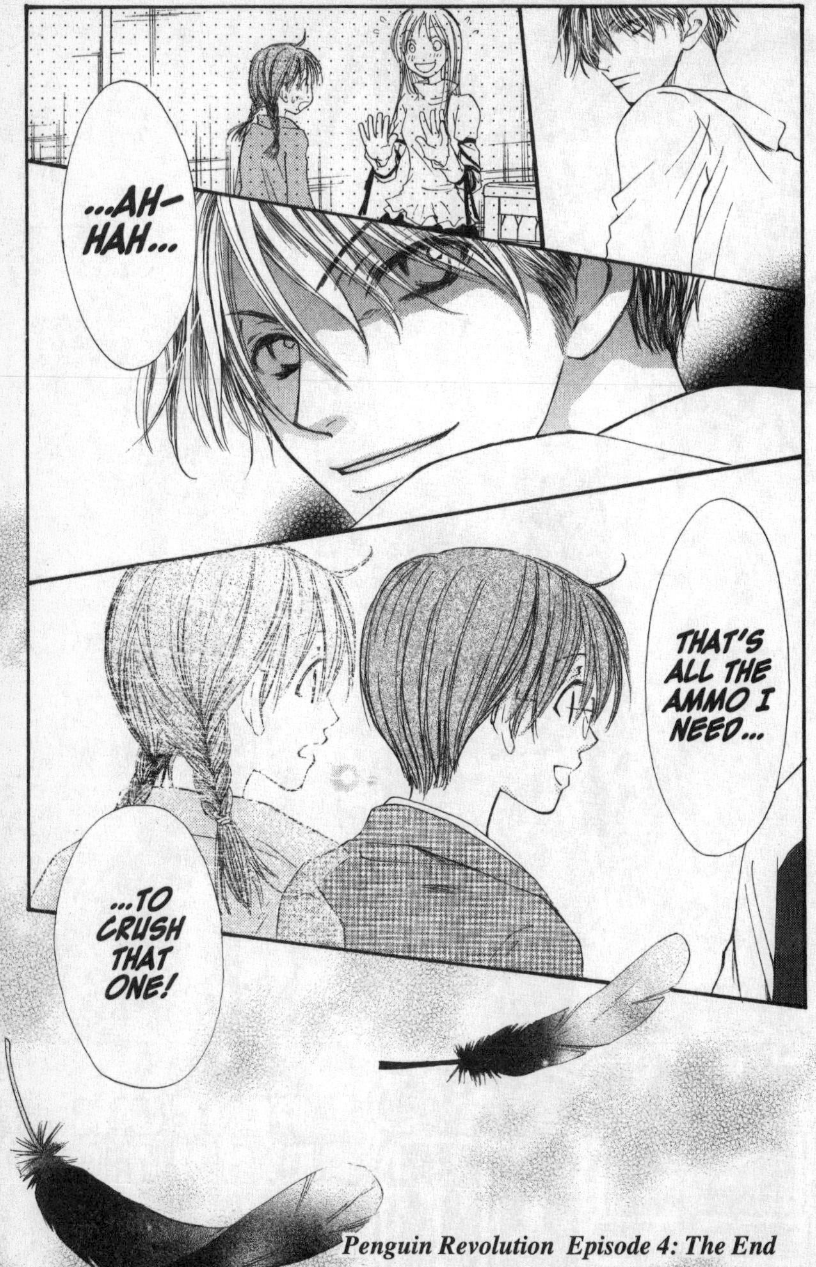
...AH-HAH...
THAT'S ALL THE AMMO I NEED...
...TO CRUSH THAT ONE!

Penguin Revolution Episode 4: The End

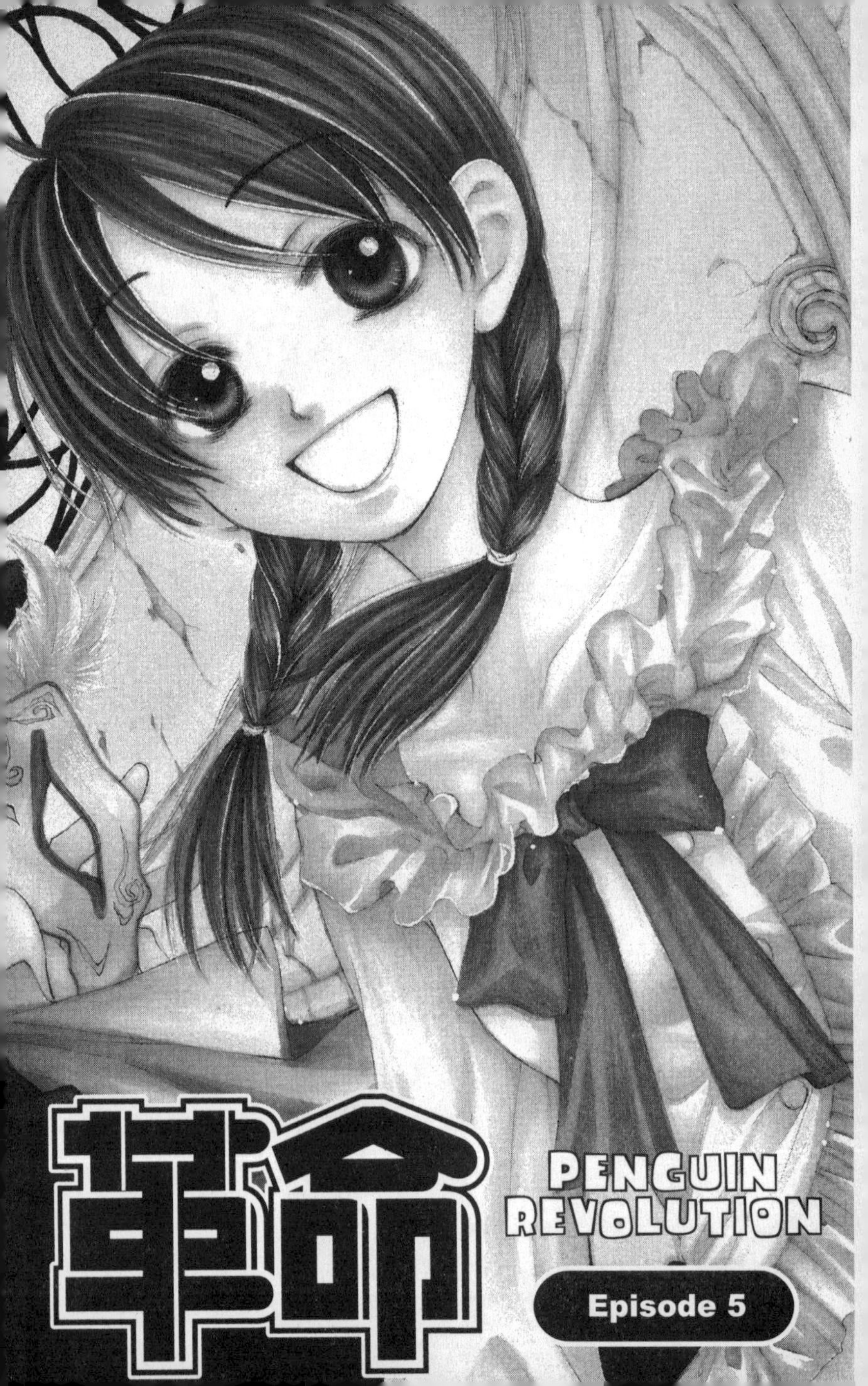

ペンギン革命
PENGUIN REVOLUTION
Episode 5

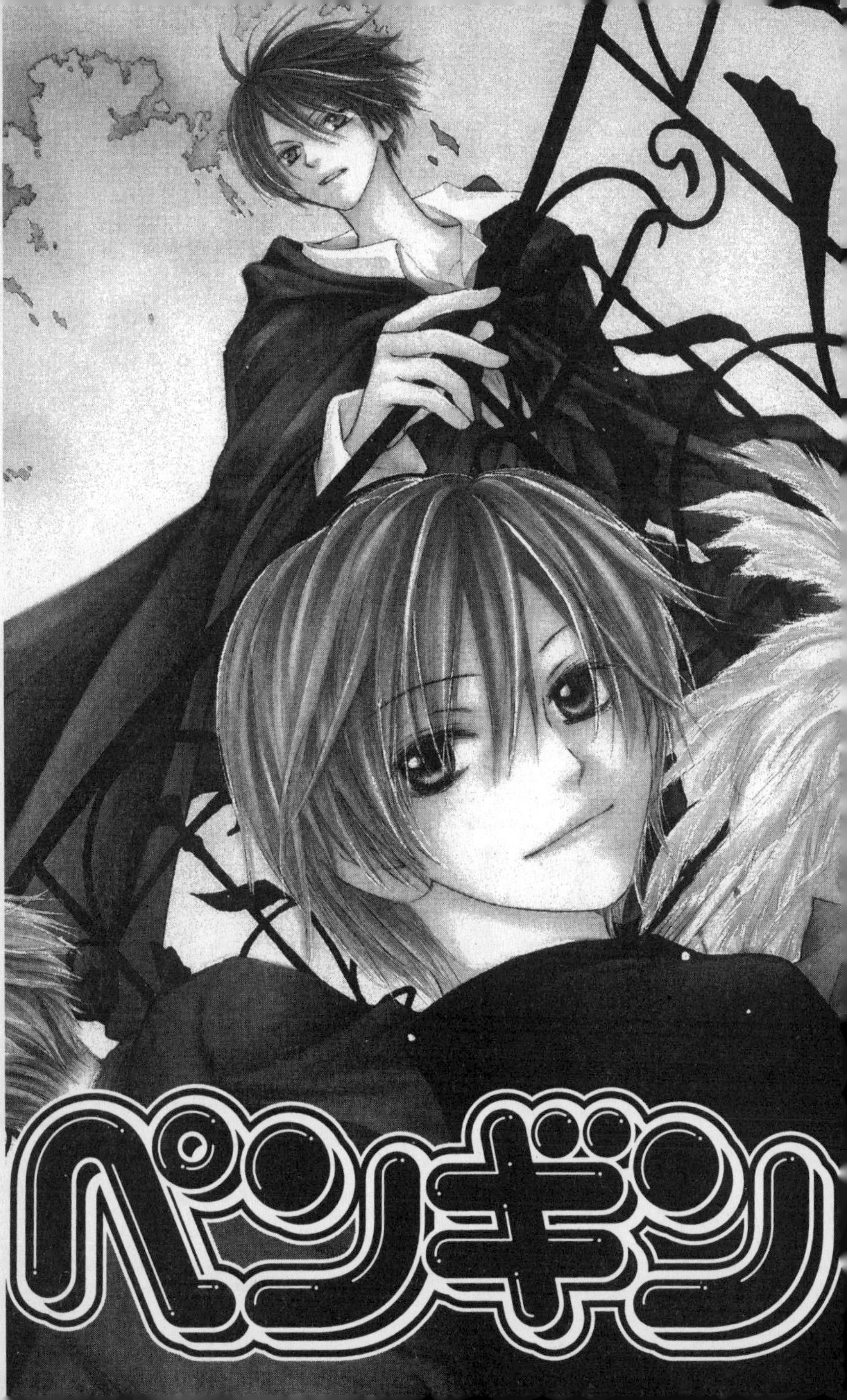
ペンギン

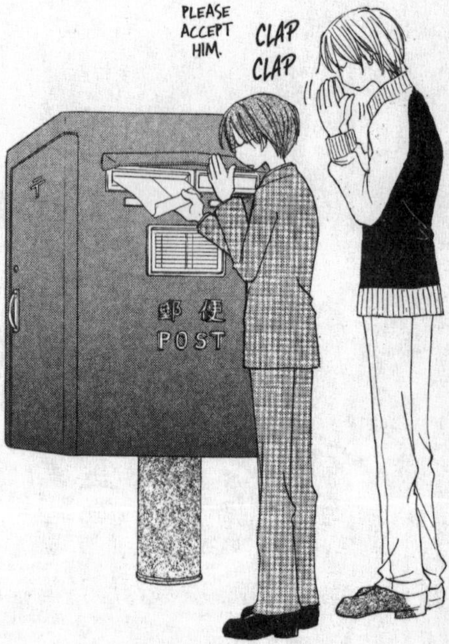
CLAP CLAP
PLEASE ACCEPT HIM.
〒
郵便
POST

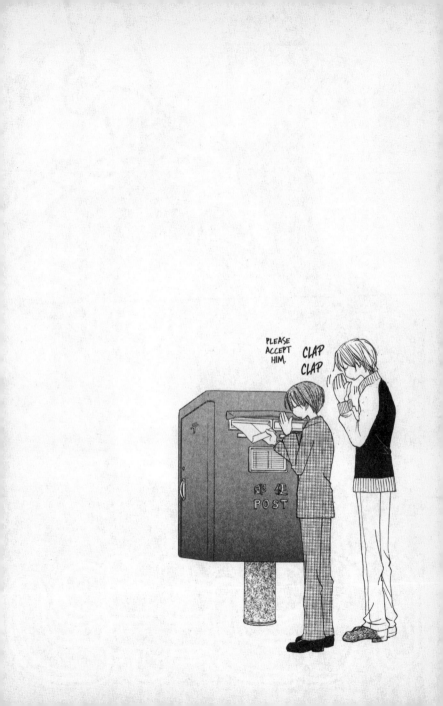

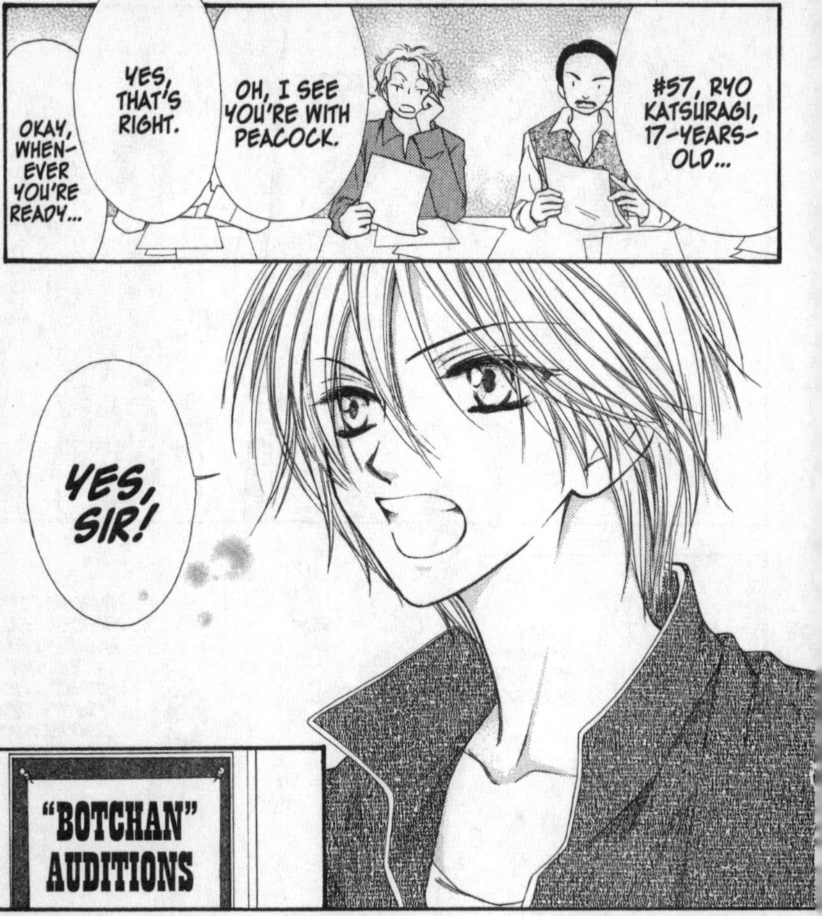
#57, RYO KATSURAGI, 17-YEARS-OLD...
OH, I SEE YOU'RE WITH PEACOCK.
YES, THAT'S RIGHT.
OKAY, WHENEVER YOU'RE READY...
YES, SIR!
"BOTCHAN" AUDITIONS

1/4 Sakura Mail

part 9

Ryo's challenges to get on the stage begins in this episode. it took me a long time to think of the play within this story, but I took a cue from Fukatsu-san's image to finally come up with "Botchan." I read Natsume Soseki's book, "Botchan", when I was a child but upon rereading it recently, I was surprised to find that "Botchan" and "Madonna" hardly had any scenes together!! My memory must have been influenced by the movie version. Interesting, in more ways than one.

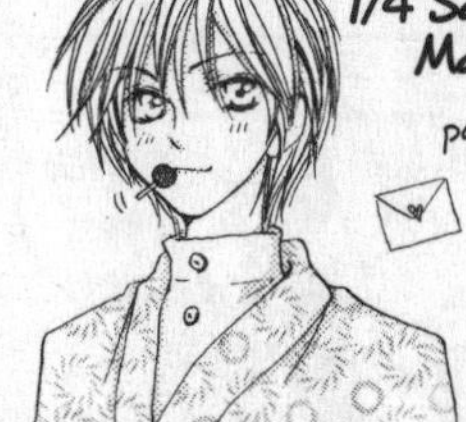

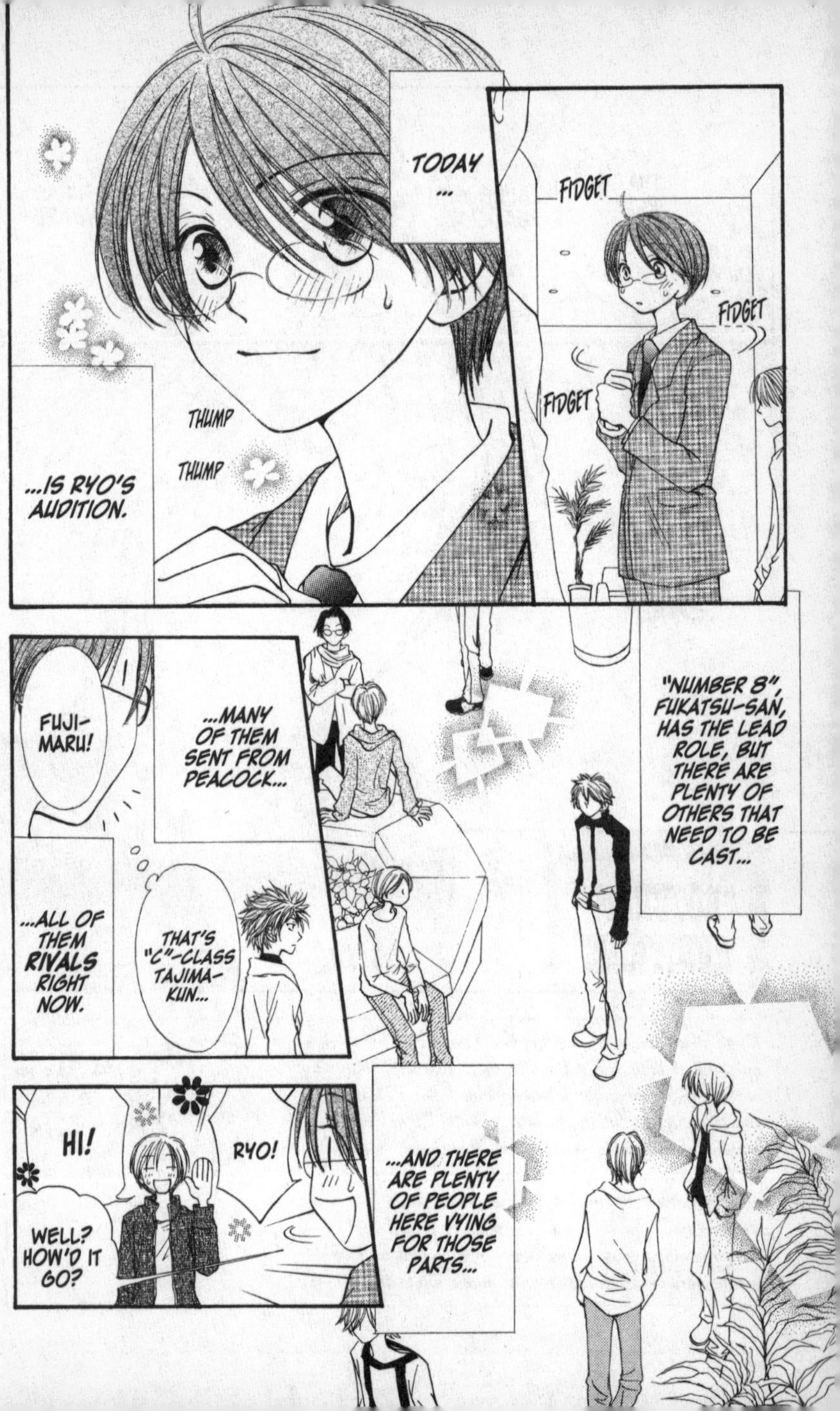
TODAY ...
FIDGET
FIDGET
FIDGET
THUMP
THUMP
...IS RYO'S AUDITION.
"NUMBER 8", FUKATSU-SAN, HAS THE LEAD ROLE, BUT THERE ARE PLENTY OF OTHERS THAT NEED TO BE CAST...
...AND THERE ARE PLENTY OF PEOPLE HERE VYING FOR THOSE PARTS...
...MANY OF THEM SENT FROM PEACOCK...
FUJI-MARU!
THAT'S "C"-CLASS TAJIMA-KUN...
...ALL OF THEM RIVALS RIGHT NOW.
RYO!
HI!
WELL? HOW'D IT GO?

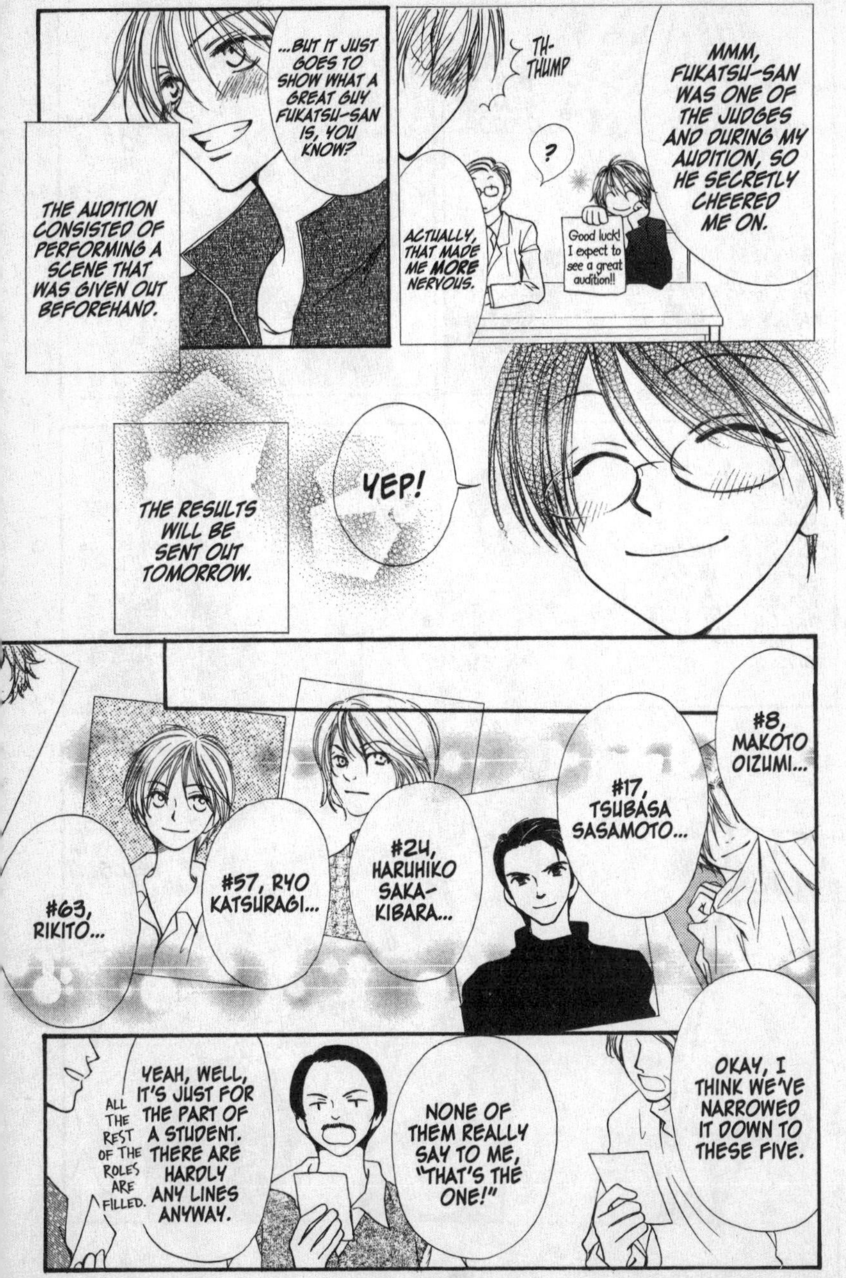
MMM, FUKATSU-SAN WAS ONE OF THE JUDGES AND DURING MY AUDITION, SO HE SECRETLY CHEERED ME ON.
TH-THUMP
?
Good luck! I expect to see a great audition!!
ACTUALLY, THAT MADE ME MORE NERVOUS.
...BUT IT JUST GOES TO SHOW WHAT A GREAT GUY FUKATSU-SAN IS, YOU KNOW?
THE AUDITION CONSISTED OF PERFORMING A SCENE THAT WAS GIVEN OUT BEFOREHAND.
YEP!
THE RESULTS WILL BE SENT OUT TOMORROW.
#8, MAKOTO OIZUMI...
#17, TSUBASA SASAMOTO...
#24, HARUHIKO SAKA-KIBARA...
#57, RYO KATSURAGI...
#63, RIKITO...
OKAY, I THINK WE'VE NARROWED IT DOWN TO THESE FIVE.
NONE OF THEM REALLY SAY TO ME, "THAT'S THE ONE!"
YEAH, WELL, IT'S JUST FOR THE PART OF A STUDENT. THERE ARE HARDLY ANY LINES ANYWAY.
ALL THE REST OF THE ROLES ARE FILLED.

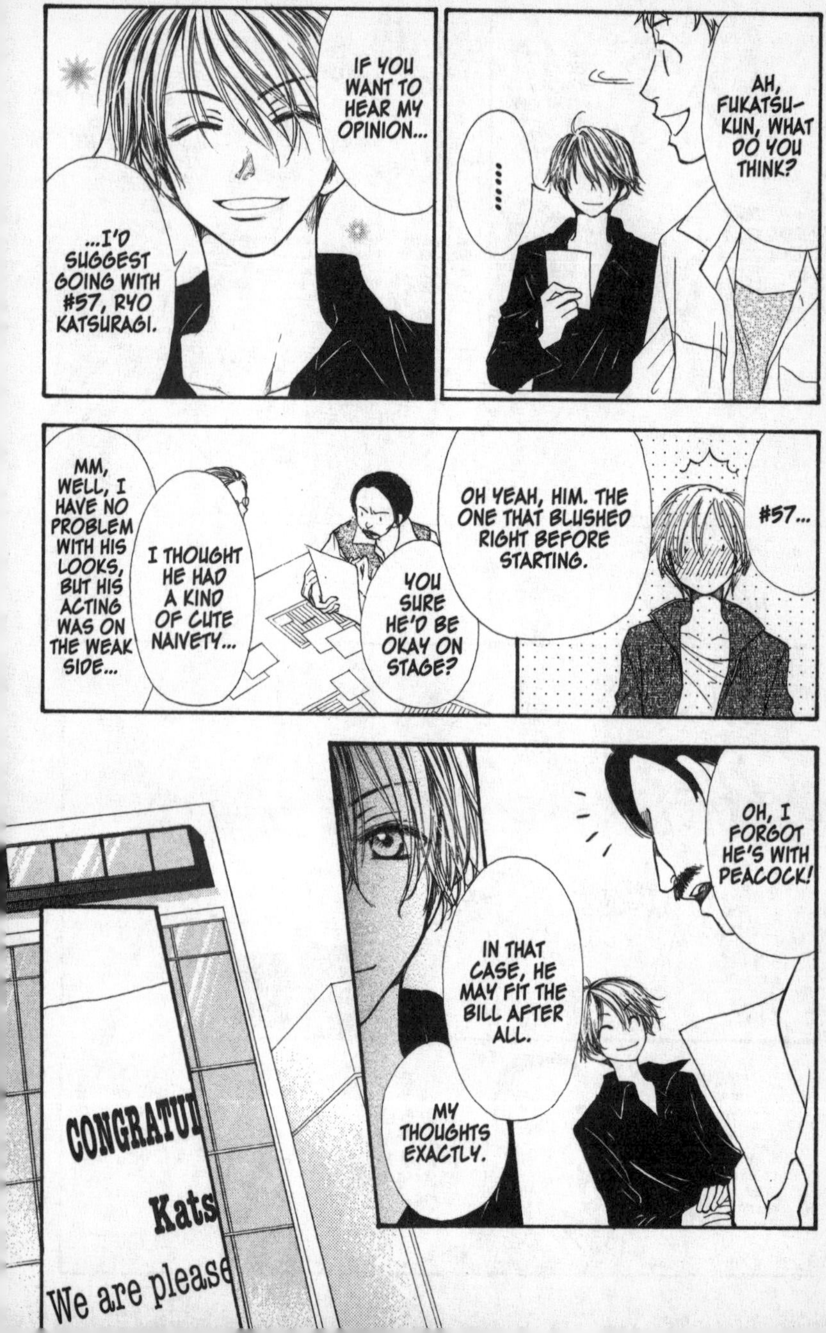
AH, FUKATSU-KUN, WHAT DO YOU THINK?
......
IF YOU WANT TO HEAR MY OPINION...
...I'D SUGGEST GOING WITH #57, RYO KATSURAGI.
#57...
OH YEAH, HIM. THE ONE THAT BLUSHED RIGHT BEFORE STARTING.
YOU SURE HE'D BE OKAY ON STAGE?
I THOUGHT HE HAD A KIND OF CUTE NAIVETY...
MM, WELL, I HAVE NO PROBLEM WITH HIS LOOKS, BUT HIS ACTING WAS ON THE WEAK SIDE...
OH, I FORGOT HE'S WITH PEACOCK!
IN THAT CASE, HE MAY FIT THE BILL AFTER ALL.
MY THOUGHTS EXACTLY.
CONGRATU
Kats
We are please

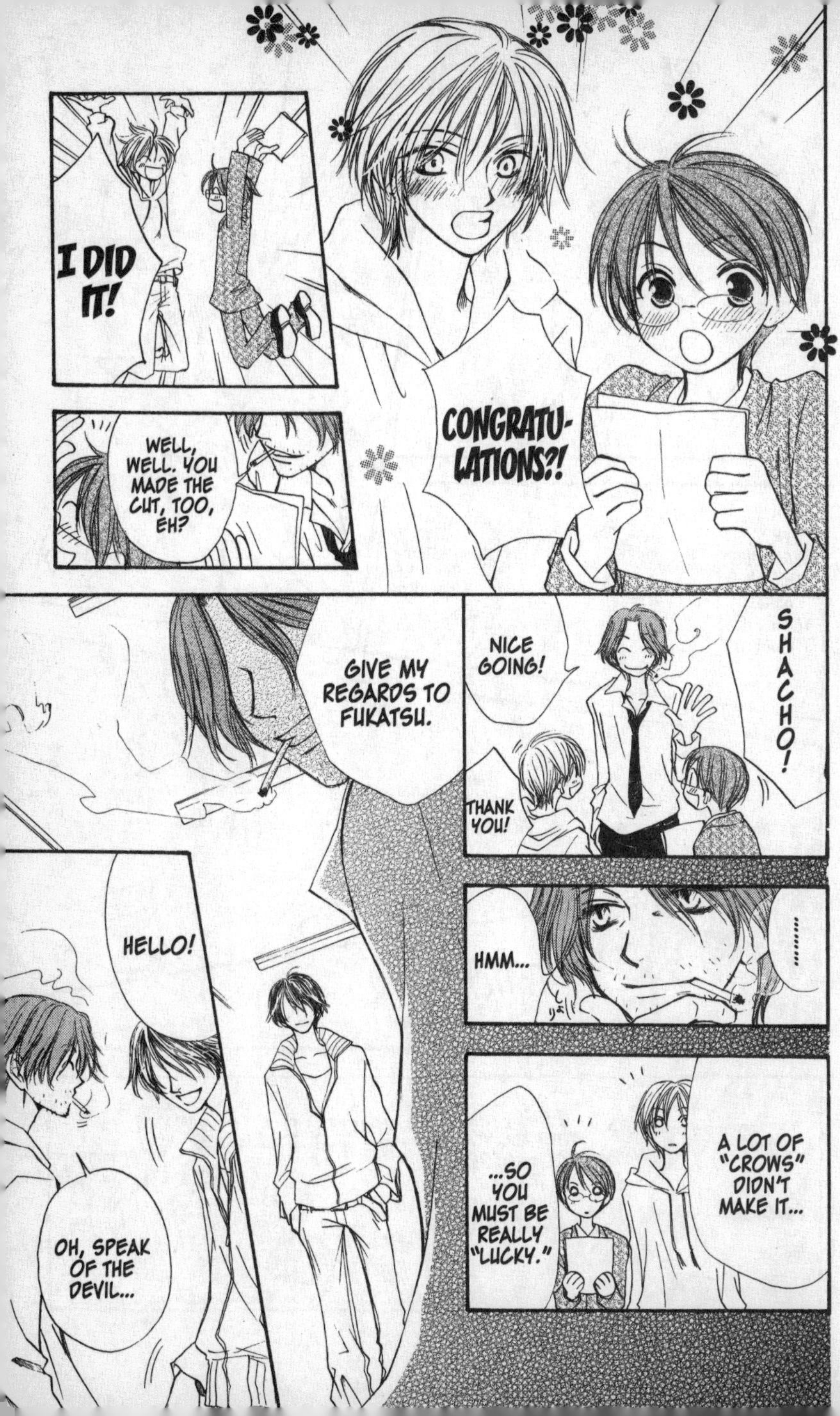
CONGRATU-LATIONS?!
I DID IT!
WELL, WELL. YOU MADE THE CUT, TOO, EH?
SHACHO!
NICE GOING!
THANK YOU!
GIVE MY REGARDS TO FUKATSU.
......
HMM...
A LOT OF "CROWS" DIDN'T MAKE IT...
...SO YOU MUST BE REALLY "LUCKY."
HELLO!
OH, SPEAK OF THE DEVIL...

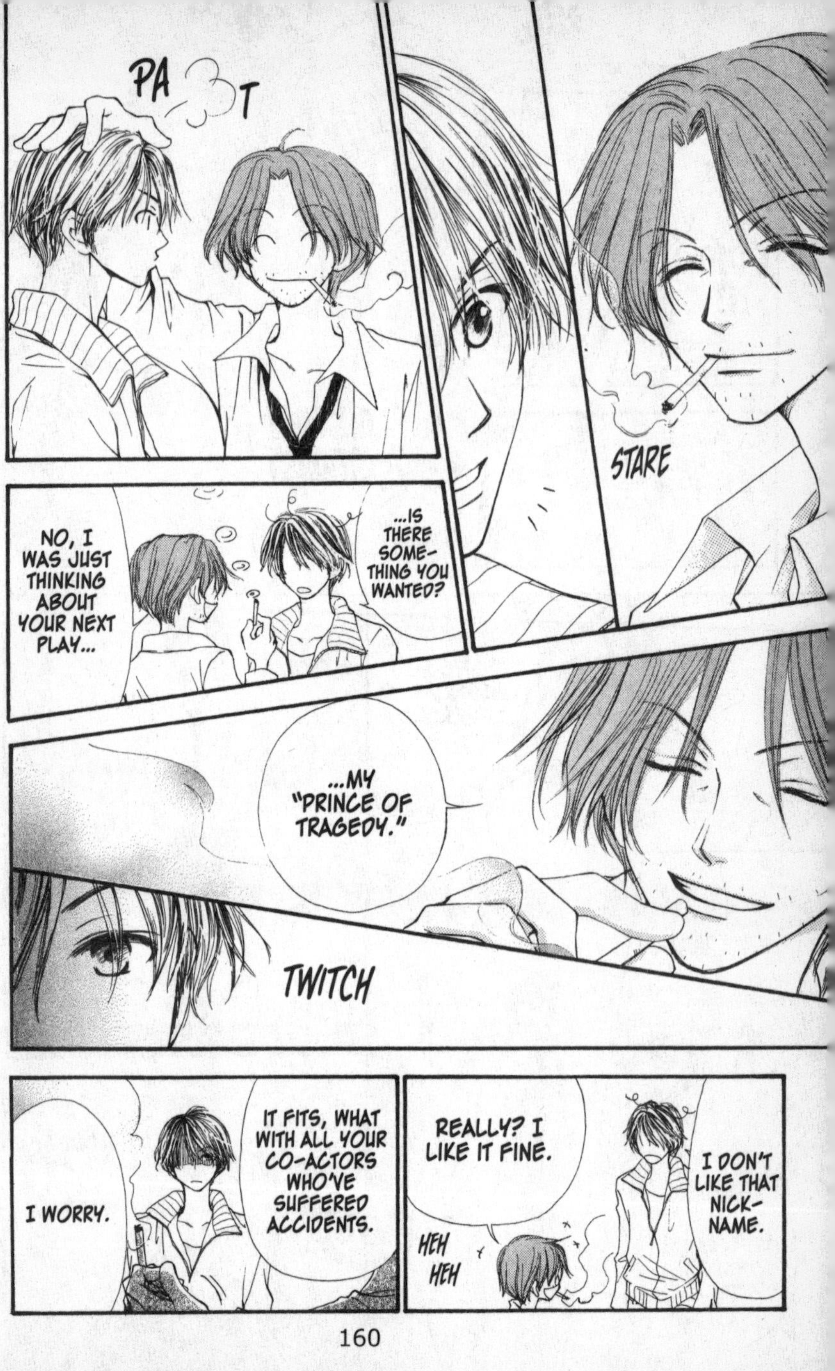
STARE
PAT
...IS THERE SOMETHING YOU WANTED?
NO, I WAS JUST THINKING ABOUT YOUR NEXT PLAY...
...MY "PRINCE OF TRAGEDY."
TWITCH
I DON'T LIKE THAT NICK-NAME.
REALLY? I LIKE IT FINE.
HEH HEH
IT FITS, WHAT WITH ALL YOUR CO-ACTORS WHO'VE SUFFERED ACCIDENTS.
I WORRY.

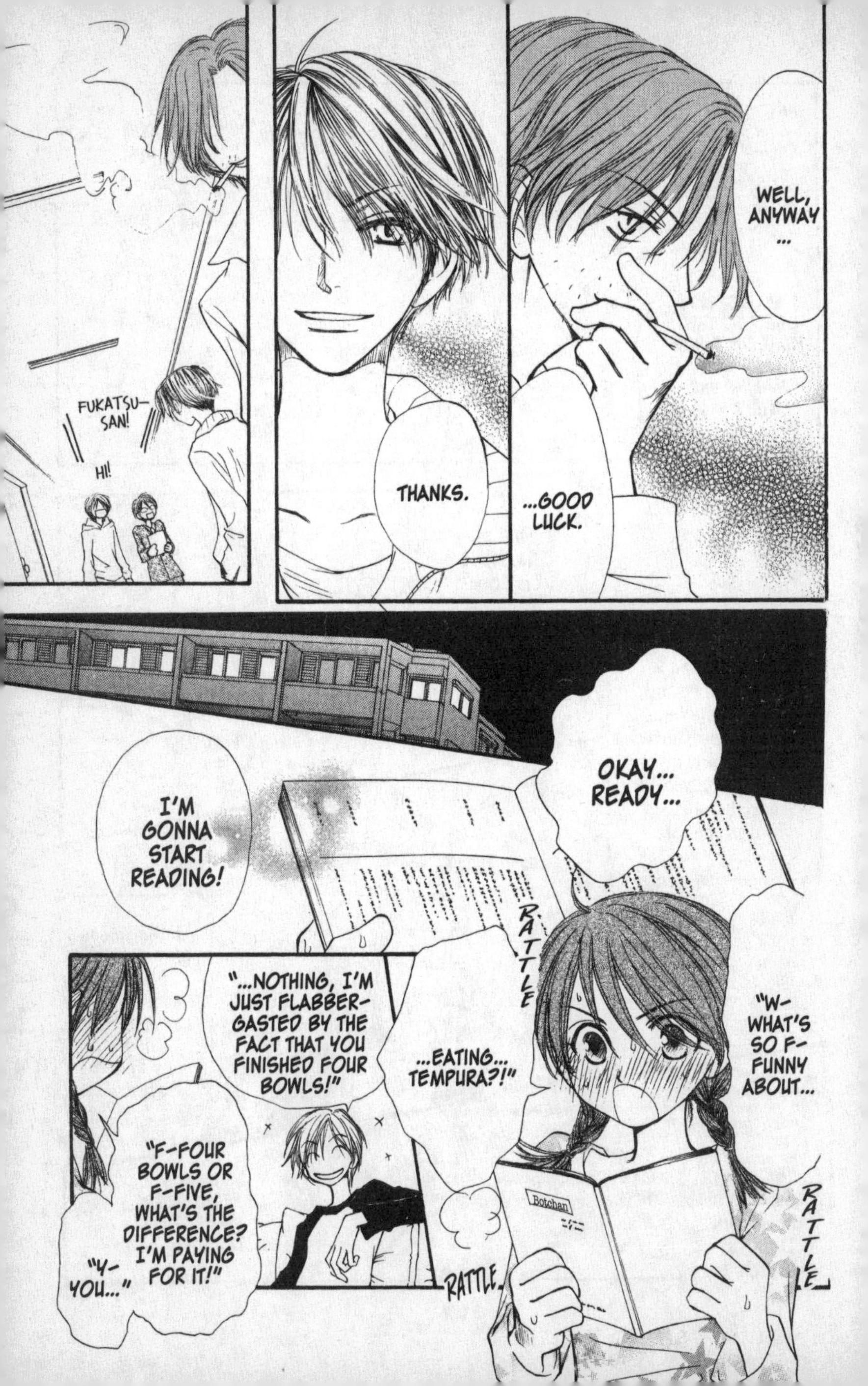
WELL, ANYWAY ...
...GOOD LUCK.
THANKS.
FUKATSU-SAN!
HI!
OKAY... READY...
I'M GONNA START READING!
RATTLE
"W-WHAT'S SO F-FUNNY ABOUT...
...EATING... TEMPURA?!"
Botchan
RATTLE
"...NOTHING, I'M JUST FLABBER-GASTED BY THE FACT THAT YOU FINISHED FOUR BOWLS!"
"F-FOUR BOWLS OR F-FIVE, WHAT'S THE DIFFERENCE? I'M PAYING FOR IT!"
"Y-YOU..."
RATTLE

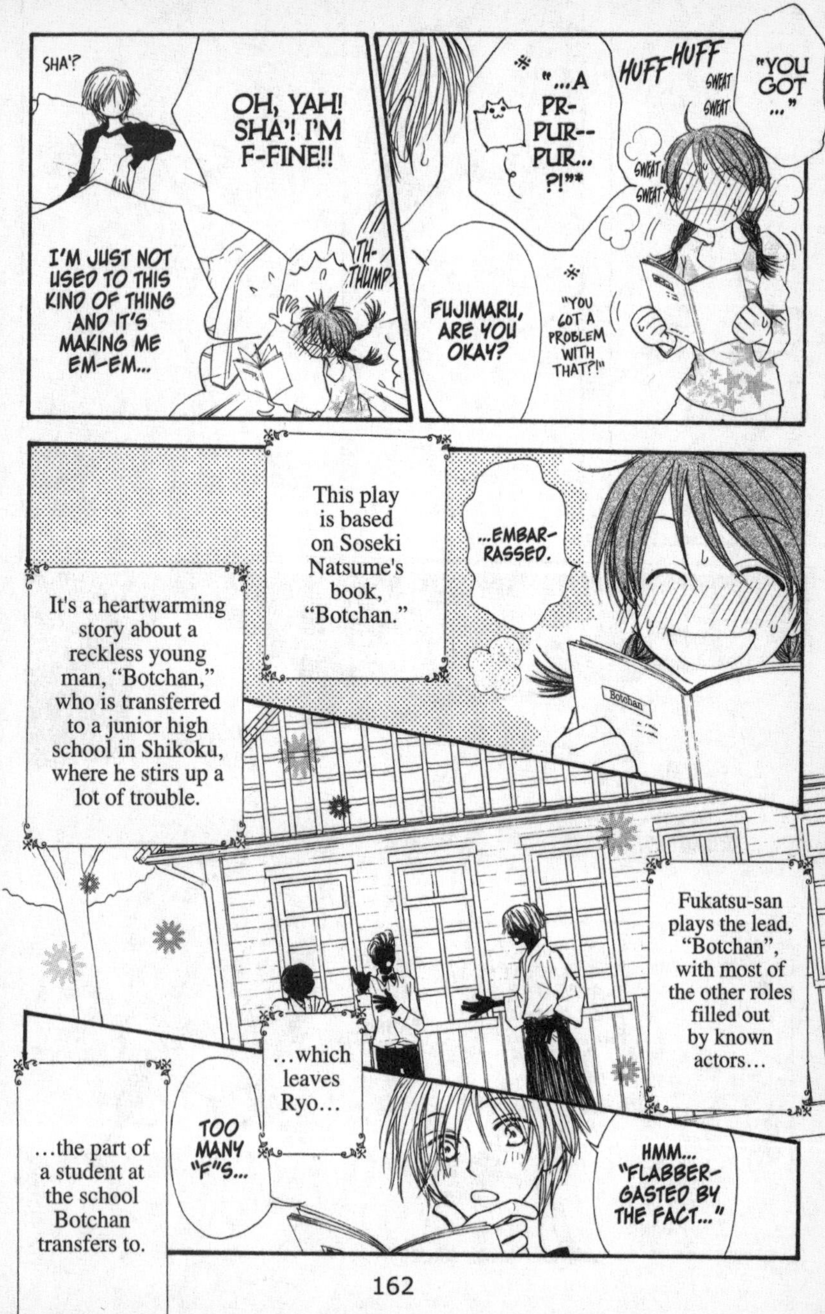
"YOU GOT ..."
HUFF HUFF
SWEAT SWEAT
※ "...A PR-PUR--PUR...?!"*
SWEAT SWEAT
FUJIMARU, ARE YOU OKAY?
※ "YOU GOT A PROBLEM WITH THAT?!"
SHA'?
OH, YAH! SHA'! I'M F-FINE!!
TH-THUMP
I'M JUST NOT USED TO THIS KIND OF THING AND IT'S MAKING ME EM-EM...
...EMBARRASSED.
Botchan
This play is based on Soseki Natsume's book, "Botchan."
It's a heartwarming story about a reckless young man, "Botchan," who is transferred to a junior high school in Shikoku, where he stirs up a lot of trouble.
Fukatsu-san plays the lead, "Botchan", with most of the other roles filled out by known actors…
…which leaves Ryo…
HMM... "FLABBERGASTED BY THE FACT..."
TOO MANY "F"S...
…the part of a student at the school Botchan transfers to.

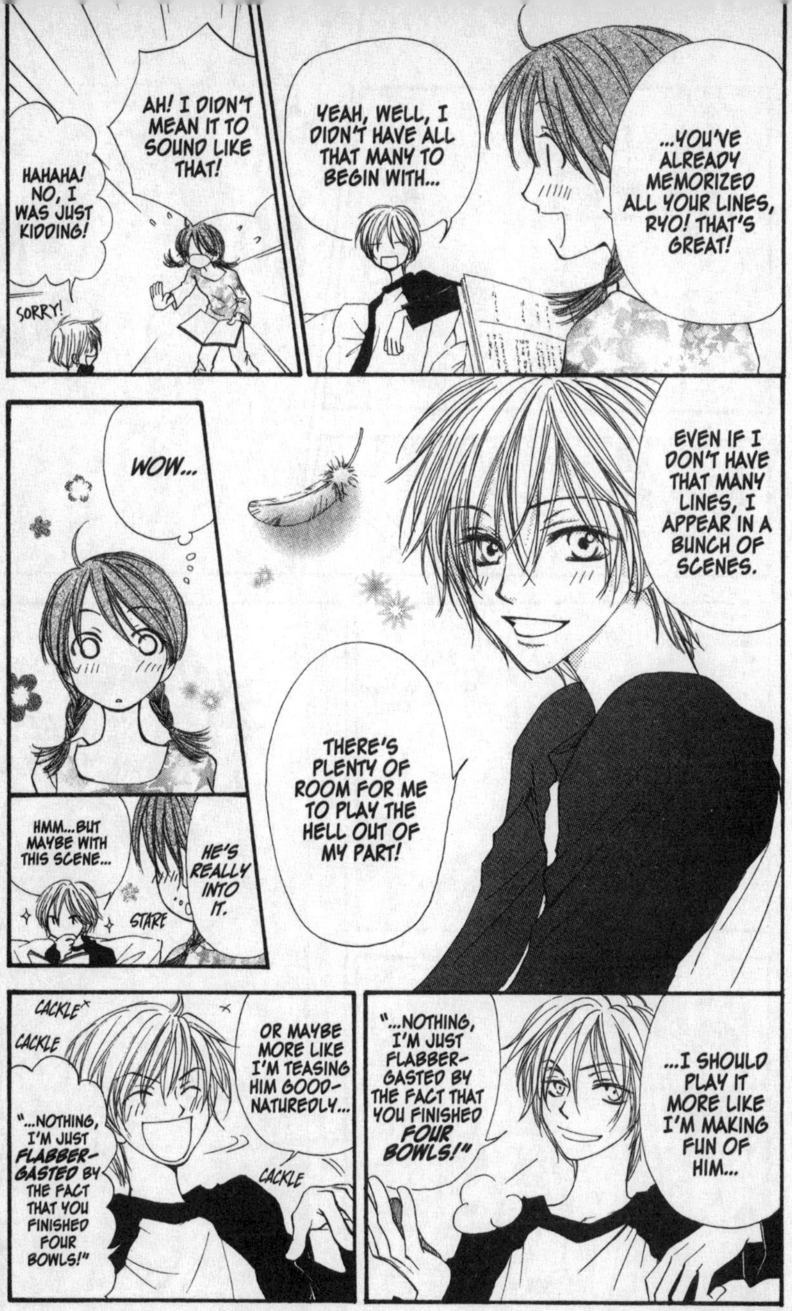
...YOU'VE ALREADY MEMORIZED ALL YOUR LINES, RYO! THAT'S GREAT!
YEAH, WELL, I DIDN'T HAVE ALL THAT MANY TO BEGIN WITH...
AH! I DIDN'T MEAN IT TO SOUND LIKE THAT!
HAHAHA! NO, I WAS JUST KIDDING!
SORRY!
EVEN IF I DON'T HAVE THAT MANY LINES, I APPEAR IN A BUNCH OF SCENES.
THERE'S PLENTY OF ROOM FOR ME TO PLAY THE HELL OUT OF MY PART!
WOW...
HE'S REALLY INTO IT.
HMM...BUT MAYBE WITH THIS SCENE...
STARE
...I SHOULD PLAY IT MORE LIKE I'M MAKING FUN OF HIM...
"...NOTHING, I'M JUST FLABBER-GASTED BY THE FACT THAT YOU FINISHED FOUR BOWLS!"
OR MAYBE MORE LIKE I'M TEASING HIM GOOD-NATUREDLY...
CACKLE
CACKLE
"...NOTHING, I'M JUST FLABBER-GASTED BY THE FACT THAT YOU FINISHED FOUR BOWLS!"
CACKLE

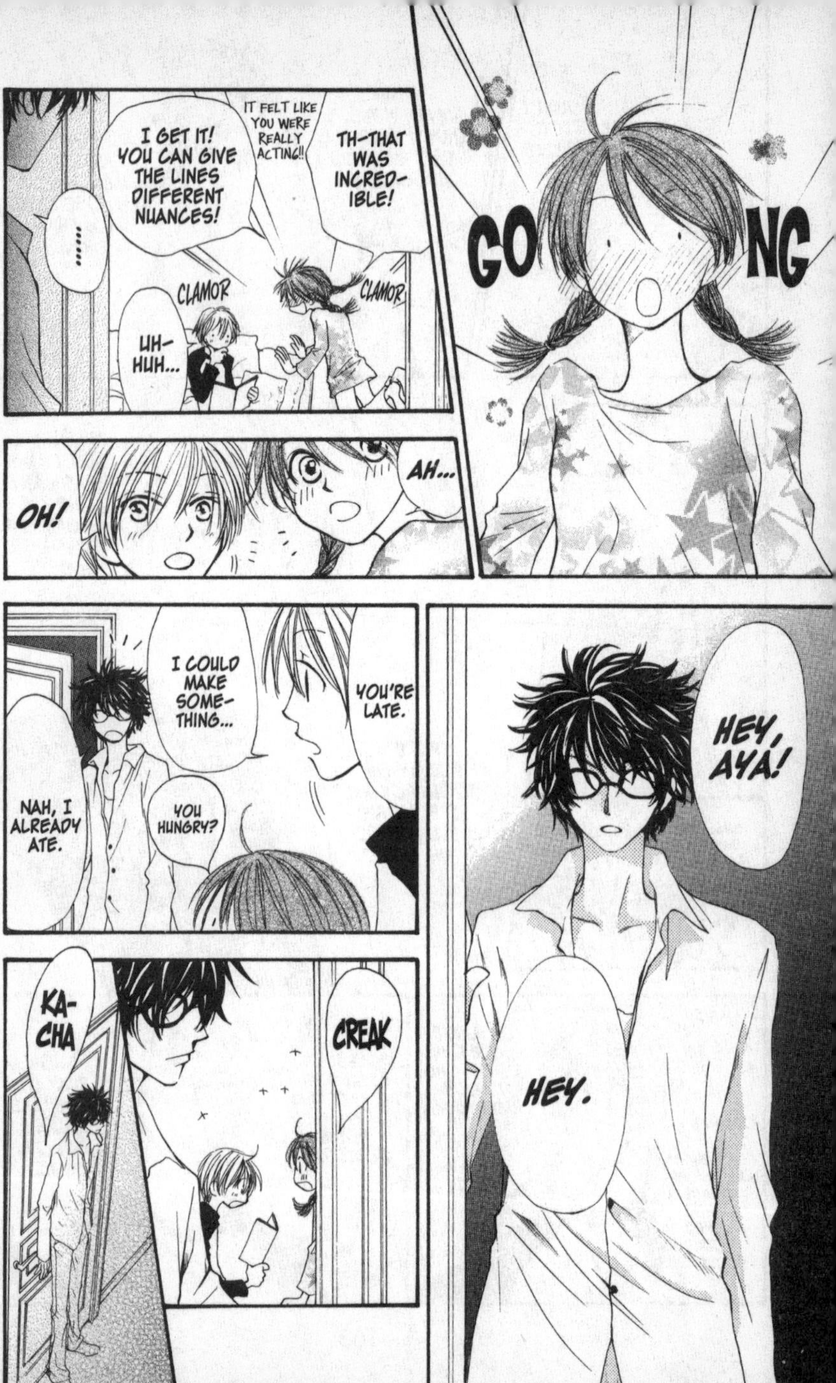
GO NG
TH-THAT WAS INCREDIBLE!
IT FELT LIKE YOU WERE REALLY ACTING!!
I GET IT! YOU CAN GIVE THE LINES DIFFERENT NUANCES!
CLAMOR
CLAMOR
......
UH-HUH...
AH...
OH!
HEY, AYA!
HEY.
YOU'RE LATE.
I COULD MAKE SOMETHING...
YOU HUNGRY?
NAH, I ALREADY ATE.
CREAK
KA-CHA

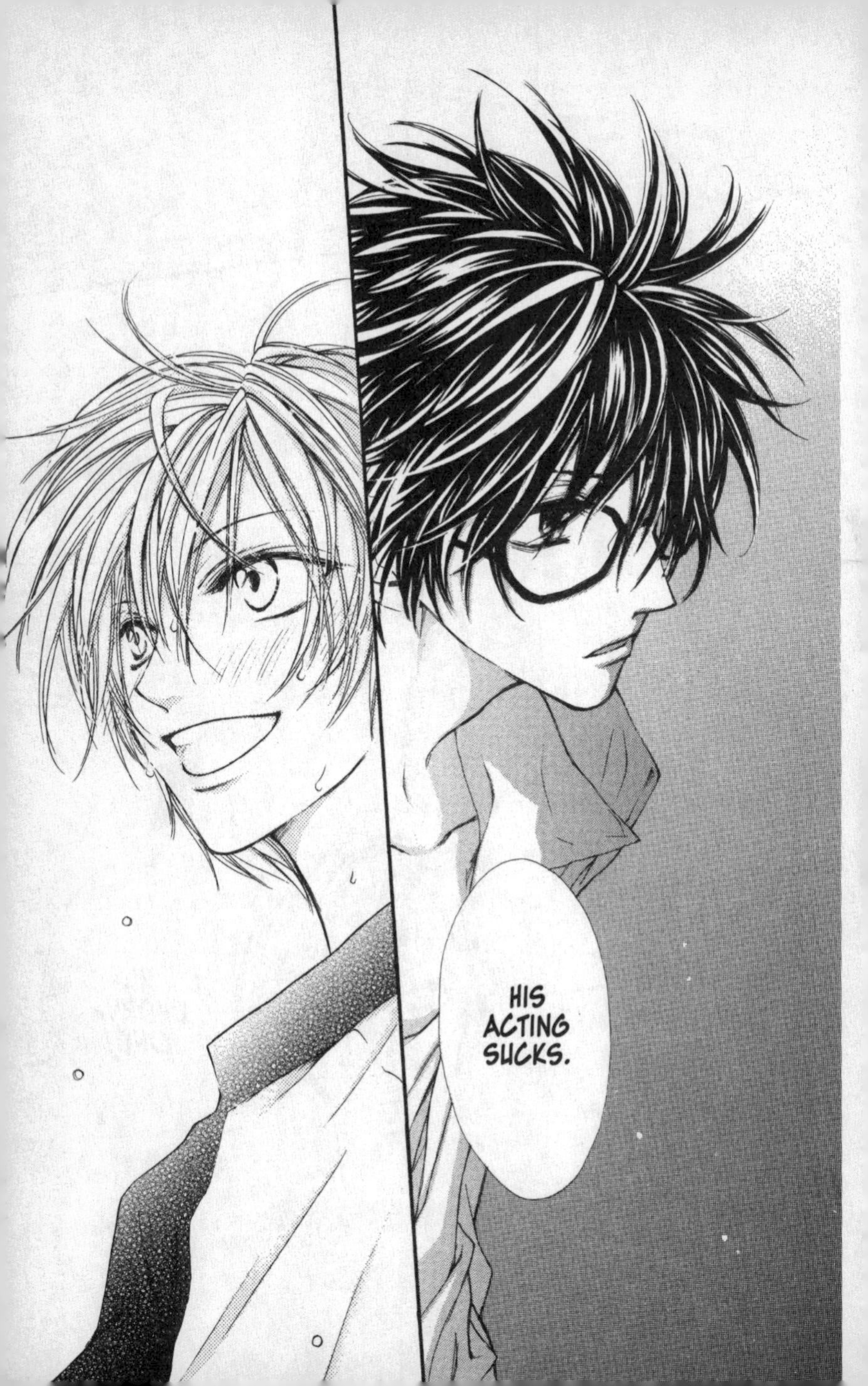
HIS ACTING SUCKS.

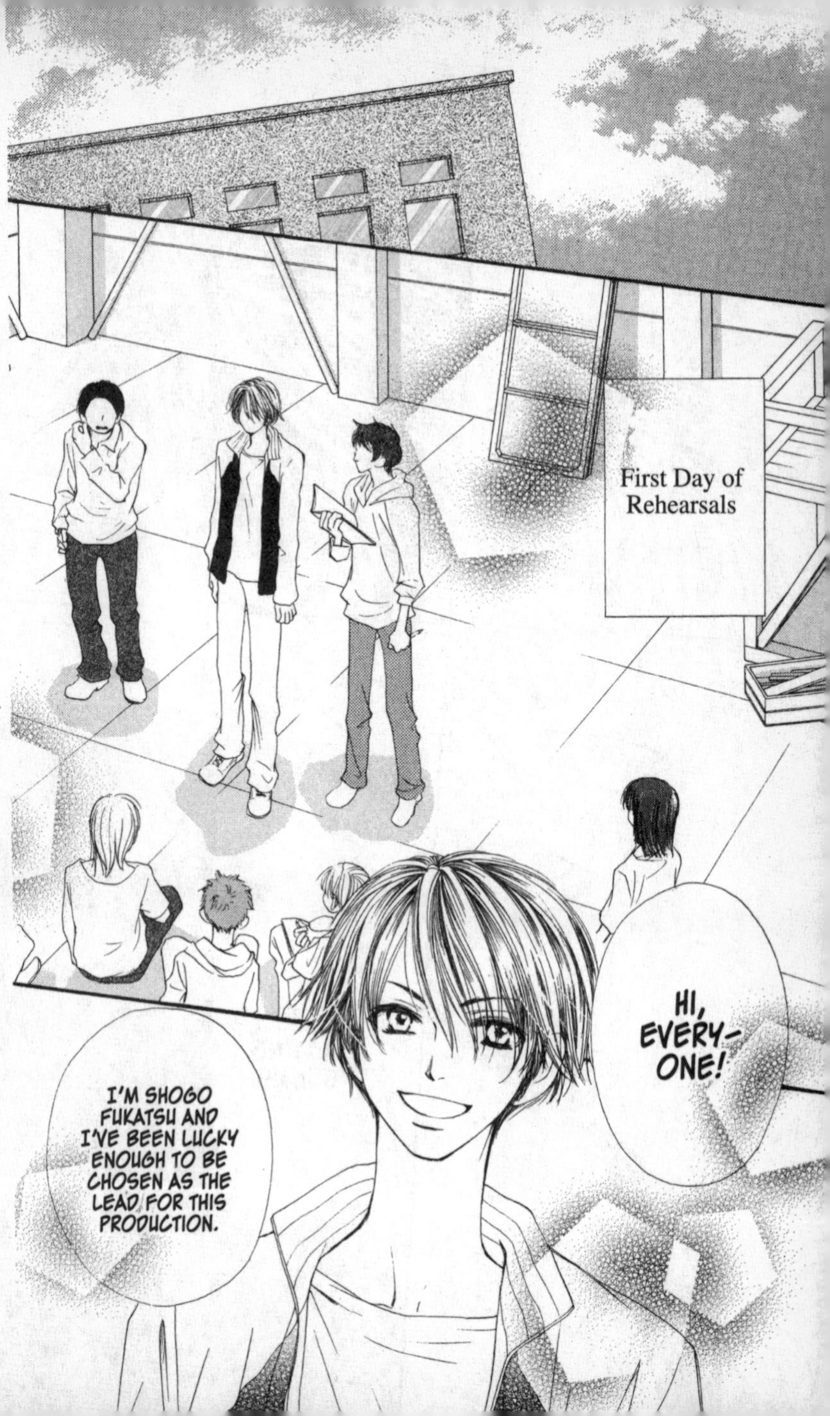
First Day of Rehearsals
HI, EVERY-ONE!
I'M SHOGO FUKATSU AND I'VE BEEN LUCKY ENOUGH TO BE CHOSEN AS THE LEAD FOR THIS PRODUCTION.

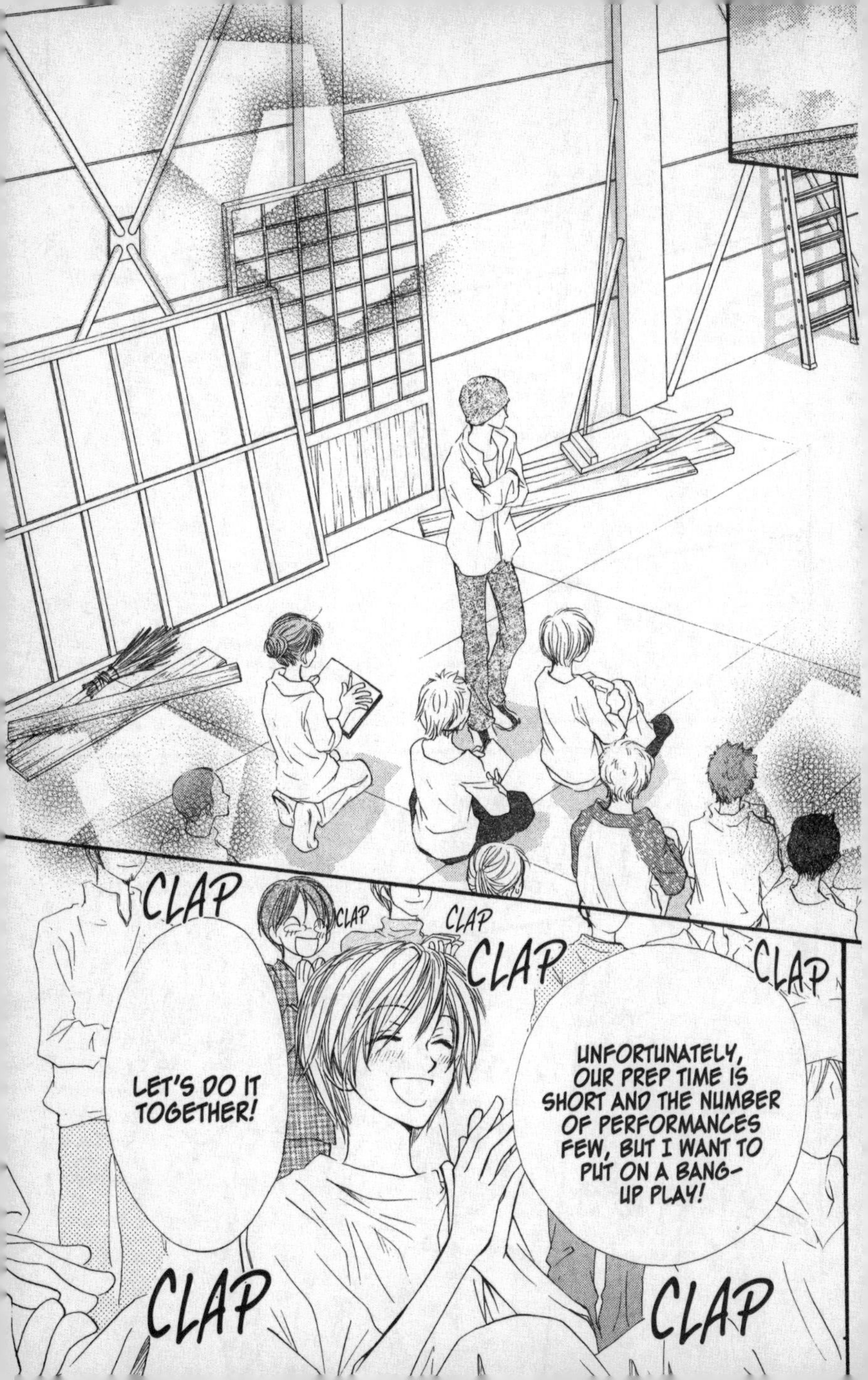
CLAP
CLAP
CLAP
CLAP
CLAP
UNFORTUNATELY, OUR PREP TIME IS SHORT AND THE NUMBER OF PERFORMANCES FEW, BUT I WANT TO PUT ON A BANG-UP PLAY!
LET'S DO IT TOGETHER!
CLAP
CLAP

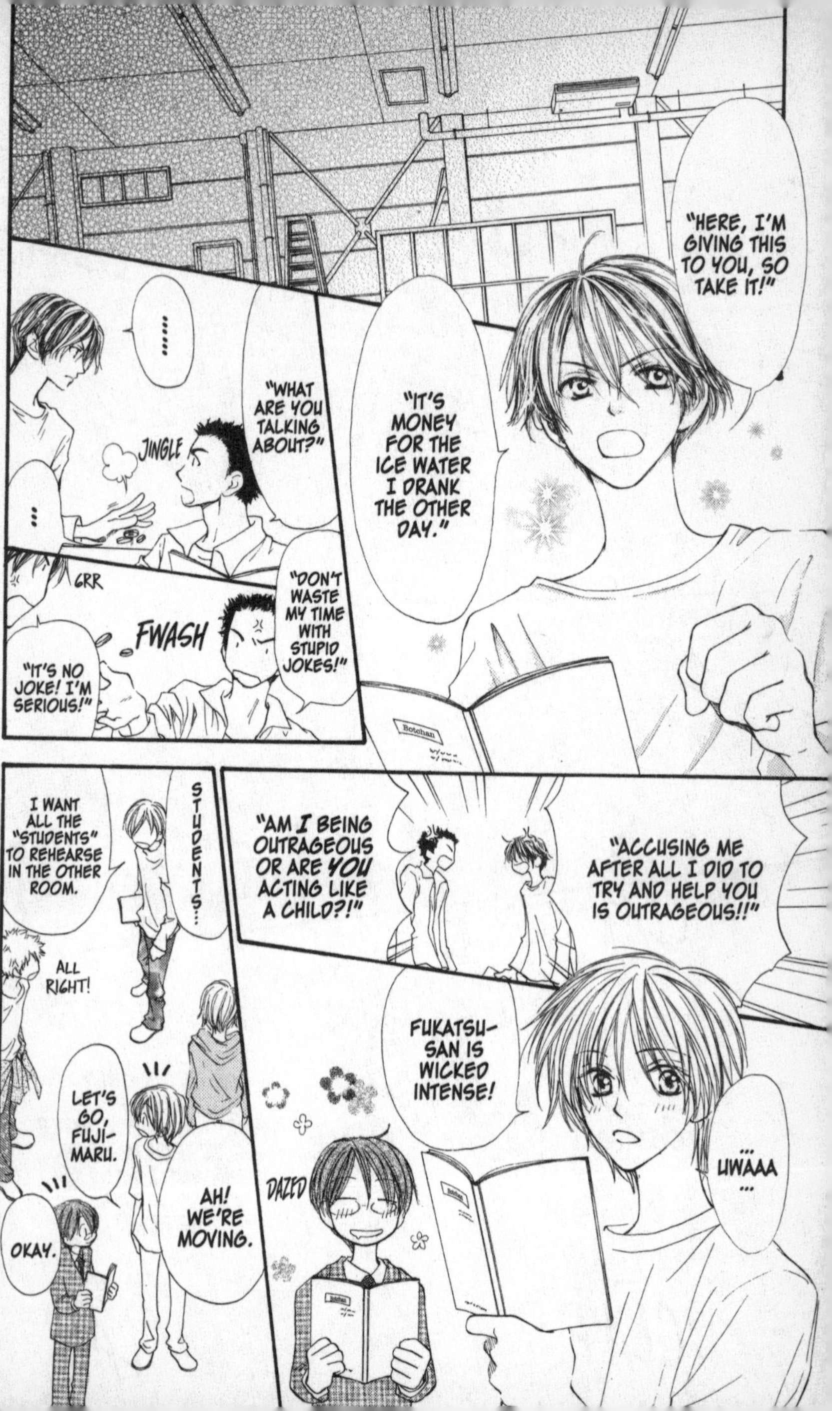

"HERE, I'M GIVING THIS TO YOU, SO TAKE IT!"
"IT'S MONEY FOR THE ICE WATER I DRANK THE OTHER DAY."
"WHAT ARE YOU TALKING ABOUT?"
......
JINGLE
...
"DON'T WASTE MY TIME WITH STUPID JOKES!"
GRR
FWASH
"IT'S NO JOKE! I'M SERIOUS!"
"ACCUSING ME AFTER ALL I DID TO TRY AND HELP YOU IS OUTRAGEOUS!!"
"AM I BEING OUTRAGEOUS OR ARE YOU ACTING LIKE A CHILD?!"
...UWAAA...
FUKATSU-SAN IS WICKED INTENSE!
DAZED
STUDENTS...
I WANT ALL THE "STUDENTS" TO REHEARSE IN THE OTHER ROOM.
ALL RIGHT!
LET'S GO, FUJI-MARU.
AH! WE'RE MOVING.
OKAY.

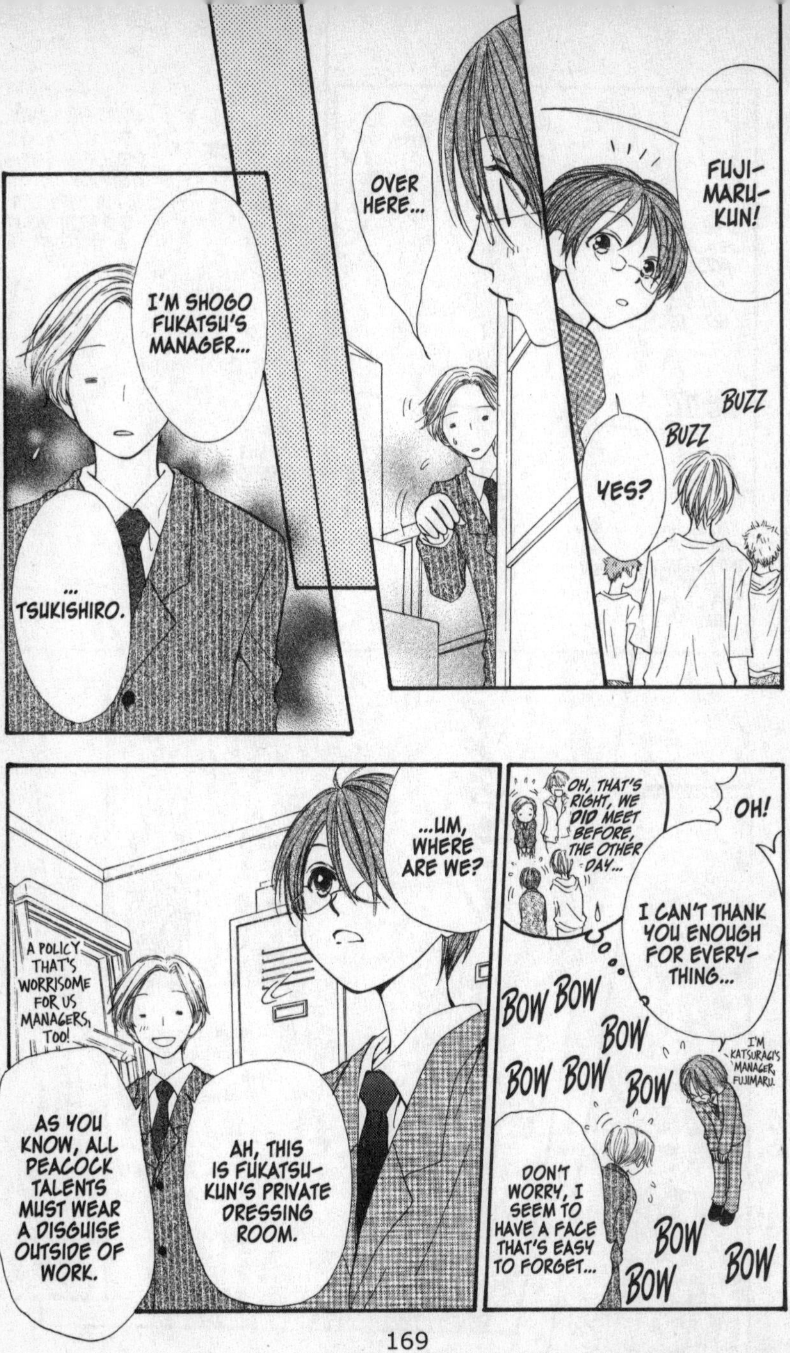
FUJI-MARU-KUN!
BUZZ
BUZZ
YES?
OVER HERE...
I'M SHOGO FUKATSU'S MANAGER...
... TSUKISHIRO.
OH!
I CAN'T THANK YOU ENOUGH FOR EVERY-THING...
OH, THAT'S RIGHT, WE DID MEET BEFORE, THE OTHER DAY...
I'M KATSURAGI'S MANAGER, FUJIMARU.
BOW BOW BOW BOW BOW BOW BOW BOW BOW
DON'T WORRY, I SEEM TO HAVE A FACE THAT'S EASY TO FORGET...
...UM, WHERE ARE WE?
AH, THIS IS FUKATSU-KUN'S PRIVATE DRESSING ROOM.
AS YOU KNOW, ALL PEACOCK TALENTS MUST WEAR A DISGUISE OUTSIDE OF WORK.
A POLICY THAT'S WORRISOME FOR US MANAGERS, TOO!

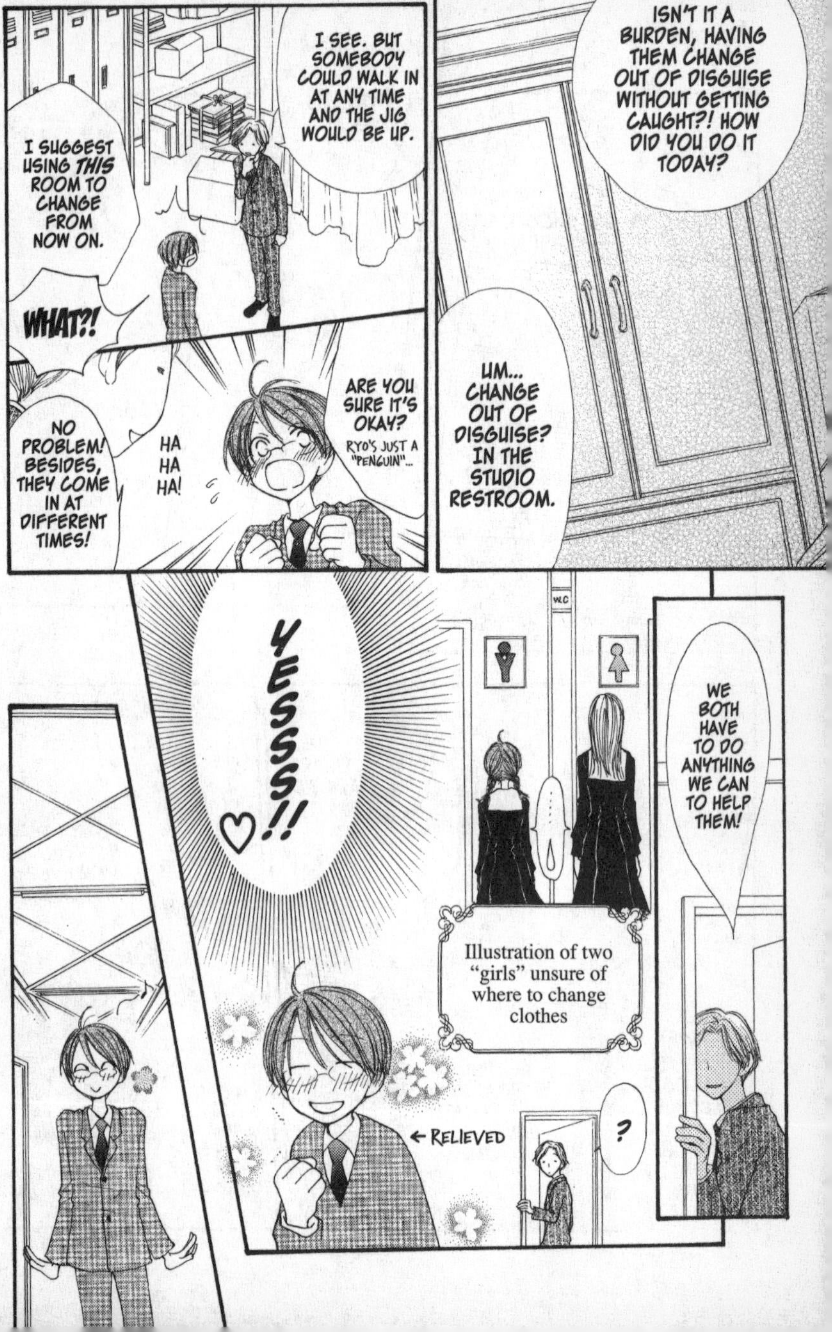
ISN'T IT A BURDEN, HAVING THEM CHANGE OUT OF DISGUISE WITHOUT GETTING CAUGHT?! HOW DID YOU DO IT TODAY?
UM... CHANGE OUT OF DISGUISE? IN THE STUDIO RESTROOM.
I SEE. BUT SOMEBODY COULD WALK IN AT ANY TIME AND THE JIG WOULD BE UP.
I SUGGEST USING *THIS* ROOM TO CHANGE FROM NOW ON.
WHAT?!
ARE YOU SURE IT'S OKAY?
RYO'S JUST A "PENGUIN"...
HA HA HA!
NO PROBLEM! BESIDES, THEY COME IN AT DIFFERENT TIMES!
WE BOTH HAVE TO DO ANYTHING WE CAN TO HELP THEM!
?
W.C
Illustration of two "girls" unsure of where to change clothes
YESSS!! ♡
← RELIEVED

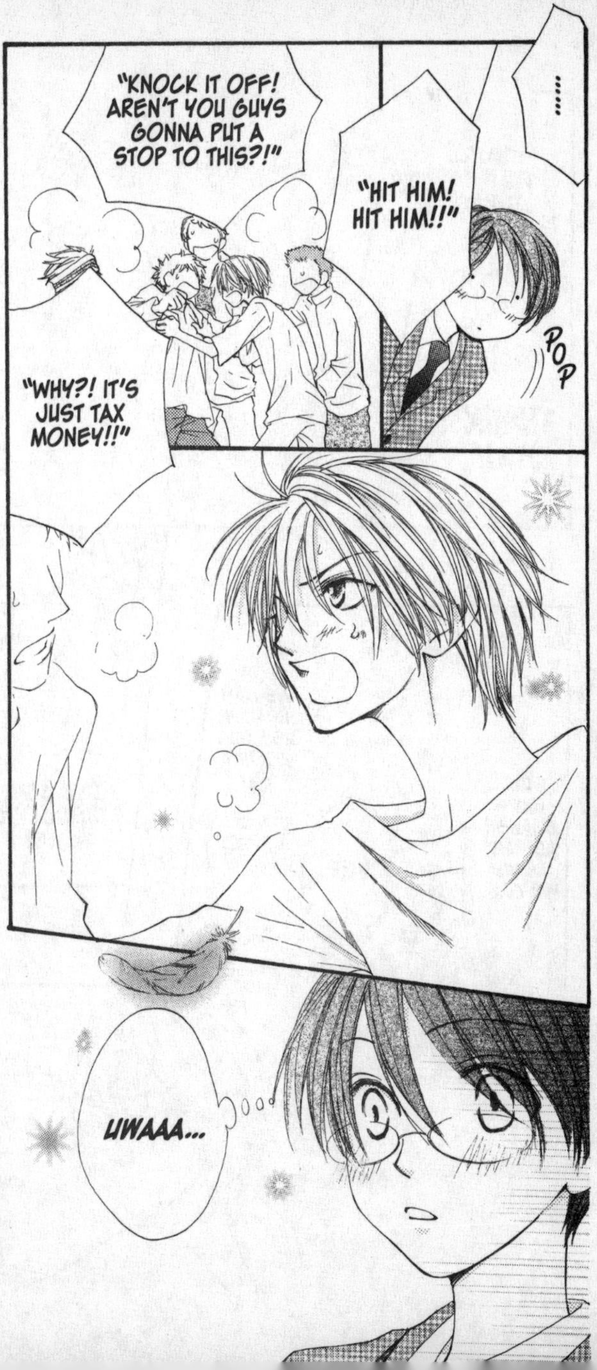
......
"HIT HIM! HIT HIM!!"
POP
"KNOCK IT OFF! AREN'T YOU GUYS GONNA PUT A STOP TO THIS?!"
"WHY?! IT'S JUST TAX MONEY!!"
UWAAA...

1/4 Sakura Mail

part 10

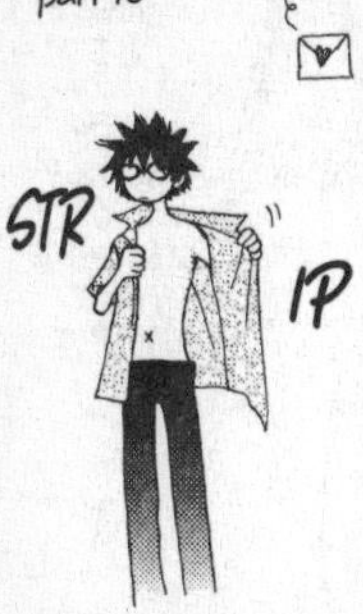
STR
IP

As I was working on this episode, the way I imagined things going veered off-course. Know what this manga is all about? Showing off skin!! Actually, I like drawing stuff like that but wasn't aware that semi-nudity would turn up in the story until I started drawing it. But it makes sense, right, with the gender-switching theme, to have lots of scenes with the characters desperately changing clothes...? **And,** most importantly for me, I have a blast drawing it!...Of course, if you have a blast reading it, then I'll **really** be thrilled...

...Well, I've run out of room, so here I'll say.

See you next time!
Sakura Tsukuba

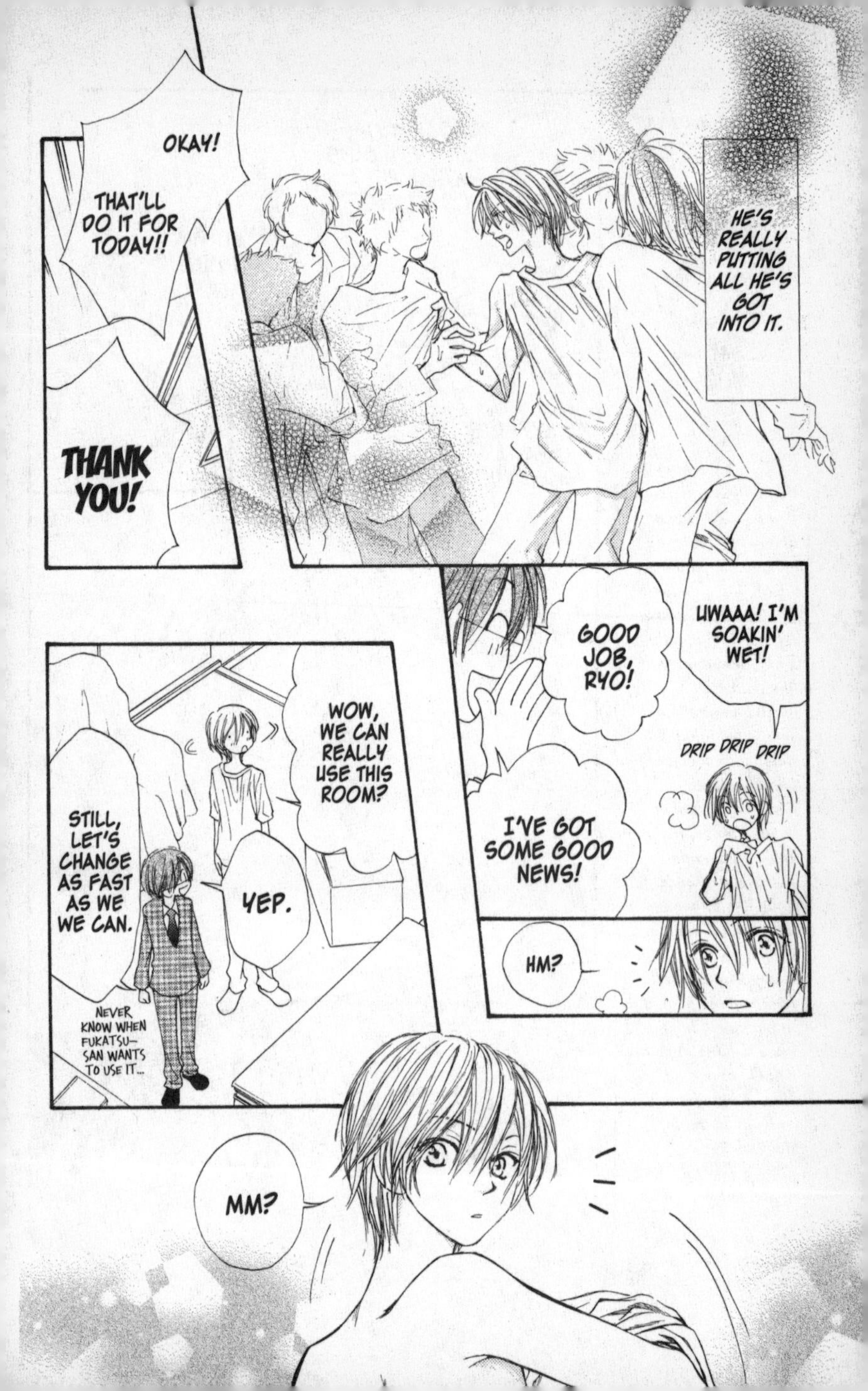
HE'S REALLY PUTTING ALL HE'S GOT INTO IT.
OKAY!
THAT'LL DO IT FOR TODAY!!
THANK YOU!
UWAAA! I'M SOAKIN' WET!
GOOD JOB, RYO!
DRIP DRIP DRIP
I'VE GOT SOME GOOD NEWS!
HM?
WOW, WE CAN REALLY USE THIS ROOM?
YEP.
STILL, LET'S CHANGE AS FAST AS WE WE CAN.
NEVER KNOW WHEN FUKATSU-SAN WANTS TO USE IT...
MM?

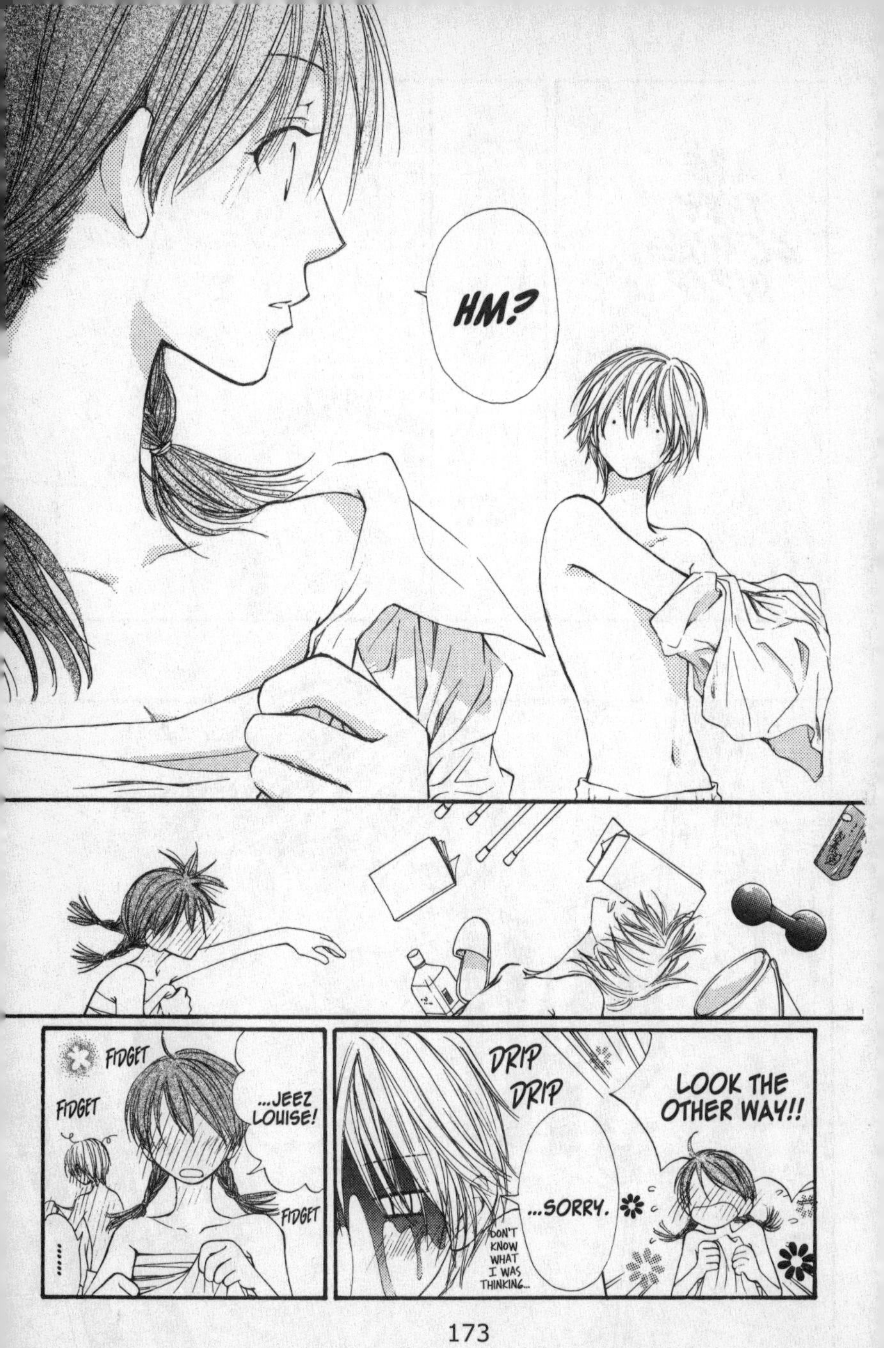
HM?
LOOK THE OTHER WAY!!
DRIP
DRIP
...SORRY.
DON'T KNOW WHAT I WAS THINKING...
...JEEZ LOUISE!
FIDGET
FIDGET
FIDGET
......

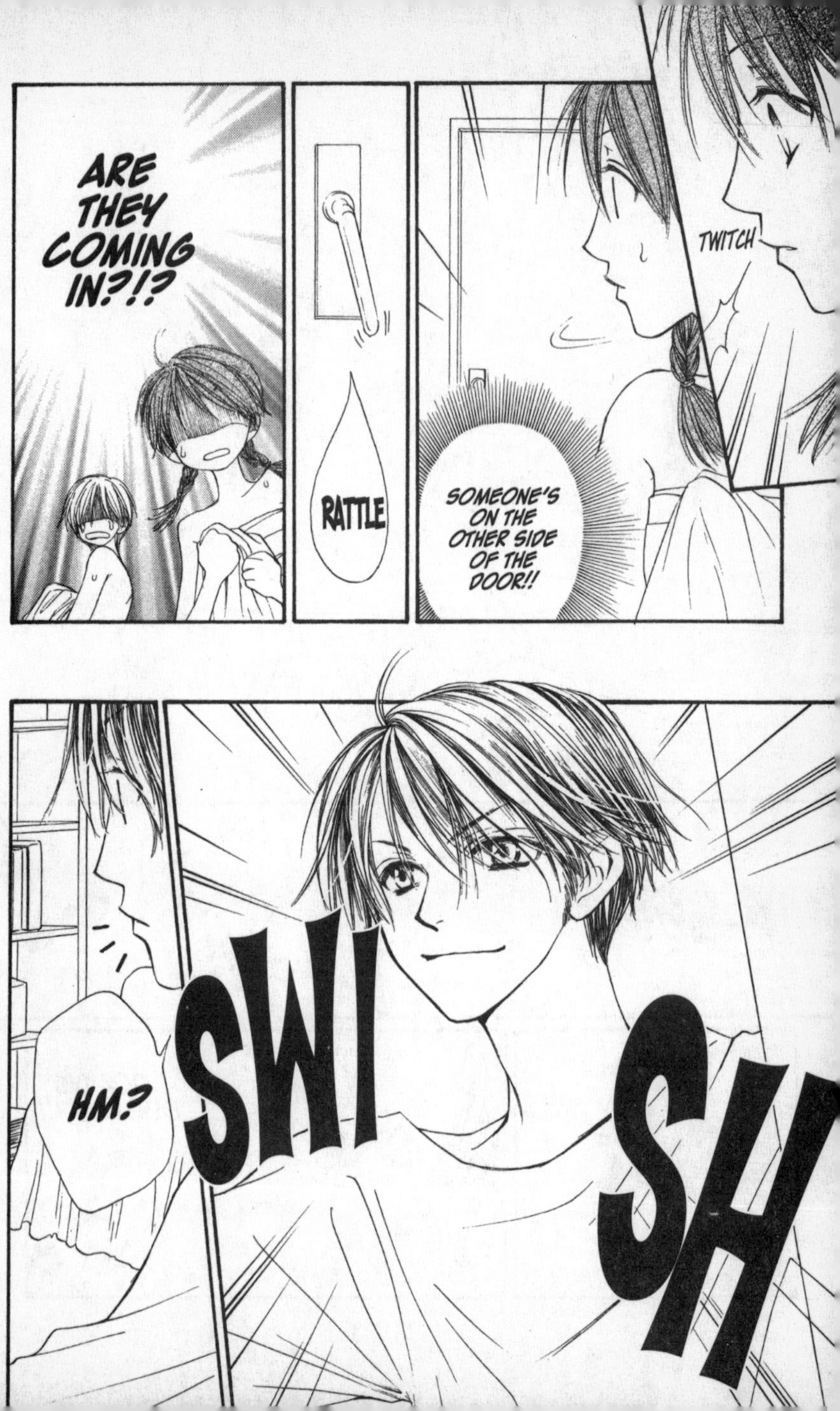
TWITCH
SOMEONE'S ON THE OTHER SIDE OF THE DOOR!!
RATTLE
ARE THEY COMING IN?!?
SWISH
HM?

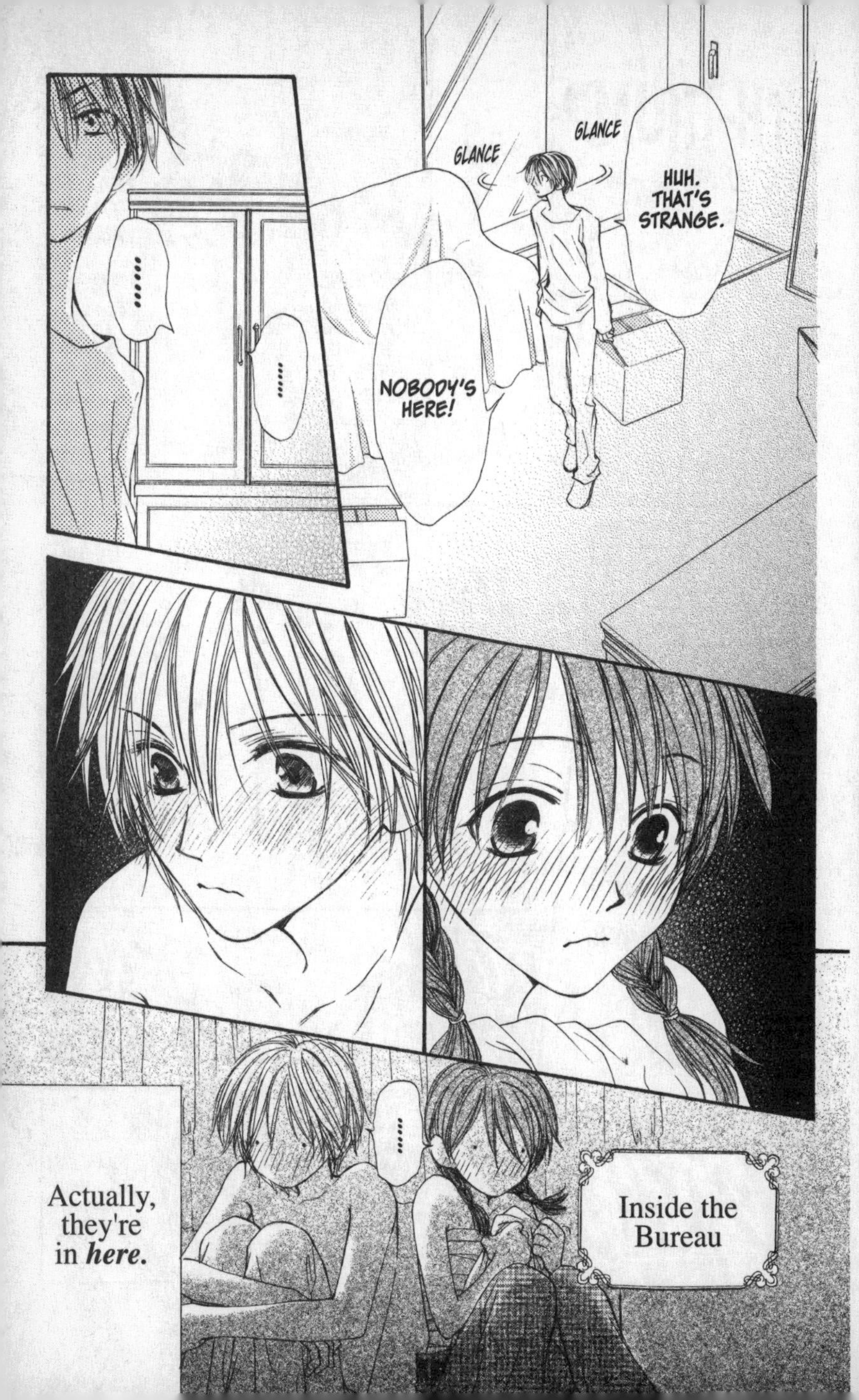
GLANCE
GLANCE
HUH. THAT'S STRANGE.
NOBODY'S HERE!
......
......
Inside the Bureau
......
Actually, they're in *here*.

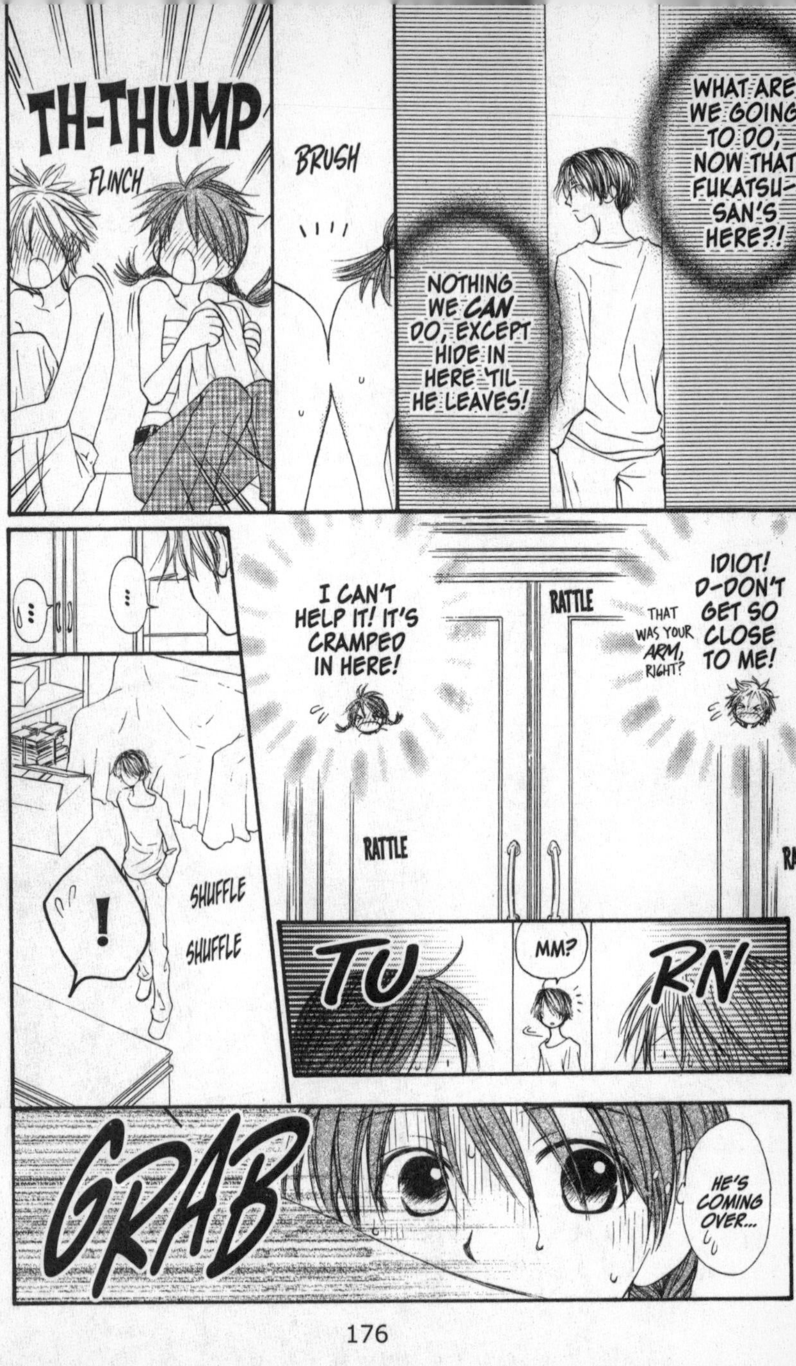
WHAT ARE WE GOING TO DO, NOW THAT FUKATSU-SAN'S HERE?!
NOTHING WE CAN DO, EXCEPT HIDE IN HERE 'TIL HE LEAVES!
BRUSH
...
TH-THUMP
FLINCH
IDIOT! D-DON'T GET SO CLOSE TO ME!
THAT WAS YOUR ARM, RIGHT?
RATTLE
I CAN'T HELP IT! IT'S CRAMPED IN HERE!
RATTLE
RATTLE
RN
MM?
TU
...
...
!
SHUFFLE
SHUFFLE
HE'S COMING OVER...
GRAB

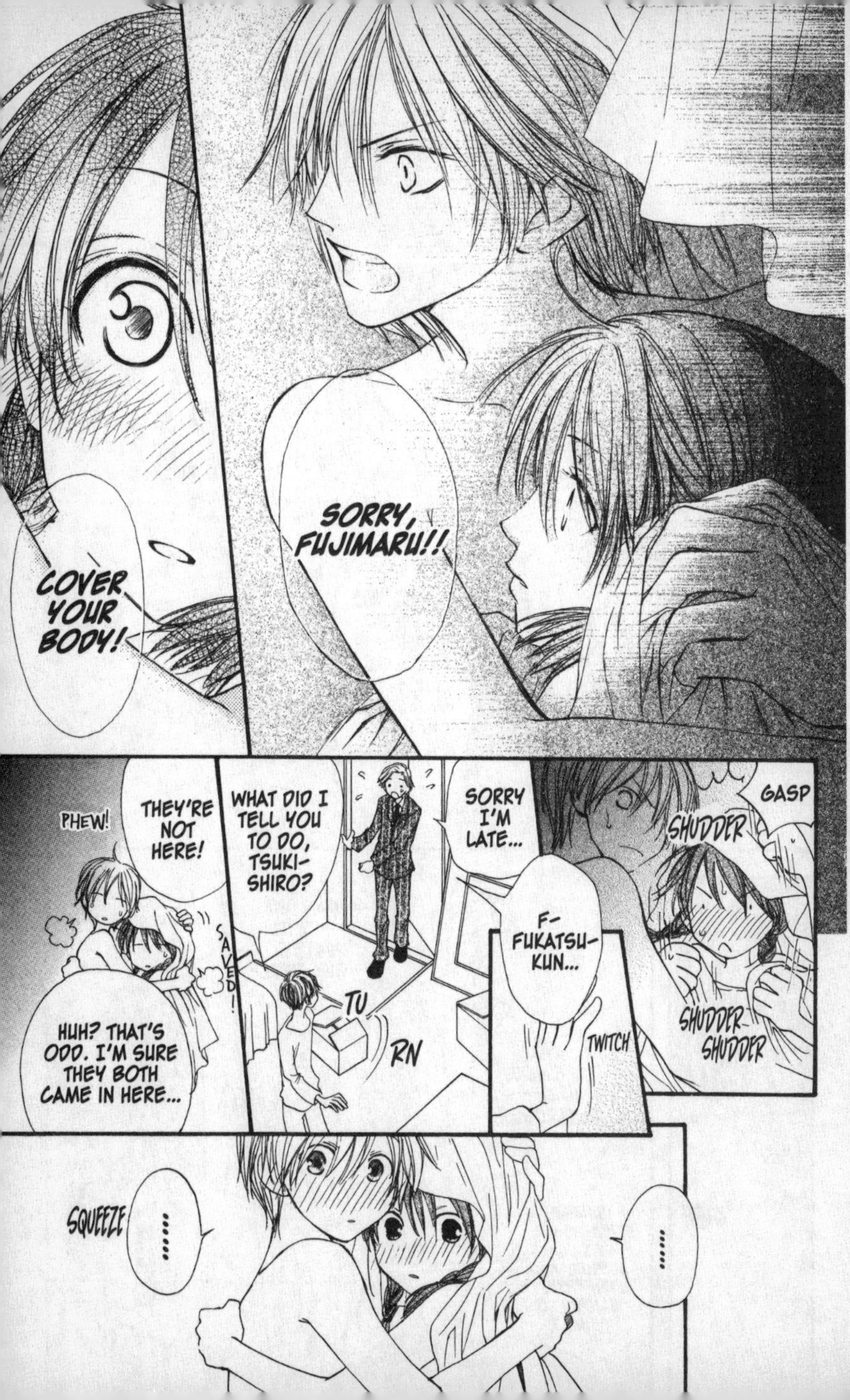
SORRY, FUJIMARU!!
COVER YOUR BODY!
GASP
SHUDDER
F-FUKATSU-KUN...
TWITCH
SHUDDER-SHUDDER
SORRY I'M LATE...
WHAT DID I TELL YOU TO DO, TSUKISHIRO?
TURN
THEY'RE NOT HERE!
PHEW!
SAVED!
HUH? THAT'S ODD. I'M SURE THEY BOTH CAME IN HERE...
......
......
SQUEEZE

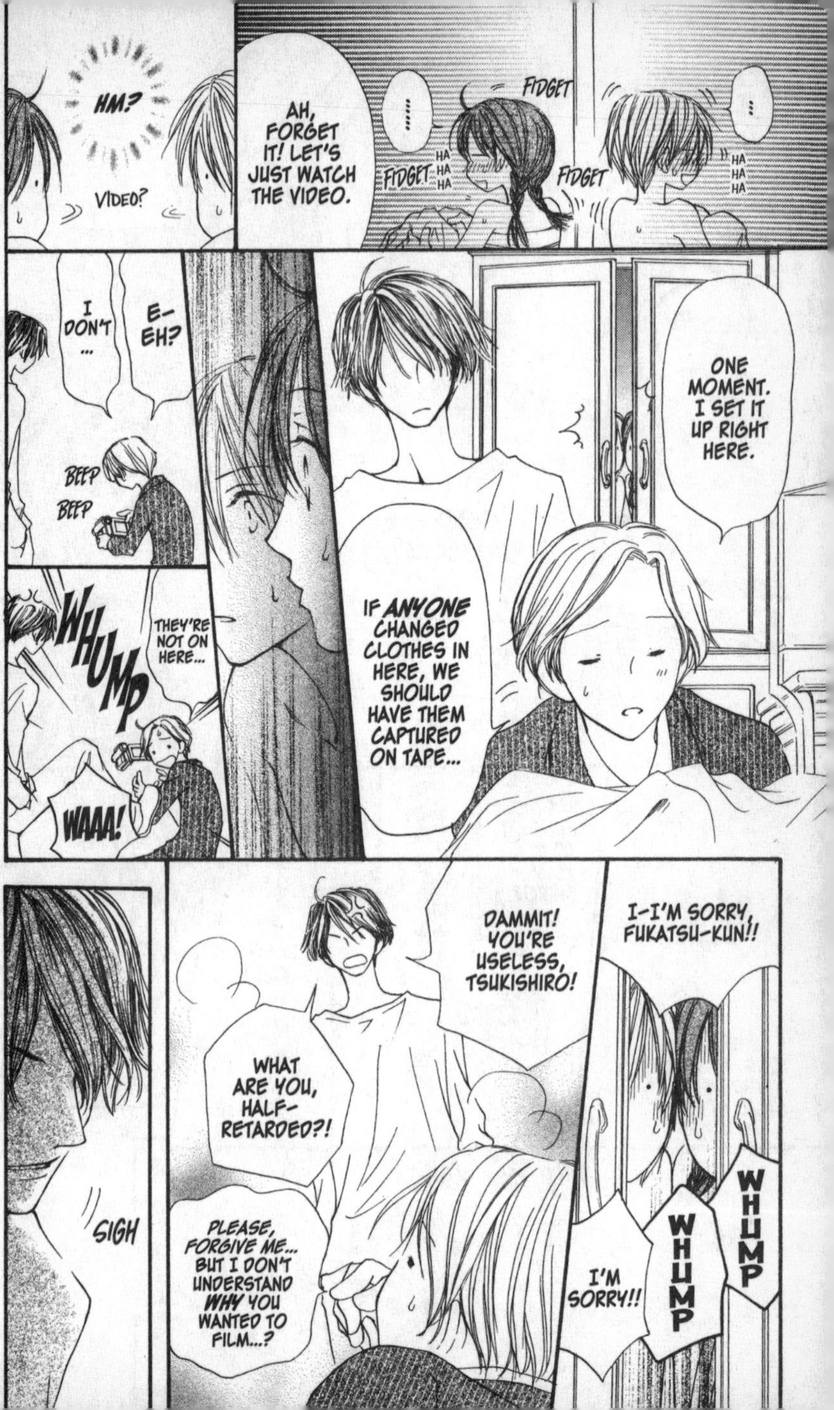
...
HA HA HA
FIDGET
......
FIDGET
HA HA HA
FIDGET
AH, FORGET IT! LET'S JUST WATCH THE VIDEO.
HM?
VIDEO?
ONE MOMENT. I SET IT UP RIGHT HERE.
IF ANYONE CHANGED CLOTHES IN HERE, WE SHOULD HAVE THEM CAPTURED ON TAPE...
E-EH?
I DON'T ...
BEEP
BEEP
THEY'RE NOT ON HERE...
WHUMP
WAAA!
I-I'M SORRY, FUKATSU-KUN!!
WHUMP
WHUMP
I'M SORRY!!
DAMMIT! YOU'RE USELESS, TSUKISHIRO!
WHAT ARE YOU, HALF-RETARDED?!
PLEASE, FORGIVE ME... BUT I DON'T UNDERSTAND WHY YOU WANTED TO FILM...?
SIGH

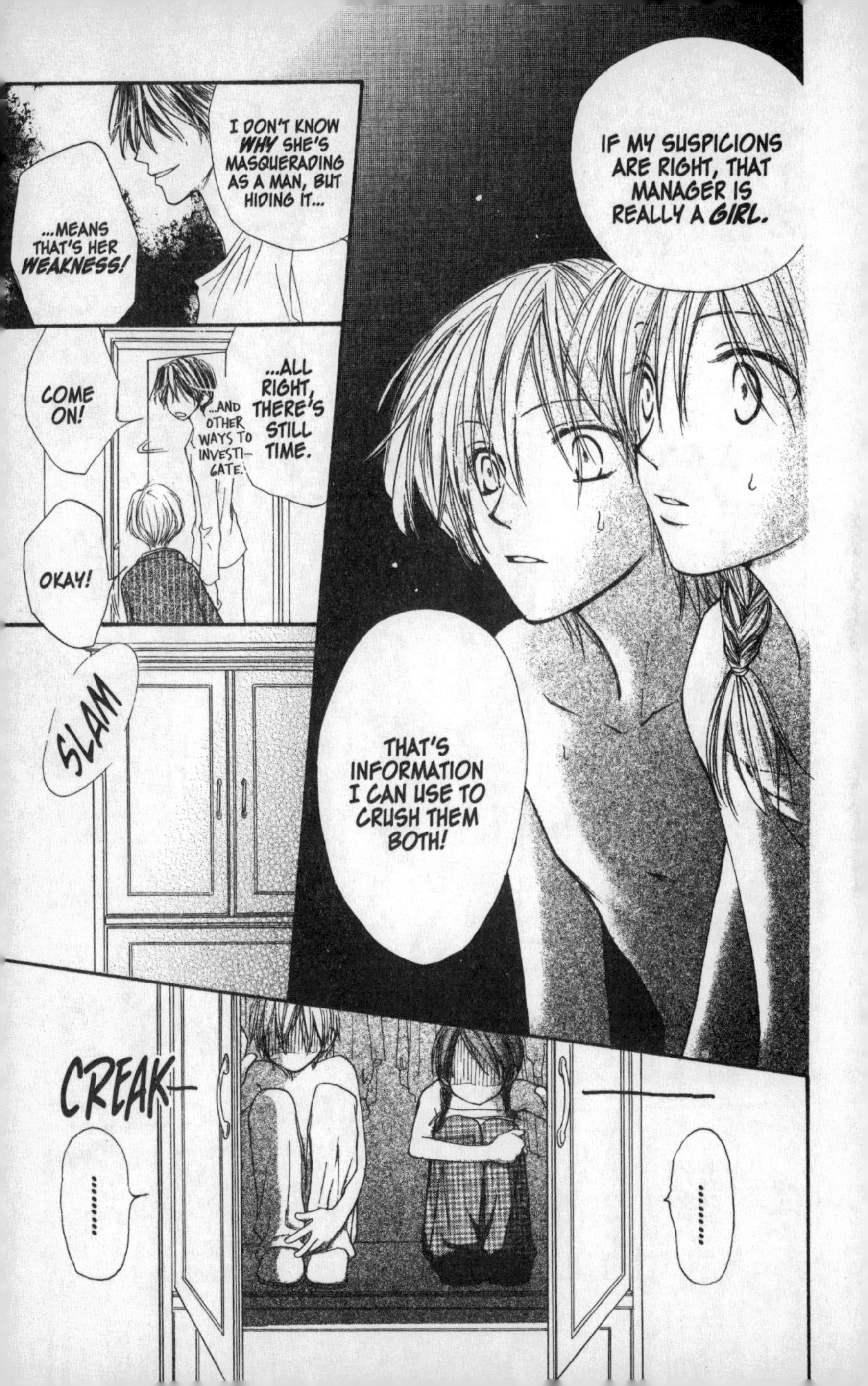
IF MY SUSPICIONS ARE RIGHT, THAT MANAGER IS REALLY A GIRL.
THAT'S INFORMATION I CAN USE TO CRUSH THEM BOTH!
I DON'T KNOW WHY SHE'S MASQUERADING AS A MAN, BUT HIDING IT...
...MEANS THAT'S HER WEAKNESS!
...ALL RIGHT, THERE'S STILL TIME.
...AND OTHER WAYS TO INVESTI-GATE.
COME ON!
OKAY!
SLAM
......
CREAK—
......

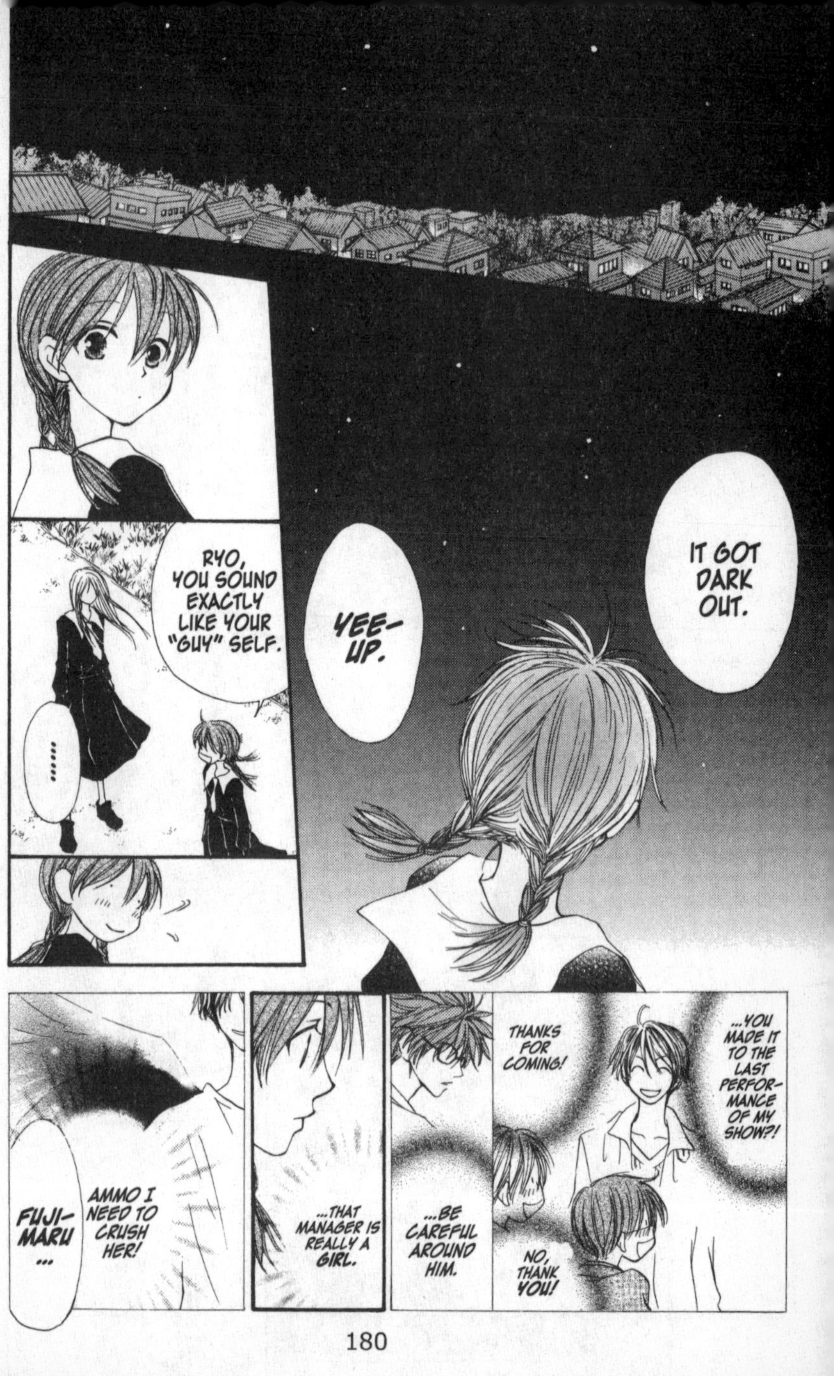
IT GOT DARK OUT.
YEE-UP.
RYO, YOU SOUND EXACTLY LIKE YOUR "GUY" SELF.
.....
...YOU MADE IT TO THE LAST PERFORMANCE OF MY SHOW?!
THANKS FOR COMING!
NO, THANK YOU!
...BE CAREFUL AROUND HIM.
...THAT MANAGER IS REALLY A GIRL.
AMMO I NEED TO CRUSH HER!
FUJI-MARU ...

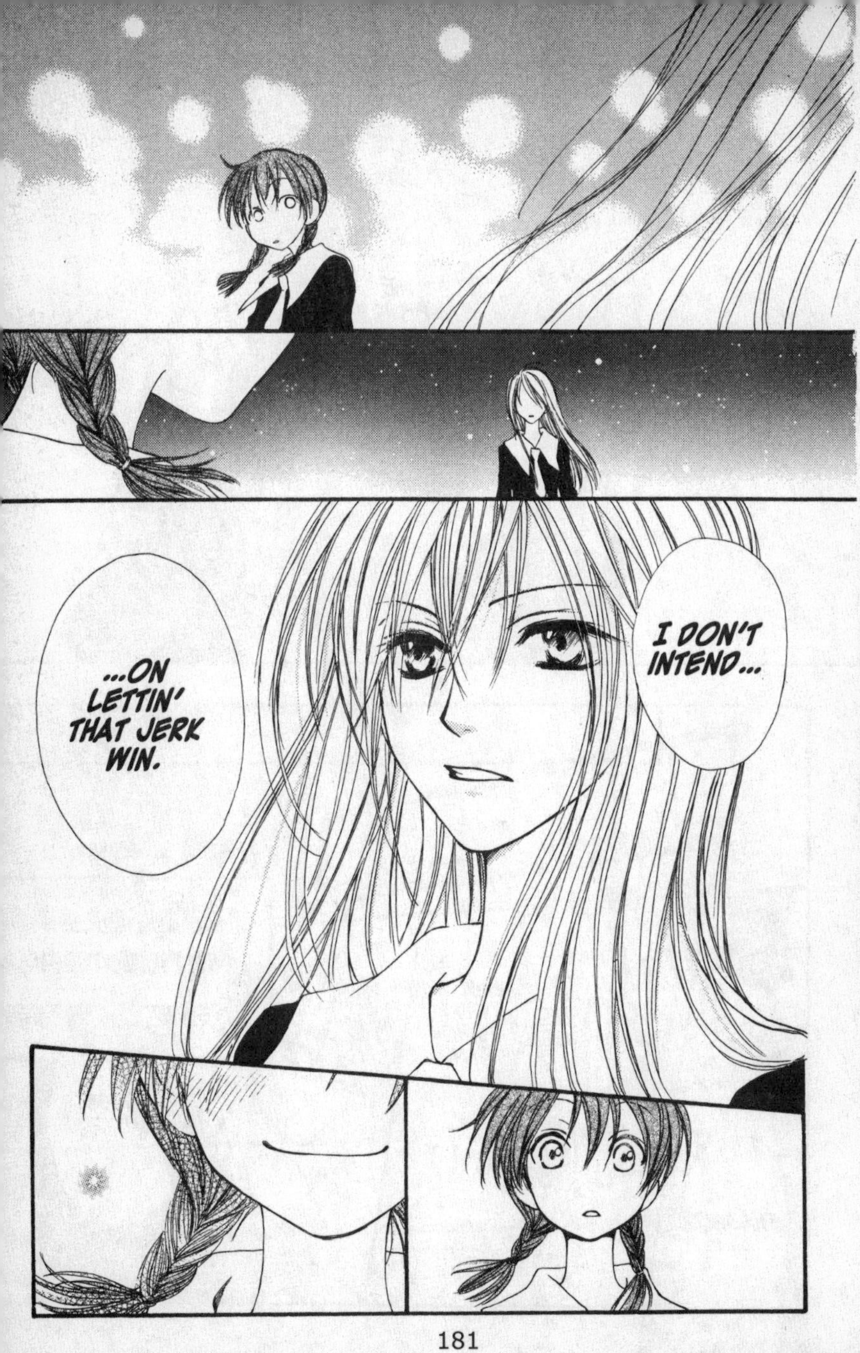
I DON'T INTEND...
...ON LETTIN' THAT JERK WIN.

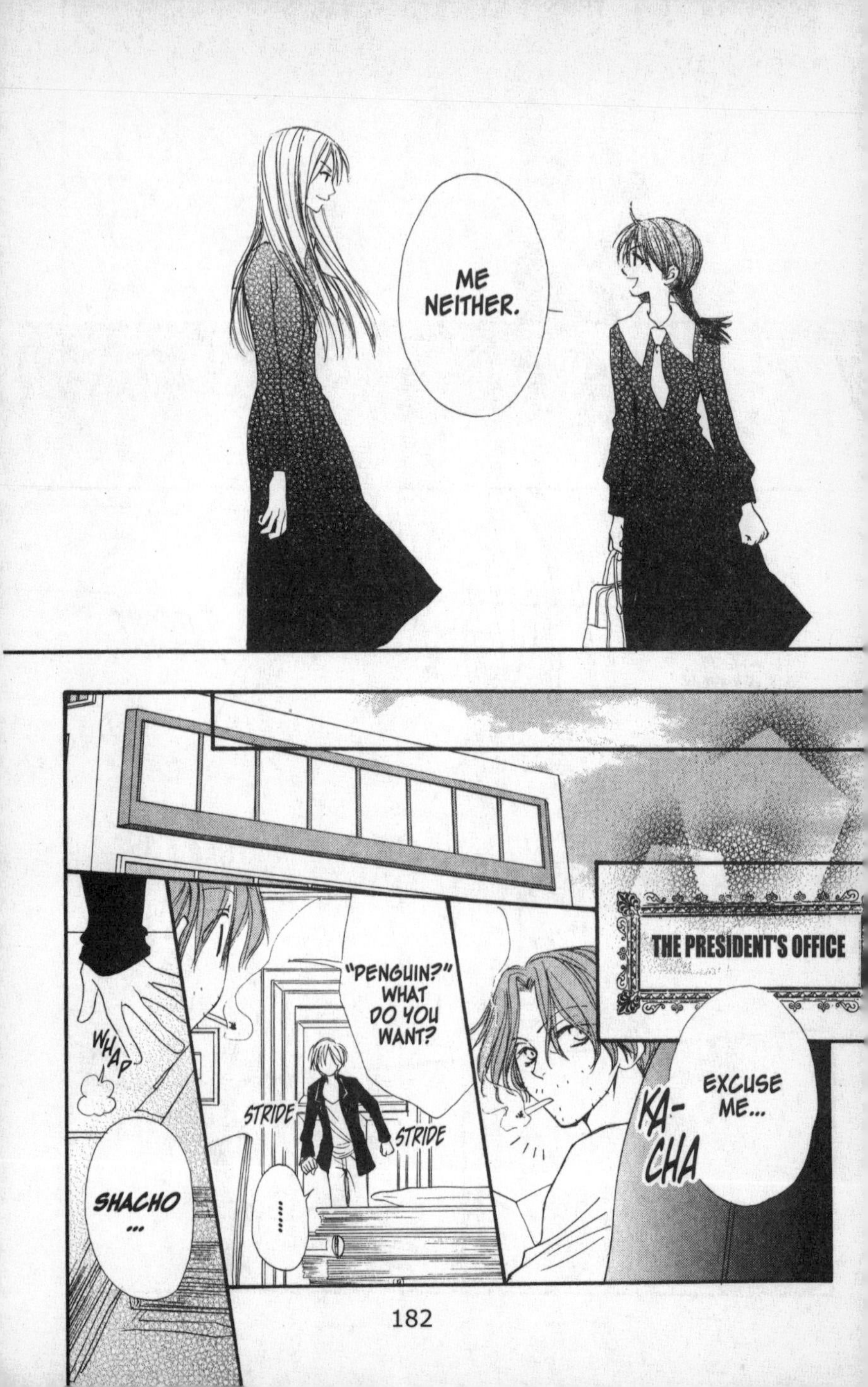
ME NEITHER.
THE PRESIDENT'S OFFICE
EXCUSE ME...
KA-CHA
"PENGUIN?" WHAT DO YOU WANT?
STRIDE
STRIDE
......
WHAP
SHACHO ...

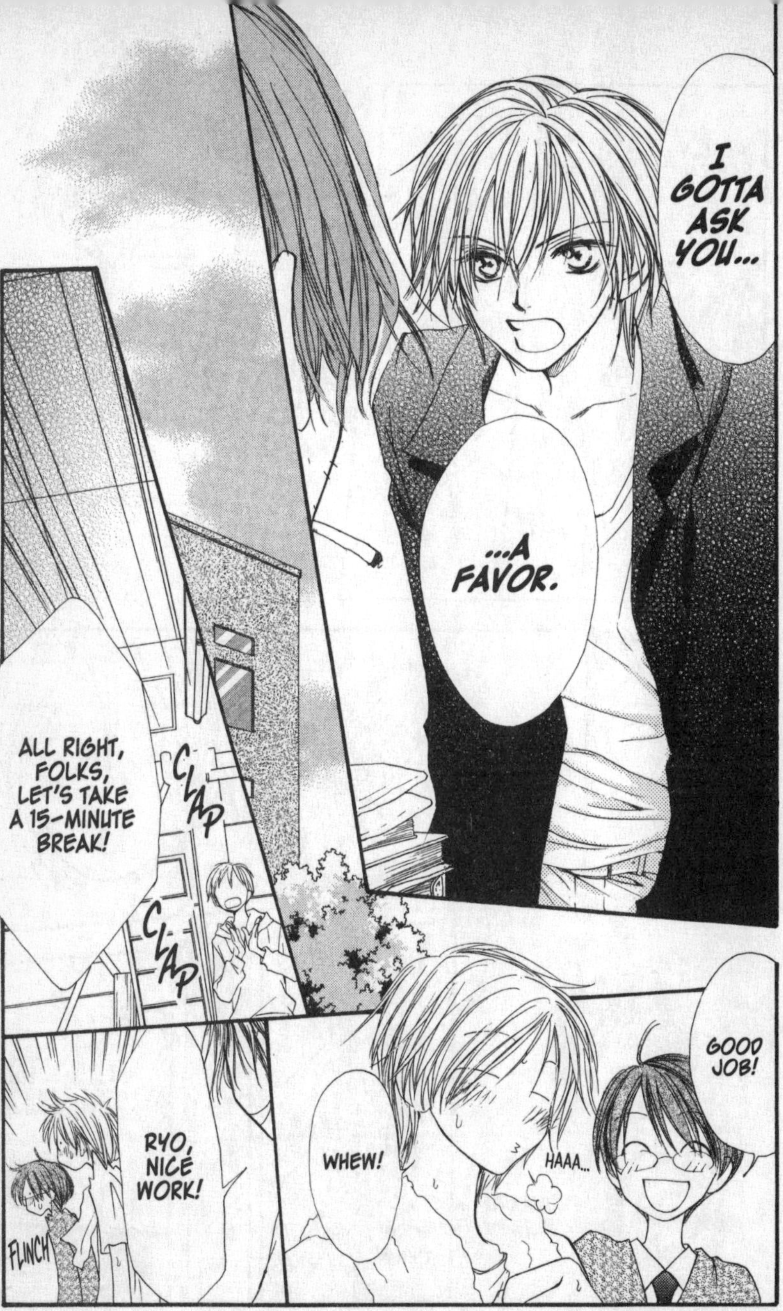
I GOTTA ASK YOU...
...A FAVOR.
ALL RIGHT, FOLKS, LET'S TAKE A 15-MINUTE BREAK!
CLAP
CLAP
GOOD JOB!
HAAA...
WHEW!
RYO, NICE WORK!
FLINCH

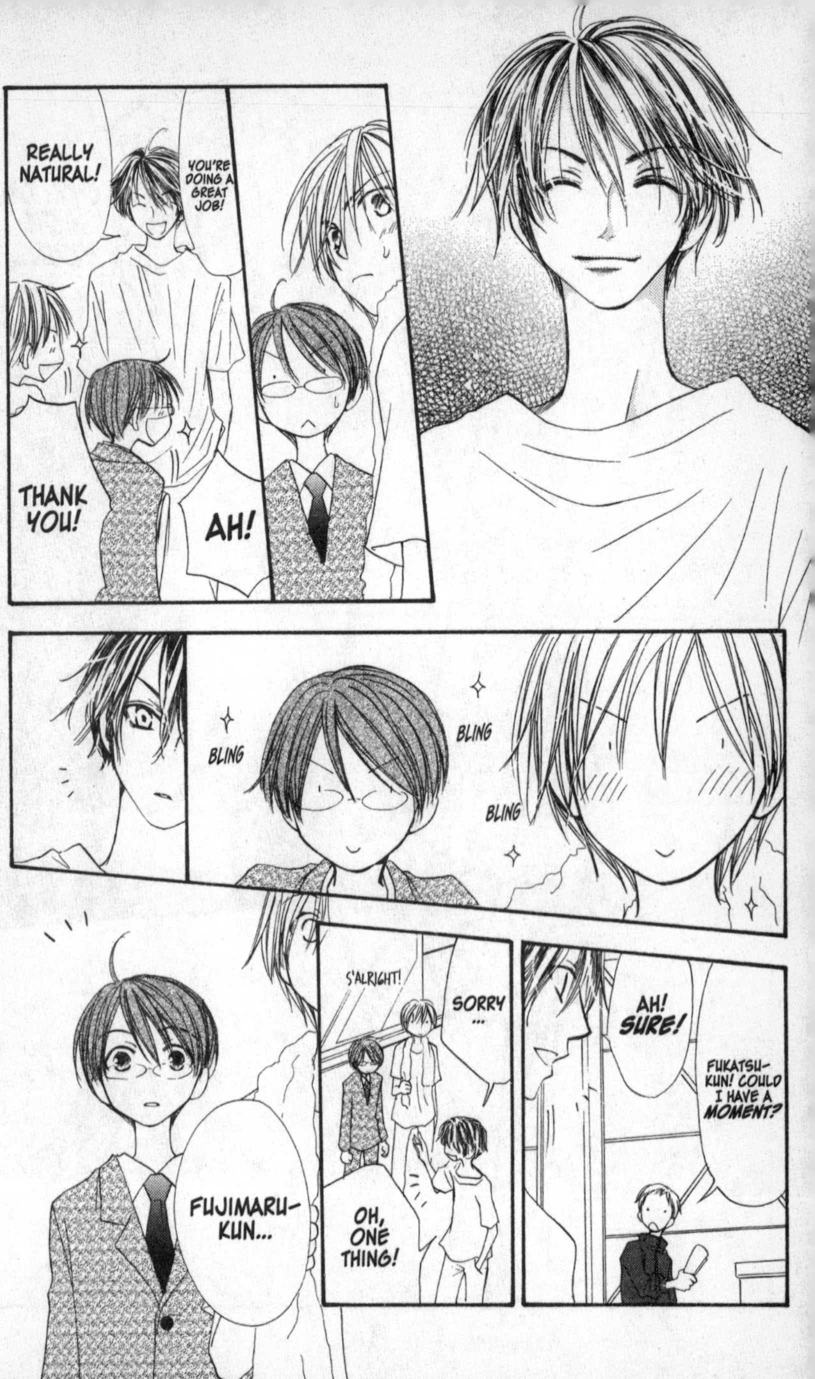
AH!
YOU'RE DOING A GREAT JOB!
REALLY NATURAL!
THANK YOU!
BLING
BLING
BLING
FUKATSU-KUN! COULD I HAVE A MOMENT?
AH! SURE!
SORRY ...
S'ALRIGHT!
OH, ONE THING!
FUJIMARU-KUN...

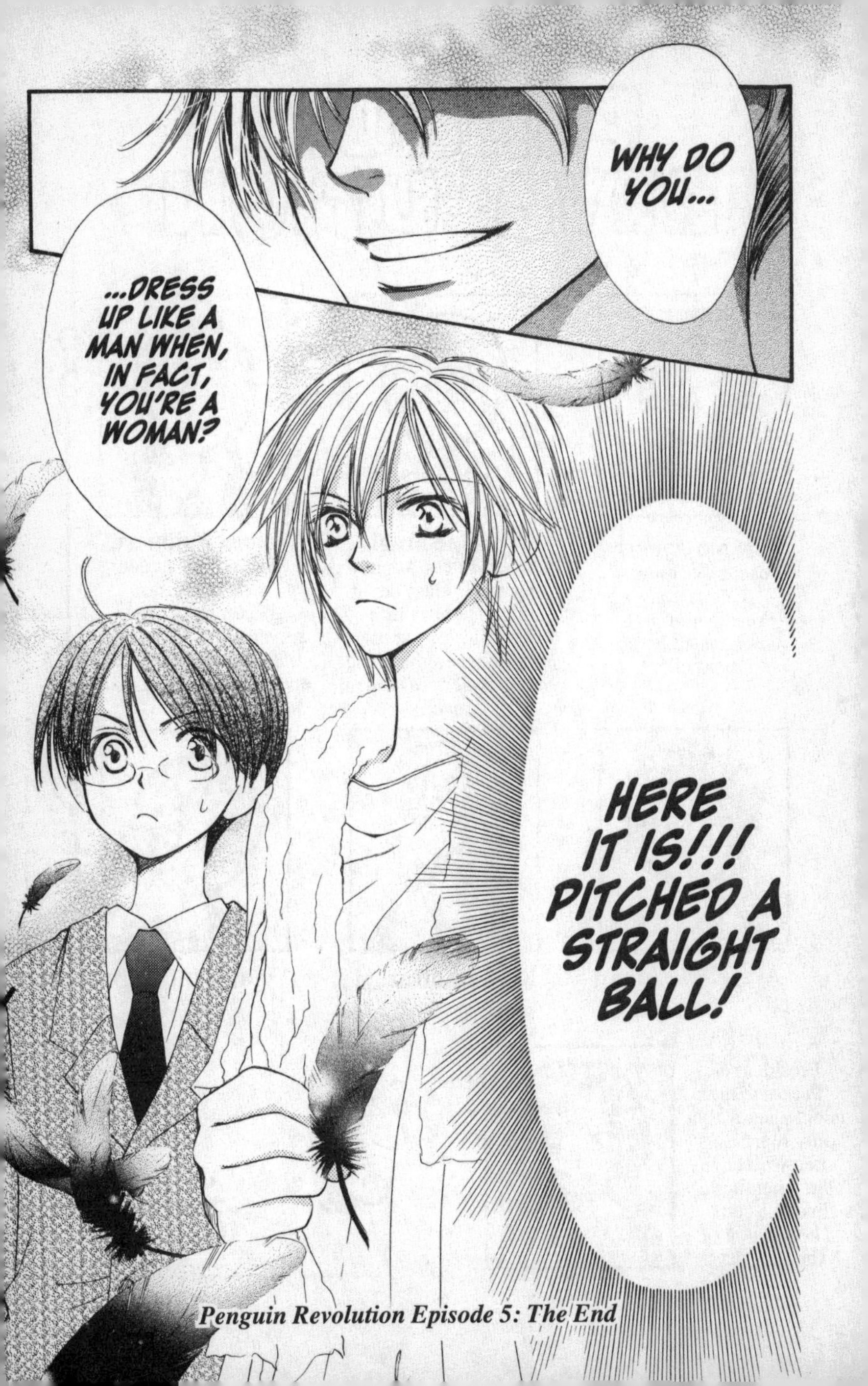
WHY DO YOU...
...DRESS UP LIKE A MAN WHEN, IN FACT, YOU'RE A WOMAN?
HERE IT IS!!! PITCHED A STRAIGHT BALL!
Penguin Revolution Episode 5: The End

PENGUIN REVOLUTION

BEFORE

Makoto Ayaori
Peacock's Number One talent. President of high school student council.

Ryo Katsuragi
Peacock Talent Agency's "Penguin"-class talent. Masquerades as a (beautiful) girl at high school, where he is the vice-president of student council.

Yukari Fujimaru
High school student who dreams of becoming a civil servant. Has had a hard life after her father ran away. Dressed as a man, she is Ryo's manager.

AFTER

Ayaori Mashiba

Ryoko Katsuragi

Yutaka Fujimaru

President of Peacock, the talent agency that only represents men who have the potential to become stars. The top dog of the industry.

Shacho

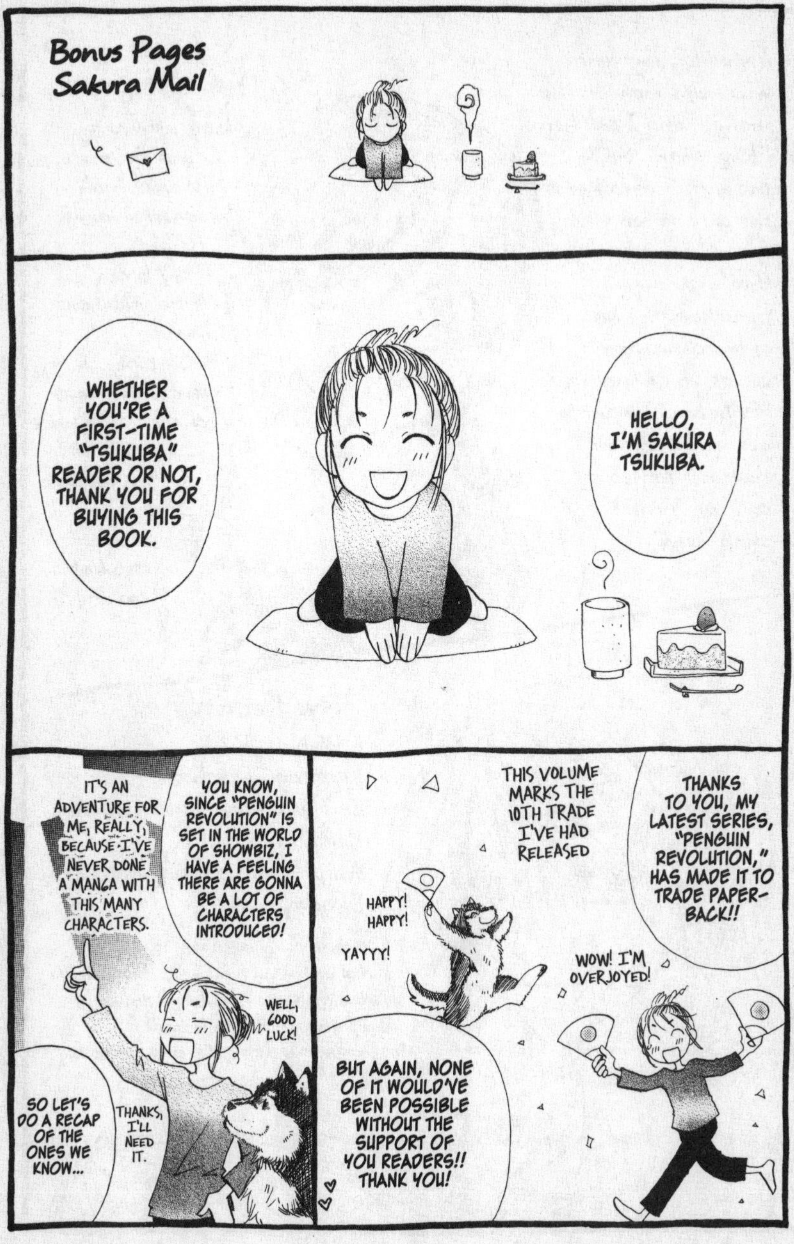
Bonus Pages
Sakura Mail
HELLO, I'M SAKURA TSUKUBA.
WHETHER YOU'RE A FIRST-TIME "TSUKUBA" READER OR NOT, THANK YOU FOR BUYING THIS BOOK.
THANKS TO YOU, MY LATEST SERIES, "PENGUIN REVOLUTION," HAS MADE IT TO TRADE PAPER-BACK!!
THIS VOLUME MARKS THE 10TH TRADE I'VE HAD RELEASED
WOW! I'M OVERJOYED!
HAPPY! HAPPY!
YAYYY!
BUT AGAIN, NONE OF IT WOULD'VE BEEN POSSIBLE WITHOUT THE SUPPORT OF YOU READERS!! THANK YOU!
YOU KNOW, SINCE "PENGUIN REVOLUTION" IS SET IN THE WORLD OF SHOWBIZ, I HAVE A FEELING THERE ARE GONNA BE A LOT OF CHARACTERS INTRODUCED!
IT'S AN ADVENTURE FOR ME, REALLY, BECAUSE I'VE NEVER DONE A MANGA WITH THIS MANY CHARACTERS.
WELL, GOOD LUCK!
THANKS, I'LL NEED IT.
SO LET'S DO A RECAP OF THE ONES WE KNOW...

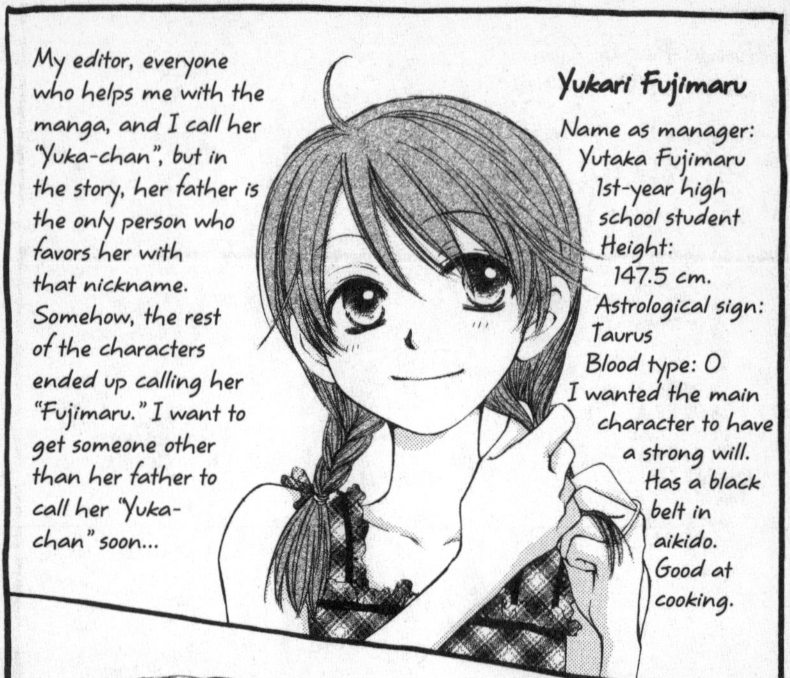
Yukari Fujimaru
Name as manager: Yutaka Fujimaru
1st-year high school student
Height: 147.5 cm.
Astrological sign: Taurus
Blood type: O
I wanted the main character to have a strong will. Has a black belt in aikido. Good at cooking.
My editor, everyone who helps me with the manga, and I call her "Yuka-chan", but in the story, her father is the only person who favors her with that nickname. Somehow, the rest of the characters ended up calling her "Fujimaru." I want to get someone other than her father to call her "Yuka-chan" soon...

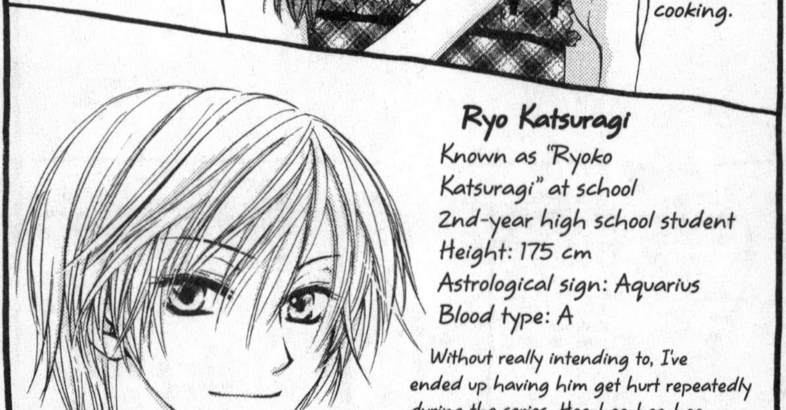
Ryo Katsuragi
Known as "Ryoko Katsuragi" at school
2nd-year high school student
Height: 175 cm
Astrological sign: Aquarius
Blood type: A
Without really intending to, I've ended up having him get hurt repeatedly during the series. Hee-hee-hee-hee. But I guess it can't be helped! Dressing up as a girl is really difficult.

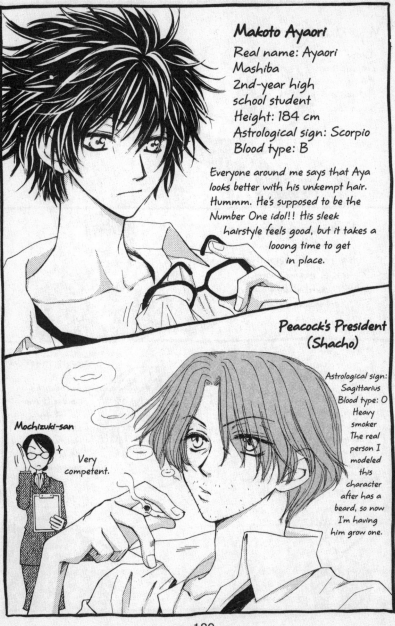

Makoto Ayaori

Real name: Ayaori
Mashiba
2nd-year high
school student
Height: 184 cm
Astrological sign: Scorpio
Blood type: B

Everyone around me says that Aya
looks better with his unkempt hair.
Hummm. He's supposed to be the
Number One idol!! His sleek
hairstyle feels good, but it takes a
looong time to get
in place.

Peacock's President
(Shacho)

Astrological sign:
Sagittarius
Blood type: O
Heavy
smoker
The real
person I
modeled
this
character
after has a
beard, so now
I'm having
him grow one.

Mochizuki-san

Very
competent.

189

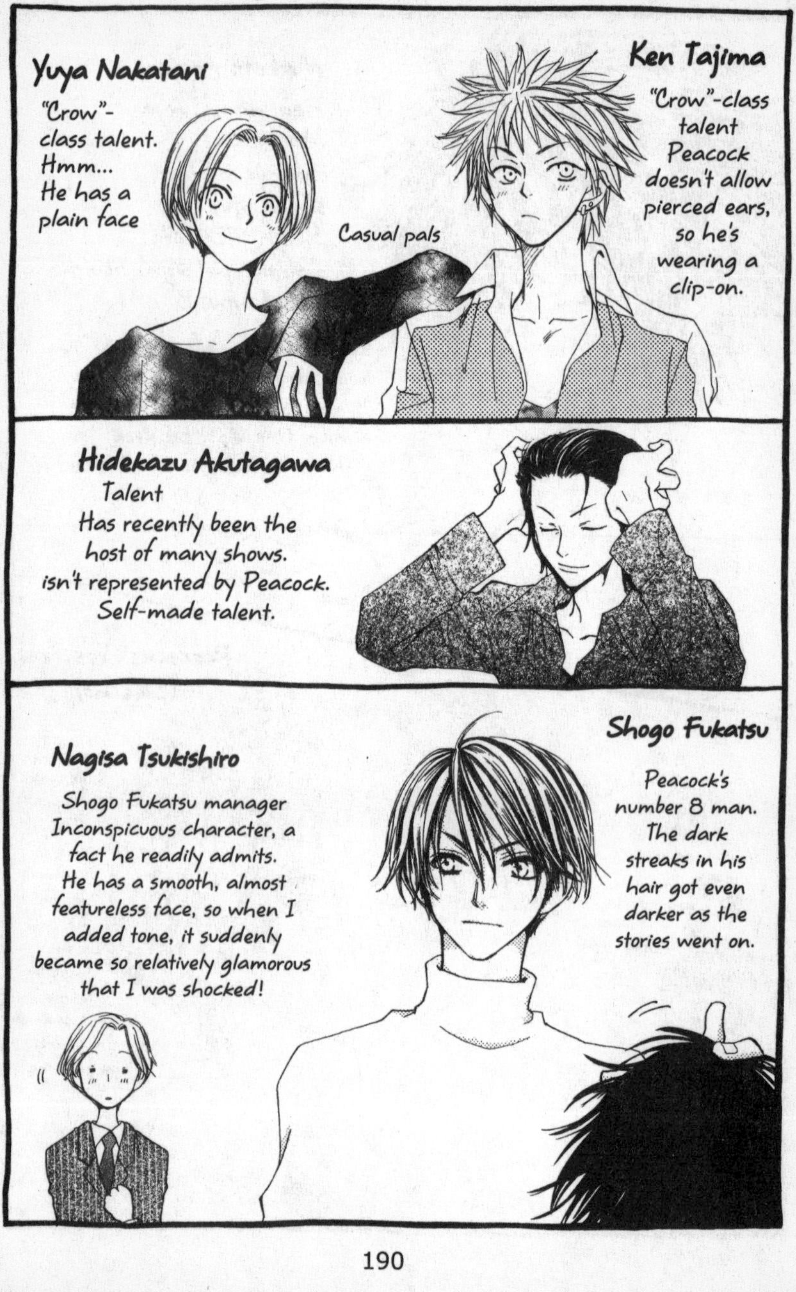
Ken Tajima
"Crow"-class talent Peacock doesn't allow pierced ears, so he's wearing a clip-on.
Yuya Nakatani
"Crow"-class talent. Hmm... He has a plain face
Casual pals
Hidekazu Akutagawa
Talent Has recently been the host of many shows. isn't represented by Peacock. Self-made talent.
Shogo Fukatsu
Peacock's number 8 man. The dark streaks in his hair got even darker as the stories went on.
Nagisa Tsukishiro
Shogo Fukatsu manager Inconspicuous character, a fact he readily admits. He has a smooth, almost featureless face, so when I added tone, it suddenly became so relatively glamorous that I was shocked!

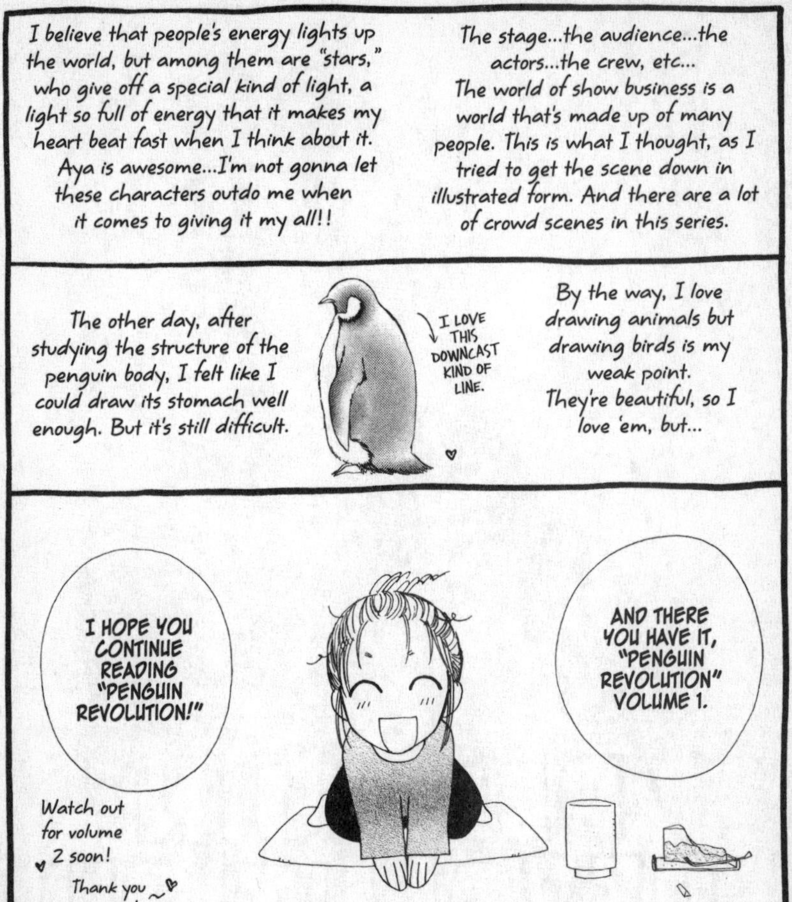
The stage...the audience...the actors...the crew, etc... The world of show business is a world that's made up of many people. This is what I thought, as I tried to get the scene down in illustrated form. And there are a lot of crowd scenes in this series.
I believe that people's energy lights up the world, but among them are "stars," who give off a special kind of light, a light so full of energy that it makes my heart beat fast when I think about it. Aya is awesome...I'm not gonna let these characters outdo me when it comes to giving it my all!!
By the way, I love drawing animals but drawing birds is my weak point. They're beautiful, so I love 'em, but...
I LOVE THIS DOWNCAST KIND OF LINE.
The other day, after studying the structure of the penguin body, I felt like I could draw its stomach well enough. But it's still difficult.
AND THERE YOU HAVE IT, "PENGUIN REVOLUTION" VOLUME 1.
I HOPE YOU CONTINUE READING "PENGUIN REVOLUTION!"
Watch out for volume 2 soon!
Thank you very much~ Sakura Tsukuba
And last but not least, a HUGE thank you to: Sakuman, Yuko-san, Mika-chan, Miho-chan, Osamin, Chito-chan, Hatsu-chan, Shino-chan, Ken-chan, Naito-san...
...my family, my friends, my editor and all of my readers!!
Wow! As usual, I've been helped by a lot of people. Thank you for helping me, everyone.
I really appreciate your help when I've got a tight deadline. See you soon.
My new editor, Ichikawa-sama.
TSUKUBA-SAN, YOU'RE TOO LATE!!
I want to thank my editor for sticking with me.
Okay, see you!!

Bonus Pages: Sakura Mail: The End

THE LIGHTS GO UP IN JANUARY!

PENGUIN REVOLUTION

Volume 2

By Sakura Tsukuba. It's Ryo's big debut on stage and he's in the lead role. Yukari's doing her best to support him, but she's busy trying to pull off her own performance as well by pretending to be a guy. Her "role" might not be as convincing as she had hoped, but Ryo seems to be bringing down the house. In fact, the lines between acting and real life might be getting a little *too* blurry.

PENGUIN KAKUMEI Volume 2 © 2005 Sakura Tsukuba/HAKUSENSHA, INC.

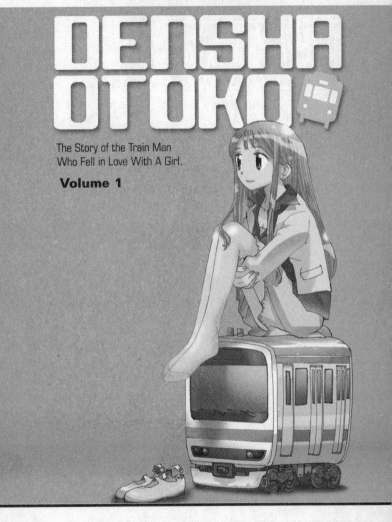

THE SAGA OF FORBIDDEN LOVE BEGINS HERE!

EMMA

Volume 1

By Kaoru Mori. In Victorian-era England, a young girl is rescued from a life of destitution and raised to become a proper British maid. Emma meets William, the eldest son of a wealthy family, and immediately falls in love with him. William shares her feelings, but the strict rules of their society may prevent their relationship from ever coming out in the open.

IF YOU LIKE PENGUIN REVOLUTION, YOU'LL LOVE THESE SERIES, TOO!

By Sakura Tsukuba
Entire Series Available

By Reiko Shimizu
4 Volumes Available

By Keiko Yamada
3 Volumes Available

By Iwahara Yuji
Entire Series Available

ONE OF THESE TITLES COULD BE YOUR NEXT FAVORITE SERIES!

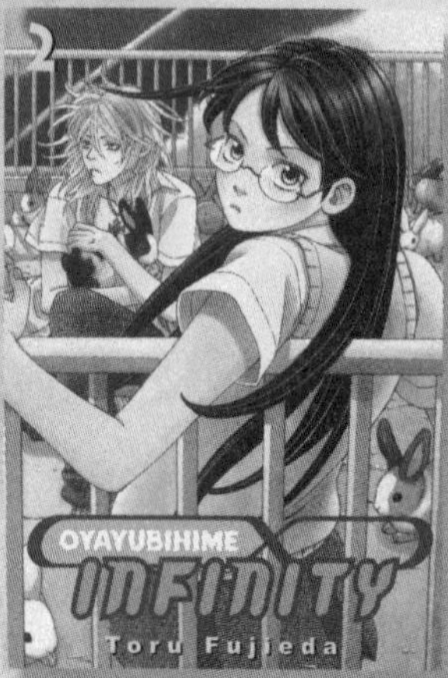
2
OYAYUBIHIME
INFINITY
Toru Fujieda

By Toru Fujieda
2 Volumes Available

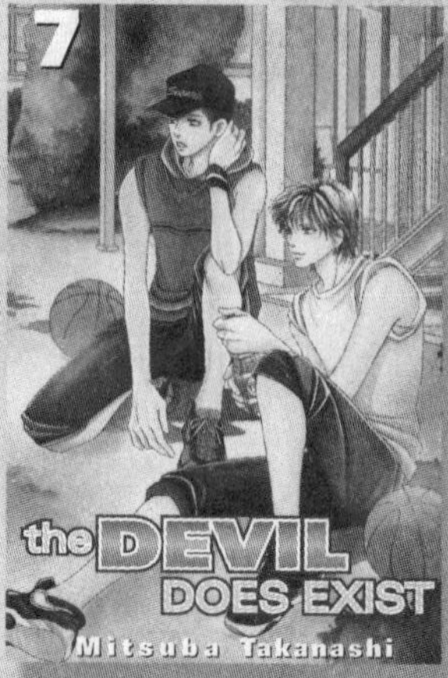
7
the DEVIL
DOES EXIST
Mitsuba Takanashi

By Mitsuba Takanashi
7 Volumes Available

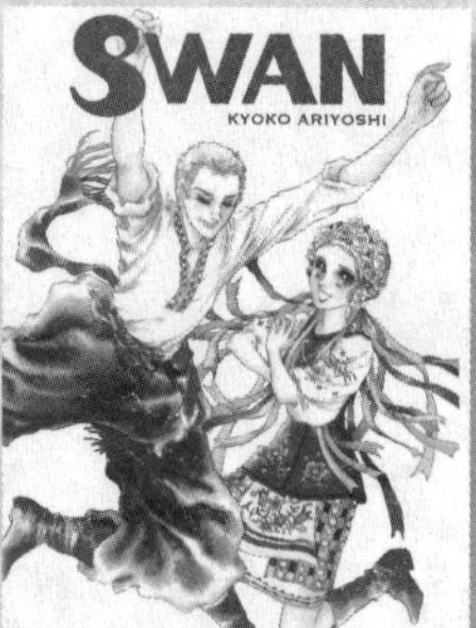
SWAN
KYOKO ARIYOSHI
8

By Kyoko Ariyoshi
8 Volumes Available

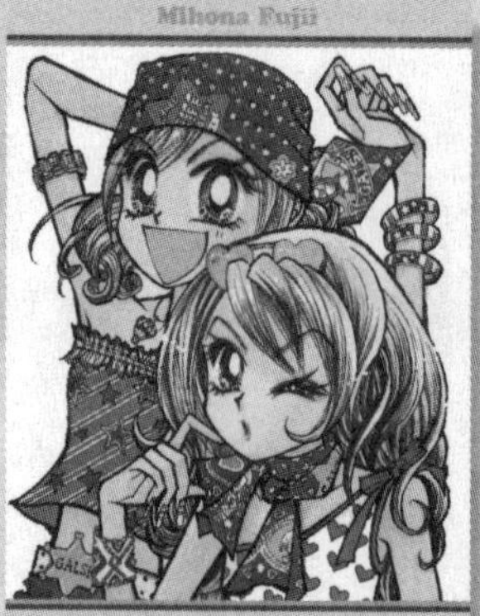
Mihona Fujii
GALS! 7

By Mihona Fujii
7 Volumes Available

For more information and sneak previews, visit cmxmanga.com. Call 1-800-COMIC BOOK for the nearest comics shop or head to your local book store.

IF YOU LIKE PENGUIN REVOLUTION, YOU'LL LOVE THESE SERIES, TOO!

By Arina Tanemura
5 Volumes Available

By Naoe Kita
1 Volume Available

By Nari Kusakawa
1 Volume Available

By Meca Tanaka
1 Volume Available

KNOW WHAT'S INSIDE

With the wide variety of manga available, CMX understands it can be confusing to determine age-appropriate material. We rate our books in four categories: EVERYONE, TEEN, TEEN + and MATURE. For the TEEN, TEEN + and MATURE categories, we include additional, specific descriptions to assist consumers in determining if the book is age appropriate. (Our MATURE books are shipped shrink-wrapped with a Parental Advisory sticker affixed to the wrapper.)

EVERYONE

Titles with this rating are appropriate for all age readers. They contain no offensive material. They may contain mild violence and/or some comic mischief.

TEEN

Titles with this rating are appropriate for a teen audience and older. They may contain some violent content, language, and/or suggestive themes.

TEEN PLUS

Titles with this rating are appropriate for an audience of 16 and older. They may contain partial nudity, mild profanity and more intense violence.

MATURE

Titles with this rating are appropriate only for mature readers. They may contain graphic violence, nudity, sex and content suitable only for older readers.

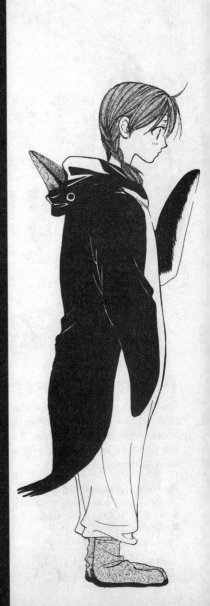

PENGUIN KAKUMEI Volume 1 © 2004 Sakura Tsukuba.
All Rights Reserved. First published in Japan in 2005 by
HAKUSENSHA, INC., Tokyo.

PENGUIN REVOLUTION Volume 1, published by WildStorm
Productions, an imprint of DC Comics, 888 Prospect St.
#240, La Jolla, CA 92037. English Translation © 2006. All
Rights Reserved. English translation rights in U.S.A. and
Canada arranged by HAKUSENSHA, INC., through Tuttle-
Mori Agency Inc., Tokyo. The stories, characters, and inci-
dents mentioned in this magazine are entirely fictional.
Printed on recyclable paper. WildStorm does not read or
accept unsolicited submissions of ideas, stories or artwork.
Printed in Canada.

DC Comics, a Warner Bros. Entertainment Company.

Sheldon Drzka – Translation and Adaptation

Deron Bennett
Sno Cone (pgs. 7-14) – Lettering

Larry Berry – Design

Jim Chadwick – Editor

ISBN:1-4012-1130-5
ISBN-13: 978-1-4012-1130-1

All the pages in this book were created—and are printed here—in Japanese RIGHT-to-LEFT format. No artwork has been reversed or altered, so you can read the stories the way the creators meant for them to be read.

RIGHT TO LEFT?!

Traditional Japanese manga starts at the upper right-hand corner, and moves right-to-left as it goes down the page. Follow this guide for an easy understanding.

For more information and sneak previews, visit cmxmanga.com. Call 1-800-COMIC BOOK for the nearest comics shop or head to your local book store.